D1806982

Embodied Nostalgia

Embodied Nostalgia is a collection of interlocking case studies that focus on how social dance in musical theatre brings forth the dancer on stage as a site of embodied history, cultural memory, and nostalgia, and asks what social dance is doing performatively, dramaturgically, and critically in musical theatre.

The case studies in this volume are all Broadway musicals set during the Jazz Age (1910–1950), however, performed and produced after that time, creating a spectrum of nostalgic impulses that are interrogated for social and political resonance and meaning. All reflect the fractures or changes in the social dance when brought to the stage and expose the complexities of the embodied nostalgia – broadly interpreted as the physicalizing of community memories, longings, and historical meaning – the dances carry with them. Particular attention is focused on the Black ownership of the social dances and the subsequent appropriation, cultural theft, and forgotten legacies.

By approaching musical theatre through this lens of social dance – always already deeply connected to notions of class and race – and the politics of choreography therein, a unique and necessary method to describing, discussing, and critically evaluating the body in motion in musical theatre is put forth.

Phoebe Rumsey is a Senior Lecturer in Musical Theatre and Course Leader of the BA (Hons) Musical Theatre degree at the University of Portsmouth in the UK. She received her PhD in Theatre and Performance from The Graduate Center, CUNY.

Routledge Advances in Theatre & Performance Studies

This series is our home for cutting-edge, upper-level scholarly studies and edited collections. Considering theatre and performance alongside topics such as religion, politics, gender, race, ecology, and the avant-garde, titles are characterized by dynamic interventions into established subjects and innovative studies on emerging topics.

Contemporary Irish Theatre and Social Change
Activist Aesthetics
Emer O'Toole

Live Digital Theatre
Interdisciplinary Performative Pedagogies
Aleksandar Sasha Dundjerović

Performance Cultures as Epistemic Cultures, Volume I
(Re)Generating Knowledges in Performance
Erika Fischer-Lichte, Torsten Jost, Milos Kosic, Astrid Schenka

Performance Cultures as Epistemic Cultures, Volume II
Interweaving Epistemologies
Erika Fischer-Lichte, Torsten Jost, Milos Kosic, Astrid Schenka

Politics of the Oberammergau Passion Play
Tradition as Trademark
Julia Stenzel and Jan Mohr

Beyoncé and Beyond
2013–2016
Naila Keleta-Mae

Reconstructing Performance Art
Practices of Historicisation, Documentation and Representation
Tancredi Gusman

For more information about this series, please visit: https://www.routledge.com/Routledge-Advances-in-Theatre–Performance-Studies/book-series/RATPS.

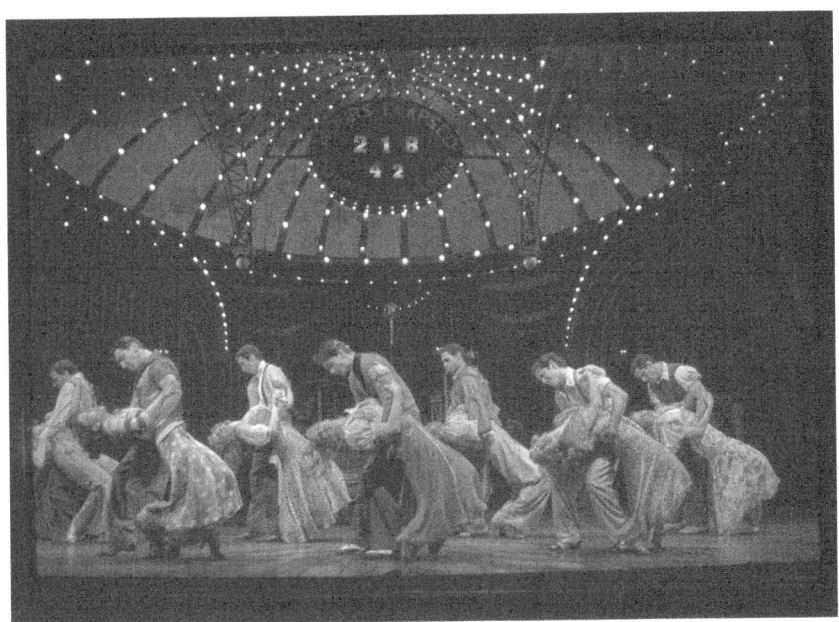

Figure 0.1 *Steel Pier* Broadway Cast, 1998
Source: Photo by Joan Marcus. New York Public Library Digital Collections

Embodied Nostalgia

Early Twentieth Century Social Dance
and the Choreographing of Broadway
Musical Theatre

Phoebe Rumsey

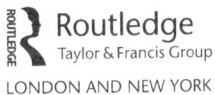

Routledge
Taylor & Francis Group

LONDON AND NEW YORK

First published 2024
by Routledge
4 Park Square, Milton Park, Abingdon, Oxon OX14 4RN

and by Routledge
605 Third Avenue, New York, NY 10158

Routledge is an imprint of the Taylor & Francis Group, an informa business

© 2024 Phoebe Rumsey

The right of Phoebe Rumsey to be identified as author of this work has been asserted in accordance with sections 77 and 78 of the Copyright, Designs and Patents Act 1988.

All rights reserved. No part of this book may be reprinted or reproduced or utilised in any form or by any electronic, mechanical, or other means, now known or hereafter invented, including photocopying and recording, or in any information storage or retrieval system, without permission in writing from the publishers.

Trademark notice: Product or corporate names may be trademarks or registered trademarks, and are used only for identification and explanation without intent to infringe.

British Library Cataloguing in Publication Data
A catalogue record for this book is available from the British Library

ISBN: 9780367757199 (hbk)
ISBN: 9780367757205 (pbk)
ISBN: 9781003163688 (ebk)

DOI: 10.4324/9781003163688

Typeset in Bembo
by Taylor & Francis Books

Contents

List of figures   ix
Acknowledgements   x

Introduction: The Nostalgic Promise of Musical Theatre   1

PART I
Ragtime – The Heartbeat of the Modern Era   21

1 "Juke Joints Supposed to be in the Woods": Nostalgia for Privacy
   and Place in *The Color Purple*   29

2 "This Was a Music That Was Theirs": *Ragtime* and the
   Breakdown of Collective Nostalgia   48

3 "Till Georgie Took 'Em Away": Counter Nostalgia and Cultural
   Theft in *Shuffle Along, Or The Making of the Musical Sensation of
   1921 and All That Followed*   65

PART II
The Charleston – Lively and Liberated   87

4 "Men Say it's Criminal What Women Will Do": *Thoroughly
   Modern Millie* and Nostalgia for the "New Woman"   103

5 "I need to do the Black Bottom!": Demystifying Nostalgia in *The
   Wild Party*   117

6 "I Don't Want To Show Off No More": Parody and Nostalgia
   Go Toe to Toe in *The Drowsy Chaperone*   134

PART III
Swing Dance – Rally and Rebound   149

  7 "Good neighbors – Good neighbors": *Wonderful Town* and
     Nostalgia for Lost Communities   159

  8 When Nostalgia is Your Only Hope: *Steel Pier* and
     Dance Marathons   182

  9 "Get in the game": Destabilizing Nostalgia in the Crisis of Identity
     in *Allegiance*   196

Conclusion "Just Like It Was Before": The Promise Continues   215

    Index   225

Figures

0.1   *Steel Pier* Broadway Cast, 1998   iii
I.1   "Scott Joplin, 'the king of ragtime composers'"   22
I.2   The Castles were applauded for their elegance and grace by white audiences in their popularizing of Black dances for white audiences. "Irene and Vernon Castle partnering each other" (1915).   23
2.1   "Dancers performing the Cakewalk" 1850   53
2.2   *Ragtime*, Broadway Cast Recording Cover, 1998   59
3.1   "Lyricist Noble Sissle and cast members from the musical 'Shuffle Along,' ca. 1921"   70
3.2   Ensemble Dancers, "Shuffle Along, or the musical sensation of 1922 and all that followed," 2016   74
4.1   *Thoroughly Modern Millie* (2002) "Thoroughly Modern Millie," Sutton Foster with cast.   104
III.1   "Jitterbug contest" The Miriam and Ira D. Wallach Division of Art, Prints and Photographs: Photography Collection, The New York Public Library   154
7.1   Rosalind Russell and chorus boys dressed as Brazilian cadets in "Wonderful Town" 1952, *Wonderful Town*, Billy Rose Theatre Division, The New York Public Library   171
8.1   Title image projected on downstage scrim at the opening of the show and mirrored on the Playbill. Design by James Candy, 1997   187
9.1   *Allegiance* (2015) "Heart Mountain Dance"   197
10.1   One of the only promotional images of the ghost soldiers in performance *Bandstand* (2017)   218
10.2   *Bandstand* (2017)   219

Acknowledgements

A truly heartfelt thank you extends to everyone who has assisted in the completion of this project. My sincere gratitude goes to the librarians at the Theatre on Film and Tape archive at the NYPL for the Performing Arts at Lincoln Center for the many viewing sessions they facilitated. Thank you to the wonderful librarians at The Schomburg Center for Research in Black Culture for helping find rare books, videos documents, and sources. Thank you to the artists I interviewed, Andy Blankenbuehler, Susan Stroman, Andrew Palermo, Lisa La Touche, and Scott Taylor who generously gave their time to share their choreographic process and experiences. Thank you to the members of my dissertation committee and all their help with the first draft of this book: David Savran, Elizabeth Wollman and Peter Eckersall. A special thank you to the anonymous peer-reviewers for the time they took to read and offer invaluable feedback at the later stages of the project, your insight has been much appreciated.

Many thanks to my wonderful friends and colleagues in the U.S.: Jennifer Thompson, Sarah Lucie, Chloe Edmonson, Ryan Donovan, Alosha Grinenko, Shane Breaux, Mara Valderama, Bhargav Rani, Sarah Lucie, Fabian Escalona, Bindi Kang, Margit Edwards, Andy Goldberg, Alison Walls, Eylul Fidan, Hansol Oh, Ugo Prasad, Kristof van Baarle, Donatella Galella and Cory Tamler. Thank you to the Martin E Segal Theatre Center and Frank Hentschker. Special thanks to Dustyn Martincich for our shared passion for dance and ongoing projects and considerations of the field. Thank you to my colleagues and friends in the UK and Europe: Erika Hughes, Kit Danowski, George Burrows, Tereza Havelková, Ben Macpherson, Millie Taylor, Nik Wakefield, Matt Smith, Paul Gerard, Doug Hamilton, Andrew Burbanks, and Tim Broom. Thank you to the University of Portsmouth, Oliver Gruner, and the coaching program that helped shape the original proposal. Thank you to Sarah Whitfield, MacMillan International, the Red Globe Press and Bloomsbury Publishing Plc. for publication of an earlier version of chapter three. Thank you to the many conference organizations where early drafts of these chapters have been presented and workshopped including, the International Federation of Theatre Research and the Music Theatre Working Group, Association for Theatre in Higher Education and the Music Theatre and

Dance Group, Canadian Association of Theatre Research, Performance Studies international, American Society for Theatre Research. Many thanks to Andrew Ku at Playbill, Matthew Murphy, Jeremy Daniel, Julieta Cervantes, and Joan Marcus for their photographs.

I am forever grateful for the support of my family. Thank you to my father, Peter Newsted for listening and offering advice as I described and re-described my project in its many iterations over many bowls of popcorn. Thank you to my mother, Jean Newsted, for being part of my dance career from the beginning and innately understanding embodiment from the get go. Finally, thank you to my husband Chuck Rumsey for the long discussions about musical theatre, dance, and the politics of performance that have been invaluable, especially when undertaken on road trips across North America, hikes in the Rockies, marches across windy New York bridges, snowy walks up Mont Royal in Montreal, and now in the U.K. – all of these journeys are greatly treasured.

Introduction

The Nostalgic Promise of Musical Theatre

The satin chrome plates of the iconic Shure 55 microphone glint in the stage lights and the clear voice of Laura Osnes rings out to the rafters. Dancers kick, swing, and rebound up and over the shoulders of their suspender and fedora clad partners. It is 1945, and soldiers have returned home. Promotional materials set the scene for the struggling World War II veterans that inhabit the world of *Bandstand*,

> Teaming up with a beautiful young war widow [...] they struggle to confront the lingering effects and secrets of the battlefield that threaten to tear them apart. Playing for every voiceless underdog in a world that has left them behind, they will risk everything [...] to redefine the meaning of victory.[1]

The promise of the 2017 Broadway musical by Richard Oberacker and Robert Taylor – passionate music, nation building, and courageous actions from spirited characters – illustrates musical theatre's ongoing and deep-seated relationship with history, memory, and ideologies of American exceptionalism. Video trailers for *Bandstand* lure audiences with a smoky jazz club filled with hot tunes and dancing bodies set in motion by Tony award-winning choreographer Andy Blankenbuehler – momentary time-travel to post World War II America is assured.

In the listings for new musicals in the 2010s over numerous Broadway seasons, from *Anastasia* to *Natasha, Pierre & The Great Comet of 1812*, *Come From Away* to *A Bronx Tale The Musical*, *Beautiful: The Carol King Musical* to *Ain't Too Proud: The Life and Times of the Temptations*, *1776*, and *Camelot*, enthusiasm for revisiting the past through the musical theatre form abounds.[2] Eleven-time Tony winner *Hamilton* may have elevated affection for the historical, but American Broadway musicals, by their notable desire to define the United States, have frequently looked to the past, both recent and distant, for answers. Not to put too fine a point on it, in *The American Musical and the Formation of National Identity*, musicologist Raymond Knapp dedicates a chapter to "Defining America," which he says is "arguably *the* central theme in American musicals, to which the other themes relate in both obvious and

DOI: 10.4324/9781003163688-1

subtle ways."[3] Likewise, the backwards glance so common in musical theatre is more often than not a means towards understanding ourselves in the present.

Musicals commonly use a combination of theatrical conventions and techniques to make these historical sojourns possible. Structurally, musicals often employ elements of scenic and costume design to create narratives set in the past. Innovative production teams may have a narrator guide the audience back in time (*Joseph and the Amazing Technicolor Dreamcoat*), rewind time as a point of the narrative (*Merrily We Roll Along*), or even create memories of an earlier history within a show by using the repetition of music and lyrics ("Can't Help Lovin' Dat Man" in *Showboat*). Beyond structural tactics however, at the heart of these backwards glances are the shared memories and emotions that musicals tap into. The descriptive language in the *Bandstand* pitch – "a truly American story of love, loss, triumph and the everyday men and women whose personal bravery defined a nation" – unabashedly invokes a sentimental mélange of U.S. mythologies and national narratives and idioms that were part of the social, cultural, and political consciousness of 1945.[4]

Markedly, these collective emotional connections and historical explorations characteristic of musical theatre constitute a nostalgic impulse dramaturgically inherent in the form. In my intervention exploring the link between nostalgia and musical theatre, I look to an area underrepresented in musical theatre scholarship – dance, in particular social dance.[5] Through a collection of case studies that focuses specifically on how social dance (and social dance-based choreography) in musical theatre brings forth the dancer on stage as a site of embodied history, cultural memory, and nostalgia, I ask what social dance is *doing* in musical theatre and how the dancing body functions as a catalyst for nostalgic thinking and feeling for the audience. U.S. social dance styles of the first half of the twentieth century, when performed in musicals written *after* that time, create a spectrum of nostalgic impulses and embodied meanings that fluctuate as a consequence of the variance and relation between the historical setting of the musical and the time of its original production on Broadway. By comparing the two timeframes, I provide a framework for how the "embodied nostalgia" – broadly interpreted as the physicalization of community memories, longings, and historical meaning – within social dance in musical theatre elucidates racial, cultural, and political consciousness. Given that the roots of jazz music and dance sit squarely within the cultural traditions of Black communities, I construct a mode of analysis that is grounded in the foundational Black legacy and lineage of social dance and jazz music in the U.S. This purposeful and essential intention helps contextualize the embodied meanings of social dance within cultural and political realms. The investigation of nostalgia through social dance in musical theatre augments the move in scholarship to consider musical theatre as a performance style that is, as David Savran has maintained, an essential "barometer of cultural and social politics."[6] Furthermore, as advocated by Liza Gennaro, and building on her substantial research, this book both helps "dispel the perception of musical theatre dance as kitsch, disposable, and created minus artistic methodology." *Embodied Nostalgia* champions the study of the body in motion on stage as a unique and significant method towards understanding ourselves, both in the past, present, and into the future.[7]

Definitions and Scope

One of the main premises of the book is the investigation of shows that are written after the era in which the narrative of the musical takes place. This choice allows for an exploration of how nostalgia becomes embedded in the show and, crucially, embodied by the performers. If I were to look at musicals written in and of their current time, such as *West Side Story*, or *On the Town* the temporal distance needed to examine the threads of nostalgia and evaluate their meaning would be lacking. Nor do such musicals allow exploration of how social dance can be, according to dance scholar Danielle Robinson, "not just a time machine…but a permeable border between the past and the present."[8] I chiefly focus on the original musical rather than revivals of the work as analyzing the work of multiple choreographers on specific social dances in one musical would overpower the historical, social, and political analysis and extends beyond the scope of this book.[9] By focusing on a diversity of narratives as opposed to reiterations of the same, I articulate varied ways the embodied nostalgia in social dance creates constructs of meaning. I look specifically at moments of choreography that happen diegetically in the narrative because of the visibility and impact of the dance in its communal setting. *Embodied Nostalgia* tells the history of social dances from a specified time frame in the United States and unpicks how and to what end these dances – and the embodied nostalgia therein – become part of the choreographic strategies and meaning making in musical theatre.

My internal choreographer and director compel me to set out the specific rules for the world of this exploration. To start, I focus on musicals *set* in the U.S. between 1910 and 1945 and produced *after* that period. I do this for several reasons. First, the American musical itself takes its shape in the earlier part of this range and the time frame is a popular era in which to situate musical theatre narratives. Further, as social dance becomes the main leisure activity for the younger generation and working class, in this time frame, the embodiment of cultural values and social attitudes is happening all round – on the streets, in dance halls, in clubs, jook joints, speakeasies, and more. The second guideline is the musical must have a narrative that includes social dance in order to explore the dramaturgical and choreographic choices made in regards to storytelling through social dance-based movement and the embodied nostalgia therein. Thirdly, in order to explore formations of personal and national identity vis a vis nostalgia, I have restricted the study to book musicals set in the United States. The fourth and final criteria is in regards to revues. While musical revues such as *Swing!* (1999), *Smokey Joe's Café* (1994), or *After Midnight* (2013) and others incorporate social dance, they do so without focus on a strong narrative, as is the purview of a revue, and so exist outside of the realm of this project.

To bring the reader into this world, for ease of reading, and as a nod to the historical aficionado, I explore the social dances in order of their emergence. I start with early ragtime dances, then move to Charleston styles, and then to swing dances. In addition to the above cues, I follow popular music's trajectory from ragtime, to early jazz, to swing, up to the beginnings of rock'n' roll, to make it possible to trace how social dances transform from one era to another and how cultural assumptions and registers of nostalgia shift along with them.[10] To set the scene then, and provide the reader with a basis of knowledge to build from, I begin with a brief grounding in social dance.

Social Dance

Social dance historian Julie Malnig defines social dance in *Ballroom, Boogie, Shimmy Sham, Shake: A Social and Popular Dance Reader* as a communal movement form "rooted in the materiality of everyday life."[11] According to Malnig, social dances do not generally involve a classical training regime or private instruction but are "essentially vernacular in the sense that they spring from the lifeblood of communities and subcultures and are generally learned informally through cultural and social networks."[12] Malnig's dedication to identifying, describing, defining, and coding the various social dances is fundamental towards understanding how social dance shapes (and is shaped by) constructs of identity and nationalism in the U.S. Not unlike following a rabbit down a hole, following changes in social dance can reveal other worlds, communities, political idioms, social constructs, and cultural idiosyncrasies. Markedly, there is not one rabbit hole, or trajectory, as social dances do not exist alone, they are part of a network of many social dances all evolving at varying rates, importing different cultural and political significance as they gain or wane in popularity.[13] It is often difficult to clearly designate moments of transition from one popular dance to another; however, it is in these interstices where cultural assumptions shift and new dance styles emerge. For the purpose of this book an interrogation of these transitions in social dance uncovers what cultural theorist Svetlana Boym in *The Future of Nostalgia* calls, "the fantasies of the age," which she argues coincide with and activate nostalgic tendencies.[14] The fantasies, desires, rituals, and the many assumptions and beliefs swirling around the body in motion are the essence of this project.

To understand, then, the significance of choreographers and directors possessing a social dance as part of the narrative and world of the musical in question, I examine how the ownership of a dance – filled with the heart and soul of a community – gets fractured in the move from dance club to stage. I explore the changes in the social dance when brought to the musical theatre stage and shed light on the dance's embodied nostalgia, particularly in regards to the Black ownership of the social dances in question. I look at the fusion of social dance styles and choreography that happen when the choreographer's voice emerges and how that choreographic agency becomes part of the operation of nostalgia in the musical. As such, I impress upon the reader a consideration of nostalgia in order to spark a curiosity and interest around the complexities of the concept that underpins the framework of the book.

Nostalgia

Nostalgia has a unique capacity to teach us about the "human predicament in the modern world"; about how we use our bodies to emotionally relate to each other, to embody our concept of home or homeland within the greater space of the world, and the significance of our physical presence as part of a community or nation.[15] The term "embodied nostalgia" can be interpreted as an amalgamation of these factors as manifested in the body, whether through postures, movement, or dance. Boym critically examines how nostalgia can be used as a way of understanding modernity. I find there to be an innate connection between how Boym engages with nostalgia and the ancillary project of musical theatre. Boym explains "nostalgia is about the relationship between individual biography and the biography of groups or nations, between personal and collective memory."[16] In like manner, the attempt to understand one's place within the complexities of the collective has often been a task of musical theatre.[17] And so, in order to investigate what social dance is *doing* in musical theatre, I overlay two frameworks of nostalgia – restorative and reflective – as set forth by Boym and put them forth for contemplation.

Restorative nostalgia "signifies a return to the original stasis," and in this return, "the past is not a duration but a perfect snapshot."[18] This idealized portrait of the past does not "reveal any signs of decay; it has to be freshly painted in its 'original image' and remain eternally young."[19] This designation, as seen in the publicity for *Bandstand,* concerns a polished vision of the past and often participates in the many mythologies that circulate in nation building.[20] In contrast, by excavating below the shiny "restorative" veneer of many historically driven musicals to critically examine the choreographic and dramaturgical nuances that use the past to comment on the present – a "reflective" nostalgia can be realized.

Reflective nostalgia suggests a meditation on and retracing of the past that introduces the possibility for considering alternate perspectives that may go on to influence future individual actions. Boym suggests reflective nostalgia "cherishes shattered fragments of memory and temporalizes space," and that this action advances the possibility for multiple consciousness and levels of meaning.[21] These two designations of nostalgia, often overlapping in musical theatre, become, as this book explores, more evident through theatricalized social dance. Whether in a fictional narrative or in actuality, the manner in which one engages with social dance in their everyday life can be seen as a visceral reaction to political and economic stresses.[22] Likewise, engagement in social dances of a previous era can be both an embrace of nostalgia and indicative of one's growing apprehension of their current time and angst concerning the future.[23] These provocations provide a schema for examining histories, identity constructions, and the socio-political impact of dancing bodies then and now. By considering how community identity and belonging emerge in social dance, crosscut with Boym's conceptualizations, I delve into how embodied nostalgia can be both an indicator of uncertainty in one's current situation, and an intuitive mode of understanding socio-cultural anxieties.

For those who might find nostalgia to be indulgent or misplaced, I point to the contemporary study of nostalgia which expands beyond ideas of melancholia and longing. New approaches to the concept operate in an involved and complex manner that recognize nostalgic impulses as entry points for a compassionate and critical rethinking of our contemporary moment, in tandem with a widening of possibilities for gaining, "a greater intimacy with the world."[24] That said, in exploring nostalgic impulses, particularly around the retrieving of memories – which is in effect where the seeds for nostalgia get planted – one is right to proceed with caution. French philosopher and sociologist, Maurice Halbwachs gestures towards the susceptibility and conscious or subconscious draw of nostalgia when he explains there is often a temptation to "touch up, shorten memories, to give them a prestige that reality did not possess." In fact, this is the action that triggers what Boym terms restorative nostalgia.[25] This polishing of memories is particularly heightened due to the sense for some that the best part of one's self was left in their youth. This is compounded by Halbwachs' argument that the majority of memories come from being part of a specific group at a specific time and is more often than not collective in nature. Considering social dance is a community experience, the scenarios they happen in are ripe with expressive meaning.[26] Markedly, the people in those dance spaces physicalize – or embody– those memories. Unpacking the concept of embodiment provides a way into how to read dance in musical theatre.

Embodiment

Embodied Nostalgia engages with the notion that the body is a prime site to examine historical agency and ownership of cultural mores.[27] This interpretation is drawn from the work of Diana Taylor, Susan Foster, and Mark Franko, who, along with Anthea Kraut and Carrie Noland to name a few, have examined how "embodied performance … makes visible an entire spectrum of attitudes and values."[28] As such, reading the body on stage becomes the challenge of studying choreography, and indeed there are a plethora of concepts to consider when engaging in movement analysis. I focus in on three from the get go to offer a tool kit for the interrogations of this book. To start, in *Choreographing Empathy: Kinesthesia in Performance*, dance scholar Susan Foster considers choreography a theorization of identity and corporeality, both individual and social. Using this connection between the self and community helps to identify the genesis of movements in social dance and their individual and collective meaning and reception. For Foster, the act of "reproducing in one's mind the kinesthetic image of the other," creates an empathy that challenges and provokes consideration of how one travels through the world physically and emotionally.[29] Keeping this emotional and affective exchange in mind and investigating how it circulates when a social dance community is seen on stage is productive when attempting to understand the dimensions of embodiment and nostalgia. How does watching dance make your body feel? And does the movement itself make you aware of your differences or similarities to the bodies on stage?

Secondly, recognizing the "body as an archive," as explored by performance studies scholar Diana Taylor helps explain how a body can hold in it the embodied memories of the past, or even the moves and style of an artist they have worked with. Taylor considers the body as an important site for the performance and re-performance of historical memory in a fluid and contingent repertoire. This insight underpins how the body holds meaning and is shaped by its surroundings.[30] In terms of the transmission of choreography, this is also a productive line of thinking. For instance, many considered Ann Reinking as the bodily archive of the work of Bob Fosse. This reasoning can be beneficial for tracking the legacy of a choreographer and how their impact and style can be so lasting outside their lifetime.[31] A third provocation to contemplate in working through not only what dance is *doing* but the *why* and the *how* is the scholarship of philosopher and feminist theorist Elizabeth Grosz who considers the body as continuously and actively produced by its the social environment.[32] As Grosz explains there is a "lack of finality" in the body, that the body is not a fixed state but "a series of processes of becoming."[33] This perspective helps to contend with the ongoing transformations within social dances and how bodies can be the carriers of social and political meanings through shifting historical eras. Following Grosz, I keep in mind that bodies "are not only inscribed, marked, engraved, by social pressures external to them but are the products, the direct effects, of the very social constitution of nature itself."[34] This awareness is productive when considering specific movements or choreographic choices and how embodied markers are present but are not static or unchanging in any choreographic analysis. Casts change, people change, attitudes shift, and so too does social dance. These transformations can happen daily, nightly, or in a slow burn over many, many evenings spent in a club or dance hall getting that warm burn at the back of the neck while dancing over and over to that one iconic song.[35]

Intersections and crossroads

At the heart of musical theatre's innate desire to reflect back to us who we are, there has always been a sense of fusion between popular dance styles and performance forms. In all likeliness, the dance one did at the ballroom or rave last night might very well be seen on stage in the hit musical of the day. This can be seen in contemporary musicals such as *Everybody's Talking About Jamie* (2017) or *Head Over Heels* (2015) and stands true for earlier musicals in their time such as *Anything Goes* (1934) or *Lady Be Good!* (1924). Dance scholar Barbara Cohen-Stratyner pinpoints the roots of this happening in the structure of musical theatre of the 1920s. She explains, the "best way to bring attention to a song was to attach a dance to it."[36] Cohen-Stratyner insists the reason for the prevalent inclusion of social dance in musical theatre at the time was because of its prominence in people's lives – "In 1920s New York, you were what you danced."[37] People were obsessed with social dance in the 1920s and it was common, if not expected, for the latest social dance and a fictionalized dance venue to be part of a musical comedy. Social dances were often part of the narrative structure of a musical and, pointedly, the venues where the dances took place were of great narrative importance as they were frequently where major conflicts, turning points, and resolutions occurred. With this emphasis on social dance as a plot device in the formative decades of the musical theatre, the dances themselves have come to define different historical and political moments and impacts of the decades. However, the sharing back and forth between the stage and real life was not always as symbiotic or harmonious as it may seem.

Theatre and performance scholar William Given suggests when social dance is taken from the dance clubs and placed in the theatricalized setting of Broadway, the distance created de-emphasizes the appropriation of the dance from its roots in the Black community.[38] He claims when a social dance is placed on stage, the "imagined community" it represents becomes "diluted by its intersection with those other communities."[39] For example, Given claims that when social dances moved out of the multiracial community of the Savoy and onto the stage, "the dance becomes more theatrical, and is supplanted with another outside discourse, the dance begins to transform from community to spectacle."[40] Given suggests through this "spectacularization," the Black ownership of the dances and sense of community fade away.[41] I build on both Given and Cohen-Straytner's claims by exploring the cultural appropriations, misappropriations, racial repressions, fusions, and social meanings that develop when theatricalized social dance is removed from its original time frame. Considering the consequences of the attempts at the protection of cultural idioms alongside the inevitable progression and transformations of social dance forms helps answer further questions such as: what are the effects of the codification and theatricalization of social dances on the Broadway stage? For example, how does a musical like *Shuffle Along, Or The Making of the Musical Sensation of 1921 and All That Followed* (2016) or *Allegiance* (2015) theatricalize social dance and how does nostalgia play a part in this "spectacularization"?[42] How do choreographic manoeuvres help realize social dance in musical theatre as an indicator of cultural identity and roots?

In the exploration of these questions, this project engages with research on the development of social dance and its racialized foundations. Robinson and dance studies scholar and cultural historian Brenda Dixon Gottschild make clear from the start that social dance is always and already deeply connected to notions of class and race.[43] One of the main interrogations of Robinson's work is how Black dances were "refined" by white dancers, teachers, choreographers, and communities.[44] Following her interpretation of the "Americanization" of social dances along with developments of national narratives helps explain the development of collective imaginations around the case studies in question.[45] Robinson upholds the ownership Black Americans have over social dance and argues that race is "an organizing principle of social dance."[46] Likewise, as with Malnig, Robinson makes clear that fluidity and flux are always a part of social dance. White communities searching for new and exciting cultural identities at the turn of the century melded, approporiated, and blended Black music and dance with European dance. Zora Neale Hurston explains this reformation of Black sensibilities by white performers in the convergence with Europeans in the migration north: "While he lives and moves in the midst of white civilization, everything that he touches is reinterpreted for his own use."[47] In such a scenario then how are, "ideas about culture and politics communicated through bodies in motion?"[48]

Continuing this line of questioning, in this socialization of bodies it is important to ask "who" is dancing and to interrogate the complexities of the cross-cultural borrowing.[49] Robinson argues that social dancers are "community members and culture bearers," and notably, explores how this consideration sets up the circular paradigm of the "nostalgic cycling and recycling" of social dances.[50] Which is to say, Black Americans use dance to both assert their heritage and seek an identity in the modern era (in a variety of manners based on a multitude of community backgrounds and histories). This foundational take on social dance as coming from the community, as community, is key towards the conceptualization and operation of nostalgia in social dance particularly in tandem with how Gottschild finds dance to function as a "mirror and measure of society."[51]

Like Robinson, Gottschild discusses the appropriation of dance styles and interrogates how Black Americans managed this ongoing conflict asking, "how did black people and white people negotiate the ground between the (exoticizing) embrace of black creative endeavor and the perpetuation of racism as standard practice?"[52] Instead of replacing cultural behaviors with another, Black communities would often try to find, through their embodied practices, such as social dance, a way to allow cultural continuation.[53] Diana Taylor interprets this "multiplication" or "simultaneity" as a way of maintaining culture within shifting political realms.[54] Pointedly, in this environment how do the aesthetics of Black social dances became signposts for modernity, embraced by white Americans and Europeans alike, while also operating under the continued racist and racialized climate of the Swing Era?[55] Jayna Brown explores the crossroad between – and impact of – Black chorus dancers on the modernization of performance and female identity on stage.[56] Daphne Brooks's *Bodies in Dissent: Spectacular Performances of Race and Freedom, 1850–1910* does valuable work in this regard as well.[57] Both Brown and Brook's insistence on the ushering in of modernity via Black cultural forms is a motivation for this book, along with inspiration from Thomas F. DeFrantz's exploration of Black dance styles, aesthetics, and dance theory.[58]

In essence, the study of social dance in the early twentieth century in the U.S. illustrates how important it was for Black Americans to maintain their cultural rhythms and bodily gestures, despite the ongoing "refinement" by white performers. *Embodied Nostalgia* investigates the ongoing cultural conflicts that physically manifest in social dance in order to understand the nostalgic affects that do or do not emerge by the inclusion of a particular social dance in a musical. What, then, are the challenges, risks, rewards, and pitfalls of this world-making so forged from how the body moves?

Choreographic Strategies in Musical Theatre

To understand the significance of choreographers and directors (and director-choreographers) possessing a social dance as part of the narrative and essence of the musicals in question, I focus in on how the ownership of the dance gets fractured in moving from dance club to stage. In the move from club to stage there "becomes a desire to lay claim to [social dance] in order to possess it once it has been objectified."[59] In this light, I analyze how choreography amplifies meaning, and what shifts in meaning occur when social dance is transferred to the stage. Looking at the fractures or changes in this move exposes the complexities of the embodied nostalgia the social dances carry with them, particularly in regards to the cultural roots of the social dances in question. Specifically, I unpick the choices made by choreographers in terms of the development of a dramaturgical strategy for social dance-based choreography and how that methodology involves, to a greater or lesser degree, a fusion of social dance styles and contemporary styles within the context of the score and libretto of the musical. Similarly, I investigate the modes of movement acquisition of the various social dances used to support the choreographic signature. As my ongoing aims are to provide a skill-set and bring confidence to others to engage in discussion and analysis of dance, a clear mapping of my parameters models how to consider dance in musical theatre.

For each chapter, I first look at the history of the social dances in question and situate them in time and place. I explain how these dances were created, to what music, and in what venues. Second, I identify the communities the dances came from and trace the appropriation, assimilation and (sometimes) cultural exchange that have been layered upon the dance as it was popularized. This process includes identifying who originally did the dance, who the character is in the narrative of the musical, and who the performer on stage is executing the dance. This identification supports a connection to how and for whom nostalgia is created in the musical. I then look at how each choreographer uses social dance as a framework upon which to build a unique movement signature that explores the visceral experience of a particular moment for a particular community.

In order to understand how embodied nostalgia can form around theatricalized social dance, I look at indications of how social dance communities get flattened in the move to the stage. Taking my initial cue from Benedict Andersons's organizing principle of "imagined communities," I draw on his methods in various instances to identify the nature and style of the social dance communities.[60] For example, the Lindy Hop community at the Savoy

Ballroom in the 1930s imagined itself a fraternal community, though what was outside the ballroom was not. When the Lindy Hop is then shown on stage in a non-Black, historical musical, is that fraternity intact or is it a "white ghosting of a Black dance?"[61] In this consideration of "imagined communities" as seen on stage and within the world of the musical, I illustrate whether merely a fraction of the identifying factors of the social dance are brought onto the stage, in the constructed choreographic performance, and what are the consequences of this possible rupture.[62] By intervening in this manner, I conceptualize the nostalgic paradigms – either restorative or reflective or both – at work when the piece is presented out of time and includes theatricalized social dance. My work is augmented by numerous interviews with choreographers and dancers and their understanding of what social dance is *doing* in their production and the creative process that led to its inclusion, adding the *how* and *why* that particular social dance is interpreted.

★

In section one, "Ragtime – The Heartbeat of the Modern Era," I investigate the ragtime dances of the early twentieth century that provided the roots of influence for the subsequent social dances of this study. The Slow Drag, the Cakewalk, and numerous Animal Dances are interrogated to show both Black influences on social dance and the counter-influence of European social dance on Black social dance styles. The three chapters that follow critically examine the following musicals: *The Color Purple* (2005), *Ragtime* (1998) and *Shuffle Along, Or The Making of the Musical Sensation of 1921 and All That Followed* (2016). In Chapter 1, *The Color Purple*, directed by Gary Griffin and choreographed by Donald Byrd, is found to be one of the only musicals to have a "jook house" as part of the narrative and to use the less known social dance, the Slow Drag. The Slow Drag characterizes how Black Americans of the time attempted to keep some physicality of their home and culture, while also trying to assimilate into the industrialized world. I interrogate the restorative and reflective nostalgic elements that emerge through the social dance and its transfer to the stage – a substantial move from the private realm to the public. In Chapter 2, I problematize the complex intersection between the different worlds of race and ethnicities of the early twentieth century in the musical *Ragtime*, directed by Frank Galati and choreographed by Graciela Daniele. I investigate how Daniele deconstructs the Cakewalk and trace how in the rupture of the collective parts of the dance, there is a consideration of the magnitude of where the dance came from. Chapter 3 investigates George C. Wolfe's *Shuffle Along, Or The Making of the Musical Sensation of 1921 and All That Followed*. Through this case study, I analyze how the embodied nostalgia embedded in the dance styles is used to shed light on the social and cultural complexities that operated in musical comedies in the original 1921 *Shuffle Along* and how choreographer Savion Glover uses dance to stake a claim for continued diversity and representation in musical theatre today. I critically examine how Glover is able to navigate and bring together the temporal divide of the show with an intense physicality that speaks to the past, present, and future.

In Part II, "The Charleston – Lively and Liberated," I explore the transition from ragtime dances into the social dances that came to define the Jazz Age, particularly the Charleston. I look at three musicals that take up the sensibilities and social dances of the time, *Thoroughly Modern Millie* (2002), Michael John LaChiusa's *The Wild Party* (2000), and *The Drowsy Chaperone* (2006). In each case study of this section, embodied meanings in the Charleston (or Black Bottom in the case of *The Wild Party*) are dramaturgically maneuvered with divergent motives that present the dance from a distinct perspective. In particular, the differing perspectives depend on how the dramatic structure of the musical – ranging from pastiche to parody – presents the world of the 1920s. In Chapter 4, I explore how the social dance on stage embodies the new rhythms and feelings of the 1920s by way of *Thoroughly Modern Millie* (2002). I connect the musical's narrative to the nostalgic essences of the flapper lifestyle, commonly fashioned in popular media as a time of jazz music, female autonomy, and Prohibition-era shenanigans, and what the transference of the dance to the stage means. I interrogate how the Charleston, which had its peak in 1926, embodies a process of exploring one's subjectivity in an increasingly modernized world. Additionally, I critically examine the problematic topic of Orientalism in the show in terms of both ethnic stereotypes and movement parodies. Chapter 5 examines, *The Wild Party*, the uncensored interpretation of Joseph Moncure March's 1928 poem and allows for a critical take on the Jazz Age. This darker perspective on the era demystifies the embodied nostalgia for the indulgences of the 1920s and exposes, through movement and music, the cultural theft at work then and now. Chapter 6 takes *The Drowsy Chaperone* (2006) as an example of how nostalgia is created onstage, and how director and choreographer Casey Nicholaw uses the popular social dance idioms of the 1920s to achieve the nostalgic affect that fuels the show. I explore how *The Drowsy Chaperone* uses a playful double coded parodic telling of 1920s musicals that re-engages affection for musical theatre by capitalizing on the thrills of the form while also reflecting on the meaning and influence of nostalgia in musical theater and life.

In the third and final part, "Swing Dance – Rally and Rebound," I consider swing dances and how they are used and interpreted in different ways in three musicals set between 1930 and 1945: *Wonderful Town* (1953), *Steel Pier* (1997), and *Allegiance* (2015). I trace how the very popular swing style social dances are used to signal historical idioms, economic survival, cultural identity, and community. I investigate how concepts of community, and thus social dance, shifted with the political and economic changes of the 1930s and early 1940s. In all three musicals swing dance is employed by the choreographer to imagine a community in the face of precarity whether in response to actions in the narrative or to sociopolitical circumstances at the time of production. The study of these shows demonstrates how social dance can embody the subtext of the story, and how the embodied nostalgia therein becomes the subversive element that can bring social and political meaning to light, even if the plot may not. Chapter 7 considers *Wonderful Town* as a comedy that uses pastiche combined with a light-hearted social satire to bring 1935 Greenwich Village to life. The opening of the show at the height of the Red Scare, however, complicates the high-spirited show, that will be shown to have subtle but critical undercurrents as manifested through movement. Chapter 8 takes on the complexities of dance marathons by looking at *Steel Pier*. This musical is set in the early 1930s, and attempts to demonstrate how swing dance helped a country escape, if only momentarily, from economic realities. I investigate how choreographer Susan Stroman puts social dance front and center and turns towards nostalgia as a way of understanding dance marathons, and the social and economic meaning rooted within them. Finally in Chapter 9 I investigate the musical *Allegiance*, set in 1941 and the 2010s, directed by Stafford Arima and choreographed by Andrew Palermo. In this chapter, I examine concepts of nationalism and geopolitics and how swing dance becomes a tenet of American identity. I argue that Japanese bodies doing American social dances challenge common assumptions about America's past, and how an embodied nostalgia inherent in the dance form recovers the notion that a Japanese body is also American.

The conclusion points towards the transition into the rock'n'roll dances and what this transition means for the embodied nostalgia derived from the dances of the Jazz Age and the World War II era. I return to *Bandstand* at the conclusion of this project because it is a musical that both builds upon and troubles the embodied nostalgia of social dance in the Jazz Age. It is my aim to illustrate how nostalgia is embodied and what this corporeal connection conveys on a larger social and political scale. I champion the study of dancing bodies and social dance choreography in musical theatre as a way to comprehend the essential impact the body has on nostalgic thinking and what that recognition means in the grand scheme of understanding popular performance as a gauge of cultural and social politics. In all, and at the most basic, I model how to talk about dance with the continued goal to persuade and excite any and all to take up the tools, methods or styles set forth and delve into the study of dance in musical theatre.

Notes

1 "Laura Osnes and Corey Cott Star in Bandstand the New Broadway Musical at the Jacobs Theatre," *The Shubert Organization,* October 21, 2016 https://shubert.nyc/p ress/laura-osnes-and-corey-cott-star-in-bandstand-the-new-broadway-musical-at-t he-jacobs-theatre/.
2 "Show Listings," *Playbill,* accessed March 25, 2017, http://www.playbill.com/p roductions; "Schedule of Upcoming and Announced Broadway Shows," *Playbill,* accessed November 20, 2018, http://www.playbill.com/article/schedule-of-upcom ing-and-announced-broadway-shows-com-113677. "Show Listings," *Playbill,* accessed April 29, 2022, https://playbill.com/productions
3 Raymond Knapp, *The American Musical and the Formation of National Identity* (Princeton University Press, 2005), 8 (Knapp's italics).

4 "Laura Osnes and Corey Cott starr in Bandstand on Broadway at the Jacobs Theatre," *The Shubert Organization*, October 21, 2016. https://shubert.nyc/press/laura-osnes-and-corey-cott-star-in-bandstand-the-new-broadway-musical-at-the-jacobs-theatre/.

5 The 2021 work of Liza Gennaro, *Making Broadway Dance* (Oxford University Press) along with Kevin Winkler's *Everything is Choreography: The Musical Theater of Tommy Tune* (Oxford University Press, 2021); Ariel Nereson's *Democracy Moving: Bill T. Jones, Contemporary American Performance, and the Racial Past* (University of Michigan Press, 2022; and Ryan Donovan's *Broadway Bodies: A Critical History of Conformity* (Oxford University Press, 2023) among others have greatly added to the examination of musical theatre dance.

6 David Savran, "The Do-Re-Mi of Musical Theatre Historiography," in *Changing the Subject: Marvin Carlson and Theatre Studies 1959–2009*, ed. Joseph Roach (Ann Arbor: University of Michigan Press, 2009), 230.

7 Liza Gennaro, *Making Broadway Dance* (Oxford University Press, 2021), 4.

8 Danielle Robinson, *Modern Moves: Dancing Race During the Ragtime and Jazz Eras* (New York: Oxford University Press), 47.

9 I make an exception to this rule with *The Color Purple* in Chapter 1 and briefly touch on the 2003 revival of *Wonderful Town* in Chapter 7.

10 I build on the scholarship of Julie Malnig who connects popular dance with American cultural identity by tracing how social dance trends "give physical and symbolic shape to social, cultural, and political issues in selected historical era," "Popular Dance and American Cultural Identity," course description, New York University, accessed April 1, 2017, http://gallatin.nyu.edu/academics/courses/2017/FA/idsem-ug1675_001.html.

11 Julie Malnig, ed. *Ballroom, Boogie, Shimmy Sham, Shake: A Social and Popular Dance Reader* (Chicago: University of Illinois Press, 2009), 6.

12 Malnig, *Ballroom, Boogie, Shimmy Sham, Shake*, 4.

13 In making this connection Malnig draws in parts of the research of Joel Dinerstein, *Swinging the Machine: Modernity, Technology, and African American Culture Between the Wars* (Amherst: University of Massachusetts Press, 2003).

14 Svetlana Boym, *The Future of Nostalgia* (New York: Basic Books. 2001), 351.

15 Boym, *The Future of Nostalgia*, 351. Historically, the term nostalgia was coined by Swiss doctor Johannes Sofer in 1688. The word is from the Greek *nostos* (return to home) and *algia* (pain, or longing). At the time it was thought that nostalgia was caused by homesickness and could be cured by a return home. Boym, *The Future of Nostalgia*, xiii, 3.

16 Boym, *The Future of Nostalgia*, xvi.

17 Some key texts that explore the search for belonging through musical theatre: Andrea Most, *Making Americans: Jews and the Broadway Musical* (Cambridge: Harvard University Press, 2004); Raymond Knapp, *The American Musical and the Performance of National Identity* (Princeton: Princeton University Press, 2005) and *The American Musical and the Performance of Personal Identity* (Princeton: Princeton University Press, 2006); John Bush Jones, *Our Musicals, Ourselves: A Social History of the American Musical Theatre* (Waltham, MA: Brandeis University Press, 2004); and David Walsh and Len Platt. *Musical Theater and American Culture* (Westport, CT: Greenwood Press, 2003).

18 Boym, *The Future of Nostalgia*, 49.

19 Ibid.

20 I am not claiming *Bandstand* only creates or operates in restorative nostalgia; however, the marketing package creates this sort of imagery to potentially attract audiences. The reflective nostalgia in *Bandstand* is explored further in the conclusion.

21 Boym, *The Future of Nostalgia*, 49.

22 The impact of social dance on everyday life has been explored by Kathy Peiss in *Cheap Amusements Working Women and Leisure in Turn-of-the-Century New York* (Philadelphia: Temple University Press, 1996) and Linda J. Tomko in *Dancing Class: Gender, Ethnicity and Social Divides in American Dance, 1890–1920* (Indianapolis: Indiana University Press, 1999).

23 Eric Martin Usner explains how a renewed interest in swing dancing in the 1990s was indicative of a rejection of the social politics of the time. Usner, "Dancing in the Past, Living in the Present: Nostalgia and Race in Southern California Neo-Swing Dance Culture," *Dance Research Journal* 33, no. 2 (2001): 87–101.

24 Boym, *The Future of Nostalgia*, 50. Other theorists studying contemporary definitions of nostalgia in congruence with Boym include: Tammy Clewell, Peter Fritzsche, Elizabeth Outka, Clay Routledge, Sean Scanlan, Susan Stewart, and others. Contemporary investigations such as these move beyond the notion of nostalgia as homesickness, and take Boym's lead that nostalgia is "coeval with modernity," and allow for secondary interpretations beyond only the "restorative" kind of nostalgia. Boym, *The Future of Nostalgia*, 8.

25 Halbwachs, Maurice, On Collective Memory (Lewis A. Coser trans. and ed.) (Chicago: University of Chicago Press, 1992), 51.

26 While this project cannot cover all areas of dance studies it is important to note that the aforementioned scholars such as Julie Malnig and Danielle Robinson are not working in isolation but part of a larger area of study called Popular Dance Studies that as Sherill Dodds explains "is key to developing a richer understanding of the distinctive characteristics of movement practices located in the public domain" Sherril Dodds, *Dancing on the Canon: Embodiments of Value in Popular Dance* (Palgrave Macmillan, 2011), 65.

27 Drawn from the work of Susan Leigh Foster, *Choreographing Empathy: Kinesthesia in Performance* (London: Routledge, 2010); Mark Franko, *The Work of Dance: Labor, Movement, and Identity in the 1930s* (Middletown, CT: Wesleyan University Press, 2002); Anthea Kraut, *Choreographing Copyright: Race, Gender, and Intellectual Property Rights in American Dance* (Oxford, UK: Oxford University Press, 2016); Carrie Noland, *Agency and Embodiment: Performing Gestures/Producing Culture* (Cambridge: Harvard University Press, 2009).

28 Diana Taylor, *Archive and the Repertoire: Performing Cultural Memory in the Americas* (Durham, NC: Duke University Press, 2003), 46.

29 Susan Foster, *Choreographing Empathy*, 28.

30 Taylor explains that the repertoire "enacts embodied memory" and "allows for individual agency." Like Malnig, Taylor recognizes the fluidity of dance and that the repertoire's meaning can shift over time. Investigating these case studies with a sense of how "the repertoire both keeps and transforms choreographies of meaning," helps to understand the transmission of dances from body to body and community to community. Taylor, *Archive and the Repertoire*, 20.

31 The legacy of the styles of Martha Graham, Merce Cunningham, Katherine Dunham, Paul Taylor come to mind, to name only a few.

32 Elizabeth Grosz, *Volatile Bodies: Toward a Corporeal Feminism* (Bloomington: Indiana University Press, 1994), x.

33 Grosz, *Volatile Bodies: Toward a Corporeal Feminism*, 12.

34 Ibid., x.

35 For extending mapping of the historical trajectory of music and dance in the Jazz Age see Ted Gioia, *The History of Jazz* (New York: Oxford University Press, 2011); Marshall and Jean Stearns, *Jazz Dance: The Story of American Vernacular Dance* (New York: Da Capo Press, 1994). See also: Scott DeVeaux and Gary Giddins, *Jazz* 2nd Ed. (New York, NY: W.W. Norton & Company, 2015) and Lewis Erenberg's *Swingin' the Dream: Big Band Jazz and the Rebirth of American Culture* (Chicago: University of Chicago Press, 1999).

36 Barbara Cohen-Stratyner, "A Thousand Raggy, Draggy Dances: Social Dance in Broadway Musical Comedy in the 1920s," in *Ballroom, Boogie, Shimmy Sham, Shake: A Social and Popular Dance Reader*, ed. Julie Malnig (Chicago: University of Illinois Press, 2009), 218.

37 Cohen-Stratyner, "A Thousand Raggy, Draggy Dances," 217.

38 William Given, "Lindy Hop, Community, and the Isolation of Appropriation," in *The Oxford Handbook of Dance and Theatre,* ed. Nadine George-Graves Given (Oxford, UK: Oxford University Press, 2015).

39 Given, "Lindy Hop, Community, and the Isolation of Appropriation," 735. Given borrows the term "imagined communities" from Benedict Anderson's *Imagined Communities: Reflections on the Origin and Spread of Nationalism* (London, UK: Verso, 1983).

40 Given, 733. He further explains, "The epicenter for the development of the Lindy Hop was at the Savoy Ballroom." describes the venue, "The Savoy Ballroom opened March 12, 1926 and occupied a full city block between 140th and 141st Street on Lenox Avenue. It closed on July 10, 1958." Given, "Lindy Hop, Community, and the Isolation of Appropriation," 750 (note 10).

41 Given designates the word "spectacularization" to describe the move of social dance from the club or dance hall to the stage. Given, "Lindy Hop, Community, and the Isolation of Appropriation," 742.

42 Ibid.

43 Robinson, *Modern Moves*, 2015; Brenda Dixon Gottschild, *Waltzing in the Dark: African American Vaudeville and Race Politics in the Swing Era* (New York: St. Martin's Press, 2000); Gottschild's *The Black Dancing Body: A Geography from Coon to Cool* (New York: Palgrave Macmillan, 2003) is also pertinent to this discussion.

44 Robinson, *Modern Moves*, 3.

45 Robinson, *Modern Moves*, 64.

46 Robinson, *Modern Moves*, 26.

47 Zora Neale Hurston, "Characteristics of Negro Expressions," in *Negro Anthology*, ed. Nancy Cunard (London, England: Wishart & Company in London, England, 1959), 28.

48 Robinson, *Modern Moves*, 17. Notable works that also discuss the implications of bodies in motion, as well as the impact of social dance on everyday life at the turn of the twentieth century include: Kathy Peiss, *Cheap Amusements Working Women and Leisure in the Turn-of-the-Century New York* (Philadelphia: Temple University Press, 1996); Linda J. Tomko, *Dancing Class: Gender, Ethnicity and Social Divides in American Dance, 1890–1920* (Indianapolis: Indiana University Press, 1999); Joel Dinerstein, *Swinging the Machine: Modernity, Technology, and African American Culture Between the Wars* (Amherst: University of Massachusetts Press, 2003).

49 Robinson, *Modern Moves*, 18.

50 See also Robinson's: "The Ugly Duckling: The Refinement of Ragtime Dancing and the Mass Production and Marketing of Modern Social Dance," *Dance Research: The Journal of the Society for Dance Research* 28, no. 2 (2010): 179–99; "Performing American: Ragtime Dancing as Participatory Minstrelsy," *Dance Chronicle* 32, no. 1 (2009): 89–126; "'Oh, You Black Bottom!' Appropriation, Authenticity, and Opportunity in the Jazz Dance Teaching of 1920s New York," *Dance Research Journal* 38, no. 1/2 (2006): 19–42.

51 Gottschild, *Waltzing in the Dark*, 6.

52 Gottschild, *Waltzing in the Dark*, 35.

53 The replacing of one cultural behavior with another has been termed "surrogation" by Joseph Roach in *Cities of the Dead: Circum-Atlantic Performance* (New York: Columbia University Press, 1996), 2. He describes it as a method of cultures attempting to "fit satisfactory alternatives" as a way of continuing cultural or societal processes, when theirs have been taken over. Roach, *Cities of the Dead,* 2.

Diana Taylor, while agreeing Roach's foundational ideas are valuable, challenges them by explaining that some cultures do follow the new status quo, but "simultaneously" find embodied ways of keeping their culture alive.

54 Taylor, *Archive and the Repertoire*, 46.

55 Gottschild defines the Swing Era as existing between 1920–1940, though recognizes historical jazz writers generally identify it as 1935–45. *Waltzing in the Dark*, 17.

56 Jayna Brown, *Babylon Girls: Black Women Performers and the Shaping of the Modern* (Durham, NC: Duke University Press, 2008).

57 Daphne Brooks, *Bodies in Dissent: Spectacular Performances of Race and Freedom, 1850-1910* (Durham, NC: Duke University Press, 2006). Brooks is also a scholar of American Studies, Women's, Gender and Sexuality Studies, and Music Studies.

58 Thomas F. DeFrantz's *Dancing Many Drums: Excavations in African American Dance* (Madison: University of Wisconsin Press, 2002) is consulted along with various articles.

59 Given, "Lindy Hop, Community, and the Isolation of Appropriation," 739.

60 Benedict Anderson states, "Communities are to be distinguished, not by their falsity/genuineness, but by the style in which they are imagined." He identifies three ways nations, (extending to communities) are imagined: they are *limited* because even the largest communities have boundaries (though elastic); they are *sovereign* or have dreams of being free standing; and as having "deep, horizontal comradeship" providing as sense of *fraternity* that dedicates or inspires one towards the community or nation. Anderson, *Imagined Communities*, 6,7 (Anderson's italics).

61 Given, "Lindy Hop, Community, and the Isolation of Appropriation," 732.

62 Given, "Lindy Hop, Community, and the Isolation of Appropriation," 737.

References

Anderson, Benedict. *Imagined Communities: Reflections on the Origin and Spread of Nationalism*. Rev. ed. London, UK: Verso, 2006.

Boym, Svetlana. *The Future of Nostalgia*. New York: Basic Books, 2001.

Brooks, Daphne. *Bodies in Dissent: Spectacular Performances of Race and Freedom, 1850–1910*. Durham, NC: Duke University Press, 2006.

Brown, Jayna. *Babylon Girls: Black Women Performers and the Shaping of the Modern*. Durham, NC: Duke University Press, 2008.

Cohen-Stratyner, Barbara. "A Thousand Raggy, Draggy Dances: Social Dance in Broadway Musical Comedy in the 1920s." In *Ballroom, Boogie, Shimmy Sham, Shake: A Social and Popular Dance Reader*, edited by Julie Malnig, 217–233. Chicago: University of Illinois Press, 2009.

DeFrantz, Thomas F. ed. *Dancing Many Drums: Excavations in African American Dance*. Madison: University of Wisconsin Press, 2002.

DeVeaux, Scott and Gary Giddins. *Jazz*. 2nd ed. New York: W.W. Norton & Company, 2015.

Dinerstein, Joel. *Swinging the Machine: Modernity, Technology, and African American Culture Between the Wars*. Amherst: University of Massachusetts Press, 2003.

Dodds, Sherril. *Dancing on the Canon: Embodiments of Value in Popular Dance*. Basingstoke, UK: Palgrave MacMillan, 2011.

Erenberg, Lewis. *Swingin' the Dream: Big Band Jazz and the Rebirth of American Culture*. Chicago: University of Chicago Press, 1999.

Gennaro, Liza. *Making Broadway Dance*. Oxford University Press, 2021.

Foster, Susan Leigh. *Choreographing Empathy: Kinesthesia in Performance*. London, UK: Routledge, 2010.

Franko, Mark. *The Work of Dance: Labor, Movement, and Identity in the 1930s*. Middletown, CT: Wesleyan University Press, 2002.

Gioia, Ted. *The History of Jazz*. New York: Oxford University Press, 2011.

Given, William. "Lindy Hop, Community, and the Isolation of Appropriation." In *The Oxford Handbook of Dance and Theatre*, edited by Nadine George-Graves, 729–749. Oxford, UK: Oxford University Press, 2015.

Gottschild, Brenda Dixon. *Digging the Africanist Presence in American Performance: Dance and Other Contexts*. Westport, CT: Greenwood Press, 1996.

Gottschild, Brenda Dixon. *The Black Dancing Body: A Geography from Coon to Cool*. New York: Palgrave Macmillan, 2003.

Gottschild, Brenda Dixon. *Waltzing in the Dark: African American Vaudeville and Race Politics in the Swing Era*. New York: St. Martin's Press, 2000.

Grosz, Elizabeth. *Volatile Bodies: Toward a Corporeal Feminism*. Bloomington: Indiana University Press, 1994.

Halbwachs, Maurice. *On Collective Memory*. Edited and translated by Lewis A. Coser. Chicago: University of Chicago Press, 1992.

Hoffman, Warren. *The Great White Way: Race and the Broadway Musical*. New Brunswick, NJ: Rutgers University Press, 2014.

Hurston, Zora Neale. "Characteristics of Negro Expressions." In *Negro Anthology*, edited by Nancy Cunard, 28–29. London, UK: Wishart & Company, 1959.

Jones, John Bush. *Our Musicals, Ourselves: A Social History of the American Musical Theatre*. Waltham, MA: Brandeis University Press, 2004.

"Laura Osnes and Corey Cott Star in Bandstand the New Broadway Musical at the Jacobs Theatre," *The Shubert Organization*, October 21, 2016. https://shubert.nyc/press/laura-osnes-and-corey-cott-star-in-bandstand-the-new-broadway-musical-at-the-jacobs-theatre/.

Knapp, Raymond. *The American Musical and the Formation of National Identity*. Princeton University Press, 2005.

Knapp, Raymond. *The American Musical and the Performance of Personal Identity*. Princeton: Princeton University Press, 2006.

Knapp, Raymond, Mitchell Morris, and Stacy Wolf. *The Oxford Handbook of The American Musical*. New York: Oxford University Press, 2011.

Kraut, Anthea. *Choreographing Copyright: Race, Gender, and Intellectual Property Rights in American Dance*. Oxford, UK: Oxford University Press, 2016.

Malnig, Julie, ed. *Ballroom, Boogie, Shimmy Sham, Shake: A Social and Popular Dance Reader*. Chicago: University of Illinois Press, 2009.

Most, Andrea. *Making Americans: Jews and the Broadway Musical*. Cambridge: Harvard University Press, 2004.

Music Division, The New York Public Library. "*The Castle walk: trot and one step*" New York Public Library Digital Collections. Accessed August 12, 2022. https://digitalcollections.nypl.org/items/793719fe-64dc-8b00-e040-e00a18066fd5.

Noland, Carrie. *Agency and Embodiment: Performing Gestures/Producing Culture*. Cambridge: Harvard University Press, 2009.

Peiss, Kathy. *Cheap Amusements Working Women and Leisure in Turn-of-the-Century New York*. Philadelphia, PA: Temple University Press, 1996.

"Popular Dance and American Cultural Identity," course description, New York University, accessed April1, 2017. http://gallatin.nyu.edu/academics/courses/2017/FA/idsem-ug1675_001.html.

Roach, Joseph. *Cities of the Dead: Circum-Atlantic Performance*. New York: Columbia University Press, 1996.

Robinson, Danielle. *Modern Moves: Dancing Race During the Ragtime and Jazz Eras* (New York: Oxford University Press).

Robinson, Danielle. "'Oh, You Black Bottom!' Appropriation, Authenticity, and Opportunity in the Jazz Dance Teaching of 1920s New York." *Dance Research Journal* 38, no. 1/2 (2006): 19–42.

Robinson, Danielle. "Performing American: Ragtime Dancing as Participatory Minstrelsy." *Dance Chronicle* 32, no. 1 (2009): 89–126.

Robinson, Danielle. "The Ugly Duckling: The Refinement of Ragtime Dancing and the Mass Production and Marketing of Modern Social Dance." *Dance Research: The Journal of the Society for Dance Research* 28, no. 2 (2010): 179–199.

Savran, David. "The Do-Re-Mi of Musical Theatre Historiography," in *Changing the Subject: Marvin Carlson and Theatre Studies 1959–2009*, edited by Joseph Roach. Ann Arbor: University of Michigan Press, 2009.

"Schedule of Upcoming and Announced Broadway Shows," *Playbill*, accessed November 20, 2018. http://www.playbill.com/article/schedule-of-upcoming-and-announced-broadway-shows-com-113677.

"Show Listings," *Playbill*, accessed March 25, 2017. http://www.playbill.com/productions.

"Show Listings," *Playbill*, accessed April 29, 2022, https://playbill.com/productions.

Stearns, Marshall, and Jean Stearns. *Jazz Dance: The Story of American Vernacular Dance*. New York: Da Capo Press, 1994.

Taylor, Diana. *Archive and the Repertoire: Performing Cultural Memory in the Americas*. Durham, NC: Duke University Press, 2003.

Tomko, Linda J. *Dancing Class: Gender, Ethnicity and Social Divides in American Dance, 1890–1920*. Indianapolis: Indiana University Press, 1999.

Usner, Eric Martin. "Dancing in the Past, Living in the Present: Nostalgia and Race in Southern California Neo-Swing Dance Culture." *Dance Research Journal* 33, no. 2 (2001): 87–101.

Walsh, David, and Len Platt. *Musical Theater and American Culture*. Westport, CT: Greenwood, 2003.

Wolf, Stacy Ellen. *Changed for Good: A Feminist History of the Broadway Musical*. New York: Oxford University Press, 2011.

Woods, Alan. "Consuming the Past: Commercial American Theatre in the Reagan Era." In *The American Stage: Social and Economic Issues from the Colonial Period to the Present*, edited by Ron Engle and Tice L. Miller, 252–266. New York: Cambridge University Press, 1993.

Part I

Ragtime – The Heartbeat of the Modern Era

When Scott Joplin moved to New York City in 1907 he had already published over 40 ragtime compositions including his famous "Maple Leaf Rag," a ringing and seamless model of the form.[1] By the middle of the first decade of the twentieth century, ragtime music had nearly obscured European waltzes and parlor music across the nation. The pulse of syncopated rhythms, the aural assault of chords activated by a lively left hand on the piano keys, the delightful melodies, and the irresistible quick dips into a minor key made ragtime "far and away the gayest, most exciting, most infectiously lilting music ever heard."[2] As the United States transitioned into the new century, ragtime music exemplified the heartbeat of the modern era. In the decade between "The Maple Leaf Rag" and Joplin's arrival in New York from Texas via Missouri, ragtime music became the sound of a new age. The "ragged" rhythms, developed from "folk melodies and from the syncopation of plantation banjos," created a unique American sound.[3] Joplin brought a sense of elegance to the rapid and complex rhythms, and unlike many of his contemporaries, he later turned towards more theatrical genres, including opera and ballet – his intent with his first piece composed for the lyric theatre – "The Ragtime Dance."[4] Joplin had an awareness of the dances that surrounded, depended on, and grew out of the music, as demonstrated by the following lyrics, "Let me see you do the 'rag time dance,' Turn left and do the 'Cake walk prance,' Turn the other way and do the and do the 'Slow drag' […] And do the 'rag time dance.'"[5] By 1907, ragtime music, generally considered to have prospered between 1898 and 1918, infiltrated all walks of life in New York City.[6]

With the toe tapping rhythms and infectious melodies of ragtime music established in Black communities, social dancing as a leisure activity exploded in cities and towns. Ragtime dances, such as the Slow Drag, the Cakewalk, and the numerous Animal Dances such as the Turkey Trot and the Grizzly Bear, all from Black communities to the rhythms of the "jubilant new music," provided the roots of the subsequent social jazz dances of the 1920s such as the Shimmy, the Charleston, and the Black Bottom.[7]

The ragtime era dance craze quickly expanded into a tangle of authorship claims of steps, cultural ownership of dances, and quests for authenticity,

DOI: 10.4324/9781003163688-2

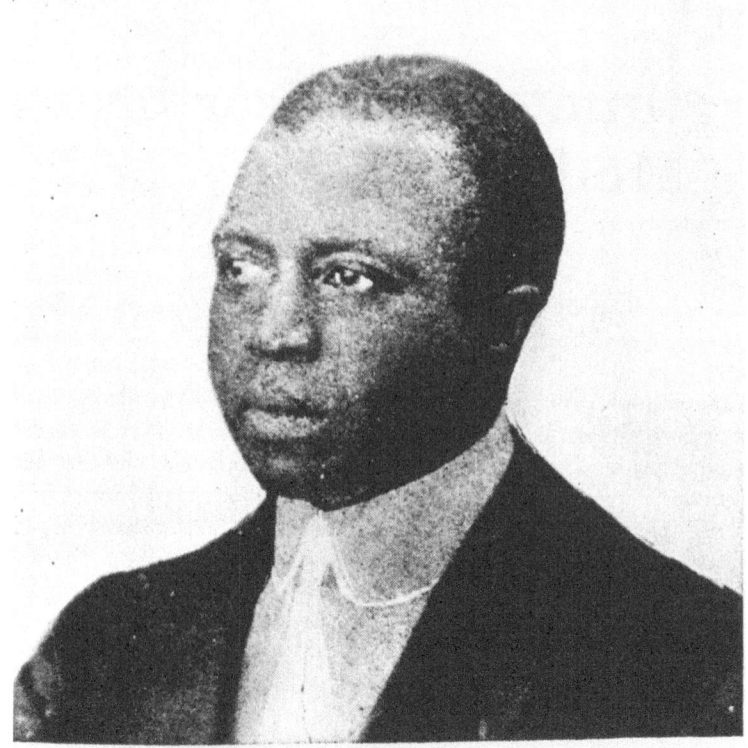

Scott Joplin about 1911

"THE KING OF RAGTIME COMPOSERS"

Figure I.1 "Scott Joplin, 'the king of ragtime composers'"
Source: Schomburg Center for Research in Black Culture, Photographs and Prints Division, The New York Public Library.

which only intensifies in the social dances of the Jazz Age.[8] Further, the deliberate "refinement" of Black dances by white artists, instigated by the immensely popular dance team Irene and Vernon Castle, heightened tensions regarding accepted styles of cultural expression for particular classes and cultures.[9]

Inevitably, the multitude of social dance fads and accompanying social politics spilled over onto the Broadway stage. In this move, social dances further shifted in style, largely due to Black dances being performed by white dancers in white musicals for white audiences.[10]

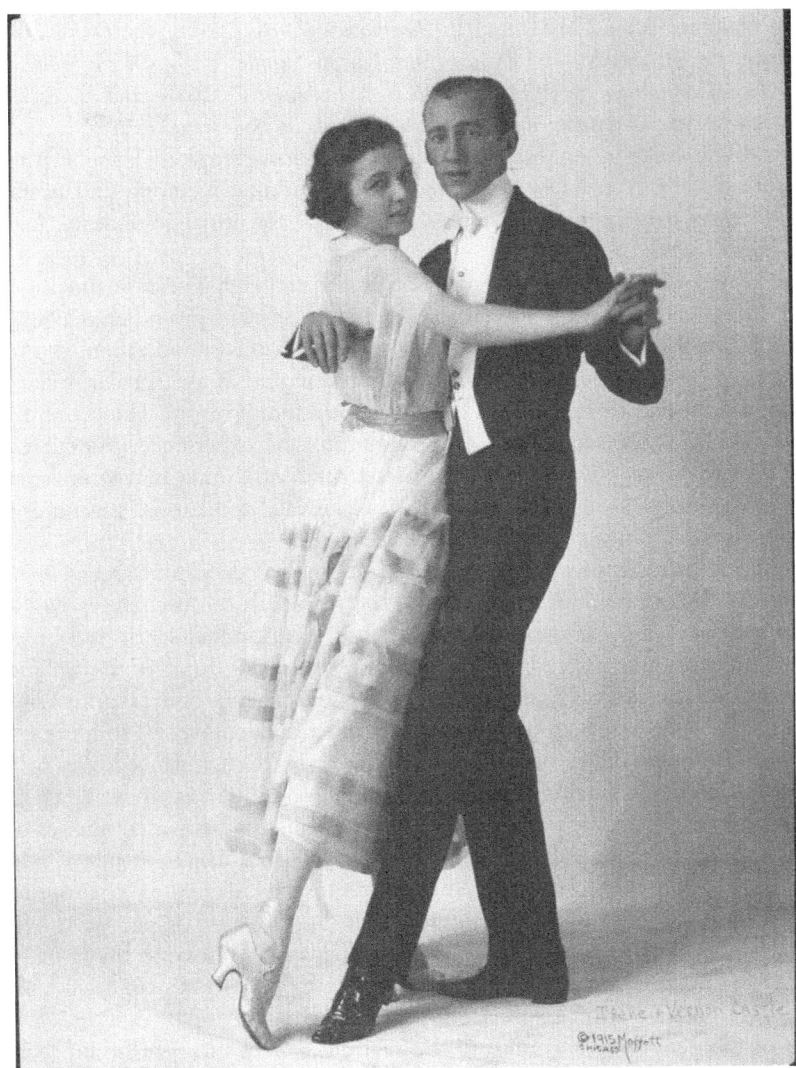

Figure I.2 The Castles were applauded for their elegance and grace by white audiences in their popularizing of Black dances for white audiences. "Irene and Vernon Castle partnering each other" (1915).
Source: Jerome Robbins Dance Division, New York Public Library Digital Collections.

Part one examines early ragtime dances in three musicals in the following three chapters – the Slow Drag in *The Color Purple* (2005), the Cakewalk in *Ragtime* (1998), and Animal Dances and Tap in *Shuffle Along, Or The Making of the Musical Sensation of 1921 and All That Followed* (2016) – and investigates what these social dances *do* when transferred to the stage nearly a century later.[11] The focus is on how the social dances interrogated bring forth the dancer on stage as a site of embodied history, cultural memory, and nostalgia and how the dancing body functions as a catalyst for nostalgic thinking for the audience.

In *Choreographing History*, dance scholar Susan Leigh Foster maintains that the body should not be considered as a "natural or absolute given but as a tangible and substantial category of cultural experience."[12] In this consideration, the stage dancer, when engaged in social dances created in and of a particular social and political moment, participates in both the communities from which the dance originated and their members' enduring historical experience. Whether the community on stage is one that populates a rural jook joint, or a white upper-class community that participates in a Cakewalk fundraiser, meanings are always already attributed to the body dancing.

All three musicals investigated in Part 1 attempt to deepen awareness of particular Black communities at the turn of the twentieth century. By way of diegetic moments of social dance in the musicals, political and social issues rooted in the body are physicalized. The embodiment in social dance of the agitations, passions, and desires of a community makes the dancing body a prime site to examine historical agency and ownership of cultural mores. Considering the body, as "unfinished," the socialization of the body through dance leaves behind physical signifiers of cultural practices and the communities from which they were derived.[13] This embodied history, emphasizing the body as a signifier of its past, is found to be most readable in moments of social dance.

Complications arise with the inclusion of social dances in the musicals, however, as the physicalized aesthetics of the social dance as put forth by the communities who created them are transformed in the move to the Broadway stage. The disparity between taking "your lady to the world's fair [...] And do [ing] the 'rag time dance,'" – a common social event Joplin describes at the turn of the century – and putting the ragtime dances on stage in another far removed era is vast.[14] Though the shift to the stage may be a tribute or celebration of the dance, the move can lead to simplification or mis-representation.[15] Creating a physical space between performer and audience in the theatre, and making a private experience more public, can reduce the social dance of its rich dimensions of cultural meaning and lineage.[16] When dancers perform facing the audience in a more presentational style, the social dances can get flattened, and cultural significance risks becoming "obscured or diluted."[17] Significantly, Black social dances are rooted in a more enclosed circular and improvisational style, thus the exhibitory alterations almost inevitably distort the movement intentions.[18] It is important to recognize, however, the genre of musical theatre has been devoted since its beginnings in musical comedy, vaudeville, and early Broadway revues to creating choreography that excites, thrills, and supports the narrative (to a greater or lesser extent). In this structural expectation, the theatricalized on-stage styles characteristically involve more precision in the placement of steps, unity in choreography across couples, and repeatable sequences in order to produce maximum theatrical and dramatic impact. The adjustments and accommodations made to the social dance are in part how the movement gets used as a foundation for the more theatricalized choreography the genre demands and is celebrated for.

The "spectacularization" of the social dances can be telling of the creative team's motives—in particular the choreographer.[19] While something gets flattened as social dances move to the stage, the social dances are also operating on a nostalgic level that can be critical and productive. In this investigation, attention is given specifically to the choreographers of the three case studies in consideration of how they use the shape and form of the social dance as a primary framework upon which to build their choreographic signature and the embodied nostalgia that is revealed from this handling. Each musical's embodiment of nostalgia is shown to persist in a divergent manner from dehistoricizing appropriation in *The Color Purple*, to deconstructing movement codes in *Ragtime*, to historical reclamation in *Shuffle Along* (2016).

The Color Purple is set prior to the Great Migration of Black Americans where social dances (in the narrative) take place in backwoods jook joints and nostalgia is evoked for an experience of relaxation and privacy from white scrutiny and control. *Ragtime* takes place in a time when the Cakewalk was a popular society dance. The deconstruction of the Cakewalk in the production meets up with two strains of nostalgia through the body. First, it evokes nostalgia in white communities for their effortless modes of living in the era. Second, it conceivably evokes a starkly contrasted two-sided nostalgia, or double consciousness for Black Americans – a nostalgia for outwitting white society through the dance, and an anti-nostalgia for the white brutality to which the roots of the Cakewalk call attention. *Shuffle Along* (2016) straddles the ragtime era and early Jazz Age and its overall essence activates the beginnings of jazz music and dance in musical theatre on Broadway. As a unique counter-example, *Shuffle Along* (2016) undercuts white nostalgic claims to the ownership and creation of musical theatre through its energetic movement style combining both tap dance and a plethora of Animal Dances.

The diverse choreographic structures of each musical require distinct approaches in order to understand the social dance being dehistoricized, deconstructed, or elevated. For this reason the order of investigation of each case study varies based on what is at stake between the dance and the narrative; the history of the Slow Drag takes precedent in *The Color Purple*, a breakdown of the choreography in *Ragtime* is used to enter into the politics of the Cakewalk, and the creative process of developing *Shuffle Along* (2016) begins the final investigation in order to critically examine the function of the choreography of tap powerhouse Savion Glover.

Part 1 concludes at the beginning of the Jazz Age, when the appropriation of Black social dances by white creatives and performers becomes a distinguishing feature. Though all social dances of this section are connected by their hybridity with other dances, what early ragtime dances do fundamentally is emphasize how Black social dances always already express a history of Black survival, endurance, and ingenuity.

Notes

1 "The Maple Leaf Rag" was published in 1899, though written several years earlier in 1896. Edward A. Berlin "Scott Joplin," *Grove Music Online*, October 16, 2013, http://www.oxfordmusiconline.com.ezproxy.gc.cuny.edu/grovemusic/view/10.10 93/gmo/9781561592630.article.A2253061.
2 Rudi Blesh, *They All Played Ragtime: The True Story of American* Music (New York: Grove Press Inc., 1959), 4.
3 Blesh, 7.
4 Joplin's first attempt at writing for the theatre was *The Ragtime Dance*, "a ballet for dancers and a singer-narrator that depicts an African American ball such as those held at Sedalia's Black 400 Club. It was first staged on 24 November 1899 at Wood's Opera House in Sedalia." Berlin, "Scott Joplin."
5 Scott Joplin, "The Ragtime Dance," 1902. Markedly the opening Introduction to the song is often overlooked in the discussion. The introductory lyrics are: "I attended a ball last Thursday night, Given by the dark town swells […] Ev'ry coon came out in full dress alright, And the girls were society belles…" Keeping this language in mind when attending to the cultural language circulating at the time is revealing of the vast difference in respect for Black and white patrons.
6 Edward A. Berlin, "Ragtime," *Grove Music Online*, October 16, 2013, http://www.oxfordmusiconline.com.ezproxy.gc.cuny.edu/grovemusic/view/10.1093.
7 Ted Gioia, *The History of Jazz* (New York: Oxford University Press, 2011), 22. The timeframe of ragtime music and dance begins over two decades before the opening of the iconic Savoy Ballroom in Harlem in 1926. Though the Savoy became the "epicenter" for the expansion and transformation of Black dance styles, the development of the earlier and foundational dances is often overlooked in importance in the historical progression of U.S. social dances. William Given, "Lindy Hop, Community, and the Isolation of Appropriation," in *The Oxford Handbook of Dance and Theatre,* ed. Nadine George-Graves Given (Oxford, UK: Oxford University Press, 2015), 733.
8 The term "Jazz Age" was coined by F. Scott Fitzgerald in his 1931 article "Echoes of the Jazz Age." Fitzgerald claims the Jazz Age began with the May Day Riots in 1919 and concluded with the Stock Market crash in 1929, Fitzgerald, "Echoes of the Jazz Age," accessed March 13, 2018. There are varying views as to the dates of the Jazz Age, Gioia places the Jazz Age beginning in the early to mid-1920s, continuing through the 1930s and early 1940s. He attributes Louis Armstrong as a strong influence in this development, though points out, "the revolution initiated by Armstrong took place in fits and starts, and with little fanfare at the time." Gioia, 56. https://pdcrodas.webs.ull.es/anglo/ScottFitzgeraldEchoesOfTheJazzAge.pdf.
9 Irene and Vernon Castle were a married ballroom dance team that refined Black dances in the early twentieth century and performed them for white audiences in the United States and Europe to much acclaim. The Castles were instrumental in teaching many of the dances to white students, particularly of high society. Megan Pugh explains, "Vernon and Irene Castle set out to change the perception that

cabarets were havens of sin. They helped sanitize social dancing, publicly rejecting the bunny hug, turkey trot, and other ragtime animal crazes." Pugh, Megan, *America Dancing: From the Cakewalk to the Moonwalk* (New Haven, CT: Yale University Press, 2015), 104.

10 For more on attempts at ownership of dances and who can claim ownership of cultural practices see: Anthea Kraut, *Choreographing Copyright: Race, Gender, and Intellectual Property Rights in American Dance* (Oxford, UK: Oxford University Press, 2016). Kraut highlights the inequities of the appropriations and the operation of the "institutional discrimination, entrenched patterns of appropriation, and insidious stereotypes," that beset Black Americans in the U.S. Kraut, *Choreographing Copyright*, 27.

11 *The Color Purple*: 2005, book by Marsha Norman, and music and lyrics by Stephen Bray, Brenda Russell and Allee Willis, based on the 1982 novel by Alice Walker; *Ragtime*: 1998, book by Terrence McNally, music by Stephen Flaherty, lyrics by Lynn Ahrens, based on the 1975 book by E.L. Doctorow, *Shuffle Along, Or The Making of the Musical Sensation of 1921 and All That Followed*: 2015, with music and lyrics by Eubie Blake and Noble Sissle, libretto by George C. Wolfe, based on the original book of the 1921 *Shuffle Along* book by Flournoy Miller and Aubrey Lyles. All musicals have been viewed at the New York Public Library's Theatre on Film and Tape Archive or seen live.

12 Susan Leigh Foster, "Introduction," in *Choreographing History*, ed. Susan Leigh Foster (Bloomington: Indiana University Press, 1995), 4.

13 Grosz, *Volatile Bodies*, x.

14 Scott Joplin, "The Ragtime Dance," 1902.

15 Joplin "The Ragtime Dance," 1902.

16 Given, 730.

17 Ibid., 735.

18 The Stearnses trace the circular dance movement from Africa to the United States by examining a variety of American dances (such as the Buzzard Lope and the Itch) that move in a circular manner common to the Ring Shout in African community movement practice. The Stearnses discuss "patterns of diffusion" of social dances and continually remind their readers circular motion in social dance can be traced back to African roots. Stearns and Stearns, *Jazz Dance*, 32, 25–42.

19 As explained in the introduction, I borrow the term "spectacularization" from William Given who uses it to describe the move of social dance from the club or dance hall to the stage.

References

Berlin, Edward A. "Ragtime." *Grove Music Online*, October 16, 2013. http://www.oxfordmusiconline.com.ezproxy.gc.cuny.edu/grovemusic/view/10.1093.

Berlin, Edward A. "Scott Joplin." *Grove Music Online*, October 16, 2013. 2017. http://www.oxfordmusiconline.com.ezproxy.gc.cuny.edu/grovemusic/view/10.1093/gmo/9781561592630.article.A2253061.

Blesh, Rudi. *They All Played Ragtime: The True Story of American Music*. New York: Grove Press Inc., 1959.

Fitzgerald, F. Scott. Echoes of the Jazz Age (1931). Accessed March 13, 2018, https://pdcrodas.webs.ull.es/anglo/ScottFitzgeraldEchoesOfTheJazzAge.pdf.

Kraut, Anthea. *Choreographing Copyright: Race, Gender, and Intellectual Property Rights in American Dance*. Oxford, UK: Oxford University Press, 2016.

McNally, Terrence, Lynn Ahrens, and Stephen Flaherty. *Ragtime*, Vocal Selections. Van Nuys, CA: Alfred Publishing, 2009.

Pugh, Megan. *America Dancing: From the Cakewalk to the Moonwalk*. New Haven, CT: Yale University Press, 2015.

Russell, Brenda, Allee Willis, Stephen Bray, *The Color Purple*, Vocal Selections. Milwaukee, WI: Hal Leonard Corporation, 2004.

Schomburg Center for Research in Black Culture, Photographs and Prints Division, The New York Public Library. "Scott Joplin, 'the king of ragtime composers'." *New York Public Library Digital Collections*. Accessed August 13, 2022. https://digitalcollec tions.nypl.org/items/61045064-83f7-cc9c-e040-e00a18062c81.

1 "Juke Joints Supposed to be in the Woods"

Nostalgia for Privacy and Place in *The Color Purple*

Shug Avery, the sultry jazz singer in *The Color Purple* encourages "Now there is something 'bout good loving [...] If you want to light your man on fire, You gotta start real slow."[1] And so, hip to hip, legs intertwined, the dancers slowly grind their pelvises together in a figure-eight pattern. Knees are loose and bent, slightly twisting, coiling clockwise until a shift in the man's hand far below the women's waist breaks the slow and sensual spiral, to grip her thigh. The man extends a leg and drags or pulls his partner sideways. In the transition, the couple deepen their connection to the floor, and move together through a low lunge to an adjacent space, merely a foot from where they first stood. A slight loosening of the embrace ensues until the women is pulled upwards, both sets of hands sliding along each other's bodies to resume the intimate and private connection, slightly to the side of where they were originally standing. The dancers are surrounded by other couples engaged in similar erotic play in the dark shadows of the jook joint. A small band, a guitar player or two and a piano player, keep a syncopated and sensuous rhythm. If the joint is popular, a singer might croon evocative and moving lyrics of the fantasies and perils of love, drawing more couples into the dance – the Slow Drag.[2]

Background of the Slow Drag

The Slow Drag, with its intimate nature, is an elusive dance to categorize, though in order to grasp its importance in *The Color Purple*, a historical overview of the dance is necessary. Likewise, comprehending how the dance was disseminated across the U.S. helps with an understanding of the emotional value and sociality of the dance for Black Americans. Danielle Robinson claims the Slow Drag "defies labels such as ragtime, blues, or jazz,"[3] though finds it to be "a key dance of this new era of African American social dancing, as a touchstone for understanding the black migration experience in early twentieth-century New York."[4] The Slow Drag was done in places where Black communities were seeking out privacy from the public politics that surrounded their presence wherever they went. Though *The Color Purple* does not take place in New York, the reasons why the dance was brought North

DOI: 10.4324/9781003163688-3

helps explain the dance's importance for Black communities. The dance is ambiguous to label and situate, however, its visceral sense of intrigue and eroticism clearly emerges in the partnerships put forth on the dance floor. Katrina Hazzard-Gordon explains in *Jookin': The Rise of Social Dance Formations in African American Culture*, "Hip shaking and pelvic innuendo were now more of a statement to one's partner than to one's community."[5]

The Slow Drag was a diversion from the public sphere, and allowed for a mingling of bodies in a particular shared private time and place for community members. For this reason, dances that happened in the jook joints, particularly the Slow Drag, "remained primarily underground, away from the American cultural and political mainstream."[6] For some members of the community attending the jook houses in the rural South, the Slow Drag likely worked to invoke a sense of freedom from the law and white oppression. The move out of the rural South dispersed communities through different migrant tributaries. Hazzard-Gordon explains the Slow Drag is a reminder that "never again would the vast majority of African Americans find themselves in such homogeneous communities."[7] The community closeness experienced in the jook house would rarely be encountered again and attending to this cultural magnitude is integral to understanding social interactions.

Migration and the Slow Drag

When the migration north of Black communities began, re-engaging with the music and dances of the jook joints helped many reimagine "the rural homes they left behind to carve out better, safer lives."[8] Music and dances from the intimate settings of jook houses and honkytonks were brought north into the public arenas of urban locales. "From mouth to mouth and from Jook to Jook," and, I propose, body to body, Black songs and dances travelled north.[9] The embodied memories the Slow Drag roused were used as coping mechanisms and a method of self-care for the new migrants who entered into unfamiliar social and political landscapes. The nostalgia embodied in the Slow Drag is for familial belonging and the routine, where one was free from white employers or authorities, if only for a few hours at the jook joint. As Robinson explains, the Slow Drag was "a powerful source of physical pleasure, recreation, and escape," which is how it is taken up in *The Color Purple*.[10] The Slow Drag was carried north as a reminder of a homeland and a sense of belonging that did not get reclaimed for many decades, if at all, in the North. Further, as a way of retaining a sense of uniqueness and to hold their community together, Black Americans "used dances like the Slow Drag to assert a black distinctiveness within American culture."[11]

The sense of belonging in the North for newly (re)forming Black communities becomes more complicated, however, as different class strata within Black communities attempted to fit into society in different ways. Before long, the Slow Drag was politically seen as a "rejection of black elitism."[12] The Slow Drag threatened to divide Black communities post-migration, where Black elites, in a move to gain respect and positioning in society, sought to move away from working-class identities and interests. To some, the Slow Drag blatantly evoked Black Americans' rural and slave roots. Robinson explains, "As a folk practice, the slow drag was publicly celebrated ... for its embodiment of 'real' black experience" – but not by all.[13] Importantly, this entanglement of meanings comes from an embodied practice, and when the social dance is reanimated in *The Color Purple* on Broadway in 2005, these ideologies rise to the surface. This history of the dance explains why the story unfolding in the musical needs to be expressed not only through the music of the time but through dance. Though the Slow Drag within the narrative of *The Color Purple* happens in the South, prior to significant northern migration, the dance is emblematic of this pride, as its inward and private focus bespeaks a sense of safety and belonging. *The Color Purple* is situated in this moment, and explores the dysfunctions, but also harmonies, within communities, focusing in on the love between the ones who stayed and those who were forced away.

The Color Purple

The musical *The Color Purple* is based on Alice Walker's 1982 novel of the same name. Walker's novel won the 1983 Pulitzer Prize for fiction and was adapted into a film in 1985, directed by Steven Spielberg.[14] The story begins in 1909 in rural Georgia and follows the life of fourteen year-old Celie, including her trials and tribulations at the hands of her abusive father and husband. The plot traces Celie's plight to reconnect with her sister Nettie and the two children she had as a result of rape by her father, who were taken from her at their birth. With the help of the uninhibited performer and singer Shug Avery, Celie learns of letters from her sister that had been kept from her by her ruthless husband. Celie's reconnection with Nettie and bond with Shug starts her on the path to personal empowerment that begins with her leaving her husband and creating her own business. The story offers the opportunity to critically rethink Celie's embodied experience, which opens with a shattered Celie singing "Somebody Gonna Love You," and concludes with "I'm Here," sung by Celie, the now successful and self-determined business woman.[15]

This frank and poignant story of the struggles of Black women in the early twentieth century was turned into a musical in 2005. *The Color Purple* is the only Broadway musical to have a jook house as part of the narrative and to use the Slow Drag.[16] The social dance occurs in one of the few moments of dance in the show, when, as previously described, the sultry Shug Avery sings the song "Push Da Button" in a jook house. The original production, directed by Gary Griffin and choreographed by Donald Byrd, ran for three years at The Broadway Theatre. The show was revived on Broadway in 2015 at the Bernard B. Jacobs Theatre, directed and staged by John Doyle.[17] The original production with music and lyrics by Stephen Bray, Brenda Russell, and Allee Willis, received ten Tony nominations though only one win (Best Actress in a

Musical for LaChanze in the role of Celie) and overall drew lukewarm reviews. The Doyle revival received tremendous praise, including four Tony nominations and the Tony award for "Best Revival of a Musical." Both productions imagine the communities of rural Georgia in disparate ways that distinctly clash in their embodied interpretation of the time.[18] There was greater diversity in the original 2005 creative team which also included, along with Byrd, Black musical director Linda Twine and producers Oprah Winfrey and Quincy Jones. The Black representation in the creative team for the revival was slightly less, though Winfrey was again involved and Jason Michael Webb took up the role as Music Director. As mentioned, Doyle took on the directing, musical staging and set design. An investigation of the revival in latter part of this chapter explores how musical theatre engages with issues of cultural, economic and political environments, and troubles how cultural bias around cultural expressions operates in theatre systems, particularly with John Doyle, a white Scottish director being appointed director for the revival.

Choreography and the original *The Color Purple* (2005)

Donald Byrd, the choreographer of the original *The Color Purple,* is a renowned contemporary concert dance choreographer who has worked with Alvin Ailey and Twyla Tharp among many others and has been the artistic director of Spectrum Dance Theatre based in Seattle, Washington since 2002. Prior to that engagement he founded Donald Byrd/The Group which performed and toured extensively or over twenty years. Byrd has a vast repertoire of choreographic works ranging over the past fifty years. Some better known of his works include *The Harlem Nutcracker* (1999) and more recently *Greenwood* (2019). He is part of a small and unique group of Black choreographers of Broadway musicals that includes, among others, Savion Glover, George Faison, and in 2017, Camille A. Brown debuting with *Once On This Island.* [19] Like Glover and George C. Wolfe, who will be explored in Chapter 3, Byrd is distinctly and steadfastly committed to social justice and in much of his work he investigates the complexities of Black performance in history with the intention to move people to action. As choreographer for the 2005 *The Color Purple,* Byrd includes his take on the Slow Drag in the scene in Harpo's jook joint in the first act. Harpo, Celie's stepson, builds the jook joint out of his broken-down house in defiance of his strong-willed wife Sophia. Byrd's intentional use of some of the basic sensibilities of the Slow Drag, such as the grinding of hips and pelvis and holding of buttocks, gestures towards the origins of the form. Byrd had a familiarity with the movement of the era, as over a decade prior to *The Color Purple* in 1991 he created *The Minstrel Show,* a complex and complicated intervention into blackface minstrelsy that utilized dances of the early twentieth century, including a pointed confrontation with the Cakewalk, in order to challenge and breakdown racial stereotypes.[20] While *The Color Purple* did not allow space for a poignant political intervention, Byrd's reputation as someone whose form has deep roots in Black aesthetics and commitment social justice circulates in the performance. The slow build and unfolding of the style of Byrd's choreography in *The Color Purple* also celebrates how "exceedingly accessible" the Slow Drag was to those in attendance at the jook house. All skill levels can join in in their own way, whether at the more complex end of the style or more subtle movement qualities. This range of participatory opportunities exists in the origins of the social dance giving it an inclusive feel from the start.[21] Shug Avery welcomes all to "Push Da Button," and all do, including the older less athletic performers.

Critical response to Byrd's choreography was generally unenthusiastic. Brian Scott Lipton found that director Gary Griffin rarely allowed Byrd to "let loose," and the moment he finally does (in the Africa montage in act two) critics felt he radically overcompensated.[22] Ben Brantley recognized his contribution only as "sprightly fits of choreography."[23] This sort of analysis is demonstrative of a partiality towards the text and score in order to illustrate community experience in the broader sense of musical theatre criticism. This minimal emphasis on the dance by the reviewers, imparts a lack of understanding of the physicalized nature of the communities that created the dances themselves and those explored in the show. "Push Da Button" is an over four-minute dance production number which involves more than "sprightly fits" of movement, its builds from Shug bringing people in and creates, without extensive sets or lighting, the atmosphere of the jook house. Choreography is more than structured, unison dances, but a movement vision that encompasses the whole movement dynamic of the scene that works in *The Color Purple* to shine a light on a community at their most carefree. In Byrd's interpretation of "Push Da Button," the group movement, whether in the more complex choreography of a highlighted dancer or the enthusiastic bump and grinds of the onlookers, creates the feel and sound of the jook joint. Overall, Byrd establishes the sense of liberty and lascivious behaviour that the jook joint gives space for.

In Byrd and Griffin's dramaturgical structure, the rural jook house provides, through lighting and simple wooden structures, a sense of escape and privacy.[24] Music historian Paul Oliver explains the jook joint, "was the final bastion for black people who want to get away from whites and the pressures of the day.[25] Furthermore, the jook house needed no assistance from public officials to function. As Hazzard-Gordon explains, "The jook provided both entertainment and an economic alternative to people excluded from the mainstream economy."[26] The dance in the jook house in the woods in *The Color Purple* shows an intimacy within the community, in a space free from the eyes of hovering authorities, even if the sense of privacy is only imagined. In "Push Da Button" there is a harmonious moment where bodies are grinding, backs are arching, and arms are swinging, where desires seem to be met and bodies of all physical sizes and abilities come together. The direct sexual metaphor of the lyrics unashamedly helps to eroticize the song in the production, "Keep on turning up that voltage [...] Like you're switchin' on a lightbulb, Watch the juice begin to flow..."[27] The song is about sexual intercourse and celebrates the freedom of unbridled desire. The dance allows and encourages bodies of all types to engage in physical contact, to feel that visceral connection with another person. Celebrating physical intuitions and connectedness through the Slow Drag awakens a sense of utopianism held in the body. The appealing number champions Black bodies dancing and demonstrates free will and sovereignty through its lack of physical inhibitions.[28] This moment further physicalizes the historical trajectory, the "tangible and substantial category of cultural experience" of Black dance styles – from indigenous African dances where connections to many subsequent social dances can be made, to plantation dances where slaves sought out any sense of community through music and dance, to backwoods jook joints and a brief sense of seclusion and privacy.[29]

Imagined Communities and Pre-Migratory Nostalgia

The notion of Black Americans escaping from white control both during slavery and after emancipation created a tight community united by the goal to preserve their culture. As Hazzard-Gordon explains, "This sense of community existed in a dynamic tension with white control and allowed for the creation of distinctly African-American cultural activities."[30] The nostalgia in this construct is for a sense of belonging and solidarity that was challenged in the years following the Civil War. As people scattered around the country, any sense of privacy was arguably gone and "strong bonds of loyalty" broke down.[31] There was uncertainty, anxiety, and as Hazzard-Gordon finds, "some were frightened by their new freedom."[32] The Slow Drag evoked the power and endurance behind communities in the face of such enormous oppression. Using the body as a conduit to the past, or at least as an embodiment of memories, makes for a unique way of knowing and situating oneself in the world.

To be sure, there is a risk of suggesting there is a nostalgia for plantation days by celebrating dances that were essentially created out of the performance practices of, or near to, that era. Byrd, however, emphatically uses the Black body in *The Color Purple* to show ownership of and pride in these dances if not the social conditions of 1907. Black performers in the 2005 production execute the social dance with grounded centers, a looseness of hips and knees, and an unrestricted sense of flow true to the origins of the dance.[33] In the jook house scene, in order to clearly represent the Black communities involved, European influences should be very minimal.[34] Though European influences had been absorbed into ragtime music, the Slow Drag, by its private nature in the remote jook house setting, would rely on Black movement sensibilities.

Nonetheless, Black social dance communities are transformed in the move to the stage in a variety of ways in *The Color Purple*. Most obviously, the rhythm of the music is sped up so there is a more extravagant and flashier feel to the piece, as opposed to the "slow, delayed sensuality," which Nadine George-Graves describes is fundamental to the Slow Drag.[35] Stephen Bray, Brenda Russell, and Allee Willis collectively share credit for creating the music and lyrics of *The Color Purple*. Due to their different musical backgrounds, Bray from rock, Russell from jazz, and Willis from a multimedia and song writing background, there is a mixing of musical styles in the musical.[36] The blues-styled music, generally sits more squarely in the era than most of the other songs in the musical that have a more contemporary R&B sound, sprinkled with simple pop rhythms and sentimental lyrics. The change in tempo, however, plays a large part in transforming the execution of the dance and shifts how the community is displayed. The increase in speed portrays the rural Black community as more outward. At jook joints, participants "were exhausted from their work and tally of the day's oppressions within their own community."[37] These conditions are very much part of the themes that circulate in *The Color Purple,* even if they are not fully embodied in the dancing in Harpo's jook joint on stage given the upbeat tempo.[38]

In addition, the dancing body in "Push Da Button" is more upright with shoulders back and the head up, a characteristic of a more European style that avoids slouched positions. This posture challenges the roots of the dance, though is part of the compensation in the theatricalization of the dance.[39] There are some attempts in "Push Da Button" to avoid European physicalities; for example, knees are flexed throughout and the sensuous pelvic circling is continuous. The Slow Drag is also reimagined by its very presentational, front-facing entertaining style. This choreographic choice alters the private and intimate nature of the dance. As dance scholars Karen Hubbard and Terry Monaghan point out in "Negotiating Compromise on a Burnished Wood Floor: Social Dancing at the Savoy," the Slow Drag is a private dance done in dark, closed venues.[40] The dances that were taken up in rural jook joints or private clubhouses were not for show or teaching but for social relations and sexual opportunities. This can be seen in the intense sensuality that surrounds the Slow Drag, described by Hubbard and Monaghan as only "marginally acceptable," when it arrived in New York.[41]

The movement style in *The Color Purple* also shifts in reaction to the tempo as bodies in motion in the number seem tuned in to a more contemporary "Dirty Dancing" style, a fusion of more vigorous Latin dances such as the Mambo and the Lambada, than the relaxed and languid Slow Drag.[42] Certainly, the odd high flying partnered lifts and kicks are out of place in the historical context of the narrative, along with partner-supported drops into the splits by some chorus members. Though, as this project explores, choreographers' may diverge from historical accuracy out of necessity to fulfil the expected conventions of the form. By the end, "Push Da Button" becomes a highly stylized Broadway number, with unison group choreography that builds to all shaking their hands, in the "jazz hands" style, towards Shug Avery before all collapsing to the ground.[43] Byrd lets loose in the last minute of the piece and over-compensates by adding in *jetés* (leaps) and other ballet-derived moves, with expert ballet skills from the dancers. However, as the act one finale nears, the need to impress audiences is critical. Understandably, this is part of the compensation that happens when social dance is transferred to the stage. However, what is pressed out of the dance by the end is its universal welcoming of all bodies and skill levels. Finely trained dancers, with taut and strong bodies, turn and kick with expertise and panache, distorting any ideas the less-skilled could join in. Publicizing or "spectacularizing" the dance imagines a different sort of experience; trained bodies replace socializing bodies.

The virtuosity on display is impressive and the one-upmanship of hot dance moves is titillating, though the relaxed and low-pressure mood of the jook house is markedly gone. There is nostalgia at work here that envisions the jook joint as a hot club more suited to 1930s Harlem than to the rural south. In this kind of nostalgia – more restorative, and in fact disruptive, than reflective – there is what Rebecca Rugg calls "a fantasy of similarity," where America is seen to be populated by people who are all alike and of equal abilities.[44] Dehistoricizing appropriation in this manner assumes that all jook joints are of this uplifted manner and reinterprets the importance of the venue to the Black experience. John Doyle, however, takes much more severe steps that demonstrates an uncertain engagement with issues of cultural, economic and political environments of the community he explores.

Choreography and *The Color Purple* Revival (2015)

In a drastic shift, the dance in the 2015 revival of *The Color Purple* is near non-existent. There is no choreographer listed as part of the production team. Scottish stage director John Doyle is credited for "Direction and Musical Staging."[45] Ann Yee was the choreographer of Doyle's initial London production of the revival in 2013, whose contributions Ben Brantley described at the time as "subtle and elegant."[46] Yee's name was removed from the production credits and the movement signature became more understated once the piece moved to Broadway.[47] The choice not to include social dances that were part of the jook joints of rural Black communities makes for an alternate interpretation of life in the early twentieth century than the original production. This move risks disregarding or redrawing rural Black communities as more austere than they were. Doyle, renowned for paring down musicals to focus on character depth and development, chooses to show minimal dance-like moves in "Push Da Button."[48] There are some shoulder shimmies, a few hip swings, and select "step-touches," but Doyle, who also designed the sparse set, uses the chairs that make up most of the environment of the play to signal the sexuality. At certain points during the song men and women sit on or straddle the chairs. The performers then rise and lower their bodies on the chairs as a stand-in for physical connection. This move undermines the possible nostalgia within the movement, creating a stiffness that, along with Jennifer Hudson's somewhat tempered performance as Shug Avery, subdues the experience of the jook house. The straddling of the chairs, while apropos in a musical such as *Cabaret* ("Mein Heir") or *Chicago* ("Cell Block Tango"), seems gratuitous and borrows a trope that works in a cabaret-like setting but not within the modest dramaturgical structure Doyle has set up in *The Color Purple*.[49] Doyle's choices in the scene fall flat, and as critic Joe Dzeimianowicz describes, his use of chairs "feels a bit gimmicky" in parts.[50] For example, chairs are shuttled around so Shug can walk along them in a line, which has been done in a variety of shows and is quite common as a choice. Further, turning the chair around and straddling it becomes much more performative than it need be in the Doyle production. When a social dance – which is characteristically in this era about a partnered pressing of bodies together – is done with an object instead, there is a awkwardness that need not be present. The stand in of a chair for the Black body devalues the embodied history of the social dance and the community from which it came and the community explored in *The Color Purple*. While Doyle uses the chairs as a stand in for other scenarios (to make a table for example), using them to stand in for bodies, that are in fact populate the space, does not engage with the cultural identity of the characters in the narrative. This choice displays a bias toward a minimalist way of theatre making that while characteristic of a more post-modern or Eurocentric style disavows the community whose story he is telling and does not fit the aesthetic of the genre he is exploring. He has however taken the time to rethink the language of the play and does not have the actors speak in dialects outside of their own personal speech pattern, thereby avoiding stereotypic performative utterance of the Black experience that is so common in past theatre, such as *Showboat* or *Porgy & Bess*.

Critics overall, however, had positive reactions to Doyle's production, all generally agreeing that it was an improvement on the original. What is noticeable across a span of a dozen different reviews is the movement is rarely mentioned, if at all. Some begin their reaction by noticing its absence: Matt Windman says, "At first, Doyle's production comes off as overtly mannered and limited in movement"; Jesse Green observes, "The songs and dialogue have been trimmed, and much of the dance music removed as fluff."[51] However, both resolve that the show works in this new manner. In fact, the dance has been drastically trimmed down and often moves are generally just suggested. Each actor portrays their own physicality as part of their character and save for the moments pointed to in this discussion, Doyle's revival is limited in movement.

What is more often recognized by reviewers is how the general conventions of musical theatre have shifted slightly under Doyle's treatment. For example, Peter Marks of the *Washington Post* describes the show as "virtually a concert version," or Charles McNulty at the *Los Angeles Times* finds that Doyle "treat[s] the show more like a church service than a traditional book musical."[52] The absence of dance does not seem to bother critics; most applaud the greater focus on Celie (Cynthia Erivo) and the vocal heft the female leads bring to the show. Green articulates most clearly that Doyle "stages the songs for their thematic content"; the staging of "Push Da Button" "separate[s] the women and the men in ways that clarify the lyrics and then bring[s] them together on equal terms. He gets the showstopper almost as a side effect."[53] There does not seem to be an equalizing in the movement, the performers are separating to give space to Shug's storytelling. This treatment, which sidelines the ensemble, turns away from the embodiment of the music and lyrics and veers the musical towards a "concert version" that keeps emphasis on the voice, over the body and choreography, to achieve success. In fact, the critics generally applaud the erasure of the movement qualities that are so part of the Black rural cultural experience, making the white critics in a way implicit in the erasure of the Black body. While it is possible that the piece could be expressed only in music which is also key to the moment, given the specific narrative designation of "Push Da Button" happening in a jook house and given the layers of embodied embedded in the history of the jook joint, the moment is puzzling.

The need for a more robust set up of the jook joint fades into the background in order to provide space for a celebrity performer. Hudson does enact a suggestive grinding atop a man laid out on a chair at one point, but for much of the song she assembles the patrons of the jook joint in chairs and sings to them in a sermon-like style. The patrons of the jook house seem more like a congregation than the denizens of a rogue gambling and drinking house. Lyrics such as, "Watch the juice begin to flow [...] Find the spot she love the best, If you don't know where it is, Give her the stick; she'll do the rest"[54] present a stark contrast to the physicality shown on stage. While the engagement with the chairs hints at some eroticism, Doyle's choice derails the nature of the jook joints. The ensemble, however, does warm up to the lascivious concepts suggested in the song. Overall, the importance of the jook house and dance in the rural community gets misrepresented as stiff and perfunctory, disassembling the imagery in Walker's novel.

Unlike Byrd, Doyle does use a variety of body types, all with less dance technicity or overt athleticism than is often the norm in many Broadway choruses. Does taking this tack make for a more sophisticated, complex, and respectable performance? Hilton Als finds that Doyle "exercise[s] empathy, critical distance, and an openness to lives and cultures other than his own."[55] This identification by Als readily captures the approach of Doyle's overall dramaturgy, however, there is not a consistency in this suggested "critical distance" later on in the play which seems to undo this openness via a minimalist approach. In the second act, Doyle uses the bodies of the ensemble purposely to invoke images of Africa. While Doyle keeps his distance from fully imagining the community in the jook house, as applauded by Als, he conceives of the "Africa" of Celie's imagination with relative abundance, as a place filled with family and tradition. This contradiction in how culture is embodied undermines nostalgia for the places and moments of respite for Black communities in the rural South. It is worth explaining the movement concept in the second act of Doyle's revival to demonstrate his puzzling use of movement.

When Celie reads though hidden letters from her sister Nettie, whom she comes to learn is living in Africa, Doyle carefully traces Celie's imaginings of Africa for the audience. In place of what had been a lengthy African dance sequence in Byrd's original choreography, that tended towards a romanticized vision of Africa, Doyle uses a much more straightforward portrayal.[56] For example, Doyle engages the female ensemble to imagine Nettie's world in Africa, whereas Byrd has a large dance chorus (who did not seem to appear in other parts of the show) take over the scene. For Doyle, the same women who have been part of Celie's life up until this point as secondary characters and community members use baskets from the previous scene to evoke images of Africa. They put the baskets on their heads and slowly promenade around the stage. They pull out bright coloured scarves and gently undulate and billow them up and down to enhance the imagery. By avoiding any compilation of African dance, but rather using gestures of everyday community tasks, the story is kept in the African paradigm and not shifted to a questioning of European influences. Still, the cutting out of traditional movements, decreases the emphasis on Black culture. This issue becomes a talking point for critics who praise the minimalism by-passing any allowance for grandeur and celebration of African movement. Critic David Rooney explains the issue in his review of the revival, "Whereas before, that narrative shift brought a jarring detour into full-on *Lion King* exotica, Doyle transports us with the simple means of basketware carried by the female ensemble members, who unfurl lengths of African-print fabric.[57] In the 2005 production, the African dance chorus, as explained by Rooney, was a distraction to the overall narrative of the show. It should be noted however, that this section of the show is uniquely Cellie's imaginative construction of her sister's experiences, and thus the sensationalism, which unfortunately Black artists such as Alvin Ailey are sometimes criticized for, should have been looked at with greater openness given the dream-like nature of the sequence to start. Conversely, the simplicity and practicality of Doyle's representation of Africa within the sparse set helps conjure up the ideas circulating in Celie's imagination without the scene feeling exoticized, which makes for an acceptable choice for a weak part in the narrative in general, however, the absence of the large dance ensemble from the original is felt. The dream-like nature of the memory does allow for both versions to work in their own way. Regardless, Doyle's treatment of the jook joint scene seems less able to "transport" the audience to a place where inhibitions are dropped and sexual energy abounds in a way that the location requires.[58]

The incompatibility of the two sections felt like a stumble in the dramaturgy of the piece. Though the revival was much more successful overall than the original, offering up the opportunity to further shape the movement in the musical to his original choreographer, Ann Yee (or another choreographer), may have provided a greater space for reflection on the Black experience. Brantley observes it is part of Doyle's style to "[make] shows smaller to demonstrate how truly big they are."[59] However, despite his paring down and reducing sensationalism, bodily meanings are unavoidably present and again bring forth "a substantial category of cultural experience" to tap into that could have deepened the experience of the jook house instead of bringing it into a more contemporary minimalist interpretation.[60] Privileging minimalism suggests, even if subtly, a more Eurocentric lens or colonial gaze which holds to a style of performance that does not fit the narrative.

In all, *The Color Purple* is a difficult show for a choreographer to take on given the minimal and differing movement requirements. The narrative of the show does not offer the opportunity to develop a choreographic through-line or cohesive movement signature. The contrast between Doyle's modest interpretation and Byrd's more spectacular methods is vast. Both approach the jook house in different ways, though neither quite captures the essence and import of the backwoods establishment. Hazzard-Gordon claims, "The African American jook may very well be the most significant development in American popular dance and popular music history."[61] The challenge of addressing this significance is complex. Byrd adds flourishes that transform the intimate dance into a more public entertainment offering expected of the genre of musical theatre, though makes the environment more public-facing than the nature of intimate location primed for physical connections between bodies, when soloists put forth virtuosic dance moves. Doyle attempts to pull back and offer a more minimalist and pedestrian interpretation but loses the essence and weakens opportunities for reflective nostalgia which demonstrates a disconnect from the embodied history of Black culture. Given the fact that the 2015 revival ran during the rise of the Black Lives Matter movement, there was perhaps a missed opportunity for Doyle to make a more emblematic statement of the importance of the jook joint to a story of the inner workings, accomplishments, and solidarity of Black communities. The embodied nostalgia within the bodies of the performers, as carriers of that tradition, could have been lifted through movement to a point where there was a more personal contemplation of Black autonomy. Hazzard-Gordon insists, "For it is in the jook that core black culture – its food, language, community fellowship, mate selection, music, and dance found sanctuary."[62] It would be possible to show a key place (or idea) of sanctuary in a time of much misalignment, with both critical distance and eloquence. Though Byrd's choreography flattens the importance of this fundamental function with an over-emphasis on flash, the jook scene is a highlight that uplifts in the original musical that brings together bodies in motion to create a community. In contrast, Doyle's scene cuts off a valuable opportunity for nostalgic enlightenment, empowerment, and a sense of belonging in the contemporary moment by not focusing in on the cultural aesthetic of movement as a way of creating community. In consideration that the body "lacks finality," troubling how the body is shaped by its social history, particularly experiences as significant as the jook joint is an essential endeavor.[63] Structurally, a greater emphasis on the bodily practices of the era throughout the entire production (not only two songs) might help to make the cultural import of the show more physically tangible and encourage greater contemplation of racial injustices. As a male non-white non-American, Doyle takes some huge risks in taking on much of the creative roles himself. With the ongoing efforts in the 2020s at decolonizing theatre practices, casting, and creative teams would this unilateral vision for the piece have been as well-received?

Notes

1 "Push Da Button," *The Color Purple*, music and lyrics by Brenda Russell, Allee Willis, Stephen Bray, 2005.
2 This description is compiled from accounts of the dance in The Mura Dehn Collection and Papers, "Papers on Afro-American Dance," circa 1869–1987, *Performing Arts Research Collections – Dance*, NYPL, box 1,3; the viewing of archival videos at the Schomburg Center for Research in Black Culture, "Ernie Smith Jazz and Dance File," Collection tape 1, 25a, SC Visual VRA; and descriptions in Danielle Robinson's Modern Moves: Dancing Race During the Ragtime and Jazz Era (New York: Oxford University Press, 2015).
3 Ibid., 28.
4 Ibid., 36.
5 Katrina Hazzard-Gordon, *Jookin':The Rise of Social Dance Formations in African American Culture* (Temple University Press: Philadelphia, 1992), 93.
6 Hazzard-Gordon, *Jookin'*, xi. The Slow Drag is not the only dance to occur in the jook joint. Hazzard-Gordon explains, "Dances in the jooks included the Charleston, the shimmy, the snake hips, the funky butt, the twist, the slow drag, the buzzard lope, the black bottom, the itch, the fish tail, and the grind." *Jookin,* 83. While many of these dances involved hip movements, the highly sexualized lyrics of "Push Da Button," in *The Color Purple* sits within the movement style of the Slow Drag.
7 Ibid., 64.
8 Robinson, Modern Moves, 35.
9 Zora Neale Hurston, "Characteristics of Negro Expressions." In *Negro Anthology*, edited by
      Nancy Cunard, 28–29 (London, UK: Wishart & Company, 1959), 29.
10 Robinson, Modern Moves, 37.
11 Ibid., 38.
12 Ibid., 37.
13 Ibid.
14 The playbills to the original musical and revival cite the basis of the musical as both the novel and the film, stating below the title: "Based upon the novel written by Alice Walker and the Warner Bros./Amblin Motion Picture," "Inside *The Color Purple*," *Playbill*, accessed March 2, 2018. http://www.playbill.com/playbillpagega llery/inside-playbill?asset=00000150-aea8-d936-a7fd-eefc72eb0004&type=Inside Playbill&slide=1.
15 "Somebody Gonna Love You," "I'm Here," music and lyrics by Brenda Russell, Allee Willis, Stephen Bray, 2005.
16 Though there are no musicals with the Slow Drag, John O. Perpener reports Wallace Thurman's 1929 play *Harlem* incorporates the Slow Drag into the narrative. *Harlem* tells the story of an African American family from South Carolina who move to Harlem and face financial difficulties as well as prejudices within the black community. In order to make ends meet the family holds rent parties; in these instances, the Slow Drag was performed. John O. Perpener, *African American Concert Dance: The Harlem Renaissance and Beyond* (Champaign, IL: University of Illinois Press, 2001), 37. The play has been the object of much controversy as to whether it

is "an honest portrayal or exploitation of African American urban life;" Linda M. Carter, "Wallace Thurman 1902–1934," in *African American Dramatists: An A-to-Z Guide* ed. Emmanuel S. Nelson (Westport, CT: Greenwood Press, 2004), 438.

17 John Doyle originally revived the musical at The Menier Chocolate Factory in London in 2013 with choreography by Ann Yee. An adjusted production was then brought to Broadway and produced by Scott Sanders, Roy Furman, and Oprah Winfrey in 2015. The Broadway revival ran just over a year closing January 8, 2017. "The Color Purple," *Playbill,* http://www.playbill.com/production/the-co lor-purple-broadway-theatre-vault-0000012250, accessed January 9, 2019.

18 The choice to include the Doyle revival is an exception to the designation to avoid revivals because of the enthusiasm and reception surrounding it in comparison to the original.

19 The small group of Black Broadway choreographers (and some of their credits) further includes the likes of Lester Wilson (*Saturday Night Fever* (Film, 1977), *Sister Act* (Film, 1992), Henry LeTang (*Black and Blue* (1989), Debbie Allen *Carrie* (1988), Hope Clarke, *Caroline or Change* (2004), *Jelly's Last Jam* (1992), Marlies Yearby, *Rent* (1991), Dianne McIntyre, *Paul Robeson* (1988), Mabel Robinson *It's So Nice to Be Civilized* (1980), and the 1976 revival of *Porgy and Bess*. Most notably, Katherine Dunham choreographed nine Broadway shows, including her uncredited work in *Cabin in the Sky* (1940) where the choreographer was listed as George Balanchine. "The List of Black Female Women Who've Choreographed for Broadway is Too Short," accessed January 16, 2022. https://www.dancemagazine.com/black-wom en-choreographers/.

20 He won a Bessie Award for *The Minstrel Show* in 2002. He revived the piece in 2015 called *The Minstrel Show Revisited* that toured throughout the U.S. The *Revisted* version involved the reading of the transcripts of the cases of the Trayvon Martin and Michael Brown shootings. "Donald Byrd."

21 Robinson, Modern Moves, 36.

22 Brian Scott Lipton describes the jook scene of act one: "One of the too-few occasions when choreographer Donald Byrd gets to let loose," Lipton further suggests he goes too far later in the Africa montage section in act two. "*The Color Purple,*" TheatreMania, December 1, 2015, http://www.theatermania.com/new-york-city-theater/reviews/12-2005/the-color-purple_7219.html.

23 Ben Brantley, "One Women's Awakening, in Double Time," *New York Times,* December 5, 2005, http://www.nytimes.com/2005/12/02/theater/reviews/one-womans-awakening-in-double-time.html.

24 John Lee Beatty's set design for *The Color Purple* (2005) frames the stage with dark wooden walls, table tops, and a make-shift bar that easily accommodates the behaviours, from gambling to drinking to dancing, apropos to a jook joint.

25 Paul Oliver, *Blues off the Record: Thirty Years of Blues Commentary* (Tunbridge Wells, Kent: Baton Press; New York, NY: Hippocrene Books, 1984), 46.
    Music Historian Paul Oliver explains the jook joint, "was the final bastion for black people who want to get away from whites and the pressures of the day."

26 Hazzard-Gordon, *Jookin',* x.

27 "Push Da Button," Music and lyrics by Brenda Russell, Allee Willis, Stephen Bray, 2005.

28 The privacy to experience physical intimacy for Black Americans is made all the more poignant keeping in mind the unofficial prohibition of serious love scenes/songs between Black characters on stage during the early twentieth century. It was not until *Shuffle Along* in 1921 (nearly a decade later than the narrative of *The Color Purple*) that a love scene and song, "Love Will Find A Way," between two Black performers was accepted and applauded by audiences. Allen Woll explains "while perfectly acceptable in white musical comedies, love scenes were taboo in black shows, since it was assumed that romancing would offend white audiences…

Despite [efforts] to revise stereotypic notions of black behavior, the love making taboo lingered into the 1920s." Allen L. Woll, *Black Musical Theatre: From "Coontown" to "Dreamgirls"* (Baton Rouge: Louisiana State University Press, 1989), 23–24. In *The Color Purple*, "Push Da Button" and the scene in the jook house celebrate physical contact free of inhibitions for Black Americans in an era where such actions were forbidden in the public sphere making the erotic-styled Slow Drag all the more affecting.

29 Susan L. Foster, Corporealities *Dancing Knowledge, Culture and Power* (New York: Routledge, 1996), 4.

30 Hazzard-Gordon, *Jookin'*, 63.

31 Ibid., 64.

32 Ibid.

33 Having a grounded center is a term that comes from African and modern dance vocabulary that means staying low to the ground, using lots of bend, flex, or looseness in the knees.

34 Nadine George-Graves, explains that as dances moved from rural to urban settings European influences were stronger. "Just Like Being at the Zoo: Primitivity and Ragtime Dances," in *Ballroom, Boogie, Shimmy Sham, Shake: A Social and Popular Dance Reader*, ed. Julie Malnig, (Chicago: University of Illinois Press, 2009), 63.

35 George-Graves, "Just Like Being at the Zoo," 59.

36 Stephen Bray is a drummer who comes from a more rock/pop background who is known for his collaborations with Madonna. Brenda Russell is a singer-songwriter and keyboardist who comes from a jazz and soul background. Allee Willis is a multi-media artist and songwriter as well as a set designer and director. "The Color Purple," *Playbill*, accessed December 18, 2017. http://www.playbill.com/production/the-color-purple-broadway-theatre-vault-0000012250.

37 George-Graves, "Just Like Being at the Zoo," 58–59.

38 The 1985 movie does find a middle ground. First, the camera takes a very narrow shot of the small venue, so the jook joint feels cramped and filled with people already very close by circumstance – an effect not necessarily possible on stage. Second, Shug Avery (Margaret Avery) sings two songs in the jook house (both composed by Quincy Jones, who was also a producer and informal musical adviser to the musical) as opposed to one in the musical. The first song, "The Dirty Dozens" is an up-tempo piece, only slightly slower than "Push Da Button" where all patrons are clapping and dancing along; several couples in the background are dancing in the Slow Drag style. The atmosphere, as per the genre of film is more relaxed – film not having the convention/expectation of a pre-intermission showstopper. The second song, "Ms. Celie's Blues" however is unique to the movie as it has a very slow and sensuous blues feel very apropos to the jook atmosphere. Shug sings the song directly to Celie, in a very playful and sexy manner, while patrons look on casually and continue their activities in the joint. A second slowed down song would have been interesting to add to the musical and help evoke the essence of the jook joint. However, the duet, "What About Love," that occurs between Shug and Celie several scenes later in the musical, likely precluded any earlier ballad between the two. Both songs available for viewing on YouTube, https://www.youtube.com/watch?v=eK3URAH760w, https://www.youtube.com/watch?v=GKc3Ht7idJU, accessed February 26, 2017. Of note, Oprah Winfrey made her acting debut in the role of Sofia, and then went on to be a producer and promoter for both Broadway productions.

39 George-Graves gives additional reasoning for the shift in posture, "the movement of the body towards a more upright stance was also influenced by the fact that more black workers were moving from agrarian lifestyles which shifted the importance of the earth and groundedness." The jook house in 1907 would have reflected a mix of these occupations and so some leeway in the stance is understandable. George-Graves, "Just Like Being at the Zoo," 63.

40 Karen Hubbard and Terry Monaghan, "Negotiating Compromise on a Burnished Floor: Social Dancing at The Savoy" in *Ballroom, Boogie, Shimmy Sham, Shake: A Social and Popular Dance Reader* ed. Julie Malnig (Chicago: University of Illinois Press, 2009), 130.

41 Hubbard and Monaghan, "Negotiating Compromise on a Burnished Floor," 130. In fact, the deliberately unhurried speed of the Slow Drag secluded it from other more upbeat dances of the time. Once the dance transitioned to New York dance clubs, and became known more publicly as "dancing-on-a-dime" or "the grind," it attracted less interest publicly and was "not as popular at venues such as the Savoy, and others because couples were to be constantly moving." Hubbard and Monaghan, "Negotiating Compromise on a Burnished Floor," 130. The very slowed down speed of the Slow Drag kept it in some ways protected from appropriation.

42 The 1987 movie *Dirty Dancing* popularized the term "Dirty Dancing," where sexual and erotic dances, such as the Lambada and the Grind were taken up and celebrated with much gusto heralding a stage version, prequel, and live concert tours. "Dirty Dancing," accessed November 26, 2017. http://www.imdb.com/title/tt0092890/.

43 "Jazz hands" are done with fingers splayed and wrists shaking. The move is often used in spoofs of musical theatre as the sole way performers show excitement on stage. In general Broadway choreographers avoid using "Jazz hands" today unless specifically as a spoof or specific stylization of the form. The use of them to conclude "Push Da Button," is not a spoof, though exaggerates the energy in the jook joint.

44 Rebecca Ann Rugg, "What it Used to Be: Nostalgia and the State of the Broadway Musical," *Theater* 32, no. 2 (2002): 46. As described in the introduction, Svetlana Boym finds reflective nostalgia can be beneficial towards understanding one's self in the contemporary moment. Reflective nostalgia suggests a meditation on and retracing of the past that opens up the possibility for considering alternate perspectives that may go on to influence future individual actions.

45 In the London production the choreography had been done by Ann Yee. Doyle adapted and paired down the choreography for Broadway, though there is no choreography credit in the Broadway Playbill. "The Color Purple," *Playbill,* accessed November 6, 2017, http://www.playbill.com/production/the-color-purple-bernard-b-jacobs-theatre-vault-0000014109, http://www.playbill.com/article/additional-casting-announced-for-broadways-the-color-purple-com-354422.

46 Ben Brantley, "Striping a Southern Musical to Its Core," London, *New York Times,* July 16, 2013, http://www.nytimes.com/2013/07/17/theater/the-color-purple-and-prudencia-hart-sing-anew-in-london.html.

47 In seeking out an interview with Yee, she was open to talking about her work and current projects. However, she did not wish to discuss the Broadway production of *The Color Purple.*

48 Doyle has received much critical acclaim for his take on Stephen Sondheim productions, such as *Sweeney Todd* (2005) and *Company* (2006) that required the actors to sing and play their musical accompaniment, drawing attention more towards the character and away from the production. For more on actor-musicianship see Jeremy Harrison's *Actor-Musicianship* (London, UK: Bloomsbury Publishing, 2016). I have written elsewhere of the considerations of musicianship as choreography in the work of John Doyle, "The New Choreography of Rodgers and Hammerstein's *Allegro*," *Studies in Musical Theatre Journal* 9, no. 3 (2016): 277–285.

49 *Chicago* (1975), music by John Kander, lyrics by Fred Ebb, book by Fred Ebb and Bob Fosse; *Cabaret* (1966), music by John Kander, lyrics by Fred Ebb, book by Joe Masteroff.

50 Joe Dzeimianowicz, "*The Color Purple*: Review," *New York Daily News*, December 10, 2015, http://www.nydailynews.com/entertainment/theater-arts/synthia-erivo-jennifer-hudson-shine-color-purple-article-1.2461515.

51 Matt Windman, *"The Color Purple* Review: Jennifer Hudson Soars in Revival," *AM New York,* December 10, 2015, https://www.amny.com/entertainment/the-color-purple-review-jennifer-hudson-soars-in-revival-1.11215876; Jesse Green, "Theater Review: *The Color Purple* Is One of the Greatest Revivals Ever," December 10, 2015, *Vulture,* http://www.vulture.com/2015/12/theater-re view-the-color-purple.html.

52 Peter Marks, "Go On. Try to Resist The Vibrant 'Color Purple' on Broadway," *Washington Post,* December 10, 2015, https://www.washingtonpost.com/news/a rts-and-entertainment/wp/2015/12/10; Charles McNulty, *"Color Purple* Musical on Broadway Has a Divine, Moving Spirit," *Los Angeles Times,* December 10, 2015, http://www.latimes.com/entertainment/arts/la-et-cm-color-purple-broadwa y-review-20151211-column.html.

53 Green, "Theater Review," 2015.

54 "Push Da Button," music and lyrics by Brenda Russell, Allee Willis, Stephen Bray, 2005.

55 Hinton Als, "Dreamgirls: Doyle's fresh and vital revival of *The Color Purple,"* *The New Yorker,* January 4, 2016, https://www.newyorker.com/magazine/2016/01/ 04/dreamgirls.

56 Brian Scott Lipton explains in his review of the African section in original pro-duction, felt Byrd's choreography was "more appropriate to 1999 that 1929," TheatreMania, December 1, 2005, http://www.theatermania.com/new-york-city-theater/reviews/12-2005/the-color-purple_7219.html.

57 David Rooney, *"The Color Purple*: Theatre Review," The Hollywood Reporter, December 10, 2015, https://www.hollywoodreporter.com/review/jennifer-hudso n-color-purple-theater-847846.

58 Rooney, December 10, 2015.

59 Ben Brantley, "Gaining Voices and Losing Inhibitions," *New York Times,* July 16, 2013, https://www.nytimes.com/2013/07/17/theater/the-color-purple-and-prude ncia-hart-sing-anew-in-london.html.

60 Foster, *Corporealities,* 4.

61 Hazzard-Gordon, *Jookin',* 76.

62 Hazzard-Gordon, *Jookin',* 173.

63 Elizabeth Grosz, *Volatile Bodies: Toward a Corporeal Feminism* (Bloomington: Indiana University Press, 1994), xi.

References

Als, Hinton. "Dreamgirls: Doyle's Fresh and Vital Revival of *The Color Purple." The New Yorker,* January 4, 2016, https://www.newyorker.com/magazine/2016/01/04/ dreamgirls.

Brantley, Ben. "One Women's Awakening, in Double Time." *New York Times,* December 5, 2005, http://www.nytimes.com/2005/12/02/theater/reviews/one-womans-awakening-in-double-time.html.

Brantley, Ben. "Gaining Voices and Losing Inhibitions." *New York Times,* July 16, 2013. https://www.nytimes.com/2013/07/17/theater/the-color-purple-and-pruden cia-hart-sing-.anew-in-london.html.

Brantley, Ben. "Striping a Southern Musical to Its Core." London, *New York Times,* July 16, 2013. http://www.nytimes.com/2013/07/17/theater/the-color-purple-a nd-prudencia-hart-sing anew in-london.html.

Carter, Linda M. "Wallace Thurman 1902–1934." In *African American Dramatists: An A-to-Z Guide,* edited by Emmanuel S. Nelson, 435–439. Westport, CT: Greenwood Press, 2004.

Dehn, Mura. Papers on Afro-American Dance. Circa 1869–1987, The Mura Dehn Collection and Papers. Performing Arts Research Collections: Dance, NYPL box 1, 3.

Dzeimianowicz, Joe. "*The Color Purple*: Review." *New York Daily News*, December 10, 2015. http://www.nydailynews.com/entertainment/theater-arts/synthia-erivo-jennifer-hudson-shine-color-purple-article-1.2461515.

Foster, Susan Leigh. *Corporealities. Dancing Knowledge, Culture and Power*. New York: Routledge, 1996.

George-Graves, Nadine. "Just Like Being at the Zoo: Primitivity and Ragtime Dances." In *Ballroom, Boogie, Shimmy Sham, Shake: A Social and Popular Dance Reader*, edited by Julie Malnig, 55–71. Chicago: University of Illinois Press, 2009.

Green, Jesse. "Theater Review: *The Color Purple* Is One of the Greatest Revivals Ever." December 10, 2015, *Vulture*. http://www.vulture.com/2015/12/theater-review-the-color-purple.html.

Grosz, Elizabeth. *Volatile Bodies: Toward a Corporeal Feminism*. Bloomington: Indiana University Press, 1994.

Harrison, Jeremy. *Actor-Musicianship*. London, UK: Bloomsbury Publishing, 2016.

Hazzard-Gordon, Katrina. *Jookin': The Rise of Social Dance Formations in African American Culture*. Philadelphia: Temple University Press, 1992.

Hubbard, Karen, and Terry Monaghan. "Negotiating Compromise on a Burnished Floor: Social Dancing at The Savoy." In *Ballroom, Boogie, Shimmy Sham, Shake: A Social and. Popular Dance Reader*, edited by Julie Malnig, 126–245. Chicago: University of Illinois Press, 2009.

Hurston, Zora Neale. "Characteristics of Negro Expressions." In *Negro Anthology*, edited by Nancy Cunard, 28–29. London, UK: Wishart & Company, 1959.

Lipton, Brian Scott. "The Color Purple." *TheatreMania*. December 1, 2015, http://www.theatermania.com/new-york-city-theater/reviews/12-2005/the-color-purple_7219.html.

McNulty, Charles. "*Color Purple Musical on Broadway Has a Divine, Moving Spirit*." December 10, 2015, http://www.latimes.com/entertainment/arts/la-et-cm-color-purple-.broadway-review-20151211-column.html.

Marks, Peter. "Go On. Try to Resist The Vibrant 'Color Purple' on Broadway." *Washington Post*, December 10, 2015. https://www.washingtonpost.com/news/arts-and entertainment/wp/2015/12/10.

Oliver, Paul. *Blues off the record: Thirty years of blues commentary*. Tunbridge Wells, Kent: Baton Press; New York, NY: Hippocrene Books, 1984.

Perpener, John O. *African American Concert Dance: The Harlem Renaissance and Beyond*. Champaign, IL: University of Illinois Press, 2001.

Playbill. "*The Color Purple*." Accessed January 9, 2019. http://www.playbill.com/production/the-color-purple-broadway-theatre-vault-.0000012250.

Playbill. "*Inside The Color Purple*." Accessed March 2, 2018. http://www.playbill.com/playbillpagegallery/inside-playbill?asset=00000150-aea8-d936-.a7fd-eefc72eb0004&type=InsidePlaybill&slide=1.

Robinson, Danielle. *Modern Moves: Dancing Race During the Ragtime and Jazz Era*. New York: Oxford University Press, 2015.

Rooney, David. "*The Color Purple*: Theatre Review." *The Hollywood Reporter*, December 10, 2015. https://www.hollywoodreporter.com/review/jennifer-hudson-color-purple-theater-847846.

Rugg, Rebecca Ann. "What it Used to Be: Nostalgia and the State of the Broadway Musical." *Theater* 32, no. 2 (2002): 44–55.

Rumsey, Phoebe. "The New Choreography of Rodgers and Hammerstein's *Allegro*." *Studies in Musical Theatre Journal* 9, no. 3 (2016): 277–285.

Smith, Ernie. "*Ernie Smith Jazz and Dance File*." Schomburg Center for Research in Black Culture, Collection tape 1, 25a, SC Visual VRA.

Spectrum Dance. "*Donald Byrd*." Accessed November 25, 2017. https://spectrumda nce.org/about/donald-byrd/.

"The List of Black Female Women Who've Choreographed for Broadway is Too Short." Accessed January 16, 2022. https://www.dancemagazine.com/black-wom en-choreographers/.

Windman, Matt. "*The Color Purple* Review: Jennifer Hudson Soars in Revival." *AM New York*. December 10, 2015. https://www.amny.com/entertainment/the-color-p urple-review-jennifer-hudson-soars-in-revival-1.11215876.

Woll, Allen L. *Black Musical Theatre: From Coontown to Dreamgirls*. Baton Rouge: Louisiana State University Press, 1989.

2 "This Was a Music That Was Theirs"

Ragtime and the Breakdown of Collective Nostalgia

In his 1975 novel, *Ragtime,* E.L. Doctorow describes the first encounter a wealthy family has with ragtime music at the turn of the 20th century as follows:

> This was a most robust composition, a vigorous music that roused the senses and never stood still a moment. The boy perceived it as light touching various places in space, accumulating in intricate patterns until the entire room was made to glow with its own being.[1]

In this excerpt, the solemn Coalhouse Walker Jr., a serious and professional musician, plays on Mother's piano. With his left hand bouncing back and forth like a sewing machine, clearly articulating the syncopated beat, he introduces the household to ragtime music. Though his attempts at drawing Sarah (with whom he has a child) downstairs continue for many more weeks, the impact of the ragtime music on the family is near-instant. Doctorow's story of the intersection of cultures in the United States at the turn of the century is the dream and rapture of *Ragtime*. Through engaging and often performative writing, Doctorow spins a story that weaves in celebrities of the time, from famous escape artist Harry Houdini to entertainer Evelyn Nesbit. Delving into the micro-histories of individual families and pulling back to the macro-history of an entire generation, *Ragtime* by construct has a syncopated rhythm in and of itself. Doctorow tells a tale of intimacy and intrigue between the unlikely connections of three families at the turn of the twentieth century.

Ragtime is a result of Doctorow intersecting fiction with traditional historical narratives. His lyricism paints a world where Americana is the lifeblood of communities and patriotic mythologies turn the motor of time. *Ragtime* is a fable that tells the story of lives, loves, and the land the American Dream was built upon. Shortly after the publication of the book in 1975, John Brooks describes the melding of the novel with the soul of the music from which it takes its title: "It is full of coincidence and implausibilities; that is because like ragtime, it is not about life but about a dream of life."[2] Doctorow reflects on an era that was both rigid, like the clipped tones of the music, and exhilarating in its newness, like the light ragtime melodies, and innovative, like the bold

DOI: 10.4324/9781003163688-4

shift in emphasis of the syncopated rhythms. There is both chaos and calmness to a story that tries to know the lives of so many people and join them in one rhythm; a contrast between the everyday and the theatrical. By its sheer expressiveness, *Ragtime* ballyhoos to be brought from page to stage. Establishing the tenets of this theatricalization prior to an examination of the Cakewalk serves to set the tone and provide a grounding knowledge for an investigation of the complexities that circulate in the popular and problematic social dance.

Ragtime the Musical

Canadian producer Garth Drabinsky and his production company LiveEnt Inc. rose to the challenge to bring the novel to life in 1996.[3] The lavish production initially opened in Toronto and, after several rounds of revisions, moved to Broadway in 1998. With music by Stephen Flaherty, lyrics by Lynn Ahrens, and book by Terrence McNally, *Ragtime* is a nearly three-hour musical that in its time was one of the most expensive musicals made.[4] *Ragtime* begins when Mother finds a baby buried, but still alive, in her garden. She takes in the baby and its mother, Sarah. Coalhouse, the father of the baby, eventually regains Sarah's trust and the two begin their lives together with the help of Mother, despite Father's disapproval of her involvement. When Will Conklin and his rogue band of volunteer firemen ransack Coalhouse's car he seeks justice, only to be ignored by authorities. Sarah is killed in her attempt to help Coalhouse, beginning his dangerous and ultimately fatal attempt at revenge. Secondary stories follow personalities of the era, including Houdini, Emma Goldman, J.P. Morgan, and Henry Ford.

Ragtime lost the Tony for Best Musical to *The Lion King,* but won Best Score, Best Book, Best Featured Actress (Audra McDonald), and Best Scenic Design. Though some critics, such as Ben Brantley, were disappointed in the less-than-subtle show, *Ragtime* ran over 800 performances.[5] While *The Lion King* is a coming-of-age tale, with a successful Disney movie behind it, what *is* this musical? *Ragtime* is epic storytelling done through heightened song and dance and is a triumphant demonstration of the magnitude of the genre (though that performative emphasis may not appeal to those who prefer a more understated style). The production is at once a dreamy, rose-colored venture into the past brought to life by exquisite costumes and impressive sets, supported by a harmonious score sung by a close to sixty-member cast; as well as a very tangled web of illusion and disillusion. Harry Houdini, singing in the third person (as all do in the prologue), hints at this complexity: "But for all his achievements [...] he was only an illusionist. But he wanted to believe there was more."[6] This distance from the self is established from the beginning and all characters introduce themselves in this impersonalized third person manner. The self-narration of how one imagines him or herself makes this musical a prime site of nostalgia. Brantley titles his review, "*Ragtime*: A Diorama With Nostalgia Rampant," and the framework he identifies is accurate.[7] The plot celebrates nation building, complete with Father making his fortune selling patriotic bunting and fireworks, however there is much more that can be discerned from the movements of the many bodies on stage. *Ragtime* offers the opportunity to explore beyond the "rampant" restorative nostalgia, and critically rethink the embodied experience of a story that begins with "small clear chords hung like flowers" in Mother's softly decorated parlour and ends with the deaths of Coalhouse, Sarah, and Father.[8] Nostalgia is part of the machinery of the show and its operation, as demonstrated through the aesthetics and the choreographic choices, produces a contemplation upon the structures of racism at the turn of the twentieth century in the United States.

Choreography and *Ragtime*

Prior to the start of the original production, directed by Frank Galati and designed by Eugene Lee, a larger-than-life sepia-toned stereopticon sits in the middle of the stage. The viewing apparatus from the late 1890s begins the trek back in time of *Ragtime*. As the introductory windup to the ragtime melody begins, the stereopticon rises into the rafters, optically dissolving within a second stereopticon image on the scrim. The transition reveals a tableau of the townspeople of New Rochelle, New York, dressed in soft white and cream costumes posing for a portrait. The photographic framing sets up a sense of doubleness and reproduction from the start. The play opens with an appropriately grand, astonishingly complex introduction to the era, and the ragtime rhythms of 1902 choreographed by Graciela Daniele.

Daniele, originally from Buenos Aires, is a ten-time Tony-nominated Broadway choreographer. She first made her mark on Broadway as an ensemble dancer, then worked as Michael Bennett's assistant (*Follies*, 1971) learning the tools and techniques of choreographing for musical theatre. Daniele developed her own movement expertise and became a substantial presence in the musical theatre field both as a choreographer and director-choreographer.[9] An immigrant herself, Daniele has the unique skill of assuming American movement styles using her outsider perspective as a grounding standpoint.[10] In a 1994 interview with Svetlana McLee Grody, Daniele explains:

> I was twenty-three, twenty-four years old before I came to this country and really got into American musical theatre. But perhaps because I am a foreigner, I can be a little more objective. From an outside culture, I can see the magnificence that could be.

Daniele hints at her skills (and style) of assembling different fragments of movements in work that involves various dance forms outside of her background, "when you go into a show that demands the flavor of a different culture, it's up to the choreographer to do the research. Not do the traditional thing, but take that influence and mix it," this sort of assembly can be seen in *Ragtime*.[11] Daniele and Galati put forth an opening sequence that introduces the main characters and establishes the tension between communities at the turn of the twentieth century in the United States.

In the prologue, titled simply "Ragtime," the singing alternates between a white chorus, a Black chorus, and an immigrant chorus – all the characters in the story are part of the ten-minute opening song. The white community of New Rochelle begin, "In 1902 Father built a house at the crest of the Brodview Avenue [...] and it seemed for some years thereafter that all the family's days would be warm and fair."[12] Already a tinge of nostalgia colors the piece in both the rose-colored outlook of the boy and the romantic notion of the house built by one person. The white ensemble then executes a very formal series of promenading steps. Performers shift their weight to one side while the alternate leg extends forward in a turned-out presentational manner, showing off the foot and ankle. The movement is carefully repeated with the other foot as the body moves forward. Some performers hold parasols, top hats, or canes. This strutting and posing is redolent of quadrilles and other European dances, and is the first hint of the movement signature in the show. When the Black ensemble enters, their execution of the same steps is spirited, has much greater panache, and embraces the syncopated rhythm in its wholeness, using the full body as opposed to merely hinting at the off-beat as the first group does. The white ensemble arcs upstage, continuing the promenade as the Black group circles downstage. Coalhouse Walker, Jr. steps out of the group and proudly states, again continuing the third person narrative style, "In Harlem, men and women of color forgot their troubles and danced and reveled to the music [...] This was a music that was theirs and no one else's."[13]

An immediate connection between the two groups is set up in the similar rhythms and melodies but the narratives of each community are drastically different. Already, the Black community needs to emphatically claim ragtime music as theirs, whereas the boy muses that the world is fair and free – a decidedly privileged, naïve and utopic perspective. A third group joins representing the immigrant population thus completing the collage effect. Tateh and his young daughter step forward to introduce themselves, "His name was Tateh [...] The Little Girl was all he had now. Together, they would escape."[14] The immigrants, keen to assimilate into their new world, not telling of what they left behind, determinedly take up a blended version of the movement styles of the two choruses.[15]

In the nearly ten-minute prologue, the parodic origins of the Cakewalk are hinted at in various fragments of movement drawn from mannered promenade styles and walking kicks. These imitative stylings make up part of the texture of the opening, with each group repeating variations on the moves of the other. From the start, the Black and white characters are compared through their movement and postures. This "mimicry with a difference" is suggestive of the challenge of tap or early jazz dances.[16] In *Ragtime*, there is a testing of the physical boundaries between groups, and an embodied tension or strain is felt between the clusters because of their visibly different interpretations of the same movements. This discomfort is further emphasized by the closeness of the clumping of each group and lack of eye contact with each other, in spite of discreet attempts to size the other up. As all sing about the new rhythm of ragtime music, the famous actress and performer of the era Evelyn Nesbit enters along with two male dancers. The trio does a very stylized dance much more common to the vaudeville stage, distinguishing themselves from the social dance-based choreography shown by the groups. Nesbit's dance includes many high can-can-like kicks, done with the leg unfolding in a *developpé* style.[17] This delineation is significant: as opposed to a straight kick from the ground, this stylization makes the move look like an exaggerated step, a sort of grotesque mirroring of the moves of the two ensembles that are executed closer to the ground. Further, Nesbit's foot in the kick is flexed as opposed to pointed, breaking the fluid line of the leg, a slight physical agitation against the charm of the opening. The affected, exaggerated, and fragmented movements displayed by the three choruses and punctuated by Nesbitt's trio (before joining the white chorus) are distinguishing factors of the movement signature Daniele builds throughout the production.

By the end of the prologue, three groups are clearly established: the white Americans, the Black Americans, and the Immigrants. The rhythm of the ragtime beat sits differently with each group. In the final chorus of the song, the Black ensemble keeps time by pulsing their heels up and down whereas the other two groups remain still. The white chorus is particularly stiff and their upright stylizations are emphasized by their crisp starched costumes. The overall conceit of the opening sets up the thematic movement code of posturing, prancing, and promenading – in essence, the Cakewalk. The deconstruction of the dance and movement codes put forth by Daniele hints at the various kinds of nostalgia revealed through the complexities of the embodied history within the dance, though pointedly does not execute a full cakewalk. The fragmented choice that withholds the complete aesthetic of the social dance invites the spectator to fill in the blanks with memories or ideologies one might have about a social dance (whether it is obviously named or not) woven into the fabric of the history of the US at the turn of the twentieth century. Further, the self-narration within the lyrics hints at a sense of self-parody that speaks back to cultural power structures in effect at the time, particularly in the exaggerated stereotypes set up from the beginning of the musical. Before proceeding to analyze the nostalgic effects of the fragmenting of the Cakewalk in *Ragtime,* a necessary understanding of the history and intricacies involved in the social dance is helpful.

Historical Background of The Cakewalk

The Cakewalk, by its parodic nature, is inevitably connected to European movement sensibilities. Created on southern plantations in the mid-nineteenth century by enslaved Black Americans at "get-togethers," the Cakewalk was a temporary diversion from the oppression slaves felt at the hands of their owners. Having observed their masters partake in celebrations or balls with much pretention and pomp, slaves invented the subversive dance involving both mimicry and parody "to ridicule their white masters."[18] Plantation owners and their friends enjoyed watching the slaves imitate them, thinking them decidedly less graceful and refined – the point of the dance being entirely missed by the observers.[19] The imitation and mockery of European styled dances was the inspiration for the form, though done in an exaggerated and outlandish manner.[20] This impersonation, however, commonly thought to have its origins drawn from the white social dances of the time was not without what Brenda Dixon Gottschild calls "Africanisms."[21] Meaning there is always and already a history of slavery embodied in the Black body dancing and these physicalized echoes are, as Gottschild describes, "the bastard child, the muffled scream that can still be heard despite efforts to hush it. They are asymmetrical threads breaking the desired and mythical uniformity of the American fabric."[22] While the performance of their masters worked to ridicule white ostentatiousness, the subtext brought forward by movement unpicks assumptions of unity, or any invented nostalgia that all were equally delighted in watching and doing the dance.

After emancipation in 1865, Black Americans continued to do aspects of the dance in various informal settings and the movement style was taken up as part

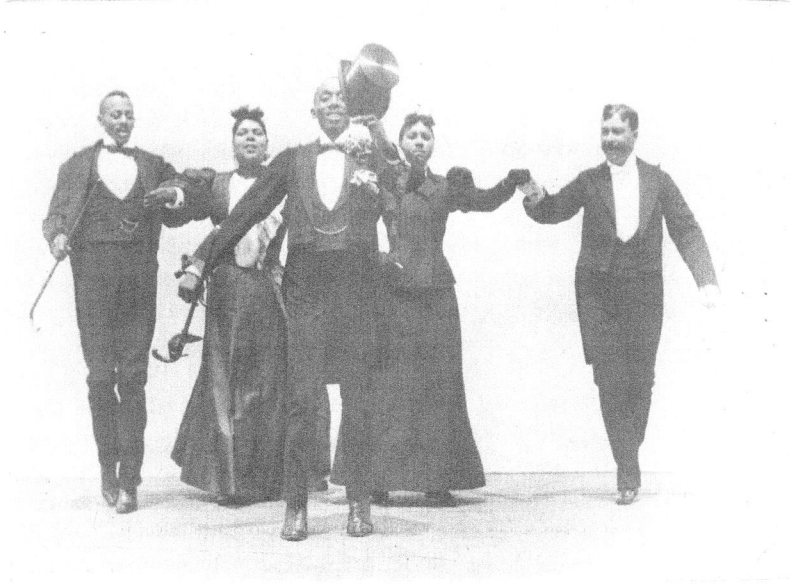

Figure 2.1 "Dancers performing the Cakewalk" 1850
Source: Schomburg Center for Research in Black Culture, Photographs and Prints Division, The New York Public Library. New York Public Library Digital Collections.

of the imitations of Black Americans in white minstrel shows. Replacing the "walkaround," where all minstrel troupe members toured the stage, the Cakewalk, in its growing popularity, became the most anticipated part of minstrel shows and spilled over into popular culture.[23] How, by whom, and where the Cakewalk is performed gets at what Megan Pugh calls the "slippery core" of the Cakewalk: "It could be performed with grace or comedy, as a sign of social aspiration, a parody of those aspirations, or a wholesale rejection of aspiration in favor of rude, freewheeling, seemingly untamed motion."[24] On the rural level, at the turn of the twentieth century, Cakewalk contests became part of community activities and fundraisers. In cities, large-scale competitions and demonstrations were organized, in many cases with both Black and white participants (though not partnering up across cultures). In New York, Madison Square Garden hosted an annual Cakewalking competition on the grandest scale. Wagers were made on prospective winners, and most knew "black superiority was a foregone conclusion."[25] In a contest between the "originators" of the dance versus the "imitators" of the dance, competitors prevailed knowing the exact nuances of the parody that enabled them to delight audiences, but also to take away the cash prize.[26]

Inevitably, the Cakewalk infiltrated entertainment venues, and revues on Broadway took it up. Productions would commonly end with a Cakewalk, or an extravagant twist on the form, performed by Black dancers, such as the "Cakewalk Jubilee" that concluded John Isham's *The Octoroons* in 1895.[27] Perhaps the most well-known of the theatricalized Cakewalks is in the 1898 musical comedy *Clorindy, or The Origin of the Cakewalk.* [28] The show was the first Broadway musical with an all-Black cast.[29] The Black writing and composing team of Will Marion Cook and Paul Lawrence wrote *Clorindy* and though, arguably, it was more of a musical revue than a complete musical, the production did elevate the pair's reputation, which came to full fruition with *In Dahomey* in 1903, which also ended with an impressive Cakewalk.[30] Importantly, the aforementioned shows were generally performed at lavish rooftop garden performance spaces in New York City, which where, as Jayna Brown describes, "a space reserved for particular enactments of modern whiteness."[31] Though Black audiences were not permitted, Black bodies were seen and applauded on stage by the white audiences that packed the sophisticated venues. This adulation of the grand Cakewalk finale – performed by well-trained Black dancers – by those who, in their efforts at modern actualization, fetishized the strength and technique needed to pull off the dance with the desired grace and nonchalance, is revealing of how Black dancers had fleeting moments of bodily empowerment.[32] Remarkably, as Brown describes, "It is a thick irony that a black dance supposedly originating on the plantation would become the era's signature performance at the heart of the metropole."[33] The continued applause for Black performers at the most fashionable performance spaces of the time troubles some of the hierarchies, if only for a moment. The Black performers' presence and expertise at movement, particularly executing the Cakewalk with such panache and virtuosity, asserted a degree of control over the space. In this structure, there is an entanglement of embodied power and strength of the Black bodies expertly performing a dance with seemingly little effort. Brown explains this complexity demonstrates "the multi-signifying power of black performance, the agile navigation of hostile territories."[34] The performative declaration of values coveted by middle and upper classes as indicators of modern sophistication by Black dancers did work to create – if only during performance – a sense of agency for Black communities.

The last show on Broadway to have a Cakewalk, and salute "the ideal bodies of urban sophistication" was *Darktown Follies* in 1913.[35] The Stearnses write:

> At the conclusion of the show the entire company got together again for a cakewalk–parading, bowling, prancing, strutting, and high-kicking with arched backs and pointed toes…. As an ensemble finale, the Cakewalk was unbeatable, and it brought *Darktown Follies* to a triumphant dancing conclusion.[36]

Markedly, the Stearnses note that it was not until "the miracle of *Shuffle Along*" that dance changed on Broadway, in touring circuits, and ballroom dance settings; the Cakewalk fell out of fashion as more rhythmic and jazz styles took over.[37]

The performance of the Cakewalk in social settings and the Cakewalk on stage exhibit only slight differences, as the dance is already in an overtly presentational style. When the Cakewalk was done in a social situation where there was little to no distance between audience and performer, secondary meanings (such as its slave origins and class oppressions) were lessened as social pursuits and community happenings were at the forefront of any social dance event of the time. When the Cakewalk was put on a professional stage however, as the grand finale of a Broadway show with audiences standing and applauding, the dance was glamorized and saluted as a national idiom. A very "House of Mirrors" feel to the dance emerges in this spectacularization – audiences are applauding professional dancers imitating the dance of the general populace, imitating the dance that slaves did, who were imitating and ridiculing their white oppressors. This "parodic shell game" becomes an entanglement of embodied experiences and histories, white obliviousness, and the drive of popular culture and capitalism, all of which risks obscuring and simplifying the slave communities from which the Cakewalk emerged.[38] How communities doing the dance imagine themselves in the game, or what role participants inhabit, becomes part of the complexity of the Cakewalk's embodied nostalgia and anti-nostalgia.

As mentioned, the sociopolitical complexities increase in the move to the stage given the increased visibility of the Black body on stage. The bodies that originally did the Cakewalk were slaves; bodies that were whipped, tortured, starved, and over-worked were the bodies that had the ingenuity to create the dance – that history is embodied in them. The community that Black Americans imagined from the beginning of the creation of the Cakewalk was founded upon collective survival and self-determination. However, as whites both in the United States and Europe take up the Cakewalk in social settings, all while enthusiastically applaud Black performers in the Cakewalk finales in the early Broadway musicals, this imagining shifts and the dance become the signifier of the cultural politics of the era. Markedly, Black creatives were aware of the growing desire of white audiences to watch Black bodies, and thus used the dance to their professional advantage. Brown explains, "playing in the field of white fantasy was stock and trade for African American variety artists."[39]

Fundamentally, the history of slavery that underlies the Cakewalk cannot be erased or overlooked. Pugh succinctly states, "The Cakewalk gets at deeper truths, and deeper patterns, all the way down to the country's great unfinished business of slavery."[40] The Cakewalk is emblematic of a double behavior from its genesis – the genuine person doing the dance and the persona or "mask donned before its white oppressors."[41] This enmeshment of identities and cultures involves an interpretation of the "Other" (or the white ruling class more specifically) that comes from a foundational place of agitation and suffering. Doctorow explores this emotional, social, and political paradigm in *Ragtime*, and Daniele physicalizes these entangled ideologies on stage by creating a movement signature built around the Cakewalk, eventually performed by the entire cast.

Ragtime, The Cakewalk, and Frictional Nostalgia

The unintended intersection of the lives of Mother and Father, and Coalhouse and Sarah is the fulcrum around which *Ragtime* operates. Mother tries to imagine a community of racial harmony whereas Father remains a symbol of antiquated ways of thinking, inevitably causing tension. The nostalgic contradictions play out in the socio-political imaginings embodied in the Cakewalk, and the deconstruction of the dance highlights the incompatibility of the four lives, reinforced by Coalhouse's death at the hand of white authorities. The continued prejudices against Black Americans, the proliferation of stereotypes, and the impulse of white communities assuming what is not theirs is what Coalhouse fights against in the narrative. The fruitlessness of Coalhouse's efforts to get the police's help for the crime against his property, and the senselessness of Sarah's death, leads to a fracturing of the mental composure of the once-respected musician. A radicalized Coalhouse powers the narrative until he is shot on the library steps at the climax of the show. This break in the harmony Mother envisions is taken up in the choreography in several ways, most strongly seen in the beginning and end of the musical.

As previously discussed, from the opening prologue an embodied sense of privilege and nationalistic pride radiates from the group and codes the white cast's movement as such. Though the anticipation for a Cakewalk hangs in the air given the music and the era, the withholding of the social dance in its entirety interrupts the spell of sentimentality. Daniele does not show a traditional Cakewalk in *Ragtime*, but rather her deconstruction of the dance gestures to the past through postures and tableaux. While tableaux were a popular theatrical form of entertainment in the nineteenth and early twentieth century, here Daniele uses the form to break the flow of movement. In the rupture of the collective parts of the dance, there is a consideration of the magnitude of where the dance came from, a sort of Brechtian-like movement effort to keep the audience from being emotionally swept away. When the Black chorus enters, the doubleness and the politics of the dance are immediately juxtaposed with the white chorus. The embodied memories of perseverance and emotional strength in Black bodies, in this particular circumstance, are suggested in their confidence and near overwhelming of the white chorus. Daniele first shows the European source of the Cakewalk in the white chorus and thereby draws on the sensibilities of the original parody, though by not allowing the white chorus to gain physical advantage, the Black chorus, by their positioning and exuberance, readily overshadows them. There is discordance to the opening, one that seems purposeful to disrupt the rose-colored and sentimental tinge that is expected to envelop the musical from the beginning. Evelyn Nesbit's flexed-foot kicks, as described earlier, add to this dislocation of movement and meaning. This bricolage is supported by the music as well, as the different groups have distinct instruments that are part of their music signature; the white group's musical line is mostly piano, the Black group's music adds drums and horns; and klezmer and flutes enhance the music for the immigrant group.[42]

In the finale of the show, the Cakewalk-like movement fragments happen upstage as performers promenade from one side of the stage to another in silhouette. Performers hold accessories that enhance the effect of the shadow, such as an umbrella or a hat. All three groups, now mixed together, are part of this promenade. All groups do the gestural maneuvers in the finale that Daniele imposes throughout the musical. Traditionally in the Cakewalk, lines between communities were clearly delineated and there was not a mixing beyond varied spectatorship of the dance. There is still an implication of discord between communities as seen in the opening, but by having this racial and cultural mixing or co-mingling on stage in the finale there is also a utopic hope for a new collective, and particularly at this closing moment of the musical, there is an attempt at resolving the doubleness that exists in the dance. As mentioned there is possibility for both a nostalgia and anti-nostalgia embedded in the Cakewalk. The heyday of all the glamorous rooftop performances, playful competitions, lavish fashions and general applauding of upper-class postures is the nostalgia white audiences had for the Cakewalk. The notion of not wanting to be reminded of, or the feigned ignorance of the conditions of the genesis of the dance causes friction against the massive popularity of the dance in its heyday. Daniele captures this tension and "the paradox of national 'representation'" by offering movements, but denying the complete and total dance.[43] The deconstruction of the cakewalk achieved by Daniele does not allow the nostalgia to fully come to fruition, or at very least makes it difficult for that nostalgic reminiscing that is so encouraged at the opening of the show to complete itself. This "frictional" sense of nostalgia, comes to mean that a sense of nostalgia is conjured up and encouraged but is unable to be fully actualized. In that cleaving, no matter how slight, a reflective space opens for contemplation of how – or if – different identities and communities can come together. In this sense, the movement signature carefully built by Daniele and threaded through the show does not quite work in tandem with the utopic current Doctorow is trying to create. As an outsider, Daniele is removed from that collective memory and nationalistic nostalgia Doctorow is drawing on and achieves a sense of bodily discordance that works to bring forth more complex themes in the story.

Some reviewers felt this break in traditional choreography and sense of flow was detrimental to the production. Lloyd Rose, while not commenting specifically on the choreography calls the pulse of the production, "faint and mechanical."[44] Ben Brantley has difficulty even identifying Daniele's role, stating: "Graciela Daniele is responsible for the 'musical staging' (a phrase, in this instance, wisely substituted for 'choreography')."[45] He adds, "The ensemble's uneasy dance and the increasingly dissonant music become an image of a melting pot whose ingredients remain unassimilated."[46] As I have argued, this dissonance is precisely the success of Daniele's choreography in *Ragtime*. The conceit of the narrative challenges the myth that the US is a melting pot, or at very least shows how difficult any sort of amalgamation is. In *The American Musical and the Performance of Personal Identity*, Raymond Knapp maintains that America's "'melting-pot' ideology [is] so obviously at odds with its history of race-based injustice."[47] This profound contradiction is at play in *Ragtime*. The line of figures that parade across the backdrop function to expose the falsities of the mythology by their very disjointed gestures that embody the complex history of the Cakewalk. The communities in *Ragtime* are not necessarily diluted or flattened by the move on stage; they are set against each other to bring deeper understanding to the surface.

The show ends with the unexpected, yet convenient marriage between Tateh and Mother, who raise Coalhouse and Sarah's child along with their own, fulfilling Doctorow's utopic desire in *Ragtime*. Doctorow's wish for an uplifting ending is also tied to the historical moment when the novel was written. In a time when the Watergate scandal was being fully exposed and the fall of Saigon was imminent, the desire to unite the country and reconcile differences was high, and Doctorow's idealism attempts to fill a void. The deconstruction of the Cakewalk in the final parade upstage breaks apart the idea of limited communities or communities with borders, for the Black, white, and immigrant communities in *Ragtime* moving together, though differently, become a society of complex cultural negotiations and adjustments. Furthermore, in consideration of the time of the premiere of the musical in 1998, people were tuned into the Bill Clinton impeachment inquiry; the Iraq disarmament crisis was ongoing; the disturbing news of Matthew Sheppard murder in Laramie, Wyoming was in the headlines (to name only several of the complex tensions circulating in society at the time) – a sense of hopefulness, as produced by the nostalgia in the happy ending was not unwelcomed.

Though *Ragtime* is thick with American idioms, its ending does not suggest, however, the "smugness" that often comes with mythologies about the United States.[48] There is a momentary hope for a new life for the younger generation. The brief picture of a patchwork-like reconciliation, seen in the mixed union of Mother, Tateh, their children, and Sarah's child, is bittersweet knowing the many obstacles that lie ahead in the continued aftermath of slavery, given the audience's knowledge when reading the novel's publication in 1975 or seeing the musical production in 1998.[49] The story of real and invented characters

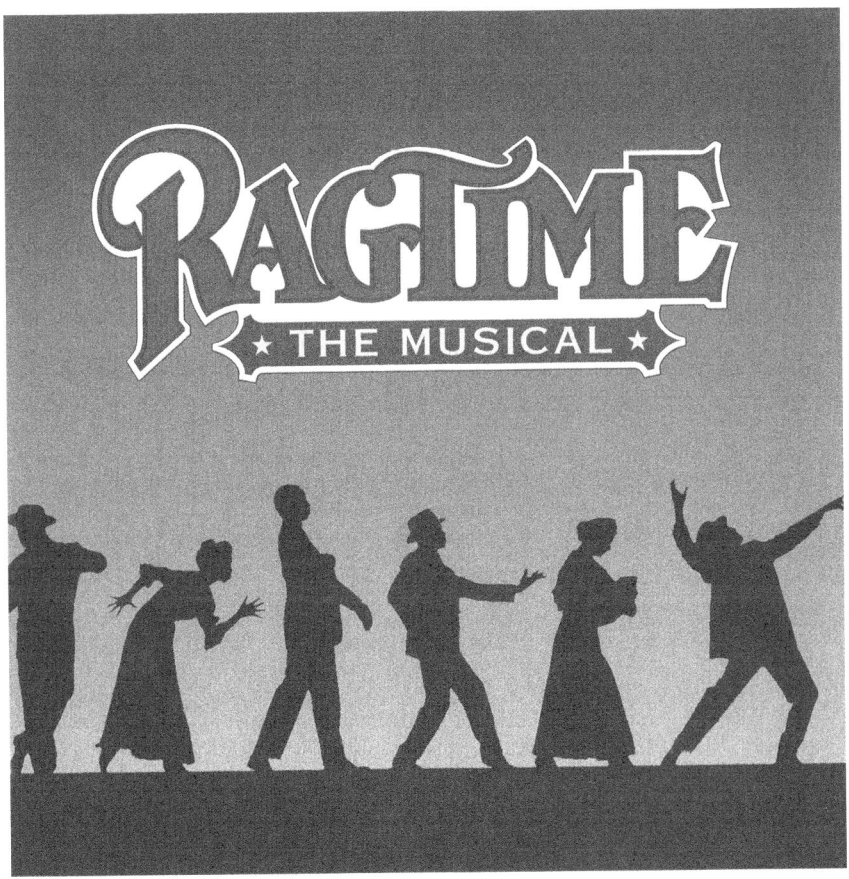

Figure 2.2 Ragtime, Broadway Cast Recording Cover, 1998, displaying closing promenade
Source: Design by Scott Thornley & Company Inc., BMG Entertainment. Courtesy of Sony Music Entertainment.

and conditions closes the show as the character simply called Boy states, "And […] the era of Ragtime had run out, as if history were no more than a tune on a player piano, But we did not know that then."[50]

Loose ends are tied together and the sentimental power ballad "Wheels of a Dream" (Coalhouse and Sarah's love ballad from the first act) has a brief reprise. The promenade of performers continues from up stage right to left. They hold sharp poses in stark black silhouette, then step forward and change into other positions in time with the syncopated beat – they appear as a ghostly row of Cakewalkers. And in this closing choreography there is an embodied power of a dance "haunted by white brutality."[51] The nostalgic framework of *Ragtime* gently begins with its photographic framing and lavish sets but then forces, by its bodily practices, a reflection and meditation on the fantasies and mythologies of an age and history that like the ragtime music are quickly obscured by the shadow of the Jazz Age.

Notes

1 E.L. Doctorow, *Ragtime* (New York: Random House, 1975), 160.
2 John Brooks, "Ragtime," *The Chicago Tribune*, 1975, accessed November 27, 2017, http://www.chicagotribune.com/lifestyles/books/ct-prj-archive-ragtime-el-doctor ow-20150305-story.html.
3 Drabinsky based the musical on the 1975 novel. There is also a 1981 movie based on the novel directed by Milos Forman starring James Cagney and Pat Obrien, with a score composed by Randy Neuman. There is no apparent connect between the movie score and the musical score.
4 Diane Haithman, "A Musical to the Tune of $10 Million," *Los Angeles Times,* June 8, 1997, http://articles.latimes.com/1997-06-08/entertainment/ca-1120_1_los-a ngeles-times.
5 *Ragtime*'s run was not enough to recoup its initial investment. Ken Mandelbaum suggests several reasons, "Reviews were very divided, with at least two negative notices in *The New York Times* and a number of unfavorable verdicts elsewhere. The show seemed to have about as many admirers as detractors. It was also a costly production to run, so even with strong grosses, it was unable to become a financial winner." Significant revivals of *Ragtime,* however, have had varying success including a scaled down version brought Broadway in 2009, with direction and choreography by Marcia Milgrom Dodge; a 2012 revival in London with direction by Timothy Sheader; numerous regional productions and concert versions have appeared since its original production. Mandelbaum, "Features," *Broadway.com,* September 22, 2004, https://www.broadway.com/buzz/10715/q-a-92204/.
6 "Ragtime," Lynn Ahrens, 1998.
7 Ben Brantley, "*Ragtime*: A Diorama With Nostalgia Rampant," *New York Times,* January 19, 1998, http://www.nytimes.com/1998/01/19/theater/theater-revie w-ragtime-a-diorama-with-nostalgia-rampant.html.
8 Doctorow, *Ragtime*, 159.
9 Select choreographic works by Graciela Daniele prior to *Ragtime* include *The Mystery of Edwin Drood* (1986), *The Goodbye Girl* (1993), both of which she received Tony award nominations; she was also the director-choreographer for *Once on This Island* (1990), *Annie Get Your Gun* (1999), *Marie Christine* (1999), *Chita Rivera: The Dancer's Life* (2005). Mervyn Rothstein, "A Life in the Theatre: Director-Choreographer Graciela Daniele," *Playbill*, June 15, 2006, http://www.playbill.com/arti

cle/a-life-in-the-theatre-director-choreographer-graciela-daniele-com-133228;
Svetlana McLee Grody and Dorothy Daniels Lister, *Conversations with Choreographers* (London: UK, Heinemann, 1996). Daniele is credited with the musical staging in the 2022 Broadway musical *Paradise Square* choreographed by Bill T. Jones and directed by Moisés Kaufman.

10 Svetlana McLee Grody, McLee and Dorothy Daniels Lister. *Conversations with Choreographers* (Portsmouth, NH: Heinemann Publishing, 1996), 157.

11 Ibid., 163.

12 Ahrens, "Ragtime," 1998.

13 Ibid..

14 Ibid.

15 For a thorough discussion of attempts of Jewish immigrants to assimilate into the United States through performance see Andrea Most's *Making Americans: Jews and the Broadway Musical* (Cambridge: Harvard University Press, 2004).

16 Anthea Kraut, Choreographing Copyright: Race, Gender, and Intellectual Property Rights in American Dance (Oxford, UK: Oxford University Press, 2016), 137.

17 *Developpé* means "to unfold" the leg in classical ballet terminology, the leg is raised by flexing the knee first up to a ninety-degree angle or more and extending the lower leg forward from there.

18 Megan Pugh, America Dancing: From the Cakewalk to the Moonwalk. New Haven, CT: Yale University Press, 2015, 17. Victor Turner explains the action of mimicry: "Through mimicry one can become an imaginary character oneself, a subject who makes believe, or makes others believe that he/she is someone other than him/herself." Adding a subtle parody to the imagining destabilizes the apparent solely imitative meaning of the dance. Turner, "Carnival in Rio: Dionysian drama in an industrializing society," in *The Celebration of Society: Perspectives on Contemporary Cultural Performance*, ed. Frank E. Manning (Bowling Green: OH, Bowling Green University Popular Press, 1983), 108.

19 The dance is so named, as owners would often award a cake to the best dancers. Pugh explains the cakes on plantations were "made up of stored-up provisions like cornmeal, baked in ashes." Pugh, *America Dancing*, 17.

20 There were a few attempts at the time of the Cakewalk's popular emergence to connect the dance to Africa as a way to deny its imitative roots. Megan Pugh reports that a *Boston Daily Globe* article from 1892, claimed the dance was "an old savage custom" from "Darkest Africa." "What Will It Be? *Boston Daily Globe*, February 23, 1892 in Pugh, *America Dancing*, 16. The Stearnses also discuss some connections of the Cakewalk to Africa such as the Ring Shout but conclude the protests of the dance being African was akin to "criticism of dancing the twist and later steps to rock-and-roll." These types of protests generally came from those opposed to popular culture and against community members dropping their duties to take up the latest craze. Marshall and Jean Stearns, *Jazz Dance: The Story of American Vernacular Dance* (New York: Da Capo Press, 1994), 123.

21 Brenda Dixon Gottschild, *Digging the Africanist Presence in American Performance: Dance and Other Contexts*. Westport, CT: Greenwood Press, 1996, 47.

22 Ibid., 47–48.

23 Though minstrel shows began with white troupes, the style was eventually taken up by Black troupes as a way to perform in the genre that drew in the most audience members. William Henry Lane was one of the first Black performers in minstrel shows. Lane worked solo, billed as "Master Juba," and went on to perform with a variety of minstrel groups. Prominent Black minstrel companies formed in the late 1860s and included, Brooker and Clayton's Georgia Minstrels, or simply the Georgia Minstrels. Companies were added to or expanded and ownership shifted, changing the names to "Haverly's European Minstrels," then "Callender's

Consolidated Spectacular Colored Minstrels," most generally had white owners and managers. Black minstrel shows became popular as they were adapted to have more song and dance in them and less "olios" or skits. Black minstrel shows were also known to have the most extravagant finales (Stearns and Stearns, 55–60). See Part Two of the Stearnses' *Jazz Dance* for a thorough investigation of dance in both early and late minstrels shows, pages 35–62.

24 Pugh, *America Dancing*, 15.
25 Ibid., 21.
26 Ibid.
27 Stearns and Stearns, *Jazz Dance*, 118.
28 Ibid., 119.
29 The show was still managed by white producers.
30 Thomas Riis explains *Clorindy, or The Origins of the Cakewalk* was not considered a complete musical as it only included five songs, and describes it more as a "song and dance medley," regardless, the show, "made history as the first thoroughly black American shows to find critical acclaim in the heart of Broadway," at the Casino Roof Garden. "Cook, Will Marion," Thomas Riis, *Grove Music Online* January 20, 2001, http://www.oxfordmusiconline.com.ezproxy.gc.cuny.edu/sub scriber/article/grove/music/06391.
31 Jayna Brown, *Babylon Girls: Black Women Performers and the Shaping of the Modern* (Durham, NC: Duke University Press, 2008), 148.
32 Ibid., 130.
33 Ibid.
34 Ibid.
35 Ibid.
36 Stearns and Stearns, *Jazz Dance*, 130–131.
37 Ibid.
38 Pugh, *America Dancing*, 23.
39 Brown, *Babylon Girls*, 142
40 Pugh, *America Dancing*, 25.
41 Michael Borshuk, "An Intelligence of the Body: Disruptive Parody through Dance in the Early Performances of Josephine Baker" in *Embodying Liberation: The Black Body in American Dance*, eds. Dorothea Fischer-Hornung and Alison D. Goeller (Piscataway, NJ: Transaction Publishers, 2001), 48.
42 For more on the juxtaposition of musical instruments and styles see Michael Lueger's interview with Adam Roberts, "Music Theatre and Musicals," *HowlRound* Podcast episode 12, November 15, 2016, https://itunes.apple.com/us/podcast/ howlrounds-podcasts/id510025281?mt=2, accessed January 25, 2018.
43 Brown, *Babylon Girls*, 135.
44 Lloyd Rose, "'Ragtime': Socially Acceptable," *The Washington Post,* January 19, 1998. https://www.washingtonpost.com/archive/lifestyle/1998/01/19/ragtime-socia lly-acceptable/5b291c2e-9e28-4f47-bb1c-d8a814008604/.
45 Brantley, *"Ragtime"*, 1998.
46 Ibid.
47 Raymond Knapp, *The American Musical and the Performance of National Identity*, (Princeton: Princeton University Press, 2005), 181.
48 In Knapp's exploration of mythologies of American and national identity, he explains there is "a smugness endemic to mythologies created, as these seem to have been, to reassure a nation of its own essential goodness." He cites examples such as *Oklahoma!* and *The Music Man* among others that function in this manner. Knapp, *The American Musical*, 122.
49 Doctorow's novel comes at the end of the first massive civil rights push in the 1950s and 1960s, and imagines how communities that come to be so diametrically opposed in his novel can find harmony by the most unexpected circumstances. His utopic wish

suggests even the mere act of imagining a sense of harmony can be one step towards achieving actual harmony. Though he "seek[s] the shelter of a bygone period," to explore racial relations, ideologies are very much being "refreshed" or reanimated for the moment in which it is written with the historical distance to allow a space for contemplation. John Updike, *The March* in *The New Yorker,* September 4, 2005, /www.newyorker.com/magazine/2005/09/12/a-cloud-of-dust/amp.

50 Ahrens, "Wheels of a Dream(Reprise)," 1998.

51 Pugh, *America Dancing,* 24.

References

Borshuk, Michael. "An Intelligence of the Body: Disruptive Parody through Dance in the Early Performances of Josephine Baker." In *Embodying Liberation: The Black Body in American Dance,* edited by Dorothea Fischer-Hornung and Alison D. Goeller, 41–58. Piscataway, NJ: Transaction Publishers, 2001.

Brown, Jayna. *Babylon Girls: Black Women Performers and the Shaping of the Modern.* Durham, NC: Duke University Press, 2008.

Brantley, Ben. "*Ragtime*: A Diorama With Nostalgia Rampant." *New York Times,* January 19, 1998. http://www.nytimes.com/1998/01/19/theater/theater-review-ra gtime-a-diorama-with-nostalgia-rampant.html.

Brooks, John. "Ragtime." *Chicago Tribune,* 1975. http://www.chicagotribune.com/lifestyles/ books/ct-prj-archive-ragtime-el-doctorow20150305-story.html, accessed November 27, 2017.

Doctorow, E.L. *Ragtime.* New York: Random House, 1975.

Gottschild, Brenda Dixon. *Digging the Africanist Presence in American Performance: Dance and Other Contexts.* Westport, CT: Greenwood Press, 1996.

Grody, Svetlana, McLee and Dorothy Daniels Lister. *Conversations with Choreographers.* Portsmouth, NH: Heinemann Publishing, 1996.

Haithman, Diane. "A Musical to the Tune of $10 Million." *Los Angeles Times,* June 8, 1997. http://articles.latimes.com/1997-06-08/entertainment/ca-1120_1_los-angeles-times.

Knapp, Raymond. *The American Musical and the Performance of Personal Identity.* Princeton: Princeton University Press, 2006.

Knapp, Raymond. *The American Musical and the Formation of National Identity.* Princeton: Princeton University Press, 2005.

Kraut, Anthea. *Choreographing Copyright: Race, Gender, and Intellectual Property Rights in American Dance.* Oxford, UK: Oxford University Press, 2016.

McNally, Terrence, Lynn Ahrens, and Stephen Flaherty. *Ragtime.* Vocal Selections. Van Nuys, CA: Alfred Publishing, 2009.

Mandelbaum, Ken. "Features." *Broadway.com,* September 22, 2004. https://www.broa dway.com/buzz/10715/q-a-92204/.

Most, Andrea. *Making Americans: Jews and the Broadway Musical.* Cambridge: Harvard University Press, 2004.

"Music Theatre and Musicals with Adam Roberts." Interview by Michael Lueger *HowlRound* Podcast episode 12, November 15, 2016. https://itunes.apple.com/us/p odcast/howlrounds-podcasts/id510025281?mt=2.

Pugh, Megan. *America Dancing: From the Cakewalk to the Moonwalk.* New Haven, CT: Yale University Press, 2015.

Riis, Thomas. "Cook, Will Marion." *Grove Music Online,* January 20, 2001. http:// www.oxfordmusiconline.com.ezproxy.gc.cuny.edu/subscriber/article/grove/music/ 06391.

Rose, Lloyd. "'Ragtime': Socially Acceptable," *The Washington Post*, January 19, 1998. https://www.washingtonpost.com/archive/lifestyle/1998/01/19/ragtime-socially-acceptable/5b291c2e-9e28-4f47-bb1c-d8a814008604/.

Rothstein, Mervyn. "*A Life in the Theatre: Director-Choreographer Graciela Daniele.*" June 15, 2006. http://www.playbill.com/article/a-life-in-the-theatre-director-choreographer-graciela-daniele-com-133228.

Schomburg Center for Research in Black Culture, Photographs and Prints Division, The New York Public Library. "*Dancers performing the Cakewalk*" New York Public Library Digital Collections. Accessed August 14, 2022. https://digitalcollections.nypl.org/items/7f1c693a-9d78-e4f8-e040-e00a18061c4a.

Stearns, Marshall, and Jean Stearns. *Jazz Dance: The Story of American Vernacular Dance.* New York: Da Capo Press, 1994.

Turner, Victor. "Carnival in Rio: Dionysian Drama in an Industrializing Society." In *The Celebration of Society: Perspectives on Contemporary Cultural Performance*, edited by Frank E. Manning, 103–124, Bowling Green: OH, Bowling Green University Popular Press, 1983.

Updike, John. "A Cloud of Dust: E.L. Doctorow's *The March.*" *The New Yorker*, September 4, 2005. www.newyorker.com/magazine/2005/09/12/a-cloud-of-dust/amp.

3 "Till Georgie Took 'Em Away"

Counter Nostalgia and Cultural Theft in *Shuffle Along, Or The Making of the Musical Sensation of 1921 and All That Followed*[1]

In a dexterous moment of storytelling in the second act of the 2016 *Shuffle Along, Or The Making of the Musical Sensation of 1921 and All That Followed*, Eubie Blake (Brandon Victor Dixon) steps forward and explains to the audience that three nights in a row, George Gershwin sat behind him not watching the stage but observing his conducting technique and a particular clarinet player, William Grant Still. The accusatory tale and song in the show, "Till Georgie Took 'Em Away," is told through a solo tap dancer "playing" clarinet in a smoky spotlight, with the Harmony Kings singing and "patting" down stage right.[2] The dancer begins with simple rhythms, and as the story of the wrongful stealing of Blake's music and style progresses, the riffs of the dancing clarinetist grow in complexity, along with the body percussion of the Harmony Kings.[3] The magnitude of the theft is felt through the commanding and forceful tap and rhythm styles. Though Blake's suggestions are done with a sly wink, the notion of appropriation is readily put forth. Certainly, lyrics such as, "steal those black notes […] write a hit song," emphasize the point.[4] Importantly, the accentuation and building of tensions in regards to the appropriation of music is done through tap and body percussion, emphatically pointing towards the unashamed borrowing of movement as well as music.

Creating Shuffle Along, Or The Making of the Musical Sensation of 1921 and All That Follows

The 2016 Broadway musical *Shuffle Along, Or The Making of the Musical Sensation of 1921 and All That Follows,* with direction and book by George C. Wolfe and choreography by Savion Glover, is a necessary and vital work in the musical theatre genre that reclaims ownership of the form for Black Americans. Wolfe and Glover achieve this through the retelling of the past that puts Black contributions to the genre firmly at the center of the conversation. In continuance with Wolfe's practice of recovery as resistance, *Shuffle Along* (2016) has a strong pedagogical and recuperative focus.[5] The original *Shuffle Along,* with music by Eubie Black, lyrics by Noble Sissle, and with the comedic narrative put together by the Flournoy Miller and Aubrey Lyles, debuted in 1921 at the 63rd Street Music Hall in New York City. The plot, based on Miller and Lyles previous play, *The Mayor of Dixie,* loosely follows

DOI: 10.4324/9781003163688-5

the story of two corrupt politicians who hatch a plot to be in control of the town and police. While they bicker amongst themselves the honest and respected Harry Walton gets the town behind him and wins the election and the girl. The show was fundamentally a vehicle for many song and dance numbers as well as tried and true vaudeville sequences. Wolfe explains in an interview with Charles McNulty how shocked he was at the lack of recognition of *Shuffle Along* in a particular history book, "*Shuffle Along* was the biggest hit, but all they had was a paragraph at the end. How could it be a footnote to 1921 when it was the biggest show in 1921? How does something that matters so much end up not mattering at all?" Wolfe was thus motivated to remind audiences how hard Black artists had to work to get recognized, stating: "These people didn't have options. They had to make their own. And they did and they changed Broadway and they empowered generation upon generation upon generation of artists, and that's an extraordinary legacy."[6] The foundational construction of the 2016 production began with the dance, movement, and music of the era, as opposed to drawing on a previously written novel as do *The Color Purple* and *Ragtime*.[7] Lisa La Touche, a dancer in the 2016 production, explains that the very first creative labs began with Glover experimenting with the dancers and orchestrator Daryl Waters (who both fortified and safe-guarded the rhythms of the 1920s) while Wolfe worked at setting the book of the 2016 show.[8] The show, in La Touche's experience in the early workshops, grew from a place of intense collaboration between Wolfe, Glover, and Waters. By (re)telling the story of the making of a show, and reimagining the artists and their labor, the bodies on stage in the 2016 *Shuffle Along* culturally and politically present the archive of this legacy, and uphold the Black foundations of U.S. musical theatre.

Markedly, the choreography in *Shuffle Along* (2016) operates in a near reverse manner from both *The Color Purple* and *Ragtime*. In consideration of Wolfe's declared intention to elevate Black artists and the music and dances from their communities, the performance of Black dances and music of the early twentieth century on stage in 2016 is part of an act of resistance to the dominant thinking of musical theater being an invention by white artists.[9] Wolfe and Glover reimagine a community of artists as sovereign and attempting to be freestanding. Glover's choreography reanimates Black dance styles, specifically tap, as an embodied and communal site of Black communication, power, and resilience. This case study demonstrates how *Shuffle Along* (2016) can be seen as a "counter-example" where the dance elevates the communities it came from rather than obscuring or flattening them and their distinguishing characteristics. The embodied nostalgia that comes with the uplifting of Black dance styles breaks down any fantasies of the current or past ages that imagine white artists as creators of the dance forms.

Glover's choreography for the production is a key element to this process. His dance palette, heavy with an assortment of tap dance and early twentieth-century social and popular dance techniques, such as Snake Hips, the Grizzly Bear, and a proto-Charleston, has an exuberance to it with the intention of recapturing the dynamism and effervescence of the mounting of the original 1921 *Shuffle Along*. Glover not only populates the piece with Black movement signatures of the 1920s, such as shoulder shimmies and early iterations of the Charleston, but he also infuses the show with his characteristic contemporary tap dance expressions as a way to connect the past to the present in a model akin to reflective nostalgia. Wolfe and Glover's dramaturgical reanimation of the original show's journey to Broadway foregrounds its significance in the contemporary moment. Kristin Moriah describes Wolfe's creation as "an act of metadrama that became a catalyst for another conversation about racial diversity on Broadway."[10] Jesse Green points towards Wolfe's reparative efforts: "Wolfe bombards a core of ideas about race and culture with a billion showbiz protons to produce both a gorgeous spectacle and a big, smoking crater where your former ideas of Broadway once stood."[11] Glover's choreographic tactic of creating movement that embodies the nostalgia of the dances from the 1920s, also expresses assertiveness with his more contemporary moves, sheds light on the social and cultural complexity that operated in musical theatre in 1921, and stakes a claim for Black foundations of musical theatre now. Further, the Black body on stage, as set forth by Wolfe and put in motion by Glover, emblematizes so much of the labor that went into the foundations of Broadway, labor which is largely unrecognized today. Glover's intensity and complexity of movement propels this show with a palpable "no holds barred" ethos that claims a futurity for tap dance and the Black body in performance. As Thomas F. De Frantz explains, "movement provokes metacommentary and suggests narratives outside the physical frame of performance."[12] In kind, Glover's insistence on paying homage to the lineage of tap in *Shuffle Along* and his assertion to "create sounds that allow one to think," reanimates the Black bodily presence on Broadway and is a critical call to challenge previous histories and systems of social beliefs that surround the emergence of modernity at the beginning of the twentieth century in the U.S.[13]

Dramaturgical Strategies

As part of Wolfe's dramaturgical framework, *Shuffle Along* (2016) addresses and then dismantles the commonly accepted historical record many have come to believe: that the foundations of musical theatre were put in place solely by white artists such as Ira and George Gershwin, Jerome Kern, Oscar Hammerstein II, and Cole Porter, among others. Wolfe's previous works, such as *The Colored Museum* (1986) and the musical *Jelly's Last Jam* (1992), come from a foundational place with the aim to "unsettle the status quo and upend racial expectations."[14] Wolfe's work in *Shuffle Along* (2016), though packaged in a more heartening manner, is no less punctuated with affirmations of Black contributions to society and theatre, and furthers his goal towards "carving a new space for African American drama."[15]

In this historicized reclamation, Wolfe ties the show together using chronological ordinances helped along by various projections of dates and places, juxtaposed with production numbers and plot points from the original 1921 show in order to reinforce the social and cultural contributions of Black Americans to musical theatre then and now. This self-referentiality (or repossession of theatre by theatre) is key in helping to reinforce to audiences just how vital theatre and its history are to the development of society and the role of social dance communities within it.[16] Wolfe details how Black composers, lyricists, comedians, singers, and dancers pushed through the segregation and elitism that surrounded Broadway at the time to come together and present a musical on their terms, and of their culture.

Wolfe's innovative weaving together of theatrical elements mixes documentary theatre with the contemporary sensibilities and technologies of current Broadway musical theatre. He includes as an insert in the Playbill a reproduction of the 1921 program in sepia tones, containing a half dozen pictures of the original artists and ensemble as well as advertisements of the era, instigating the nostalgic framework. The show alternates between scenes following the plot of the original show (the story of the shenanigans behind a quasi-fixed mayoral race), and those depicting the staging of that show on tour and the struggle to secure a Broadway venue. In the historical restructuring, Wolfe's collaboration with Glover, a Tony award-winning choreographer for his work in *Bring in 'da Noise, Bring in 'da Funk* (1996), is able both to navigate and knit together the temporal divide of the show with an intense physicality that speaks to the past, present, and future.

Choreography and *Shuffle Along* (2016)

The dance styles of the early twentieth century, when performed in Wolfe's *Shuffle Along*, rich in the flairs and fashions of the 1920s, create the possibility of nostalgic impulses in the audience – longings for a personal or public past, envisioning an alternate or preferred past, seeking a sense of home – that help them to connect to the reparative message of the production. Further, in this historical vein, the collective emotional associations and historical explorations of the past Wolfe takes on in *Shuffle Along* set up a nostalgic impulse inherent in the show. This desire however does not constitute a longing for the past or a looking back at the past through rose-colored glasses, but adopts a reflective nostalgia; a meditation on and retracing of the past that recognizes the possibility of alternate perspectives that – and this seems to be Wolfe's hope – may go on to influence future individual actions and reparations. As Wolfe explains in an interview with playwright Tony Kushner, "the show is a great place to tell the story of how far we had come, how far we needed to go, and nearly a century later, how much remains unchanged."[17]

Glover's choreography has an embodied nostalgia and boldness to it that directly re-declares Black ownership of tap in musical theatre. Brian Seibert describes the many layers in Glover's work: "Glover's choreography, in its wordless eloquence, convey[s] the resilience of African Americans in a form at once symbolic and physical."[18] This embodied nostalgia within the dancing bodies connects to the present moment by its strategic layering of tap, Black social dance styles, and Glover's modern innovations, expertly executed by the highly skilled cast. This juxtaposition of the new and the old demonstrates the dimension and embodied meaning in tap in Broadway musical theatre. This is different from Daniele's deconstruction of movement codes in *Ragtime* as there is a melding and modulation that happens between past and present styles in *Shuffle Along*, as opposed to assembling fragments alongside each other to enhance the contrast and embedded meanings. In an interview with Adam Green, Glover explains his process of amalgamating the old with the new within one body dancing:

> It's adding the steps and style of the past to the rhythms and sounds of today. It's performing an old-school step with a new-school style – or maybe you take a step from today and execute it in a style from the past.[19]

Through this blending, Glover's choreography is both an homage to the past and an attempt towards righting the historical record. This move is particularly poignant and steeped in social and political resonance given the cultural forces at work today in conjunction with social equality movements like Black Lives Matter. As DeFrantz observes in a lecture on the work and mission of choreographer Jawole Willa Jo, "our bodies are profound not just in the metaphors they inspire but in the memories they contain."[20] *Shuffle Along* (2016) shows Black bodies relentlessly striving for fairness and justice, pushing on through exhaustion and inequality. Wolfe reminds us that this has always been the struggle of Black Americans; for all the style, innovations, and foundations they brought to musical theatre, the stories need to be told and retold in order to inscribe them in the vernacular.

Decisively, *Shuffle Along* (2016) looks to the past as a way of moving forward in regards to Black Americans' historical roles as cultural innovators. Moriah observes, "In staging their awareness of the dynamics of the popular stage and the limitations of its tropes, black performers in *The Making Of* appeared not just as consumable products but as cultural agents."[21] Markedly, the dancers and choreography of the 2016 *Shuffle Along* bring these ideas of ushering in the modern flair so coveted at the time by white audiences forward for consideration. As Jayna Brown describes in *Babylon Girls: Black Women Performers and the Shaping of the Modern* the female chorus of the original *Shuffle Along* helped shape modernity. She observes, "the meanings of the black woman's body in motion were central to the anxieties and hopes imbedded in white ideas of the modern city space as well as the politics of black cultural self-referentiality."[22] Glover, through his complex choreographic signature, is pointedly staking a claim that Black performers of the past, particularly the female chorus dancers, were agents of change both on stage and off. The exuberance, energy and dynamism of the original female chorus in *Shuffle Along*, to draw on the work of Daphne Brooks, "crafted new forms of narrative agency and corporeal representation in theatricalized spaces."[23] Indeed, the 1921 *Shuffle Along* increased the visibility of Black female dancers and launched the career of numerous famous performers that emerged from the chorus, including Josephine Baker, Adelaide Hall, and Florence Mills. Brown further explains the "New Woman" of the 1920s "embraced black expressive forms, adopting racialized gestural vocabularies to shape and redefine their own bodies as modern."[24] The immense success of the original *Shuffle Along* thrust these movement and aesthetic styles into mainstream culture to enormous effect and subsequent consumption.

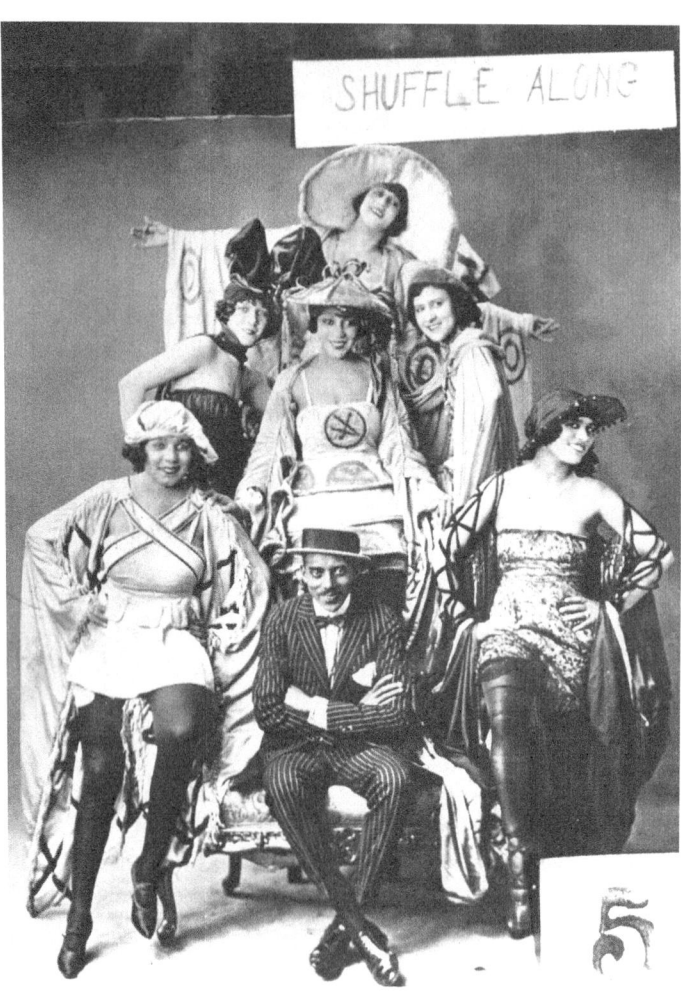

Figure 3.1 "Lyricist Noble Sissle and cast members from the musical 'Shuffle Along,' ca. 1921"
Source: New York Public Library Digital Collections. Image Schomburg Center for Research in Black Culture, Photographs and Prints Division, The New York Public Library.

As Brenda Dixon Gottschild describes, "these aesthetic principles became integral signifiers of modernism and were embraced by white Americans as well as Europeans."[25] The assumption of Black styles emphatically linked, as Gottschild observes, "the black swing era aesthetic and global trends in modernism movements of African American on stage."[26] The complexity within Glover's choreography in the 2016 *Shuffle Along* explicitly gestures to what a landmark production the original was, one that David Savran states, "made jazz and tap dancing obligatory on Broadway."[27] Glover's choreography punctuates that point nearly a century later by situating the female ensemble in the 2016 version with a dominance and dynamism reminiscent of the original chorus.

Background: Savion Glover and Tap Dance

Glover's history in tap circles and dance communities is well known. He appeared on Broadway at ten years old in *The Tap Dance Kid* (1985) and went on to *Black and Blue* in 1989, when he was the youngest person at the time to get nominated for a Tony Award. His first collaboration with director and writer George C. Wolfe was in *Jelly's Last Jam* (1992), where he performed with his teacher and tap icon Gregory Hines. His first choreography credit on Broadway was for *Bring in 'da Noise, Bring in 'da Funk* (1996), where he again collaborated with Wolfe. Described by Joan Acocella of the *New Yorker* as "the greatest tap virtuoso of our time, perhaps of all time," and given his training by the fathers and grandfathers of tap, Glover, born in 1973, is in effect the bodily archive or physical repository of tap dance.[28] Glover's main mentors, along with Hines, include tap dance greats Buster Brown, Chuck Green, Jimmy Slyde and Lon Chaney. From them (and others) he developed a well-rounded understanding of the form. La Touche, who worked with Glover on *Shuffle Along* from the very beginning of the initial workshops explains: "anytime I've ever been in a studio with him, I just get this tiniest window of what this could have been like with any of those guys."[29] The embodied history that travelled through the bodies of the greats – from Brown's subtle shuffles (the brushing back and forth of the sole of the foot to achieve two quick noises) where feet barely come off the floor, to the slides across the floor of Jimmy Slyde, to the fully physicalized style of Hines, where the percussiveness of the taps extended through his whole body – is all present in Glover. Through his work with these early innovators, Glover acquired a fine-tuned knowledge of the history of tap, against which he was able to push and pull en route to devising his own intense, hard-hitting, and grounded style of movement. His bent-over, highly percussive style emerged as very different from the upright-postured, early tap dance sounds, derived from the loose swinging shuffles and soft-shoe methods. Seibert suggests perhaps Glover's greatest contribution to the genre is that he "made tap a young person's game."[30] Glover made it acceptable to internalize the form, to move away from the presentational style previously associated with tap and movie musicals that privileged the visual or scenographic into a mode of interpretation that shared many sensibilities with more modern aesthetics, such as hip-hop and street dance. Young dancers were inspired by the more authoritative urban style of percussive and hard-hitting dance, performed to modern music.

Wolfe describes the dualities and depth within Glover: "Savion is a living repository of the history of rhythm … He got it from the guys who got it from the guys who got it from the guys. But he's also a bridge to the future."[31] Having Glover at the creative helm of the movement signature and choreographic structure of the 2016 musical offers an often-overlooked epistemology of the foundations of musical theatre in the United States. Wolfe explains his goal with the show was to "reach into the past and bring back to life the ebullient spirit of a groundbreaking hit musical."[32] Glover's choreography embodies this resurrection (and innovation) by his taking full advantage of the dynamics and depth of tap dancing as a repository of the original movement styles of the production, and melding them with contemporary urban sensibilities largely derived from Black influences. Liza Gennaro contends, "Glover's choreography was a triumph of rhythm, technique, style, innovation, and artistry. He honors the pasts while creating the future."[33] Glover's choreography functions in this assembly to both shed light on the social and cultural complexity that operated in the performance of musical theatre then (1921) and to stake a claim for the choreographic contributions, historical and ongoing, of Black artistry in musical theatre.

Shuffle Along (2016), Tap Dance, and Counter Nostalgia

The confluence of the artistry of Glover, the dramaturgical vision of Wolfe, and the on-stage contributions of some of the most talented and accomplished performers on Broadway (Audra McDonald, Brian Stokes Mitchell, Billy Porter, Brandon Victor Dixon, Joshua Henry and Adrienne Warren – all either Tony Award winners or nominees) makes *Shuffle Along* a tour de force that emphasizes the fundamental foundation Black Americans laid, and the vital contributions they continue to make to musical theatre. The revised musical, "one of the season's essential tickets," as described by Ben Brantley, signals a move to both remind and redefine the foundation of musical theatre and champion the voices and bodies that made significant inroads at a time when musical theatre was in its nascent form.[34]

What cannot be overlooked in this discussion is that, unlike the original *Shuffle Along* of 1921 that enjoyed a 504-performance run, tours for nearly three years after, and numerous revivals, the 2016 *Shuffle Along* played only 100 performances and thirty-three previews. Much press circulated around Audra McDonald's pregnancy as the cause for the show's early closure. However, McDonald was always planning to leave the show for some time to reprise her 2014 Tony Award-winning role in *Lady Day At Emerson Bar & Grill* in London. The news of her pregnancy nonetheless seemed to have stalled ticket sales, though an excellent replacement, Grammy award winner

Rhiannon Giddons was ready to step in. Catherine M. Young gives three more plausible reasons for the show's closure:

> There are three important reasons a show as great as *Shuffle Along* is closing and they don't involve a pregnant star. The show is expensive to run, may be too "inside" for the casual Broadway consumer, and it could not get out of the long shadow cast by *Hamilton*. [35]

These pragmatic reasonings ring true and help to explain the broader socioeconomic functioning of Broadway. Kristin Moriah further explains the complexity surrounding the closure: "In *The Making Of*'s closing we are witness to some of the paradoxes behind the seeming ascendance of ethnic diversity on the popular stage."[36] Moriah explains the continued challenges to navigating race and ethnicity in popular entertainment, observing, "embodied performances of blackness and nuanced depictions of African American History are still at odds with audience expectations."[37] This lack of alignment, however, should not be a reason to stall the creation of works about the Black experience, as is explained be Sandra Seaton, whose great uncle was Flournoy E. Miller.[38] Seaton describes in a 2016 article in *The Dramatist* that when artistic director Jack Viertel was thinking of reviving the original *Shuffle Along* in 2002 as part of the *Encores!* series, he communicated his worries of receiving "political resistance, especially from the very population we'd be trying to honor" in conversation with playwright August Wilson.[39] Wilson replied:

> Its presentation would be a historical reminder of that contribution, and its images and portrayal of blacks, though less than sterling, would not be a perpetuation of the images, but a historical reminder of a time when such portrayals were part of the popular culture.[40]

Though the numerous and complex reasons behind the closure "demonstrates the unsteady role that race and ethnicity continue to play in popular entertainment," avoiding these encounters all together further underserves those communities.[41]

The ephemeral nature of live performance is felt in the disappointment professed by heartbroken cast members and fan groups. In effect, this twist of fate has not allowed *Shuffle Along, Or The Making Of The Musical Sensation of 1921 And All That Follows* to be seen by a vast number of people, inevitably lessening its intended impact. The lack of a cast album and readily available libretto add to the difficulty of reviving the show. La Touche talks about the double meaning within the narrative of the original show being forgotten and the 2016 one coming to a close:

> We lived our version of it, some really dark corners that turned and some huge celebrations and the fact that our cast, our ensemble really stuck together. We became so close throughout the whole process, everyone looked out for one another and it really mattered.

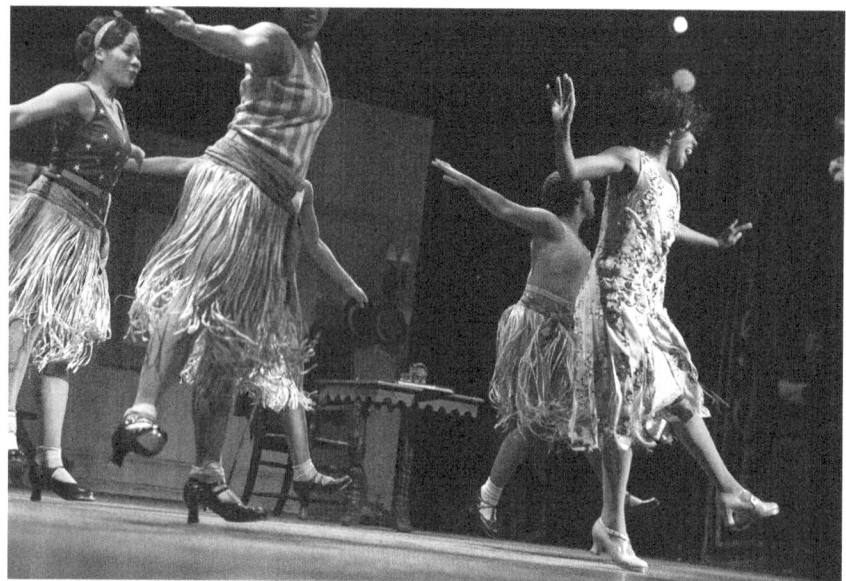

Figure 3.2 Ensemble Dancers, "Shuffle Along, or the musical sensation of 1922 and all
        that followed," 2016
Source: Julieta Cervantes Photography

She explains the significance of the show, "Obviously, any gig that you have is
super significant but you could tell there was a certain vibe that everyone had to
be able to tell this story. It was more – we get to tell the story versus we get to
be on Broadway."[42] Some of the methods used to raise the level of significance
of the dancing Black body were to engage with the history at every level and
counter any nostalgia for the white artists creating the foundations of the form.
Wolfe was determined to make people understand the stakes at play at the time
of the original. La Touche describes how the show's dramaturg explained the
history leading up to the original show. She refers to how various assistants
would put up newspapers on the rehearsal room walls each day reporting news
from the same day ninety-six years before. Wolfe comments,

> Prior to this show happening, X number of people knew about *Shuffle
> Along* …people don't know everything about it, but it's there. The cast
> knows; they are finding out about people they didn't know, the people
> who went before them, when the stakes were more violent.[43]

The crisis in *Shuffle Along* (2016) is not in the flattening of social dance communities but the missed opportunity to bring this elevation of Black history
nationwide.

Though *Shuffle Along* (1921) often receives accolades as the first popular
Black musical on Broadway, it is important to note for the sake of

understanding the artistic environment at the time, that it was not a standalone event created by Black composers and artists.[44] In his lifetime, *Shuffle Along* composer Eubie Blake consistently protested the many "firsts" commonly attached to the 1921 show, insisting they were owed to, or should be shared with, others. He continually reminded journalists throughout his lengthy career of those involved in the ongoing creation of musical theatre in the first third of the twentieth century from Bob Cole, Will Marion Cook, Billy Johnson and J. Rosamond Johnson to Ernest Hogan, George Walker, and Bert Williams.[45] *Shuffle Along* (1921) did not just appear out of the ether – it was a high moment in a time of much effort and dedication to Black music and performance in general. Wolfe's production brings this vital information front and center and describes how the original *Shuffle Along* shifted the tenor of musical comedy and the influence of jazz music on Broadway.

David Savran specifies the impact of jazz music to musical theatre resulting from the original show: "*Shuffle Along* modernized musical comedy by intro-ducing a sparkling mélange of ragtime, operetta, and jazz that did more than carry audiences away."[46] This crossover of music styles extended to the show's physical movement, as in effect social dances and movement rhythms evolved alongside jazz music (as seen with ragtime and the Cakewalk, the blues and the Slow Drag, and now with tap and jazz music). European dances of the time such as the waltz or the Schottische were over taken by more popular and physically liberating dances of the times, such as the numerous Animal Dances (the Turkey Trot, the Grizzly Bear, etc.), and eventually the high-energy Charleston and Black Bottom. And, as the Stearnses explained, the dynamism and innovation of the dancing in the 1921 *Shuffle Along* changed the structure of shows.[47] The original *Shuffle Along* was not solely a tap musical; it was a mix of many strands of music, comedy routines and even costumes, a sort of patchwork of sounds and movements that had worked before in other venues.[48] Glover's choreography today has similarities: it encompasses the many different movement dimensions from the past as well as contemporary, of-the-moment dances, just as in the original *Shuffle Along*.

Wolfe is certainly attuned to the mark *Shuffle Along* made on Broadway in 1921 in terms of changes in music styles. He includes a clever moment in the show when Lottie Gee (Audra McDonald) is rehearsing a song to be put in the show – "I'm Just Wild About Harry" (Harry being a third candidate that enters the mayoral race and comes to win the hearts of citizens, while the two crooked candidates fight amongst themselves). The song is presented for Lottie to sing as a waltz, one of the common musical structures used in European-styled musical comedy at the time. The song, which has gone on to become one of the most recognizable songs of *Shuffle Along* and often a standalone hit, is practically unrecognizable as a waltz, comical in its construction as a lilting three-quarter time composition. Lottie protests that no one is doing waltzes anymore and asks if some swing could be injected into it. In this moment in the 2016 show there is both humor and artistry on a larger level regarding the style shift that nods to the proliferation of jazz rhythms into musical comedy.

"I'm Just Wild About Harry" expands into a larger production number as Gertrude Saunders and numerous ensemble members join Lottie. The song is resplendent with the dynamism of jazz and rhythmic complexities, rising to be one of the highlights to the show.

Wolfe is attempting to capture and showcase the transition in musical styles in this scene, as in others such as the moment with the clarinettist mentioned earlier. This dramaturgical choice reminds audiences of the aural depth of the shift, demonstrating how musical comedy sounded before and after the influence of jazz music.[49] Wolfe describes the magnitude of this event: "Once you teach syncopation, everybody can syncopate – George Gershwin, Irving Berlin ... Jazz gave Broadway – and America – its own musical language. It liberated American Music."[50] The timing of this move coincided with the increased and rapidly growing mechanization of America since the late-nineteenth century. The rhythm of America was changing and nothing symbolized this more than jazz music.[51] Wolfe explains that this shift in rhythms and the move away from European sensibilities was new yet felt natural in the progressive moment of the 1920s: "These rhythms were alien but intrinsic to who we are as a culture, and they were on Broadway ... and they were changing Broadway."[52] The infiltration of jazz was unavoidable in the many aspects of daily life and when *Shuffle Along* came along there was an abundance of sounds and physicalities that Wolfe and Glover successfully recreate and recall in *Shuffle Along*, telegraphed from the start in the lengthy subtitle – *Or The Making Of The Musical Sensation of 1921 And All That Followed*.

Tap as a Conversation

One of the most striking moments in the musical comes when there is a stand-off between those performers who went on to work on the musical *The Chocolate Dandies* (1924) and those who went on to the musical *Rang Tang* (1927). This split of the cast signaled the end of the collaboration between the foursome, as they parted ways to pursue separate projects. Wolfe has Glover embody the break-up (played up in the 2016 show for theatrical effect) between Blake and Sissle and Miller and Lyles, using the ensemble to perform a sort of competition, or challenge dance, between the casts of the two shows. By creating a physical argument or competition between performers, Glover does two things. First, he both celebrates and underlines the importance of the conversational style that already existed in tap dance. Much like improvisation in jazz music, there exists in tap dance a fundamental passing back and forth of rhythms, or call and response, as a mode of showmanship and physical communication. In so doing, Glover makes sure that this basic characteristic of tap dance is represented. Second, in this conversation there is a trading and negotiating back and forth of styles, beginning with more traditional styles that increase to more contemporary tap modulations showing the progressive nature of tap dancing.

While tap dance is not specifically considered a social dance in a partnered sense, its origins and roots in physicalized conversations through challenge dances and the building upon of each other's steps, grounds it as a vital part of the "lifeblood of communities" often "learned informally through cultural and social networks."[53] There is a contradiction in the form as indeed the training necessary for tap dance requires the articulation of a physical technique based on looseness of ankles and hips, an understanding of complex rhythms, and a continued practice of steps and progressions. However, within the culture of the form there is very much a sharing and showing off of newly invented steps, and styles. Tap dance has both an oral and aural method of communicating based on the gathering of people in the space in a social setting. La Touche explains the social dance aspects of tap dance are rooted in the communication and challenge feature of the form. This social structure brings people together who would gather to show moves and "show up" other dancers. She explains, "What they would do is congregate. Just like hip hop dancers. They would congregate and always have these challenges ... like Charleston competitions in the 20s and 30s."[54] This communicative style is foundational to the form and deeply embedded in Glover's style. Furthermore, the social practice of soloing or showing off for each other salutes the improvisational nature of the form, which allows a space to experiment even in a solo in a performance setting. Dance scholar Constance Valis Hill expands on the social nature of the form, "tap dance developed from people listening to and watching each other in the street, dance hall, or social club where steps were shared, stolen and reinvented... .There were also displays of one-upmanship in social clubs: juried buck-and-wing contests on theatre stages after a show."[55] The essence of the "tap challenges," where dancers try to outdo each other comes from the social gatherings encouraged on by cheering crowds. Hill explain how skills are passed on, "Technique is transmitted visually, aurally, and corporeally."[56] This synergy, as expressed by La Touche makes for a unique art form that while not adhering to traditions of partnered social dances, the development of the form comes from social experience and exchange.

The back-and-forth dance-off, or "tap challenge" happening mid-way through the second act of *Shuffle Along* (2016), becomes a stepping off point towards more contemporary choreography in the show and demonstrates this kind of social exchange. Later in the second act, Glover has the ensemble, dressed in long pants and flat shoes, performing behind and around a scrim. This space, removed from the main focus of action, functions as a framing device to the growing complications between the artists. The ensemble, no longer in the 1920s makeshift costumes, or everyday wear of chorus dancers of the 1921 narrative, execute more percussive and rhythmic moves that have a force and dynamism; this brings the Black tenure of the form distinctly into the twenty-first century. Stomps are louder, arms ricochet forward and back in reaction to moves that bound or slide further from the body using greater complications of rhythms and taking greater physical risks. The dance becomes more authoritative, as it is executed in a position lower to the ground, with knees deeply bent and shoulders hunched. These physicalities support the growing tension in the narrative that sees the break down in the collaboration between the creative team and an increase in the competition between casts.

As mentioned, Glover's work in *Shuffle Along* (2016) is a compilation of styles and methods, each with their own historical resonance. In order to uphold this history in musical theatre, one must continuously acknowledge the complicated roots of tap dance. Hill explains that any tidy or brief explanation of the history of tap overlooks the

> more complex intercultural fusions, which occurred through the interactions of Irish indentured servants and enslaved West Africans in the Caribbean during the 1600s, African American folk and Irish American laborers in the southern United States during the 1700s, and African American freemen and Irish American performers ...in the 1800s.[57]

Keeping this Afro-Irish fusion in mind helps to understand the back and forth of movement between ethnicities and how the notion of exchange, or a conversation or competition, is always at the forefront of the form. Hill reminds that the challenge nature of tap is "a battle for virtuosity and authority, [and] puts into focus issues of race and ethnicity; it inevitably takes on the history of race, racism, and race relations in America."[58] *Shuffle Along* (2016) does not chart the complicated historical dimensions of tap, and that is not the task of the show, however, any movement analysis must recognize the complexity embedded in the art form. The production does not cover the contributions the Irish (and other cultures) made to tap dance. There is a sense that in the reparation of Black ownership of musical theatre, tap dance is carried along with it, the multiple ethnicities involved in its roots are not explored.[59] Wolfe's task for *Shuffle Along* is focused on resurrecting Black American contributions to the musical theatre, and the complications in this journey.

Two Styles of Tap

As the fashion for tap-dancing grew throughout the twentieth century, many dancers, both Black and white, learned tap at a ballet barre from a white teacher; particularly as white dancers and teachers took up the style. This style was not the grounded percussive style of tap dance passed down through generations of Black dancers, as Glover had learned. Glover's style has its roots in the social and shared communication of tap through jam sessions and communal gatherings, as described above. Though, as the popularity for tap increased more extensive training regimes were developed. As much as Black jazz music was readily taken up by white musicians, so too was the path for tap. As such the different styles of tap dance are commonly divided into two broad categories – "Broadway Style" and "Hoofing" – and what performers learned first varies depending on a variety of factors including economic backgrounds, geographic locale, and popular fads. The "Broadway Style" is more lifted with greater emphasis placed on arm gestures redolent of Fred Astaire, and largely derived from the "spectacularization" of the move to the stage.[60] The "Hoofing" style is much lower and the center of gravity is decidedly toward the floor with the arms as a manifestation of the movement not placed in accordance with a specific syllabus or standardized method. Glover has essentially embodied this more exploratory, rhythmically focused, hard-hitting style over his career. His abilities in all designations of tap however, are astonishing. Glover's melding of these two above-mentioned styles is the unique approach he brings to *Shuffle Along*. In many cases, the two styles can often be separated into the tap dance performed by female dancers wearing shoes with high heels, or men in more supple jazz oxfords, to both men and women wearing flatter, harder, square-heeled shoes, often built up in the sole to be quite heavy on their own, the weight decidedly helping to punctuate heel drops and stamps. The ensemble, particularly noticeable in the women, switch from the former shoe to the latter later in the show. Hill, also suggests that the differentiation between the forms were, "not along racial lines but rhythmic sensibilities."[61] In this consideration, Glover has a remarkable capacity to combine the intricate rhythmic details of tap with the musical elements of the musical movements of the time. He does not interpret jazz dances elements, such as turns, kicks, and transition steps separately but fuses everything together. This *mélange* of styles is embedded in the original *Shuffle Along* as the musical made its mark by evolving from the aforementioned early jazz and social dances into tap dance. There was a fusion then and Glover brings that fusion of style into the 2016 production. His choreographic voice is attuned to this need for a melding of styles shaped by his experience in Broadway shows from an early age. Pointedly, those shows explored the roots of the form, jazz music, and the Black experience which fostered an environment for him to develop the embodied skillset that helps bring Wolfe's vision alive.

Returning then to the narrative of the 2016 production. As the breakup of the four creators is looming, *Shuffle Along* stages a significant historical conversation. One reports that "Flo Ziegfeld" hired the chorus girls to teach his dancers to stomp, shimmy and shake.[62] What perhaps seems flattering at first became the beginning of cultural appropriation of tap dance by white dancers. White dancers eventually passed down their styles or interpretation of Black styles through the ranks of teachers to Broadway performers who learn a transformed version many decades later.[63]

Though Glover recognizes this differentiation, he explains this inevitable evolution of tap in performance:

> There's the Tommy Tune or Susan Stroman approach versus the Henry LeTang, Cholly Atkins, Honi Coles style – both lend themselves to the excitement and invite the audience in…*Noise/Funk* came with a different approach. I'm looking forward to… reminding people of the greats of the past.[64]

In Glover's choreography for *Shuffle Along* there is both a sense of homage to the moves and styles of the trailblazers, and his own unique contributions. Surprisingly, one of the main headliners of the show, McDonald, was not completely aware of the intricacies in bringing the musical back to the stage. She explains, "I didn't know anything about *Shuffle Along* and its influence … not many people do. That's the reason I signed on before there was even a complete script – I want to be a part of telling that story. It's a way of honoring our ancestors."[65] By recognizing the fusion of the two styles of tap, one more grounded and authoritative and one more lifted and presentational, a space opens for nostalgia that gestures toward the journey of tap, from Black culture as an initial social dance, to being an expectation on Broadway in the first half of the twentieth century.

The Cast of *Shuffle Along* (2016)

Beyond the star-studded list of principal players, the chorus brings the energy and dynamism that captures the resilience and determination of the original cast. The physicality provided by Glover encompasses the desperations and high stakes of the trials and tribulations the cast went through en route to the historic Broadway premiere. In the production numbers from the original 1921 musical (within the 2016 musical), the dancers embody an "old-fash-ionedness" in their earnestness and youthful execution. This movement dynamic (visible in the overall lightness, abandon, and presentational style) used to evoke the qualities of the original show, stands in contrast to the more powerful dancing in the second act when the cast of *Shuffle Along* is split up, and enters into the previously described dance-off, or "tap-challenge," outside the story of the original musical, but within Wolfe's narrative.[66] The physica-lized turn towards the past has a reflective element to it in the nostalgic manner suggested by Boym. There is a contemplative look at conditions of the past and meditations on their magnitude in relation to contemporary society.

While the chorus of the 2016 *Shuffle Along* is all Black, like the original 1921 cast, their collective presence hints at the continued difficulties on Broadway today for non-white dancers. Though a musical like *Hamilton* is celebrated for its mixed-race cast, there is still much to do beyond casting to repair the historical record, including using more Black composers, choreo-graphers and directors. Glover, who at one point planned to go into the cast himself, works the ensemble hard throughout – an action that "transforms syncopated tap into a widely expressive force of giddy liberation and focused determination, of exaltation and anger, in numbers that include the knockout opener, "Broadway Blues," and a fierce, competitive dance-off in the second act."[67]

Wolfe's reincarnation of *Shuffle Along* is a necessary and reparative rekindling of the historical momentum in musical theatre instigated by Black Americans. The sensational and determined 2016 *Shuffle Along* blows the dust off the archival files for scholars and practitioners alike and allows not only for the recognition of the tremendous effort of those involved in *Shuffle Along* (both in the 1921 original and 2016 revisioning) but also reinstates the historical importance and foundational contributions that Black Americans made and continue to make toward the development of U.S. musical theatre. Much like the original *Shuffle Along* on tour in the 1920s helped in part to desegregate theatre around the United States, Wolfe and Glover's 2016 *Shuffle Along* in future revivals or tours will help to restore the status of the original and solidify a more honest and inclusive history. La Touche explains Wolfe's mission to keep the past alive, "George always said, 'Please remember why we are doing this, we are doing it for them.'"[68]

In all three musicals investigated in this section, there are efforts within the narrative to deepen awareness of particular Black communities at the turn of the twentieth century. These explorations are at their most effective during moments of social dance, or at the very least at community gatherings in the narrative where dance and music happen. In these diegetic moments of social dance, political, and social issues rooted in the body are physicalized and assume a more tangible form, putting forth a complex subtext for consideration. This chapter identified what gets left behind, altered or added in the social dance's transfer to the stage, and the social and political repercussions of this "spectaculariztion." In particular, this chapter has evidenced that Black bodies dancing on stage hold within them the history of the social dance in question. In all three musicals, when the nostalgia is investigated through the bodily practices and choreography in the production, the corporeal connection conveys deeper social and political meanings.

The following section investigates the entanglement of authorship and ownership of dances, and quests for authenticity that besiege the dances of the Jazz Age, and how those social and political dimensions are embodied within the dance. Moreover, when nostalgia is investigated through the bodily practices and choreography in the next chapter a further critical analysis can be taken up as to what this corporeal connection conveys on a larger social and political scale, particularly as European and white American influences descend upon Black dances.

Notes

1 A version of this chapter has been published in *Reframing the Musical: Race, Culture and Identity.* Edited by Sarah Whitfield, 2019, Chapter title, "Reparation and Reanimation: Savion Glover's Choreography of *Shuffle Along, Or The Making of the Musical Sensation of 1921 and All That Followed*," Red Globe Press, an imprint of Bloomsbury Publishing Plc.

2 Patting is the use of handclaps and body percussion to imitate sounds of drums. Patting was originated by Black Americans out of necessity when drumming was banned in cities and on plantations. The Stearnses describe patting started, "as any kind of clapping with any dance to encourage another dancer, [and] became a special routine of slapping the hands, knees, thighs, and body in rhythmic display." The moves are often called "Patting Juba" as William Henry Lane (nicknamed "Juba") brought it into a solo performance. Patting also "became part of the more

pretentious style of the Charleston: crossing and uncrossing the hands on the knees as they fan back and forth." Marshall and Jean Stearns, *Jazz Dance: The Story of American Vernacular Dance*. New York: Da Capo Press, 1994), 29.

3 The Harmony Kings were a vocal quartet that grew out of a gospel group. Their professional status was solidified by their involvement in the original *Shuffle Along*, "Review of *Shuffle Along* and the Saga of the Four Harmony Kings: Group Harmony Pioneers," http://classicurbanharmony.net/2016/05/10/review-of-shuffle-a long-and-the-saga-of-the-four-harmony-kings-group-harmony-pioneers/, accessed December 10, 2017.

4 *Shuffle Along, Or The Making of the Musical Sensation of 1921 and All That Followed*: 2016, with music and lyrics by Eubie Blake and Noble Sissle, libretto by George C. Wolfe, based on the original book of the 1921 *Shuffle Along* book by Flournoy Miller and Aubrey Lyles; musical supervision, arrangement, orchestrations by Daryl Waters.

5 George C. Wolfe has a history of directing more radically themed works that comment on the struggles and injustices put upon Black Americans and under-represented communities. He is also dedicated to exploring and restoring the historical record with Black Americans firmly centered in the picture. As will be seen in *The Wild Party* in chapter two (also directed by Wolfe), he is interested in exploring below the surface of historical givens, assumptions, or mythologies. Previous shows include: *Jelly's Last Jam*, 1992; *Angels in America: Millennium Approaches, Angels in America: Perestroika*, 1993, *The Colored Museum*, 1986.

6 Charles McNulty, "How *Shuffle Along* director George C. Wolfe brought back the 1921 show that changed Broadway forever," *Los Angeles Times*, April 25, 2016.

7 The musical *The Color Purple* is based on both the novel and film.

8 Author interview with Lisa La Touche, *Shuffle Along* cast member, September 17, 2017.

9 Some scholars of musical theatre such as Geoffrey Block and Lehman Engels among others privilege a more "well-made" musical such as *Showboat* (1929) by Jerome Kern and Oscar Hammerstein II, or go further ahead to *Oklahoma!* as the basis for the genre. Overall, there is a tendency to assign the foundations of musical theatre to white artists such as Ira and George Gershwin, Jerome Kern, Oscar Hammerstein II, and Cole Porter, among others. This has changed in the past fifteen years as musical theatre scholarship has become more distinctive.

10 Kristin Moriah, "Shuffle and Repeat: The Making of Shuffle Along," *American Quarterly* 69, no. 1 (March 2017): 178.

11 Jesse Green, "*Shuffle Along* is a Gorgeously Staged, Life-Changing Show," *Vulture*, April 28, 2016, http://www.vulture.com/2016/04/theater-review-shuffle-along.html.

12 Thomas F. DeFrantz, "Introduction," *Dancing Many Drums: Excavations in African American Dance* (Madison: University of Wisconsin Press, 2002), 14.

13 Pia Catton, "Savion Glover on Choreographing *Shuffle Along*," *Wall Street Journal*, April 13, 2016, https://www.wsj.com/articles/savion-glover-choreographs-shuf fle-along-1460561090.

14 Harry J. Elam Jr. "Post-World War II African American Theatre," *The Oxford Handbook of American Drama*, eds. Jeffrey H. Richards and Heather S. Nathans, Oxford Handbooks Online, http://www.oxfordhandbooks.com.ezproxy.gc.cuny.edu/view/ 10.1093/oxfordhb/9780199731497.001.0001/oxfordhb-9780199731497-e-006?rskey= oJpAc7&result=1, accessed October 2, 2017, 384.

15 Elam Jr., "Post-World War II African American Theatre," 384.

16 Paula Vogel's 2016 play *Indecent*, which resurrects the story of the cast and performances of Sholem Asch's *God of Vengeance* (1907), does similar restorative work in regards to telling the story of censorship surrounding the play upon its arrival in the United States. Wolfe, like Vogel, sheds light on the injustices that operated in U.S. theatre, engaging the audience on both an intellectual and visceral level incorporating music and movement in the retelling of historical incidents.

17 Tony Kushner, "George C. Wolfe," *Interview Magazine,* May 6, 2016, https://www.interviewmagazine.com/culture/george-c-wolfe, accessed December 20, 2017.

18 Brian Seibert, *What The Eye Hears: A History of Tap Dancing* (New York: Farrar, Straus and Giroux Books, 2015), 469.

19 Adam Green, "Tap-Dancing Legend Savion Glover Reanimates the Game-Changing Broadway Musical Shuffle Along," *Vogue* 207, no. 5 (2016), 210.

20 Thomas F. DeFrantz, "Booty Control," in *Dancing Many Drums* (Madison: University of Wisconsin Press, 2002), 25.

21 Moriah, "Shuffle and Repeat: The Making of Shuffle Along," 181.

22 Jayna Brown, *Babylon Girls: Black Women Performers and the Shaping of the Modern.* (Durham, NC: Duke University Press, 2008), 2.

23 Daphne Brook, *Bodies in Dissent: Spectacular Performances of Race and Freedom, 1850–1910* (Durham, NC: Duke University Press, 2006), 11.

24 Brown, *Babylon Girls,* 3.

25 Brenda Dixon Gottschild, *Waltzing in the Dark: African American Vaudeville and Race Politics in the Swing Era* (New York: St. Martin's Press, 2000), 11.

26 Ibid., 5.

27 David Savran, *Highbrow/Lowdown: Theater, Jazz, and the Making of the New Middle Class.* (Ann Arbor: The University of Michigan Press, 2009), 76.

28 Joan Acocella, "Soaring Savion Glover in 'OM,'" July 8 2014, *The New Yorker.*https://www.newyorker.com/culture/culture-desk/soaring-savion-glover-in-om. Glover's extensive time as a young cast member of the 1985 musical Black and Blue allowed him to have contact with the older generation of tap dancers such as Jimmy Slyde and Bunny Briggs, among others.

29 Interview by author, September 19, 2017.

30 Seibert, *What the Eye Hears,* 463.

31 Adam Green, "Tap-Dancing Legend," 210.

32 Jesse Green, "Theatre Review," 2016.

33 Liza Gennaro, *Making Broadway Dance* (Oxford University Press, 2021), 206.

34 Ben Brantley, "*Shuffle Along* Return to Broadway's Embrace" *New York Times,* 28 April 2016. http://www.nytimes.com/2016/04/29/theater/review-shuffle-along-returns-to-broadways-embrace.html.

35 Catherine Young, "Don't Blame a Pregnant Star for *Shuffle Along* Closing," *Howlround Theatre Commons,* July 18, 2016, http://howlround.com/don-t-blame-pregnancy-for-shuffle-along-closing.

36 Moriah, "Shuffle and Repeat: The Making of Shuffle Along," 179.

37 Ibid.

38 Flournoy E. Miller along with Aubrey Lyles wrote the original book of the 1921 *Shuffle Along* and is a character in the 2016 show played by Brian Stokes Mitchell.

39 Sandra Seaton, "*Shuffle Along* and Ethic Humor: 'The Proper Push,'" *The Dramatist* 18, no.5 (May 2016): 47.

40 August Wilson in Seaton, "*Shuffle Along* and Ethic Humor," (2016), 50.

41 Moriah, "Shuffle and Repeat: The Making of Shuffle Along," 179.

42 Interview with author, September 19, 2017.

43 Kushner, *Interview Magazine,* May 6, 2016.

44 While the original 1921 *Shuffle Along* was the most long-running and popular African American musical of the early twentieth century and the first to have a love scene/song between two African Americans, Will Marion Cook's 1898 *Clorindy, or The Origins of the Cakewalk* "made history as the first thoroughly black American show to find critical acclaim in the heart of Broadway." It is important to note that *Clorindy* contained only five songs so is often considered a sketch or song-and-dance, further, it was performed at the less formal Casino Roof Garden (Riis, *Oxford Music Online*). Cook's *In Dahomey* (1903) however had a more substantial

full-length structure and is considered "the first all-black show to play a major Broadway theatre." *Shuffle Along* pointedly made a place for African American shows to not be such a rarity on Broadway breaking ground for, "black writers and performers be both welcomed and acclaimed on Broadway." Allen L. Woll, *Black Musical Theatre: From Coontown to Dreamgirls* (Baton Rouge: Louisiana State University Press, 1989), 38, 57.

45 Ibid., xi.
46 Savran, *Highbrow/Lowdown*, 76.
47 Stearns and Stearns, *Jazz Dance*, 130–131.
48 Savran, *Highbrow/Lowdown*, 74.
49 The transition in musical styles is emblematic of greater changes taking place at the time such as the financial boom, developments in technology, greater consumerism, increased freedoms for the younger generation, the intellectual and artistic contributions of the Harlem Renaissance, continued women's suffrage, and women in the work place.
50 Adam Green, *Vogue* 207.
51 The Jazz Age was a time of much change in society. The financial and technological boom of the early 1920s, along with new freedom for young people, the Harlem Renaissance, increasing liberties for women, made for alterations in everyday life and leisure activities. Despite socioeconomic developments happening at the time, for at least the 1920s, tickets remained affordable on Broadway, so attendance remained high and attending the theatre was a regular social activity. John Bush Jones explains, "The 1920s was one of the last decades of the century when ticket prices rose so slowly that the incomes of working-class and middle-class Americans could more than keep up with them." He adds, the general frivolous and carefree attitude of the 1920s, "fostered hundreds of 'mindless' musicals –diversionary shows intended purely as entertainment," a musical theatre phenomenon not experienced to that extent since. *Our Musicals, Ourselves: A Social History of the American Musical Theatre,* (Waltham, MA: Brandeis University Press), 61, 52.
52 Adam Green, *Vogue* 207.
53 These tenants that define social dance are put forth by Julie Malnig and explored in the introduction. Malnig explains social dances: "spring[s] from the lifeblood of communities and subcultures and are generally learned informally through cultural and social networks." Malnig, *Ballroom, Boogie, Shimmy Sham, Shake: A Social and Popular Dance Reader* (Chicago: University of Illinois Press, 2009), 4.
54 Interview with author, September 19, 2017.
55 Constance Valis Hill, *Tap Dancing America: A cultural history* (Oxford University Press, 2014), 3.
56 Ibid.
57 Ibid., 2.
58 Ibid., 3.
59 The melding of cultural contributions also happens with jazz music. Ted Gioia explains that from jazz's early beginnings there was an "Americanization of African music" (and an "Africanization of African music"), referring to it as a "synergistic process … the blending together of cultural elements that previously existed separately. He also reminds that in New Orleans where a lot of early jazz music was happening there was a lot of mixing of cultures, and a broader range of influences are often not mentioned in the popular history of jazz music. Gioia states, "settlers from Germany, Italy, England, Ireland, and Scotland also made substantial contributions to the local culture." Gioia, *The History of Jazz* (New York: Oxford University Press, 2011), 5–6.
60 Though it is of note that Fred Astaire and other white tappers of the 1920s and 30s learned many of their moves from Black Hoofers of the time. For more on the development of Fred Astaire's style see Chapter 10, "How to Hoof in Hollywood" in Brian Seibert's *What the Eye Hears: A History of Tap Dancing*. (Macmillan, 2015).

61 For more on this separation and further discussion particularly histories, roots and influences, that the space of this chapter does not allow for see "Chapter 1, 1990–1900) Trickster God and Reparees" in Constance Valis Hill, *Tap dancing America: A cultural history* (Oxford University Press, 2014).

62 The Stearnses describes how Florenz Ziegfeld purchased routines. Dancer Ethel Williams describes, "I went down to the New York Theatre and showed the cast how to dance it … they were having trouble. None of us was hired for the show." Stearns and Stearns, *Jazz Dance*, 130.

63 La Touche explains of the diversity of tap styles in the cast: "There were some that had been in theater for a while, two that were Rockettes who had tap dancing training but they had to learn tap dance from Savion. Everybody was broken down, whatever Savion is doing is like nothing we have ever done before so everyone had to learn and unlearn some stuff. That brought on everybody's unique style, you would have some very beautiful long-legged performer in the Rockettes [and] have to surrender that and kind of get down and dirty." Interview with author.

64 Emily Macel Theys, "Ten Minutes With Savion Glover," *Dance Magazine* 89 no. 7 (2015), 18. https://www.google.ca/amp/www.dancemagazine.com/10-minutes-with-savion-glover-2306965504.amp.html, accessed July 3, 2017.

65 Adam Green, *Vogue,* 210.

66 Hill, *Tap Dancing America*, 2–3.

67 Brantley, *New York Times*, 28 April 2016.

68 Interview with author, September 19, 2017.

References

Acocella, Joan. "Soaring Savion Glover in 'OM.'" *The New Yorker*, July 8, 2014. https://www.newyorker.com/culture/culture-desk/soaring-savion-glover-in-om.

Brantley, Ben. "*Shuffle Along* Return to Broadway's Embrace." *New York Times*, April 28, 2016. http://www.nytimes.com/2016/04/29/theater/review-shuffle-along-returns-to-broadways-embrace.html.

Brown, Jayna. *Babylon Girls: Black Women Performers and the Shaping of the Modern.* Durham, NC: Duke University Press, 2008.

Brooks, Daphne. *Bodies in Dissent: Spectacular Performances of Race and Freedom, 1850–1910.* Durham, NC: Duke University Press, 2006.

Gottschild, Brenda Dixon *Waltzing in the Dark: African American Vaudeville and Race Politics in the Swing Era.* New York: St. Martin's Press, 2000.

Catton, Pia. "Savion Glover on Choreographing *Shuffle Along.*" *Wall Street Journal*, April 13 2016. https://www.wsj.com/articles/savion-glover-choreographs-shuffle-along-.1460561090.

DeFrantz, Thomas F. ed. *Dancing Many Drums: Excavations in African American Dance.* Madison: University of Wisconsin Press, 2002.

ElamJr., Harry J. "Post–World War II African American Theatre." In *The Oxford Handbook of American Drama*, edited by Jeffrey H. Richards and Heather S. Nathans, Oxford Handbooks Online. http://www.oxfordhandbooks.com.ezproxy.gc.cuny.edu/view/10.1093/oxfordhb/9780199731497.001.0001/oxfordhb-9780199731497-e-006?rskey=oJpAc7&result=12.

Gennaro, Liza. *Making Broadway Dance.* New York: Oxford University Press, 2021.

Gioia, Ted. *The History of Jazz.* New York: Oxford University Press, 2011.

Green, Adam. "Tap-Dancing Legend Savion Glover Reanimates the Game-Changing Broadway Musical *Shuffle Along.*" *Vogue* 207, no. 5 (2016), 210. https://www.

google.ca/amp/www.vogue.com/article/tap-dance-legend-savion-glover-broadway-musical-shuffle-along/amp.

Green, Jesse. "Theater Review: *Shuffle Along* Is a Gorgeously Staged, Life-Changing Show." *Vulture*, April 28, 2016. http://www.vulture.com/2016/04/theatre-e-review-shuffle-along-html.

Hill, Constance Valis. *Tap dancing America: A cultural history*. Oxford: Oxford University Press, 2014.

Jones, John Bush. *Our Musicals, Ourselves: A Social History of the American Musical Theatre*. Waltham, MA: Brandeis University Press, 2004.

Kushner, Tony. "George C. Wolfe." *Interview Magazine*, May 6, 2016. https://www.interviewmagazine.com/culture/george-c-wolfe.

Malnig, Julie, ed. *Ballroom, Boogie, Shimmy Sham, Shake: A Social and Popular Dance Reader*. Chicago: University of Illinois Press, 2009.

McNulty, Charles. "How *Shuffle Along* Director George C. Wolfe Brought Back the 1921 Show that Changed Broadway Forever." in *Los Angeles Times*, April 25, 2016. http://www.latimes.com/entertainment/arts/theater/la-et-cm-george-wolfe-20160425 column.html.

Moriah, Kristin. "Shuffle and Repeat: The Making of Shuffle Along." *American Quarterly* 69, no. 1 (March 2017): 177–186.

Savran, David. *Highbrow/Lowdown: Theater, Jazz, and the Making of the New Middle Class*. Ann Arbor: University of Michigan Press, 2009.

Seibert, Brian. *What The Eye Hears: A History of Tap Dancing*. New York: Farrar, Straus and Giroux Books, 2015.

Schomburg Center for Research in Black Culture, Photographs and Prints Division, The New York Public Library. "Lyricist Noble Sissle and cast members from the musical 'Shuffle Along,' ca. 1921" New York Public Library Digital Collections. https://digitalcollections.nypl.org/items/7f1bb8a9-55cd-d324-e040-e00a18061c0a, accessed August 15, 2022.

Stearns, Marshall, and Jean Stearns. *Jazz Dance: The Story of American Vernacular Dance*. New York: Da Capo Press, 1994.

"Review of Shuffle Along and the Saga of the Four Harmony Kings: Group Harmony Pioneers," http://classicurbanharmony.net/2016/05/10/review-of-shuffle-along-and-the-saga-of-the-four-harmony-kings-group-harmony-pioneers/, accessed December 10, 2017.

Rumsey, Phoebe. Reparation and Reanimation: Savion Glover's Choreography of Shuffle Along, Or The Making of the Musical Sensation of 1921 and All That Followed, in *Reframing the Musical: Race, Culture and Identity*. Edited by Sarah Whitfield, Red Globe Press, an imprint of Bloomsbury Publishing Plc, 2019.

Seaton, Sandra. "*Shuffle Along* and Ethnic Humor: 'The Proper Push.'" *The Dramatist* 18, no. 5 (May 2016): 45–50.

Theys, Emily Macel. "Ten Minutes With Savion Glover." *Dance Magazine* 89, no. 7 (2015), https://www.google.ca/amp/www.dancemagazine.com/10-minutes-with-savion-glover-2306965504.amp.html, accessed July 3, 2017.

Woll, Allen L. *Black Musical Theatre: From Coontown to Dreamgirls*. Baton Rouge: Louisiana State University Press, 1989.

Young, Catherine. "Don't Blame a Pregnant Star for *Shuffle Along* Closing." *Howlround*, July 18, 2016. http://howlround.com/don-t-blame-pregnancy-for-shuffle-along-closing.

Part II

The Charleston – Lively and Liberated

When *Runnin' Wild* opened on Broadway in 1923 the Charleston became an "official" popular dance phenomenon on stage and off.[1] Cecil Mack and James B. Johnson's hit song in *Runnin' Wild* "The Charleston" unabashedly identified the heel kicking, knee-twisting dance in the musical and spoke to its openness with these encouraging lyrics, "With a new tune, funny blue tune [...] If you've not got religion in your feet, You can do this prance and do it neat."[2] In the musical, Elisabeth Welch sang the song backed up by a chorus line of dancers kicking and hopping in time.[3] As described in welcoming lyrics, the Charleston had a particular musical rhythm that could be danced by nearly everyone.[4] With a lessening of social dance rules in the 1920s which came along with the new sense of freedom and prosperity that proceeded World War I, participants needed not worry as much about the variety and rhythm of steps or the complexities of how to partner properly. While the Charleston does get "refined" and codified by dancing masters, the general populace, socializing outside the regulations of formal ballrooms, took up the dance in their individualized manner; shaking, wiggling, and twisting their heels in time to the catchy tunes. Even those "without religion in their feet," as Mack and Johnson prompt, could participate without the need to learn extensive flourishes as seen in the early ragtime dances.[5] Mack and Johnson encouraged everyone to get up, dress up, grab a partner, and give the dance a whirl. A veritable dance craze ensued and the Charleston, with its turned-in knees and heel flicks influenced by dances such as the "Jay Bird" and the Shimmy, became emblematic of the Jazz Age.[6] What was it about this eclectic dance that drew people in with such enthusiasm and continues even today to set off a spectrum of nostalgic longings?

The Charleston was energetic and exciting like the jazz music it accompanied. The movement qualities were appealing in their individuality and loosening of previous dance codes. The suppleness of movement of men and women in fashionably loose clothing came off as both playful and chic. The wildness of the quirky heel kicks and carefree knee bounces set the body a thrill from head to toe. The saucy shoulder-shrugs, provocative shimmies, and bright-eyed glances about the dance floor gave the dance a flirty and lively quality. The multi-directional kicks that lifted fringed hems of women's skirts

DOI: 10.4324/9781003163688-6

high above the knee were sure to turn heads. Dancing bodies were liberated like never before. Arms would swing wildly right and left, and short bobbed hair would escape from its pins and headbands – uninhibitedness was the order of the day. The Charleston showcased a level of permissiveness and a carefree and playful attitude that was as intoxicating as the alcohol that flowed in the many speakeasies where the Charleston often took place.[7] Author, dance critic, historian, and Black Studies scholar James Haskins in *Black Dance in America* explains, "It was an exhibition dance, that used the whole body in shimmying motions, included a fast kicking step, both forward and backward, and featured slapping the hands on the body, especially on the knees."[8] The youthfulness, vim, and undeniable allure of the Charleston made it *the* iconic dance of the 1920s.

This wild era championed physical abandon and excitement, applauded cunning choices and bold initiative, and gave birth to numerous mythologies and expressions of nostalgia for the 1920s that continue to circulate today. The conservative voices at the time that claimed the Charleston was dangerous and put people on a "path to vice," only enhanced the appeal of the dance and fueled the stories that grew up around the dance and its dancers.[9] When a current film or stage production advertises itself as set in the Roaring Twenties, images of bathtub gin parties, flapper girls, and outrageous celebrations *à la* Jay Gatsby quickly come to mind. A continued nostalgia for the Roaring Twenties can be seen in recent and past decades in the many films set in this era and in the long-running success of Broadway musicals set in the 1920s like *Chicago* and the various iterations of Gershwin musicals over the years, such as *Crazy for You* (1992) or *Nice Work If You Can Get It* (2012).[10]

This section examines the Charleston, and other dances rooted in the form such as the Black Bottom, in three musicals – *Thoroughly Modern Millie* (2002), Michael John LaChiusa's *The Wild Party* (2000), and *The Drowsy Chaperone* (2006) – and investigates what these social dances *do* when transferred to the stage nearly a century later.[11] I focus on how and why the body, particularly the female dancing body, is thrust front and center as an emblem of the Roaring Twenties. The female body in the 1920s – confident, daring, outward, free, and supple – is less rigid and more exposed than in any previous era. The choreographers of the above musicals draw on the freedom and permissiveness embodied in social dances and dancing bodies of the 1920s to form the thematic and dramaturgical structure of the musical.

Expectedly, in the transfer of the Charleston (and Black Bottom) to the stage, the improvised and chaotic essence of the dance tends to get lost.[12] Furthermore, what is gained in this move varies depending on the molding and manipulation of the dance by the choreographer. For instance, though the organization of the dance into repeatable sequences alters the improvised nature of the dance in a venue such as the speakeasy, it also amplifies bodily meanings at a grander scale. In addition, the separation between the social dance ethos and the theatricalized, highly choreographed adaptation of the dance creates an embodied nostalgia that emerges when the experiences and related mythologies of the past are put on stage alongside or within the dance. The exaggeration of the already theatricalized elements in the dance within the frame of highly choreographed sequences differs from the flattening of social dance communities seen in Chapter 1. This variance is in part because there seems to be more fluidity between the dance hall and the stage in the emergence of the Charleston.[13] As a result, the continued transformations of the dance in the public sphere and its improvised and varying nature opens up a broad range of choreographic material from which contemporary choreographers can draw.

In each case study of this section, embodied meanings in the Charleston (or Black Bottom in *The Wild Party*) are developed by the choreographers from distinct standpoints. The differing perspectives, depend not only on the choreographer's vision and methods but also how the dramatic structure of the musical – ranging from pastiche to parody – presents the world of the 1920s. In turn, the mode of the comedic structure sets up how the social dance is used to create nostalgia. For instance, in *Thoroughly Modern Millie*, pastiche (and misfire at parody to be discussed) creates an embodied nostalgia used to embolden feminine modernity and champion frivolity and newness. In *The Wild Party* the uncensored interpretation of Joseph Moncure March's 1928 poem allows for a critical take on the Jazz Age disguised as pastiche. This "dangerous" angle demystifies the embodied nostalgia for the indulgences of the 1920s and exposes, through movement and music, the cultural theft at work then and now.[14] *The Drowsy Chaperone* uses a playful double coded parodic telling of 1920s musicals that re-engages affection for musical theatre by capitalizing on the thrills of the form while also reflecting on the meaning and influence of nostalgia in musical theater and life.[15]

In particular, the use of parody in musical theatre, whether it be poking fun at, familiarizing, or admiring a social concept (such as the "new woman" in *Thoroughly Modern Millie*), a character trait or flaw (as in *The Wild Party*), or conventions of the form itself (as in *The Drowsy* Chaperone), sets in motion the machinery of nostalgia. This engagement with parody, "one of the major forms of modern self-reflexivity" according to Linda Hutcheon, is based on several factors.[16] Parody opens up a space in the musical where one is given license to delight in the excess of excess, to enjoy the silliness, and to be nostalgic. The nostalgia may have a referential quality, involve a moment of self-reflexivity, or create a desire for a simpler time whether imagined or not. Furthermore, there is a wish in parody for an understanding of the present moment or considerations of future paths using our collective past as material, albeit in a comedic manner – a nostalgic maneuver that can allow for critical distance.[17]

In this regard, movement and social dance-based choreography can be considered to share in the workings of the parodies.[18] As social dances of the 1920s were both expanded in and learned from musical theatre productions, the connection between dance and parody is seen already in the performative style of the dances from their earliest iterations.[19] The embodiment of nostalgia is made possible by the physical exaggerations, imitations, repetitions, and accentuated dance moves that are part of the parody in operation with the historical resonance of the social dance itself.

Of note in this section, I focus in on gender and the privileging of the female body on stage. This choice is for two reasons. First, the lead character in each show is a woman, likewise, in two out of the three cases the female protagonist is also a dancer by profession. Second, the female body (more so than the male body) is liberated from the previous constraints of society in the 1920s. Women gaining the right to vote in 1920 in the U.S. brought about "a new way of thinking about what it meant to be a woman and a citizen of the United States."[20] Linda Tomko explains women achieved greater freedom and rights in the U.S. (and internationally) through "bodily perseverance," whether in suffrage marches or labor protests.[21] The endurance and presence of women is implicit in the 1920s and in this new era, women "forged ways of comprehending their changing experiences through a variety of danced embodiments."[22] Although the youthful generation of both men and women in the 1920s experienced new and exciting physical freedoms, particularly in social dances, tracing the development of the female body in motion, the iconic "flapper" of the 1920s, helps to support how identity, particularly the "new woman," is formed through physical behaviors.[23] The "new woman," however, should not be understood only as the iconic "flapper" that can get romanticized and stereotyped. In fact, there are various contradictions within the transformations that occurred from the beginning of women's suffrage in the mid-nineteenth century to the 1920s. Carroll Smith-Rosenberg explains how at the turn of the century the "new woman" was "unmarried, career oriented, politically active," but by the 1920s, "both women and men transposed the New Woman into a sexually freighted metaphor for social disorder and protest."[24] The shifts in women's motivations, along with changes in the expectations and interpretations of women's roles unfold in tandem with a variety of factors in the 1920s including an increase in women in the work force, mechanization, and growing consumerism. Markedly, this experience does not align for Black and white communities, a contradiction explored in the following chapter.

Equally important for the overall trajectory of this project is to recognize from the start that most of the dancers doing the social dances in the three musicals of this section are white. This is a distinct shift from the previous section that showed Black dancers doing Black dances. The near obsession with which the Charleston is taken up by white dancers in the 1920s pulls the dance away from its roots in the Black American milieu. In this move there is a decreased emphasis on inward looking community ownership or expression for Black Americans, and an increased emphasis on the latest physical ingenuities, social dance narratives, and the desire to seek one's identity through the "new," i.e., the latest social dance created in Black communities. The dances attracted so much interest by whites that they were vociferously and brazenly taken up and transferred to the stage and screen. I interrogate the intricacies of this move by outlining the history of the Charleston and mapping how movement practices are transferred to and transformed on stage in the 1920s. This consideration helps us to understand the obliviousness and escapism that permeated the Charleston and the Jazz Age. Following this history, I explore the wonder of the Jazz Age then and thus nostalgia for it now to launch this section into the exploration of three musicals that are wrapped up in the thrills, enchantments, and turmoil of the time seen most vividly in the body.

Background of the Charleston

Despite the official song and debut of the Charleston in *Runnin' Wild*, Elida Webb, the choreographer of *Runnin' Wild*, is not exclusively credited for inventing the Charleston.[25] There is a more varied history of how the dance developed and travelled. True, the many patrons who saw *Runnin' Wild* on Broadway aided in the dissemination and popularization of the dance across the nation, however, fragmented forms of the Charleston had been seen and experienced prior to the 1923 musical. Elements of the dance are generally agreed to have emerged at the turn of the twentieth century in the South and carried North with the Great Migration. The most well-known of the "proto" forms of the Charleston was in the original 1921 *Shuffle Along* where different movement fragments familiar to the Charleston, such as the Shimmy and Snake Hips, were blended with tap dance.[26] The Stearnses trace the Charleston to 1903 in Savannah, Georgia, noting how the call and response-like structure of nascent forms of the Charleston can be drawn back to the African "Juba" influence.[27] Composer and lyricist Noble Sissle explains his experiences with the Charleston, "It's a real old Southern dance… . I remember learning it in Savannah around 1905."[28] James B. Johnson, the composer of *Runnin' Wild*, explains that similar movements to those in the Charleston were common around 1913 and that the dance had many variations including tamer versions that were often part of cotillion dances.[29] Additionally, various dancers of the time recall participating in Charleston contests in the early 1920s.[30]

One of the main curiosities of the Charleston as a partner dance is that the male dancer did not necessarily lead the movements. Couples would dance together but there were many moments to express individuality. The shoulder shaking, the pedestrian-like swinging of arms in opposition, the twisting of the heels, the teeter-totter-like up and down of the torso, and the opportunities for surprise "breakaways" from one's partner "freed the body publicly."[31] The woman was not seen as "following" the man, equating the dance with a politicization of the body where female autonomy becomes evident.

At the same time, with some of the openness of movement within the Charleston, as compared to earlier dances such as the foxtrot, vestiges of other dances or movement skills can creep in. Theatre and performance studies scholar Carol Martin explains this historical embodiment: "Dances come and go even as the physical memory of individual dances persists in individual

bodies long beyond their moment of popularity."[32] There is not an instanta-
neous switch over to a new dance, communities absorb the moves into their
world, and in the embrace of the new dance style a cross-fertilization happens
between previous dances embedded in the body. Movement styles people
grew up with or did in earlier eras and locales remain part of their bodily
repertoire and influence how they move or take on a new dance.[33] In this
manner one of the most distinctive aspects of the Charleston (outside the
formal ballroom) is its lack of uniformity that allows for individual personalities
and physicalities to come through.[34] Some might add an enhanced double-
bounce to the dance that makes clothing and jewelry come to life, others
might keep elbows up high by their shoulders, rarely bending the knees giving
the dance a more pogo-stick feel. The multi-layered characteristics and openness to the dance generally made it accessible to a broader audience, though
embodying the fast rhythms and free styles came more easily to some than
others.

Transmission of Dances

Though none of the musicals in this section delve into how white dancers
learned the Charleston, at the height of the Charleston in the first half of the
decade there was an active community of Black dance teachers who were in
high demand to instruct white dancers, actors, and socialites in the dance form.
A general understanding of the transmission of the dances helps to highlight
the embodied history of the dance and how ownership gets troubled as the
dance evolves.

One of the main characteristics of the Jazz Age, as it progresses into the
decade, is the increasing invisibility of the Black dancer. Ironically, this move
happens with the rising social and cultural desires for trends and fashions
coming from Black communities. In a telling moment in *The Wild Party* the
D'Armono brothers, Oscar and Phil, sing of this shift:

> Black folks, Are sounding more like, White folks, Who are sounding
> more like, black folks in every way![35]

White patrons were fascinated with jazz music and dance and rushed to learn
methods for themselves. Danielle Robinson explains that there was a "superficial but overt embracing of 'blackness' that occurred during the Jazz age."[36]
The "superficial" assumption of the dance, which is lampooned in the
LaChiusa lyrics above, is in reference to the "celebration" and simulation of
Black dances and music by whites. *The Wild Party* director George C. Wolfe
makes a direct and critical comment on this artistic theft and racial impersonation by using blackface in the lead male character's opening song.[37] White
performers, as is explicitly seen in *The Wild Party*, simultaneously learned and
adopted the dances that in turn became more or less a "celebration" of themselves. Though the Harlem Renaissance, beginning in the late 1910s, seemed

like a turning point for integration, acceptance, respect, and moving beyond Black stereotypes, there was a desire on the part of white dancers to learn Black dances and music and attempt to carry them off as part of their own lifestyle and community.

Furthermore, white performers wanting to rise out of the general dance crowd and appear on screen or stage had to learn more impressive intricacies that were being developed by Black dancers in the various dance halls in Harlem. However, in order for white dancers, particularly film stars (or would-be film stars) to excel at the Black dances, they needed the best teachers to teach them. Robinson describes how dance instruction provided a considerable amount of employment for Black dancers, unfortunately credit for the teaching and choreographing is rarely, if ever, given. When the social dances of the 1920s were on film or on stage the "whiteness of the dancer and the blackness of the dancing [is] often highlighted."[38] Jayna Brown explains this imbalance, "Such moments of cultural transfer were not celebrations of African American cultural resistance. Instead they affirmed a politics of white racial privilege, cultural access, and wilful misrecognition."[39] This contrast in fact increased, rather than lessened, the distance between the two groups.[40]

Black dancers were the experts and celebrities people rushed to see at the large ballrooms in Harlem, like the Savoy and the Cotton Club. White dancers attending these venues began to take up, borrow, and appropriate the dances for their own use and benefit. Many of the big revue shows, such as George White's *Scandals* or the various iterations of the *Ziegfeld Follies,* included the Charleston (and the Black Bottom) and celebrated them as their own. In so doing, the work of Black dancers and teachers, especially women, gets obscured, an action Brown refers to as "female minstrelsy."[41] Brown explains, many of the teaching sessions were quite secretive and executed out of the public eye. She observes that this practice was "a kind of minstrelsy that did not require cork."[42] White dancers engaged in the practice of movement acquisition in a private manner to then perform the new styles at an accomplished level in the public domain. "For white people," explains Brown, "versions of black dance practices served a particular function as they reshaped their sense of individual self to the changing larger social and geopolitical bodies."[43] This process was so sought after, not only for the expertise and virtuosic flair but because the ability to move in the manner of Black performers was a way to express feminine modernity.

Even though the appropriation of dances is not the main emphasis of this section, it must be established as an undeniable aspect of the landscape of the 1920s–1930s and is part of the embodied nostalgia. When white dancers execute Black social dances on stage, whether in the 1920s or nearly a hundred years later, there is a sense that the trajectory of history and deeper meaning of the dance is being over-written, and, once again, white performers build success from the labor of Black communities. By the 1940s, Black contributions seemed to fade further into the background as dances continued to be taken up and adapted by white dancers.[44] Further, the transformation of the dance into a cleaner, more straightened up or "cute" dance does a disservice to the fact that dancers had individual subjectivity.[45] A wider view of the Jazz Age helps to understand the construction of the social, cultural, and political climate when these borrowings occurred and the mythologies that arose around the era.

The Jazz Age

On February 16, 1926 the New York Times reported, "GIRL DEAD FROM CHARLESTON: DOCTOR CALLS DANCE DANGEROUS."[46] Dr. Boyer declared that the extreme physical exercise of the Charleston is particularly dangerous for young women. Indeed, the Jazz Age was a wild time. With "a whole race going hedonistic, deciding on pleasure," people took the lifestyle, the drinking, and the dances to the extreme.[47] Though F. Scott Fitzgerald declared in his 1931 essay "Echoes of the Jazz Age," "It was an age of miracles, it was an age of art, it was an age of excess, and it was an age of satire," not all agreed.[48] A variety of medical accounts from the time show community leaders and physicians declaring the overindulgences of the time to be harmful, particularly for dancing women.[49] However, the more social dances and their accompanying lifestyle were broadcast as damaging, the greater the dance's intrigue for young people. After World War I, and with the achievements of the women's suffrage movement, the added possibility that couples did not have to marry in order to engage in physical contact linked the Charleston with casual intimacy and shifts in social behaviors. These changes in leisure pursuits characterized the era.

Fitzgerald coined the term "Jazz Age" to describe the period, which he defined as beginning with the May Day Riots of 1919 and ending with the Stock Market Crash of 1929. The Jazz Age emerged and rapidly came into full swing along with the prohibition of alcohol in 1920. For the younger generation, a prime motive of deciding one's movement through the world was based on a deep desire for pleasure. Fitzgerald contends this urge was not entirely spurred by the ban on alcohol and the tantalizing underground nightlife it created. He explains, "The precious intimacies of the younger generation would have come about with or without prohibition," contending, "the general decision to be amused that began with the cocktail parties of 1921 had more complicated origins."[50] The freneticism within the dance and the intensity with which people took it up is telling of the fear young people had of being tamed or controlled – a prelude to what was coming ahead. The wildness of the 1920s was also in part catalyzed by an overt clash of generations. Amy Koritz explains in *Culture Makers: Urban Performance and Literature of the 1920s*:

> Beyond the icon of the flapper, with its image of youthful irresponsibility and conspicuous consumption, there is a strong presence in the 1920s of a belief in the power of rational elites to control human destiny, and a terror

on the part of those would be so controlled, that they might in fact succeed.[51]

Different generations professed opinions on how the world should function and what one's responsibilities to the self and society were at any given moment.

How people envisioned themselves and behaved in the 1920s was largely attributed to age, experience, and one's respect for or rebellion against the conventions with which they were raised. What one did in their leisure time (a relatively new concept in the 1920s) interconnected with how one's individual identity was formed.[52] The younger generation was ready to break free from the more puritan ideals, while the older generation sought to justify the work ethic they had embraced and precautions they had taken to ensure economic survival. If one was not connected to a sense of duty to family and society, he or she was prime for the indulgences of the time. The social developments of the Jazz Age, such as Prohibition, opened up a space for more unruly activities.[53]

The increase in social pursuits by the younger generation was of great curiosity to community leaders and the older generation. How people responded to pleasure and physical enjoyment caused much consternation between factions and much of this debate almost always pivoted around the consumption and enjoyment of alcohol. The shift of alcohol to underground or private venues created a world of secretive and clandestine behaviors as well as increased corruption and crime. Quite quickly secret-drinking venues – namely the speakeasy – became one of the signature locales of the Jazz Age. With nearly 100,000 speakeasies in New York City alone, drinking, dancing, and jazz music became the order of the day.[54] The spectrum of experiences in this social landscape ranged from upper-class white patrons visiting and taking in the dance venues before retreating to the safety of their homes; to gangsters and criminals seeking to profit from the illegal sale of alcohol; to the enjoyments of the musicians, dancers, and performers that worked and often lived at or near the venues. A private drinking party in one's apartment was also common fare, the experience and consequences of which are explored in *The Wild Party*.

The sense of individuality and experimentation that inhabited the Jazz Age is embodied in the Charleston. Barbara Cohen-Stratyner explains, "More than any other dance, it defined the performer as young and willing to take chances on modern life."[55] The Charleston physicalized the whimsy and wildness of the era. The dance allowed participants to let loose and experience the thrills of modern times. This adventurous, and sometimes desperate, attitude is most palpable in the upcoming case studies in moments of dance when the abandonment of previous social restrictions and inhibitions is embodied by the choreography.

The Charleston Then and Now – Consumerism and Nostalgia

The debates the Charleston ignited in the 1920s make the dance also a potential indicator of the economic and sociopolitical climate of the era. Koritz explains the Charleston in its time "generated a discourse that intertwined

apprehension about gender, class, race, and aesthetic value with both invoca-
tions of expertise and consumerist imperatives."[56] The Charleston was about
more than sexuality and freedom, it was also about consumption and the
development of mass culture. Markedly, this mass culture is based in the pur-
chasing power and consumption on the part of the middle-class and thus still
subject to delineations of class and race. Chip Rhodes explains in *Structures of
the Jazz Age: Mass Culture, Progressive Education and Racial Discourses*, "the fundamental contradiction between mass culture's democratic promises and the
inegalitarian class structure from which these promises are inseparable."[57]
Fortunately, the availability of affordable mass entertainment kept a level of
social interaction between classes and communities.[58] Koritz observes the link
between the celebration of individualism in the Charleston and consumerism
in the 1920s "contributed to the attenuation of the vibrant public sphere"
while also encouraging people to embrace their individual desires "at the
expense of the community."[59] Life for the younger generation in the 1920s
was less about contributing to the greater good or community causes than
fulfilling one's individual desires. Spending habits in this age of department
stores and shopping as a leisure activity became how people defined themselves
in society, beginning the contemporary phenomenon of self-identification in
relation to modes of consumption. In effect, the novelty of the Charleston
inspired a celebration of the self on show and in motion, particularly for
women, where one could be *fêted* by friends and lovers for the fashion
embellishments and trinkets they wore on the dance floor.

The notion that people were more fearless, both with their bodies and
money, in the 1920s creates a sense of nostalgia in the twentieth century,
particularly looking back from a time when the pressure to keep up with the
forward moving economy led many to believe they could handle extensive
credit card debt, steep interest rates and long term-mortgages.[60] The heady
time of economic obliviousness in the 1920s is folded into the dramaturgical
structure of each case study in this section, as the main characters in the
musicals generally overlook the financial repercussions of their indulgences.[61]

To investigate the interconnectedness between and among the aforementioned
themes, I begin with a look at the choreographic strategies in *Thoroughly Modern
Millie*. I interrogate how the Charleston, by way of the playful pastiche of the
show, embodies a process of exploring one's subjectivity in an increasingly modernized world. I then examine the nostalgic inclinations this self-reflexivity and
imitation creates in the twenty-first century.[62] Next, I turn to Michael John
LaChiusa's *The Wild Party* that confronts an older, more jaded and run-down
group of people, helmed by the strung-out and broken Queenie.[63] The pastiche-
like structure of the piece provides the framework to explore the misplaced nostalgia for a time of cultural theft, over-indulgence, and self-inflicted harm. Finally,
I look to *The Drowsy Chaperone* as a unique example of how nostalgia is created
onstage and used to re-engage one's affection for musical theatre, a form of nostalgia, which is shown to be a survival tactic for the protagonist (and us) in an
increasingly complex and unsettling world.

Notes

1 The Charleston had been previously "introduced" in shows such as *Liza* in 1923 and fragments of the dance were peppered throughout the 1921 *Shuffle Along*, however, it did not become a wide spread, prevalent, and popular dance until *Runnin' Wild* in 1923. James Haskins, *Black Dance in America: A History Through Its People* (New York: Harper Collins Publishers,1990), 43.

2 Cecil Mack and James B. Johnson. "The Charleston." Runnin' Wild, 1923, http://lyricsplayground.com/alpha/songs/c/charleston.html, accessed February 7, 2018.

3 "Charleston (ii)," by Claude Conyers, *Grove Music Online,* November 26, 2013 https://doi-org.ezproxy.gc.cuny.edu/10.1093/gmo/9781561592,630.article.A2218810.

4 Pauline Norton identifies the song and music as "fast, about 50–60 bars per minute," with a "characteristic syncopated" or "clave" rhythm: "A rhythmic concept underpinning performances of Salsa and related jazz styles" making it easy to dance to. "Charleston (ii)," *Grove Music Online*, January 20, 2001, http://www.oxfordmusiconline.com.ezproxy.gc.cuny.edu/grovemusic/view/10.1093;   "Clave (jazz)," *Grove Music Online*, January 20, 2002, http://www.oxfordmusiconline.com.ezproxy.gc.cuny.edu/grovemusic/view/10.1093/gmo/978156

5 Jayna Brown explains that refinement rules and expectations of dance mastery also depended on the social class taking up the dance and the venue. For example, in the formal ballroom, Irene and Vernon Castle "would model elegant deportment, a new etiquette for an upper-class clientele." Additionally, the Castles established strict rules for the ballroom: "Do not wriggle the shoulders. Do not shake the hips. Do not twist the body." These rules helped to "ameliorate the moral panic" surrounding social dance. At more casual venues such as gymnasiums, dance halls, and speak-easies rules were much more lax or disregarded all together. Brown, *Babylon Girls: Black Women Performers and the Shaping of the Modern* (Durham, NC: Duke University Press, 2008), 171, 173.

6 The "Jay Bird" is a slower dance where knees are held together while heels flick backwards or sideways giving a bird pecking or bird-like quality to the movement. James Haskins explains that the slower speed of the Jay Bird would make it loosely recognizable to the Charleston, however the earlier dance is only one of the influences of the unique style of the Charleston. Haskins, *Black Dance in America*. For further information on how the dance can be traced back to Africa see the Stearnses' *Jazz Dance: The Story of American Vernacular Dance*, 13 and Haskins, *Black Dance in America*, 42.

7 The Charleston was by no means confined to the speakeasy. Ralph G. Giordano explains the ubiquitous nature of the Charleston, "Americans danced the Charleston in dance halls, on college campuses, outside, on roofs, on boardwalks, on the beach, on the street, within their homes." Giordano, *Satan in the Dance Hall: Rev. John Roach Straton, Social Dancing and Morality in 1920s New York City* (Lanham, MD: The Scarecrow Press Inc., 2008), 83.

8 Haskins, *Black Dance in America*, 43.

9 Amy Koritz, *Culture Makers: Urban Performance and Literature of the 1920s* (Urbana: University of Illinois Press, 2009), 74.

10 Movies that celebrate the 1920s included: *The Great Gatsby* (2013), *The Artist* (2011), *Midnight in Paris,* (2011), *Chicago* (2002), *The Cat's Meow* (2002); less recent, but no less emblematic, movies about the 1920s include: *Some Like It Hot* (1959), *The Great Gatsby* with screenplay by Francis Ford Coppola (1974), and *Thoroughly Modern Millie* (1967). Successful musicals/revivals in the twenty-first century that explore the Jazz Age include: 42nd*Street* (revival, 2001), *Gypsy* (revival, 2003, 2008), *Pal Joey* (revival, 2008), *Ragtime,* (revival, 2009), *Anything Goes* (revival, 2011). The success of *Chicago* opening in 1996 on Broadway and continuing at present is also indicative of an interest in the sounds, styles, and feelings of the Jazz Age.

11 *The Wild Party*: 2000, book by George C. Wolfe and John LaChiusa, music and lyrics by John LaChiusa, based on the 1928 poem *The Wild Party* by John Moncure March; *Thoroughly Modern Millie*: 2000, book by Richard Morris and Dick Scanlan, music by Jeanine Tesori, lyrics by Dick Scanlan, based on the 1967 movie of the same name; *The Drowsy Chaperone*: 2006, book by Bob Martin and Don McKeller, music and lyrics by Lisa Lambert and Greg Morrison.

12 As will be explained in further detail, the Black Bottom is a more sensual social dance than the Charleston and was named for the neighborhood in which it was created in Nashville, Tennessee.

13 John Bush Jones observes in regards to the circulation of social dances, "If the Americans of the '20s were the thrill-seeking folks the social historians say they were, here was a chance for them to take a piece of theatre home with them." Jones, *Our Musicals, Ourselves: A Social History of the American Musical Theatre* (Hanover: University Press of New England, 2003), 64–65.

14 John Heilpern titles his review: "Welcome to The Wild Party! Dangerous, Seedy ... Fantastic," and states, "Its demimonde of second-rate showbiz performers, of fallen angels, pushers, pederasts, gays, dykes and straights (straightish, anyway) is of a world without boundaries, colliding and dangerous, in loveless America." *The Observer,* April 24, 2000, http://observer.com/2000/04/welcome-to-the-wild-party-dangerous-seedy-fantastic.

15 I draw on the work of Linda Hutcheon who uses the term "parodic double coding" to explain how the text parodied is often a parody itself; essentially the form and the subject are both sources of parody, and the "double-voiced," or multiple perspectives helps to "pay homage" to the form. Though *The Drowsy Chaperone* is not a parody in technical terms, it does take on some of the comical behaviors of parody such as exaggeration and self-realization to be examined further in chapter six. Hutcheon, *A Theory of Parody: The Teachings of Twentieth-Century Art Forms* (Urbana, IL: Chicago University Press, 2000), 14, xiv, 46.

16 Hutcheon, *A Theory of Parody*, 2.

17 This intent would depend on the degree of critical stance and the dramaturgical imperatives of the show in question.

18 Movement and dance as part of parody can be seen from early developments of the form often in tandem with the music. Elizabeth L. Wollman explains the operation of parody in burlesque and vaudeville, "Musical numbers often featured traditional or popular melodies that audiences would have recognized, set with new lyrics or newly layered with sly double entendre. Dance numbers, too, poked fun at various folk and classical styles." Wollman, *A Critical Companion to The American Stage Musical* (London, UK: Bloomsbury Publishing, Plc, 2017), 23.

19 This embodied parody is seen most readily in the work of Josephine Baker, but also in the rage for Charleston contests in the 1920s and the desire to be noticed using dance, as is shown to be one of the main motives of the Black Bottom.

20 "Women's Suffrage," History.com, https://www.history.com/topics/womens-history/the-fight-for-womens-suffrage, accessed July 27, 2018.

21 Linda J. Tomko, *Dancing Class: Gender, Ethnicity and Social Divides in American Dance, 1890–1920* (Indianapolis: Indiana University Press, 1999), 7.

22 Ibid., 7.

23 The term "new woman" was popularized by Henry James in 1877 and encompasses how women pushed against Victorian ideals and expectations. Hugh Stevens explains: "The New Woman, in her demands for education, and the right to pursue a career rather than marriage, her rejection of the patriarchal family and life of domesticity, and her demand for political power, actively questioned the biological determinism and gender assumptions of the Victorian era." Stevens, *Henry James and Sexuality* (New York: Cambridge University Press, 1998), 27.

24 Carroll Smith-Rosenberg, *Disorderly Conduct: Visions of Gender in Victorian America* (New York: Oxford University Press, 1985), 246.

25 Elida Webb is recognized by several different spellings of her first name. Claude Conyers uses Lyda, "Charleston (ii)," *Grove Music Online*, November 26, 2013, http://www.oxfordmusiconline.com.ezproxy.gc.cuny.edu/grovemusic/view/10.1093.

26 Snake Hips is a loose-jointed dance made popular in the early 1920s by Earl Tucker. The dance involves a fluid motion of legs in the hip sockets that gave the illusion of a "boneless' leg and swirly hips, an effect in part taken up by Josephine Baker in her solo performance career. Stearns and Stearns, *Jazz Dance*, 12.

27 The "Juba" is described "as going around in a circle with one foot raised – a sort of eccentric shuffle." As mentioned in chapter one the Juba step is also connected to "Patting Juba" that can be seen in variations of the Charleston that involve the "crossing and uncrossing the hands on the knees as they fan back and forth." Stearns and Stearns, *Jazz Dance*, 28, 29.

28 Stearns and Stearns, *Jazz Dance*, 112.

29 Ibid.

30 When discussing the transmission of dances and culture the mid-nineteenth century the notion of "slumming" should be mentioned as it is in part how white communities learned of the artistic practices of other cultures within the city. Chad Heap explains, "slumming became central to the emergence of the commercialized leisure industry, prompting the creation of a variety of new public amusements that promoted the crossing of racial and sexual boundaries. Heap further observes the complicated relationships slumming involved: "Travelling to Harlem and Bronzeville like other slummers to partake of jazz, liquor, and other forbidden pleasures, these musicians, literati, and socialites struck up significant cross-racial relationships with the Black women and men they met on their visits. While such relationships often remained fraught with racialist, and sometimes even racist, implications, they far exceeded the exoticism that motivated most whites to visit Black neighborhoods." Heap, *Slumming: Sexual and Racial Encounters in American Nightlife (1885–1940)* (Chicago: IL, University of Chicago Press, 2010), 7, 211. For more on slumming and Harlem Cabarets see Heap's Chapter 5 in *Slumming*, 189–230.

31 Halifu Osumare, "The Dance Archeology of Rennie Harris: Hip-Hop or Postmodern?" in *Ballroom, Boogie, Shimmy Sham, Shake: A Social and Popular Dance Reader*, ed. Julie Malnig (Chicago: University of Illinois Press, 2009), 55–71.

32 Carol Martin, "American Dance Marathons" in *Ballroom, Boogie, Shimmy Sham, Shake: A Social and Popular Dance Reader*, ed. Julie Malnig (Chicago: University of Illinois Press, 2009), 97.

33 For example, those who grew up with the waltz or foxtrot (both dances done in a closed position) may naturally embrace their partner in a similar manner while kicking heels up. The younger generation would be used to a looser hold. In all, there would be an overlap of older and newer styles of social dance.

34 As mentioned, stricter rules for body movements were enforced in more formal social dance settings. The moments of choreography in the upcoming case studies take place in informal, private, or even outdoor settings – all locales where there would be a lessening of rules. Markedly, the blending of social dance with the theatricalized embellishment is expected in the musical theatre genre, making the strict rules less significant.

35 "Uptown," Michael John LaChiusa, *The Wild Party*, in *The New American Musical: An Anthology From the End of The Century*, ed. by Wiley Hausam (New York: Theatre Communication Group, 2003), 379.

36 Danielle Robinson, "'Oh, You Black Bottom!' Appropriation, Authenticity, and Opportunity in the Jazz Dance Teaching of 1920s New York," *Dance Research Journal, Dance Research Journal* 38, no. 1/2 (2006): 25.

37 The use of blackface by George C. Wolfe in *The Wild Party* is explored in greater depth in the forthcoming analysis of the musical in Chapter 5.

38 Robinson, "Oh, You Black Bottom!", 37.

39 Jayna Brown, *Babylon Girls*, 174.
40 Robinson explains this increased margin of difference: "the performances of appropriated, 'authentic' black dancing promoted the recognition of racial differences between the dancer and the dance rather than the similarities." Robinson, "Oh, You Black Bottom!", 37.
41 Brown, *Babylon Girls*, 157.
42 Ibid.
43 Ibid., 158.
44 Perhaps the most obvious example of a shift in a Black dance to a supposed white creation is the Lindy Hop that becomes the "whitened" Jitterbug, often mistakenly understood as a solely white invention. The Lindy Hop is explored further in section three.
45 An increased "cuteness" to the dance also risks infantilizing and commodifying the dancers. For more on the commodity aesthetics of cuteness see: Sianne Ngai's *Our Aesthetic Categories: Zany, Cute, Interesting* (Cambridge, MA: Harvard University Press), 2012.
46 "Girl Dead From Charleston: Doctor Calls Dance Dangerous," *The New York Times*, February 16, 1926, pg. 27. https://timesmachine.nytimes.com/timesmachine/1926/02/16/99378979.html?pageNumber=27.
47 F. Scott Fitzgerald, "Echoes of the Jazz Age, 1931," 3, accessed March 13, 2018, https://pdcrodas.webs.ull.es/anglo/ScottFitzgeraldEchoesOfTheJazzAge.pdf.
48 Fitzgerald, "Echoes of the Jazz Age, 1931," 2.
49 Further accounts from the era describe various illnesses associated with social dancing. Most were largely unsubstantiated, though the reports themselves point to ways conservatives tried to bridle the dance. A plausible injury that could be the result of too much dancing, however, is the "Charleston Knee." *The New York Times* reported in 1928, that a Paris physician, "condemns the Charleston and Black Bottom from a new point of view." The physician explained the knee joint should only hinge back and forth and the circling of the knee (often called the "Cow Tail" for the circular motion of the knee towards the back) common in the Charleston can cause damage to ligaments which he thus diagnosed as "Charleston Knee;" in "Jazz Dance 'Dangerous Sports,' Says Doctor, Adding 'Charleston Knee to Mankind's Ills'," *New York Times*, April 29, 1928.
50 Fitzgerald, "Echoes of the Jazz Age, 1931," 3.
51 Koritz, *Culture Makers*, 2.
52 Ibid., 5. Though this manner of identification is often the norm today, at the turn of the twentieth century the concept of "leisure time" was a new phenomenon. How one chose to spend their leisure time was how urban communities came to define themselves.
53 Prohibition in the U.S. banned the sale and production of alcohol from 1920–1933. This choice was inspired by what many conservatives felt was blatant drunkenness that was beginning to spread across much of the U.S., in big cities in particular. This behavior inevitably went on to affect the family unit. The move to restrict alcohol consumption did not necessarily rid society of public drunkenness, it merely drove drinking underground, creating increased problems of corruption and crime.
54 Wayne B. Wheeler, "Is There Prohibition? And to What extent?" *The North American Review* 222, no. 828 (Sept-Nov. 1925) Cedar Falls: University of Northern Iowa, 29–35, Accessed July 12, 2018. https://www.jstor.org/stable/25113449.
55 Barbara Cohen-Stratyner, "A Thousand Raggy, Draggy Dances: Social Dance in Broadway Musical Comedy in the 1920s." In *Ballroom, Boogie, Shimmy Sham, Shake: A Social and Popular Dance Reader*, edited by Julie Malnig, (Chicago: University of Illinois Press, 2009), 222.
56 Koritz, *Culture Makers*, 65.
57 Chip Rhodes, *Structures of the Jazz Age: Mass Culture, Progressive Education and Racial Discourses* (London: UK, Verso Books, 1998), 138.

58 Koritz, *Culture Makers,* 65. For more on cultural mixing at entertainment venues see: Chad Heap's *Slumming: Sexual and Racial Encounters in American Nightlife (1885–1940).*

59 Ibid., 10.

60 A nationalist angle to this paradigm was added post-9/11 where leaders suggested it was one's patriotic duty to help reinvigorate business and the economy in New York and across the nation.

61 This is complicated in *The Drowsy Chaperone* as the characters in the show-within-a-show disregard economic circumstances, whereas the narrator Man in Chair in the 2000s seems to live by minimal or frugal means.

62 The musical, *The Grand Hotel* (1989) with music and lyrics by Robert Wright, George Forrest, Maury Yeston, and book by Luther Davis, based on the 1929 novel by Vicki Baum, takes place in 1928 Berlin and celebrates the liveliness of Roaring Twenties as well. Given its European locale, the show is out of the purview of my analysis, however it is important to note that there is nostalgia in *The Grand Hotel* for the Roaring Twenties and the Jazz Age, as well as the faded glory of the hotel and the episodes that took place within it. Tommy Tune's choreography embodied the freedom of the age (much as in *Millie*) paired with the mechanization of the buildcup to World War II, by using chairs and synchronized movements. The song, "H-A-P-P-Y," specifically celebrates the Charleston, and describes the dissemination of the dance worldwide, its lyrics stating: "What began in Charleston is now done in London, ev'rywhere from Ku'damm to Paris […] Why do I feel dandy when I dance the Charleston?"

63 In the year 2000 there were two composers who decided to turn March's poem into a musical, one by Michael John LaChiusa and one by Andrew Lippa. Lippa's version was the first to open Off-Broadway in February 2000, directed by Gabriel Barre, choreographed by Mark Dendy with Julia Murney, Brian D'Arcy James, Idina Menzel, and Taye Diggs. The second production was composed by Michael John LaChiusa and opened on Broadway in April of 2000, George C. Wolfe directed and wrote the book, Joey McKneely was the choreographer, The show starred Toni Collette, Mandy Patinkin, Yancy Arias, and Eartha Kitt. The Lippa version ran 54 shows, and the LaChiusa 36 previews and 68 shows. The purview of this project is to analyze Broadway shows not Off-Broadway.

References

Brown, Jayna. *Babylon Girls: Black Women Performers and the Shaping of the Modern.* Durham, NC: Duke University Press, 2008.

Cohen-Stratyner, Barbara. "A Thousand Raggy, Draggy Dances: Social Dance in Broadway Musical Comedy in the 1920s." In *Ballroom, Boogie, Shimmy Sham, Shake: A Social and Popular Dance Reader,* edited by Julie Malnig, 217–233. Chicago: University of Illinois Press, 2009.

Conyers, Claude. "Charleston (ii)." *Grove Music Online,* November 26, 2013. https://doi-org.ezproxy.gc.cuny.edu/10.1093/gmo/9781561592630.article.A2218810.

Fitzgerald, F. Scott. *Echoes of the Jazz Age (1931).* Accessed March 13, 2018. https://pdcrodas.webs.ull.es/anglo/ScottFitzgeraldEchoesOfTheJazzAge.pdf.

Giordano, Ralph G. *Social Dancing in America: Lindy Hop to Hip Hop 1901–2000.* Santa Barbara, CA: Greenwood Press, 2007.

Grove Music Online. "*Clave (jazz).*" January 20, 2002. http://www.oxfordmusiconline.com.ezproxy.gc.cuny.edu/grovemusic/view/10.1093/gmo/9781561592630.001.0001/omo-9781561592630-e-2000766600.

Haskins, James. *Black Dance in America: A History Through Its People*. New York: Harper Collins Publishers, 1990.

Heap, Chad. *Slumming: Sexual and Racial Encounters in American Nightlife (1885–1940)*. Chicago: IL, University of Chicago Press, 2010.

Heilpern, John. "Welcome to The Wild Party! Dangerous, Seedy … Fantastic." *The Observer*, April 24, 2000. http://observer.com/2000/04/welcome-to-the-wild-party-dangerous-seedy-fantastic/.

Hutcheon, Linda. *A Theory of Parody: The Teachings of Twentieth-Century Art Forms*. Urbana, IL: Chicago University Press, 2000.

"Jazz Dance 'Dangerous Sports,' Says Doctor, Adding "Charleston Knee to Mankind's Ills." *New York Times*, April 29, 1928.

Jones, John Bush. *Our Musicals, Ourselves: A Social History of the American Musical Theatre*. Waltham, MA: Brandeis University Press, 2004.

Koritz, Amy. *Culture Makers: Urban Performance and Literature of the 1920s*. Urbana: IL: University of Illinois Press, 2009.

LaChiusa, Michael John. *The Wild Party*. Vocal Selections. Van Nuys, CA: Alfred Publishing, 2009.

Mack, Cecil, and James B. Johnson. "The Charleston." *Runnin' Wild*, 1923, http://lyricsplayground.com/alpha/songs/c/charleston.html, accessed February 7, 2018.

Martin, Carol. "American Dance Marathons." In *Ballroom, Boogie, Shimmy Sham, Shake: A Social and Popular Dance Reader*, edited by Julie Malnig, 93–108. Chicago: University of Illinois Press, 2009.

Ngai, Sianne. *Our Aesthetic Categories: Zany, Cute, Interesting*. Cambridge, MA: Harvard University Press, 2012.

Norton, Pauline. "Charleston (ii)," January 20, 2001, *Grove Music Online*, http://www.oxfordmusiconline.com.ezproxy.gc.cuny.edu/grovemusic.

Osumare, Halifu. "The Dance Archeology of Rennie Harris: Hip-Hop or Post-modern?" In *Ballroom, Boogie, Shimmy Sham, Shake: A Social and Popular Dance Reader*, edited by Julie Malnig, 55–71, Chicago: University of Illinois Press, 2009.

Rhodes, Chip. *Structures of the Jazz Age: Mass Culture, Progressive Education and Racial Discourses*. London: UK, Verso Books, 1998.

Robinson, Danielle. "'Oh, You Black Bottom!' Appropriation, Authenticity, and Opportunity in the Jazz Dance Teaching of 1920s New York." *Dance Research Journal* 38, no. 1/2 (2006): 19–42.

Smith-Rosenberg, Caroll. *Disorderly Conduct: Visions of Gender in Victorian America*. New York: Oxford University Press, 1985.

Stearns, Marshall, and Jean Stearns. *Jazz Dance: The Story of American Vernacular Dance*. New York: Da Capo Press, 1994.

Stevens, Hugh. *Henry James and Sexuality*. New York: Cambridge University Press, 1998.

Tomko, Linda J. *Dancing Class: Gender, Ethnicity and Social Divides in American Dance, 1890–1920*. Indianapolis: Indiana University Press, 1999.

Wheeler, Wayne B. "Is There Prohibition? And to What extent?" *The North American Review* 222, no. 828 (Sep–Nov. 1925): 29–35, https://www.jstor.org/stable/25113449, accessed July 12, 2018.

Wollman, Elizabeth L. *A Critical Companion to The American Stage Musical*. London, UK: Bloomsbury Publishing, Plc, 2017.

"Women's Suffrage," *History.com*, https://www.history.com/topics/womens-history/the-fight-for-womens-suffrage, accessed July 27, 2018.

4 "Men Say it's Criminal What Women Will Do"

Thoroughly Modern Millie and Nostalgia for the "New Woman"

One arm wraps tightly around the waist; the other drapes seductively over the head; both wrists flap in double time to the building jazz music; legs flick front, side, and across to the right; a heeled and bedazzled foot comes up to the knee, swiveling the body around, leaving the head behind, until eye contact must finally be broken with the audience; short hair whirls around while shoulders pulse and knees pop and twizzle. A thoroughly modern Millie (Sutton Foster), dressed in an amber cloche hat and matching drop-waist, above-the-knee dress, makes her way through the "spiffy" dancers and sings "Men say it's criminal what women'll do, what they're forgetting [...] this is 1922!"[1] The highly choreographed opening of the 2002 Broadway musical *Thoroughly Modern Millie* imagines the height of 1922, the year Fitzgerald claimed as the exhibit of youth.[2] The ebullient cast executes exaggerated Charleston-like movements sprinkled with a variety of twists and turns, that moments earlier left Millie with her mouth gaping as she tried to pick up the new "modern" style. Millie dashes out a revolving door center stage and returns moments later in a chic 1920s dress and joins in. Millie wants to fit it and be "modern," and in the whirlwind of the opening number of the show—so do we.

Prior to this theatricalized pinpoint of the apparent peak of freedom and frivolity for the younger generation in 1922, audiences awaiting the opening of the show are presented with a dictionary definition of the word "modern" projected on the scrim covering the stage. The definition reminds the audience that to be modern is to be "a member of the modern school of thought in relation to any subject."[3] The scrim cycles through a rainbow of colors and the projection remains for contemplation throughout the playing of the overture. The description of what it means to be modern helps familiarize the audience with the early twentieth century era in which the musical is set, when female modernism was in full swing and cultural trends involved the bold salutation of all things new. Further down in the definition the audience is reminded that modernity is also "characteristic of present and recent times: not obsolete."[4] With a wink, the creative team boosts the emphasis on just how "thoroughly modern" this musical will be.

The scrim rises and an innocent and naïve looking Millie stands upstage center, wearing a long dress, her brown tresses clipped back, shoulders

DOI: 10.4324/9781003163688-7

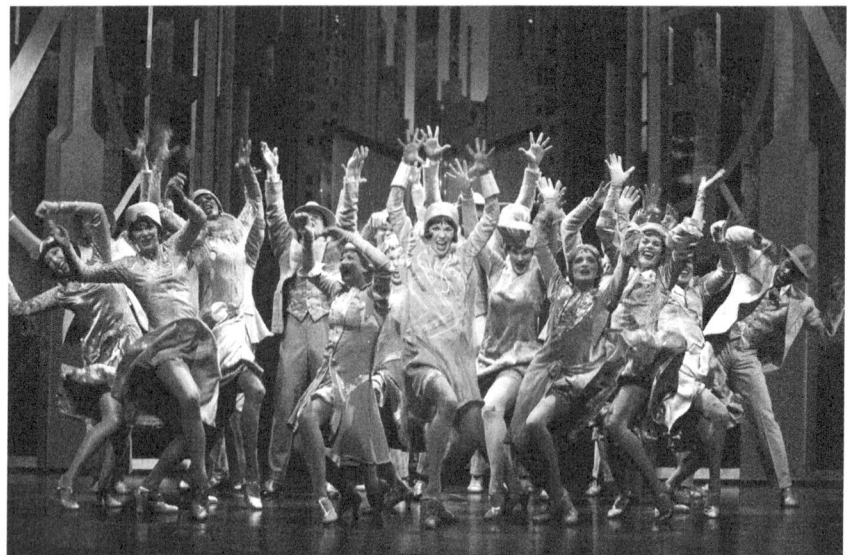

Figure 4.1 Thoroughly Modern Millie (2002) "Thoroughly Modern Millie," Sutton Foster
    with cast.
Source: Photo by Joan Marcus.

slouched. She walks slowly center stage and explains how she has planned for
this trip, studied the maps of New York City, and has "prepared" for the city
("Not For The Life of Me"). She explains that her family back home insisted
she would be lonely and homesick. She produces the return ticket they sent
along from her pocket. The music is soft and melodic until she tears the ticket
in two; jazz rhythms drop in and she proclaims, "Burn the bridge, [...] Baby's
comin' home no more, Not for the life of me."[5] This is the last we hear of
Millie's family or the older generation. The once empty stage populates with
stylish dancers, dressed in the luxurious finery of the 1920s – satin lapels of
well-tailored suits for the men and dropped waist dresses in satiny champagne
colors, accented by trim hair styles and chic accessories for the women. The
small, fast-moving kicks of the Charleston immediately bring the space and the
costumes to life. Dancers walk forward on their heels, push flexed hands
overhead, swish hips side-to-side, all while pumping knees up and down and
waving arms. The synchronization of the large ensemble amplifies the buoyant
mood and their tight formation is indicative of the increasingly mechanized
world.

An emphatic focus on, and imitation of, the playfulness and boldness of the
1920s builds from the beginning, and if the point is at all missed the lyrics of
the opening number conclude: "So beat the drums 'cause here comes thoroughly, Hot off the press! One step ahead! Jazz age! [...] We're so thoroughly
modern [Millie] Now!"[6] The charm of the era, the follies of youth, the

general casting off of one's past and embracing the new and the modern is the essence of *Thoroughly Modern Millie.*

Background of Thoroughly Modern Millie

Thoroughly Modern Millie opened on Broadway in 2002. Jeanine Tesori composed the music, with lyrics by Dick Scanlan, and a book written by Richard Morris and Scanlan. The musical was directed by Michael Mayer and choreographed by Rob Ashford.[7] The show is based on the 1967 movie of the same name and starred Julie Andrews.[8] The plot follows the dreams of newcomer Millie to New York, who gets a job in a secretary pool in order to carry out her plan to marry her rich boss. The story itself is a bit convoluted, with a secondary plot line involving the landlady of a women's rooming house who kidnaps young women and sells them into the sex trade outside the country. The success of the show lies in the treatment of the era, the dances, the music, the large personalities, and the celebration of a time of change, and pleasure, especially for women. Millie has the idea that the "new woman" of the 1920s does not need to marry for love and to marry a man for his money is quite forward thinking. Expectedly, she comes to love a man who has no prospects, only to find out in the end he is in fact the heir to a massive fortune. The musical is melodramatic and sensational; it is a period piece of the early 1920s that embraces many conventions of musical theatre.[9] From Millie's opening "I want" song ("Not For The Life Of Me") to the "11 o'clock" number ("Gimme, Gimme") the musical fills its role as a highly entertaining piece of escapism and a pastiche of the 1920s. What makes the show of critical interest is how the movement is used to unfold the story of the life of the "new woman" in 1922 within the pastiche style of the score.[10] By investigating the female body in motion we can discern how women worked around the rules set in place by the older patriarchal generation in the 1920s. In *Millie* there is a celebration of youthfulness, freedom and engagement in the novelty of life, despite living in a world run by men.

The Choreography of Thoroughly Modern Millie

Choreographer Rob Ashford has a lengthy list of Broadway choreography credits to his name – including the Disney blockbuster musical *Frozen* (2018). Like most Broadway choreographers he began as a dancer.[11] Ashford is highly interdisciplinary, often directing non-musicals and working in film. He is known for his storytelling capabilities using dance. He describes his creative process, "I work really hard to make dance an essential part in my musical. Dance isn't extra; it should be part of the story. Audiences are smart: you need only about 15 seconds of dance to establish a mood or atmosphere."[12] He continues on to explain, "the steps are always last. When you do a new show its always about the story, what do you want to get across at a particular moment, how the characters move – that's where the most production time is spent – then the steps."[13]

Ashford captures the innocence and youth of the early Jazz Age in *Millie* by creating a spectrum of body movement beyond the stereotypical kicks and swinging arms of the Charleston. His choreographic palette for both men and women in the opening includes wrist flicks and circles, shoulder twitches and shrugs, hip circles, ankle flexes, as well as a subtle exoticism that permeates the dance, with articulated fingers and arms squaring around the face suggestive of Spanish or Polynesian dance styles. This shift in style is seen in the bridge of the titular song when the ensemble sings, "What we think is chic, unique, [...] They think is odd and 'Sodom and Gomorrah'-ble."[14] Dancers travel around in an oval formation, alternating male and female dancer. They do a series of touches with the toe, and then stepping on the full foot, a move that accentuates the syncopated beat of the music. While this stepping occurs, hips swivel around towards the front while arms, hands, and wrists circle and twist in a Flamenco-like manner. The collaged movement sequence is repeated with the next step. This short section picks up the drum line and more mysterious or minor sound of the bridge and uses the switch in movement to briefly parody the wicked habits the older generation believes them to have taken on. Dancers then chassé (step-together-step) while flapping arms to a tight wedge formation and execute a series of sharp and accentuated dance moves that build in intensity. These quick moves are still in the 1920s style, but engaging the ensemble of sixteen dancers in unison and in close proximity amplifies the communal desire for the latest new and exciting trend. The machine-like quality of this section also reminds one of the urbanization, mechanization, and the fast pace of the modern era. Movement defines how Millie situates herself in the city; for example, in order to activate the elevator in her rooming house occupants must tap dance. Additionally, in the typing pool where many women work, the action of work is not typing, but tap dancing, while seated at a typewriter. The female body in motion is how the women in the piece are shown to be part of the working community, not to mention a clever production number. In regard to the two styles of tap discussed form the previous chapter, Ashford's choreography is more in line with the "Broadway Style" which is more stylized and lifted with greater emphasis placed on arm gestures and synchronization of the ensemble building towards a large spectacle. The meaning in Ashford's moves skirts the line of being both novel and in service to the various narrative twists and turns of the musical comedy. This is in opposition to Glover's engagement with the embodied history in tap and social dances to reclaim ownership of the form for Black performers and point toward the roots of appropriation that began in the early twentieth century – indeed in the era of *Millie*. Ashford does not take on these questions of authorship in his choreography. Moreover, there are some troublesome uses of a variety of cultural styles in the ethnic parody that unfolds in the musical that warrants unpacking.

Soon after "Not for the Life of Me," we are introduced to Ching Ho and Bun Foo, who work for Mrs. Meers, the leader of a "white slavery" ring. The two Chinese immigrants are trying to earn enough money to bring their mother from Hong Kong to New York. Disheartened by their work with Mrs. Meers they break into a Mandarin version of "Not For the Life of Me." Despite the absence of any choreography in their version the jazzy essence of the piece is felt with the same vocal intonations of the "bo-do-dee-dohs." Later in the musical they also tap dance to move the elevator as Millie does. Pointedly, the repetition by Ching Ho and Bun Foo of the opening number and some of Millie's moves brings up the problematic topic of Orientalism in the show.[15]

Angela C. Pao explores the concept of ethnic parody in "Green Glass and Emeralds: Citation, Performance, and the Dynamics of Ethnic Parody in *Thoroughly Modern Millie*."[16] Pao finds the musical is more about a community of migrants than ethnic stereotypes. She claims the musical "operates in the mode of second-order parody using over-emphatic citations and performances within performances to deconstruct stereotypes and reformulate social relations," and is generally a drastic improvement on the 1967 film.[17] In this consideration, the overt exaggeration is meant to "denounce racism," and as Pao claims, "Asian characters are treated no worse and no better than anyone else in the show."[18] If the Orientalism is supposed to be a spoof or parody of 1920s movie stereotypes as the creative team claims, then we need, as Hutcheon explains, "signals from the text to guide our interpretation, and the degree of visibility of these signals determines their potential for assisting us."[19] *Millie* does not offer this guidance, and Pao does reprimand the production team for not having more visible cues of the parody itself. All things considered, and without prior knowledge of the film, the Orientalist stereotypes remain of concern with or without additional background knowledge.

In terms of movement, the Orientalist stereotypes draw some attention to various Eastern or "exotic" dance styles. These flourishes are part of the mélange of 1920s styles Ashford uses in the opening dance number and are not found in any significance elsewhere in the musical. The hip rolls and wrist swirling redolent of Egyptian-styled belly dancing do, by nature of their popularity, fit within the historical era as exoticized "Salome" dances were part of popular vaudeville performance at the turn of the nineteenth century that seeped into stage performance.[20] Douglas Gilbert explains the usage: "the Salome fad became an important vehicle in vaudeville for women to showcase their female sexuality and independence."[21] The "exotic" dance elements are minimal in *Millie* and though they "point to the emergence of the New Woman," Jayna Brown reminds they are also "an eroticized enactment of European colonial access."[22] Keeping this in mind, Ashford seems more focused on imitating the thrills of the dances of the 1920s rather than parodying the "exotic" style.[23] Some critics of *Millie* acknowledged the Orientalist stereotypes in the show but, as mentioned, most were not generally that disturbed by them, given most knew of the original movie.[24]

The critics, however, are not so soft on Ashford's choreography. Though Ashford received the Tony Award for Best Choreography for *Millie,* his work on the show received mixed reviews. While some consider the choreographic moments as extra fluff, Ashford explains he strives to create movements that "grow organically from the characters and the plot."[25] Ashford has certainly created a complex movement palette that puts the entire body, particularly female bodies, in constant motion. Notwithstanding, critics debated the degree to which he achieved his goal. In order to understand Ashford's choreographic choices and methodology in the musical, I consider the operation of embodied meaning created by his use of the Charleston as base material or framework in tandem with various critiques.

Thoroughly Modern Millie and Nostalgia for the "New Woman"

With her chin thrust forward and shoulders squared, Millie belts out: "Goodbye, […] goody girl, I'm changing and how."[26] From the beginning Millie defies expectations of family members back home and joins up with the other young and resourceful women making changes in their lives in the early 1920s. What is the nature of this transformation and how is it manifested in the body? For Millie the "change" involves breaking free from traditional and conservative middle-class values and embracing independence and liberal views (and the distinct fashions of the 1920s). Importantly, the change for women at the time was also about exploring what the body can do, and the dance in *Millie* allows for this exploration, particularly as Sutton Foster, a very adept dancer, easily brings the embodied transformation to her character.[27] Millie arrives in New York at the height of the Jazz Age. The musical explores how she navigates the thrills of the time, but generally avoids questioning what is at work economically or politically. Millie expresses her experiences as new and fresh; there is an absence of cynicism and anxiety (as is seen in *The Wild Party*). This emphasis on the bright, lively, and chipper extends through the music, costumes, and movement and amplifies how female bodies moved through the world with flair and flourish.[28] The "anything goes" zeitgeist circulating at the time created, especially for women – mostly white women – a utopic few years of imagining and acting out one's autonomy without much thought for the future.

Likewise, the nostalgic inclinations created in *Millie* are for the luxury of self-reflexivity, self-exploration, and mobility – concepts not necessarily available to all audience members in the twenty-first century. The character of Miss Dorothy who joins Millie at her rooming house emphasizes this point, with ironic flair, as she comes from a wealthy background, but wants to be part of the excitement and "See a new world unfurl," as she sings in her opening song, "How the Other Half Lives."[29] The insertion of a wealthy character that wants to experience being poor offers an amusing, though blatantly naive, parody of the pursuit of economic status. Indeed, the saccharine sweet sensibilities in *Millie* do come off as too intense or self-indulgent at times. Certainly, Charles Isherwood tires of Foster's "overdetermined" smile and "pearly whites," stating "she bares her splendid assortment so insistently, so ingratiatingly, that by the end of the evening you'll either be smiling right back or reaching for sunglasses."[30] Yet, the exaggerations serve to remind one of the magnitude of the shift in the roles and behavior of women in the 1920s. The female ensemble state in the opening, "Men say it's criminal what women will do," pointing out just how opinioned men were to the ongoing changes in women's behavior.[31]

The excessiveness of the movement, as described at the top of the chapter, above other theatrical elements in *Millie,* captures this sense of detail, extravagance, and margin of change, which fits within the pastiche quality of the show. Critics seemed to agree that the larger-than-life personalities of the lead performers carry the show, and I would add that the personalities are drawn from the inflated physical sensibilities and mind-sets of the era created by the focus on the liberated-self, particularly for women. Foster amplifies the joyous shenanigans by a continued use of loose body language, and near rubbery posture and cartoonish movement styles. Thomas Burke explains Sutton Foster "drive[s] [the show] forward by sheer force of personality."[32] Yes, the shiny veneer of the show can be considered too much at times and does operate in a sort of dramaturgical impetus that can only be described as "over-the-top," however, the early part of the 1920s *was* outrageous and shameless, as wistfully described by Fitzgerald. Foster's quasi-parody of the styles helps enhance the nostalgia for the era. While Isherwood labels Ashford's choreography as "heavy on the insistently flapping hands and feet, low on distinctiveness," and Burke calls it "derivative," I posit the dance's insistence serves to support the scale of change for women's physical freedom; further, the dance is imitative by design.[33]

In the beginning of the 1920s copying, parodying, and parroting others en route to forming one's own identity was how the Charleston broke barriers towards allowing women a freedom of the body. As mentioned, this experience is markedly different for Black and white communities. Brown explains, for white women, "Imitating black women allowed them certain expressive freedoms, such as the right to be verbally and physically unrestrained, to be sexually frank and opinionated, to be figures of female independence. This process operated solely in relation to a white idle-class subject." For Black dancers at the time, the experience of doing the Charleston and related dances was much different and involved "claiming community," sustaining a livelihood, and creating a sense of comradery within the overtly racialized structures of the time.[34] This culturally ingrained suppression did not allow Black women to experience the freedom of this "new woman" of the 1920s. Brown explains the contradiction, "However 'black' infractions were shaded, in this discursive framework black women were denied subjecthood, so the rule breaking was always on the white side of the color line."[35] As a point of contrast, Glover's presentation of tap and the proto-Charleston in chapter three involves an uplifting and re-claiming of the Black body with choreographic choices that thrill and excite, yet press against "affirming the racial and sexual accessibility of black bodies."[36] Glover's choreographic authority undoes this gaze put onto black bodies and sees them presented with strength, integrity and personhood. This styling is particularly strong in the tap challenge between the cast of *The Chocolate Dandies* and *Rang Tang* as described in the previous chapter. Returning to explore some of Ashford's choreographic choice demonstrates these inconsistencies, particularly in the use of a more theatrical tap, and a zany take on ballet.

The "Nuttycracker Suite" in *Millie* emphasizes this outrageousness and imitative learning and enjoyment. An analysis of the bizarre scene helps to substantiate the idea that the early 1920s were a time of incredible chaos and exploration of the body. The "Nuttycracker Suite" is an instrumental section in the musical where Millie and her friends visit their first speakeasy. The music throughout the entire scene is a jazzed-up and amusing imitation of Pytor Illyich Tchaikovsky's *Nutcracker Suite* written in 1892. The showy piece also contributes to the cartoonish and extravagant style the musical is trying to take on. The citation of the Nutcracker also evokes a fantasy world, or "Land of the Sweets," that Millie and her friends inhabit, which works well in service to the pastiche of 1920s-styled films both the original 1967 movie and musical attempt. The diegetic dance scene involves a comic treatment of ballet, jazz dance, and social dance styles that teases out the exchanges between the dance hall and concert or stage dance, along with a demonstration of how identity can be developed through social dance (and alcohol).

As Millie and her friends enter the speakeasy, a multitude of dancers are already moving in couples using a combination of Charleston and Tango-like choreography, keeping their focus towards the floor. The dancers are hunched over, hopping and kicking one foot to the front and back, with plenty of breakaways and sensual transitions using deep lunges side to side. Their passionate dancing draws attention to the physical awkwardness of Millie and her friends upon their arrival. The lack of lyrics in the scene helps express how social dance venues from the beginning of the Jazz Age forward were about music, body language, and one's innate physicality.

Unexpectedly, Miss Dorothy grabs a flask from Jimmy and takes a swig. She instantly begins to move in a distorted and stiff manner, the alcohol apparently causing convulsions and twitches. Each girl takes a drink and the same thing happens. The jerky movement twists into ballet arabesques and other sharp movements from the classical repertoire. When Millie takes a swig, her knees immediately become rubbery and she noodles about the stage with flailing kicks and spaghetti arms. The music turns bluesy and Jimmy and an unknown partner begin a sultry and sensuous dance, close to the Slow Drag, connected by a string of pearls. Millie tries to do the same but is strangely stiff and shocked when her companion grabs her buttocks. Partners switch and Millie is now paired with Jimmy. Millie is surprised to find herself dancing with confidence and sensuality. Millie reconsiders her relationship with Jimmy, who she had butted heads with earlier, based on the shift in her physicality (and lowered inhibitions from the drinks).

Millie is pulled back in with her girlfriends for a frenzy of dancing center stage while the men circle and leap around – late night mayhem has taken over. Further alcohol is guzzled and competitions between Millie and other performers showcase Foster's dancing skills, but also show how open Millie (the "new woman") is to trying the latest moves, music and drinks. Dancers move about in low lunges with weight on the ball of the foot, adding in lots of small kicks and Charleston strides swinging forward and back. The whole concept of organized chaos is turned on its head, as the music shifts to an intense and pulsing version of the final adagio music of the ballet. A flask is passed down the line, to the Tchaikovsky *pas de deux* finale. The mayhem is put to a stop when Millie passes the flask mistakenly to a police officer and the same drinking line becomes a line up for mug shots leading to a night in jail.

In this section, one's experience of physical and social awakening is expressed through dance.[37] This strategy physicalizes the shift in Millie and her friends from first-time attendees at a speakeasy to seasoned participants and part of a new community. Adding in a ballet-meets-jazz "mash-up" alludes to how unhinged a speakeasy might have been. The juxtaposition of high and low dance forms brings up the diversity of patrons at speakeasies that could range from high society to lower classes, as well as a mix of gangsters and criminals. While the dance is somewhat presentational to the audience there are multiple points of focus, along with inward facings to one's dancing partner that altogether make this moment of mayhem believable – when the police raid the joint and everyone gets arrested, the absurdity of the situation and the outpouring of bodily freedom is very much felt by the abrupt halt in the music and movement. There is no attempt at sophistication in the "Nuttycracker Suite"; the choreography is "exuberant and playful."[38] While it may be derivative, the choreography is unrestricted and the lack of self-consciousness of the performers by the end captures the spirit of the early 1920s and the gutsy "new woman."

A more subtle but effective choice, not mentioned by critics, that Ashford uses to bring out the "social" in social dance happens at a cocktail party hosted by the wealthy Muzzy Van Hossmere. While a private conversation is going on between Muzzy and Jimmy (her secret step-son) the guests at the party engage in a light one-step behind them. There are a dozen couples all mechanically doing the dance in time, standing a foot away from each other with arms placed in the couples' dance position but not touching. This robotic and fragmented dance occurs when the guests (including Millie) are not involved in the conversation but are eavesdropping. The dancers, with their backs to the audience, go through the motions of the dance but the lack of physical contact makes for a very austere mood. The stiff movement is a nod to the refined and stiff nature of the dances when taken up by the wealthy elite and is a stark contrast to the chaos and physical abandon in the speakeasy, the domain of the uninhibited.

Critics Barbara and Scott Siegle take a more consolatory angle to the show stating director Michael Mayer "does an exceptional job of keeping the audience's mind off the show's limitations and stressing its strengths: color, pacing, laughs."[39] Indeed, the strength of *Millie* is its driving rhythm and embodiment of the thrills and merriments of the era. *Variety* calls the show a "gleefully nostalgic concoction," and in the post-9/11 world of the production (the musical opened on Broadway seven months after the attacks) the need for a turn away from present anxieties in order to contemplate one's place in the world, if just for a few hours at the theatre, becomes quite desirable.[40] A backwards glance, particularly one so sentimental and frivolous as *Millie,* offers a nostalgic reflection on the "new women" that punctuated change in a positive manner giving confidence at a particularly anxious time.

Thoroughly Modern Millie closes with a tableau of a kiss between Jimmy and Millie and a proposal. As they head off on their new lives, another young woman shows up, suitcase in hand, dressed in a plain and unfashionable outfit, just as Millie did in the opening of the musical. The chorus begins to welcome thoroughly modern "Maude" through the same up-tempo choreography they did Millie – and the cycle begins again. The circular nature of the narrative salutes continued feminine modernity and the ongoing quest for the next novelty and trend. This fanciful send-off is rich with nostalgia and unabashedly champions a rose-colored backward glance. This glance, however, illustrates bodies constantly in motion (tap dancing in moving desks in the typing pool for example), offering a sense of momentum to a society that was lacking any sense of certainty in the future in 2002. As Fitzgerald claimed in 1931, "We were the most powerful nation. Who could tell us any longer what was fashionable and what was fun."[41] Director Michael Mayer drives this point home in his enthusiastic production, largely brought to life by Ashford's choreography that has bodies in motion throughout to emphasize one must move to live and to love (and to operate an elevator).

To the above point, the speed and mechanization of the modern era was interpreted through bodies in motion in the growing cities. Mark Franko describes the dance of the early twentieth century: "the ostensibly ludic qualities of dance were there and then transformed into social energy."[42] The intensification of all kinetic and mechanized motion brought forth by Ashford's highly detailed and hectic choreography celebrates the social energy of 1922. The pastiche quality of *Thoroughly Modern Millie* uses the moves, sounds, and images of the 1920s to create the excitement of the early Jazz Age, though without any political punch. Still, instead of a "random cannibalizing of all styles of the past," as per Fredric Jameson's description of pastiche, there is a focus on recreating (through highly theatricalized dance) the social and physical energy that surrounded modernization when a sense of newness was achievable.[43] Creating nostalgia for that sense of individuality and change in this story about the "new woman" – makes *Thoroughly Modern Millie* a gesture towards the absence of the newness and ease of exploring one's subjectivity in the contemporary era. The nostalgic vision may be enticing to contemporary audiences as modernity in the 1920s had a resounding influence on bodies in motion, and shifted our understanding of how bodies, particularly female bodies, moved through the world. While it is true that technological advancement is ever more a factor of contemporary life, its presence in the 2020s is felt in the ether – the cyber and the virtual world. In contrast, the embodiment of the "new" in *Millie* resonates on a human, physical, and tactile level that can be hard to find in an increasingly mediated world.

Notes

1 These lyrics are from the second song of the musical, "Thoroughly Modern Millie," Lyrics by Dick Scanlan, music by Jeanine Tesori, 2002.

2 F. Scott Fitzgerald, *Echoes of the Jazz Age (1931).* Accessed March 13, 2018, http s://pdcrodas.webs.ull.es/anglo/ScottFitzgeraldEchoesOfTheJazzAge.pdf.

3 Opening projection of *Thoroughly Modern Millie,* as viewed at the New York Public Library Performing Art Library, Theatre on Film and Tape, January 18, 2018.

4 Ibid.

5 Scanlan and Tesori, "Not for The Life of Me," 2002.

6 Scanlan and Tesori, "Thoroughly Modern Millie," 2002.

7 The musical won six Tony awards including Best Musical and Best Choreography.

8 The 1967 movie was directed by George Roy Hill. Along with Julie Andrews, the movie also starred Mary Tyler Moore, as Miss Dorothy Brown and James Fox, as Jimmy Smith. Elmer Bernstein composed the music in the film, some of which is interpolated into the musical. *Thoroughly Modern Millie*, George Roy Hill, Universal City, CA: Universal Studios, 1967, http://www.imdb.com/title/tt0062362/full credits?ref_=tt_ov_st_sm, accessed March 26, 2018. The 1967 movie is loosely based on the 1956 British musical, *Chrysanthemum* by Neville Phillips and Robin Chancellor: Music by Robb Stewart. "Chrysanthemum," http://www.guidetom usicaltheatre.com/shows_c/chrysanthemum.htm, accessed July 28, 2017.

9 Some of the standard conventions of musical theatre include: a big opening number to introduce the world of the musical; the "I want" song where early on a character sings about what they want or desire; the act 1 finale that sends the audience to the intermission with a desire to return; the "11 o'clock number is a big showstopper towards the end of act two where a main character comes to an integral realization. For more specific conventions and further details see: Stacy Wolf's *Changed for Good: A Feminist History of the Broadway Musical* (New York: Oxford University Press, 2011).

10 Composer Jeanine Tesori and lyricist Dick Scanlan added their own songs to the musical style of the score from the film.

11 *Crazy for You* (1992), *Victor/Victoria* (1995), *Parade* (1998).

12 Interview with Jenny Dalzell, "Rob Ashford: Making *Evita* Tango Again on Broadway," *Dance Teacher Magazine*, April 1, 2012, https://jennydalzellouellette. wordpress.com/2012/04/01/interview-broadways-rob-ashford/.

13 Ibid.

14 Scanlan and Tesori, "Thoroughly Modern Millie," 2002.

15 Mrs. Meers in played by a white actress in a Chinese-styled costume, with heavy eye makeup, and an exaggerated English-Mandarin accent. Ching Ho and Bun Foo are played by Asian American actors.

16 Angela C. Pao, "Green Glass and Emeralds: Citation, Performance, and the Dynamics of Ethnic Parody in *Thoroughly Modern Millie,*" *Multi-Ethnic Literature in the U.S. Volume* 36, Number 4, Winter 2011, 35–60.

17 Angela C. Pao, "Green Glass and Emeralds," 36. Pao explains the musical has in fact done much to repair the overt racism in the movie, however those unfamiliar with the movie would not know of the improvements and are left to judge the structural logic of including the characters themselves. She explains, "Scanlan's goal was to embody the spirit of the present multiracial and multicultural era of American society and American theatre." Pao, "Green Glass and Emeralds," 36. Changes from the movie to the stage include: Scanlan and Richard Morris (co-writers of the

book) give Ching Ho and Bun Foo names (previously called Oriental 1 and 2) and motives in the show (to bring their mother to America); by the end Ching Ho ends up in a relationship with Miss Dorothy.

18 Ibid., 4.

19 Linda Hutcheon, *A Theory of Parody: The Teachings of Twentieth-Century Art Forms* (Urbana, IL: Chicago University Press, 2000), xvi.

20 Salome dances were essentially an exotic dance performed while removing veils and scarves, traditionally done to invoke desire and gain favor, "Dance of the Seven Veils," http://www.shira.net/sevenveils.htm, accessed July 2018.

21 Douglas Gilbert, *American Vaudeville: Its Life and Times* (New York: Dover Publishing, 1940), 190. Ruth St. Denis and Fahruda Manzar were some of the most famous performers of the "Salome" style and the trend grew in such popularity that there were "Salome" dance schools in various large cities.

22 Jayna Brown, *Babylon Girls: Black Women Performers and the Shaping of the Modern* (Durham, NC: Duke University Press, 2008), 175.

23 As for the racial makeup of the cast: the majority of the original ensemble was white, though there were several Asian American and Black performers in both the men and women's chorus. Some of the Asian American cast members also understudied Ching Ho and Bun Foo, including a female member of the chorus Jo Ann M Hunter and Kim Varhola. *Playbill*, accessed July 28, 2018, http://www.playbill.com/production/thoroughly-modern-millie-marquis-theatre-vault-0000008183.

24 Steven Oxman states, "Scanlan does what he can to temper the racism of the movie … [They] achieve a very layered, of still potentially controversial form of satire," "Thoroughly Modern Millie," *Variety*, October 30, 2000, https://variety.com/2000/legit/reviews/thoroughly-modern-millie-2-1200464478/. Ben Brantley states, "It's possible that some theatre goers may object to perceived racism in the portrayal of Mrs. Meers's Chinese assistants … But Mr. Morris and Mr. Scanlan have made them virtuous chaps, after all, who have a worthy place in the New York melting pot." "Alright, Everyone: Smile!" *New York Times*, April 19, 2002, https://www.nytimes.com/2002/04/19/movies/theater-review-all-right-everyone-smile.html.

25 Interview with Jenny Dalzell, *Dance Teacher Magazine*, April 1, 2012.

26 Scanlan and Tesori, "Thoroughly Modern Millie," 2002.

27 Foster has appeared in eleven Broadway shows and won two Tony Awards for *Thoroughly Modern Millie* (2002) and *Anything Goes* (2011). Trained from an early age in ballet and tap, Sutton began training intensely in high school entering numerous competitions, including Star-Search at fifteen. Her first professional jobs were as a dancer in touring musicals, then eventually as an ensemble member/understudy in a variety of Broadway shows (*Les Miserable, Grease, The Scarlet Pimpernel*). Her first major role was in *Millie*, where she got promoted from the chorus to understudy to lead. Sylviane Gold, "She's the Top," *Dance Magazine* 85, no. 12 (December 2011): 26–30.

28 Stiff corsets, long skirts, and the conventional behaviors of society in general bound bodies prior to the 1920s. When the Charleston was done in the growing number dance halls in urban areas and beyond, it enhanced the already emerging process of female autonomy in an increasingly modernized world. For more on changes in social and physical behaviors of women in the early twentieth century see: Linda J. Tomko's *Dancing Class: Gender, Ethnicity and Social Divides in American Dance, 1890–1920* (Indianapolis: Indiana University Press, 1999) and Kathy Peiss *Cheap Amusements Working Women and Leisure in Turn-of-the-Century New York* (Philadelphia, PA: Temple University Press, 1996).

29 "How the Other Half Lives," Scanlan and Tesori, 2002.

30 Charles Isherwood, "Thoroughly Modern Millie," *Variety*, April 18, 2002, https://variety.com/2002/legit/reviews/thoroughly-modern-millie-6-1200550210/.

31 Scanlan and Tesori, "Thoroughly Modern Millie," 2002. Again, what is markedly absent from the discussion of the "new woman" in *Thoroughly Modern Millie* is that much of the new movement and energy was derived from Black female artists that "helped to shape and define conceptions of the modern." Farrah Jasmine Griffin, "Cake Walk, Shimmy, and Charleston: *Babylon Girls: Black Women Performers and the Shaping of the Modern*, Review," *The Women's Review of Books*, 26, no. 4 (July/August 2009), 12.

32 Thomas Burke, "Broadway Reviews: 'Thoroughly Modern Millie," April 18, 2002, *Broadway.com*https://www.talkinbroadway.com/page/world/TMMillie.html.

33 Isherwood, "Thoroughly Modern Millie," 2002; Burke, "Broadway Reviews".

34 Brown, *Babylon Girls*, 162, 204.

35 Ibid., 215.

36 Ibid.

37 Marya Annette McQuirter observes, "Social dance figured as one of the central arenas in which the process of identity formation became manifest," in "Awkward Moves: Dance Lessons from the 1940s," in *Dancing Many Drums: Excavation in African American Dance,* ed. Thomas F. DeFrantz (Madison, WI: The University of Wisconsin Press, 2002), 81. Adding in the "Nuttycracker Suite" section in *Millie* helps to show how social dance venues helped participants find a sense of belonging within a community.

38 Barbara Siegle and Scott Siegle, *"Thoroughly Modern Millie,"* Theatremania, April 19, 2002, https://www.theatermania.com/new-york-city-theater/reviews/thoroughly-modern-millie_2097.html.

39 Ibid.

40 Isherwood, "Thoroughly Modern Millie".

41 Fitzgerald, *Echoes*, 2.

42 Mark Franko, *The Work of Dance: Labor, Movement, and Identity in the 1930s*. Middletown (CT: Wesleyan University Press, 2002), 2.

43 Frederic Jameson, *Postmodernism, Or, The Cultural Logic of Late Capitalism* (Durham, NC: Duke University Press, 1991), 18.

References

Brantley, Ben. "Alright, Everyone: Smile!" *New York Times*, April 19, 2002, https://www.nytimes.com/2002/04/19/movies/theater-review-all-right-everyone-smile.html.

Brown, Jayna. *Babylon Girls: Black Women Performers and the Shaping of the Modern.* Durham, NC: Duke University Press, 2008.

Burke, Thomas. "Broadway Reviews: 'Thoroughly Modern Millie.'" *Broadway.com*, April 18, 2002. https://www.talkinbroadway.com/page/world/TMMillie.html.

Dalzell, Jenny. "Rob Ashford: Making *Evita* Tango Again on Broadway." *Dance Teacher Magazine*, April 1, 2012. https://jennydalzellouellette.wordpress.com/2012/04/01/interview-broadways-rob-ashford/.

Gilbert, Douglas. *American Vaudeville: Its Life and Times.* New York: Dover Publishing, 1940.

Guide to Musical Theatre. "Chrysanthemum." Accessed July 28, 2017, http://www.guidetomusicaltheatre.com/shows_c/chrysanthemum.htm.

Gold, Sylviane. "She's the Top." *Dance Magazine* 85, no. 12 (December 2011): 26–30.

Fitzgerald, F. Scott. *Echoes of the Jazz Age (1931).* Accessed March 13, 2018. https://pdcrodas.webs.ull.es/anglo/ScottFitzgeraldEchoesOfTheJazzAge.pdf.

Franko, Mark. *The Work of Dance: Labor, Movement, and Identity in the 1930s.* Middletown, CT: Wesleyan University Press, 2002.

Griffin, Farrah Jasmine. "Cake Walk, Shimmy, and Charleston: *Babylon Girls: Black Women Performers and the Shaping of the Modern*, Review." *The Women's Review of Books* 26, no. 4 (July/August 2009): 12–13.

Hutcheon, Linda. *A Theory of Parody: The Teachings of Twentieth-Century Art Forms.* Urbana, IL: Chicago University Press, 2000.

Isherwood, Charles. "Thoroughly Modern Millie." *Variety*, April 18, 2002. http://variety.com/2002/legit/reviews/thoroughly-modern-millie-6-1200550210/.

Jameson, Fredric. *Postmodernism, Or, The Cultural Logic of Late Capitalism.* Durham, NC: Duke University Press, 1991.

McQuirter, Marya A. "Awkward Moves: Dance Lessons from the 1940s." In *Dancing Many Drums: Excavation in African American Dance*, edited by Thomas F. DeFrantz, Madison, WI: The University of Wisconsin Press, 2002, 81–104.

Oxman, Steven. "Thoroughly Modern Millie." *Variety*, October 30, 2000. https://variety.com/2000/legit/reviews/thoroughly-modern-millie-2-1200464478/.

Pao, Angela, C. "Green Glass and Emeralds: Citation, Performance, and the Dynamics of Ethnic Parody in *Thoroughly Modern Millie*," *Multi-Ethnic Literature in the U.S. Volume* 36, no. 4 (Winter 2011): 35–60.

Peiss, Kathy. *Cheap Amusements Working Women and Leisure in Turn-of-the-Century New York.* Philadelphia, PA: Temple University Press, 1996.

Playbill. "*Thoroughly Modern Millie*." Accessed July 28, 2018. http://www.playbill.com/production/thoroughly-modern-millie-marquis-theatre-vault-0000008183.

Siegle, Barbara, and Scott Siegle. "*Thoroughly Modern Millie*." *Theatremania.com*, April 19, 2002. https://www.theatermania.com/new-york-city-theater/reviews/thoroughly-modern-millie_2097.html.

Shira. "*Dance of the Seven Veils.*" Accessed July 8, 2018, http://www.shira.net/sevenveils.htm.

Tesori, Jeanine, Dick Scanlan, Donald Sosin, and Milton Okun. *Thoroughly Modern Millie*, Vocal Selections, New York, NY: Cherry Lane Publishing, 2003.

Thoroughly Modern Millie. Directed by George Roy Hill, Universal City, CA: Universal Studios, 1967, http://www.imdb.com/title/tt0062362/fullcredits?ref_=tt_ov_st_sm, accessed March 26, 2018.

Tomko, Linda J. *Dancing Class: Gender, Ethnicity and Social Divides in American Dance, 1890–1920.* Indianapolis: Indiana University Press, 1999.

Wolf, Stacy Ellen. *Changed for Good: A Feminist History of the Broadway Musical.* New York: Oxford University Press, 2011.

5 "I need to do the Black Bottom!"

Demystifying Nostalgia in *The Wild Party*

An embittered and tight-jawed Dolores (Eartha Kitt) intones a derisive warning, "So you think the party's gonna last forever, […] you'll always fly this high, but that depends. The higher the high, the harder you're gonna, Crash back down, When it ends."[1] And thus, a faint dawn light creeps over the half-naked and drunk bodies strewn about Queenie and Burrs's dilapidated New York apartment. Lipstick is smeared on women's faces and smudged on men's stretched-out undershirts. Some guests are passed out, some crawl half-heartedly towards their belongings, and others cast glazed eyes around the trashed apartment, taking in the aftermath of a rogue gathering, alcohol bash, drug binge, and orgy – a wild party. The merrymaking and indulgence is long over, Queenie (Toni Collette) stands alone center stage; the pre-dawn light glints off her flushed skin and dishevelled hair. She is momentarily lost in revelry. An allusion to the opening vaudeville number of the musical assembles in silhouette behind her, a tableau of dance hall girls takes up seductive postures seen earlier on. Queenie resists being drawn back into her old burlesque routine – but what a routine it had been! The image of Queenie's sexy and rough striptease with her fellow vaudeville dancers begins to pulse behind her. Just two hours earlier, horns had wailed in delight to signal Queenie's upcoming striptease, and now instruments sustain long and low tones. What happened to these characters and bodies on stage? What caused the wild and rowdy high to turn to such a somber and still low?

The Wild Party – A Poem and a Musical

At the top the 2000 Broadway musical *The Wild Party,* by composer and lyricist Michael John LaChiusa and director George C. Wolfe, six men stroll on stage and describe the yet-to-be-seen Queenie, "Gray eyes, Lips like coals aglow. Her face was a tinted, mask of snow."[2] Queenie and her chorus of dancers enter; they take up wide stances, they dip and grind their hips through deep carnal lunges; they stroke their supple bodies; they take charge of the men. Queenie struts and poses. She wears cheap satin tap shorts over her black stockings and garter belt; her gaudy top exposes pale skin and deep cleavage. She walks upstage and sits on the knee of a male patron while the others explain, "Queenie was sexually

DOI: 10.4324/9781003163688-8

ambitious."[3] This statement is chanted in a round as all gather to grab and pet Queenie. The dancers and patrons of the vaudeville venue take up the throbbing beat as their bodies press together. Blaring horns and percussive drums bring the song to a climax and the group explodes forward to form a line at the footlights. The burlesque dancers, lit from below, are sexy, yet garish. The music is bold, brassy, and at times discordant. Queenie removes her top with little flourish. The men sing, "She never inquired of the men she desired; [...] she liked her lovers violent and vicious" to describe her taste in men.[4] Queenie soaks up the attention, struts downstage center, and swings her hips in a figure-eight motion as her waving arms cast sinister shadows upstage. Queenie is a sexual animal who thrives on attention and pleasure – the men's leers and thirsty grimaces seem to suit her just fine. It's a regular day on the job for Queenie, the protagonist in Joseph Moncure March's controversial 1928 poem *The Wild Party,* upon which the musical is based.

March's poem is a book length portrayal of the deteriorating decadence of the Jazz Age as illustrated by a party gone wrong. The book was banned in Boston for "sexual reference and booze-drenched scenes," though published and released outside of the Boston area in 1928.[5] March opens the poem, "Queenie was a blonde and her age stood still, and she danced twice a day in vaudeville."[6] The language of the poem, written mostly in rhyming couplets, is described as "dynamic, quick, witty, sinister and concise."[7] March creates a portrait of the Jazz Age in his description of the music: "A chord rang out: turned blue, and ran, Through a syncopating vamp, And the song began, The verse was nothing – but the chorus was Art; And its music was enough to tear you apart."[8] The description of the music captures the tension between the joyful anguish of splendour and the boredom with the routine that inhabits the characters in the story.

The tension in the music March describes bleeds over into Queenie's clash between her desires and her despondencies. The contrast between the opening and ending of both the poem and musical is vast but not surprising. Queenie begins her initial conversation with Burrs, her live-in lover, asking "When was the last time we had a real party?" and ends the play standing in the morning light and removing her make-up with Burrs dead on the floor of the apartment.[9] The betrayal of lovers, the decay of once decadent indulgences, and the search for bodily contact with anyone meaningful has come to an end for Queenie; Mr. Black, her object of lust for the night, has run off to escape the police and Burrs is dead. March ends the poem, "The door sprang open, And the cops rushed in."[10] The abrupt end emblematically closes the door on the Jazz Age. March's writing, erotic and dark, leaves the reader with a cold image of the law taking over and shutting down the wild party, and ultimately the era.

On stage, the ending is decidedly more ambiguous. After Burrs is shot, Queenie walks out of the swirl of vaudeville performances forming behind her (recharged by Burrs's drunken performance of his vaudeville routine in smeared blackface). Queenie gestures a goodbye to Burrs, Kate, and the others. She sings, "This is what it is [...] This is what it is to be scared," and begins to remove her make-up, something Black had tried to do, which she sharply drew away from.[11]

She whispers, "This is what it is to live in light."[12] The final stage directions read: "*Queenie is bathed in morning light.*"[13] Wolfe and LaChiusa create a softer yet more perplexing end to the piece by having Queenie stand contemplating her life, with sirens in the distance. Having finally hit rock bottom, there is the suggestion, in an upward glance and slight lift in the chest from Queenie, that the only direction for her to go at the end of the party is up. Perhaps in that look, in the slow-fade to black, there is a suggestion that the consideration of rebuilding or starting fresh is crossing her mind. Queenie's experience echoes the expiration of heady and hedonistic times, overdue at the close of the 1920s, and also a similar consideration or warning in the present moment of the 2000 production, which was still a time of relative economic boom. The ending is certainly ambiguous, and leaves us wondering – what next?

Even more, why explore the train wreck of Queenie's life in the first place? What sort of bodily experience is happening in the second half of the Roaring Twenties that differs from the first half? How does the youthful and exuberant "Millie" morph into a washed up and gin-soaked "Queenie"? An interrogation of how bodies move through *The Wild Party* helps get at humanity's continued search and desire for sexual and intellectual intimacy and how a nostalgia for this sort of hyper-indulgence can be misplaced. John Heilpern describes the frightening truth to the musical, "Wild Party is the underbelly of America's meltdown into self-gratification and blurred identities, of party time and exploding violence, of forbidden fruit and the price we pay."[14] LaChiusa's music and lyrics and Wolfe's dramaturgy lure the audience in by harnessing desire as a nostalgic impulse. Like March's poem, in his theatricalization Wolfe appeals to an inadmissible longing for forbidden and indulgent activities of the past (one's own or in general). The re-release of March's poem with seventy-five drawings by Art Spiegelman in 1994 created a renewed interest in the dark poetry, and the clandestine behavior of the Jazz Age.[15] The poem, now in the graphic novel style presented by Spiegelman, was the inspiration for two musical interpretations of the poem.[16]

The fascination for the hedonism of the jazz age on paper is brought to life on stage with a sense of exaggeration and cynicism that slowly wears away at our expected reminiscence of the Jazz Age. That amplification in the poem of character and era, vividly brought to life in Spiegelman's drawings was attractive to LaChiusa as "the 1920s milieu and the bigger-than-life personalities offer him the chance to write set pieces, or "numbers."[17] Furthermore, as he explains, he was keen to "write in the jazz style of the twenties," about a party, that was not just a "wild" party but "a metaphor for our day-to-day existence."[18] With Wolfe at the directorial helm, he explores the lure of the era, and demystifies previously constructed assumptions and mythologies. By way of music and movement, *The Wild Party* entices one in to a nostalgia for an age of indulgence and wildness. The subsequent breaking down of those desires in the same manner (via the choreography and score) invites reflection on the consequences of acting on emotions while oblivious to surrounding people and cultures.

Wolfe's dramaturgical strategy is to dive into the highs and lows of Queenie's life and use the microcosm of the party and personalities of the partygoers as a kind of super-structure for the early 2000s (the time of the production), particularly regarding the continuing neo-liberalization of the U.S. since the 1970s. Through the physicalized sleaziness and depraved posturing of many of the characters, Wolfe points to a necessity for an inventory of the self and society. In the aftermath of the first Iraq War and the Clinton scandals, along with other abuses of power, as described by Heilpern, taking a look at self and society is a needed and courageous venture. Wolfe explains the essence of the poem that attracted him, "that all of us cultivate weapons to survive, and at some point in our lives those weapons stand in the way of our growth."[19] A way into the earlier question regarding the bodily experience at the end of the Jazz Age, is to explore how choreographer Joey McKneely embodies the themes of March's poem on stage, particularly through Queenie's dancing of the Black Bottom and the overall treatment of the dance in the musical.

Before analyzing the movement in the musical, tracing the origins of the Black Bottom helps situate the social dance in the era. This also helps one understand how the movement is an integral part of Wolfe's secondary dramaturgical imperative to consider how the self-destructive and indulgent behavior of the partygoers is at the cost of cultural theft of Black performance forms. Wolfe makes his point concerning appropriation early on in the show, setting a bold and disturbing tone from the start. Burrs's (Mandy Patinkin) clown piece "Marie is Tricky" that follows Queenie's opening performance is done in blackface and is a combination of insult, satire, and physical comedy. The choice to include the blackface is an extreme reminder of the insensitivities and self-interest the characters inhabit and follows Wolfe's dramaturgy to show the rawness of self-indulgence.[20] The blackface is performed by Mandy Patinkin in a sort of minstrel show-like manner complete with a title board on an easel. This framing evokes Jewish vaudeville performer Al Jolson who made a substantial career performing in blackface. This connection points to the cultural theft and appropriation of Black art by white artists.[21] The connection to Al Jolson and emphasis on whiteness is picked up by Heilpern who describes, "The idea of him playing Burrs the entertainer in Jolsonesque blackface is brilliantly creepy."[22] Indeed, the blackface is disturbing, and introducing it with such force so early on in the show is a move by Wolfe that functions to remind where ownership of jazz music and movement lies – a reclaiming he fully realizes with *Shuffle Along* in 2016. Wolfe creates his own "pocket of resistance" as the poem does not have this reference.[23] His choice to include blackface provides a stark reminder of the contestation between race, performance, and appropriation in the 1920s.

Background of the Black Bottom

Prior to throwing a party, Queenie asks Burrs, "When was the last time I danced the Black Bottom?" to which he replies, "You're not gettin' any younger [...] child."[24] Queenie stands in front of Burrs snaking her hips back and forth, and twisting her heels, anxious to jump into the untamed and often licentious dance of the 1920s. Her opportunity to perform comes in a moment of awkwardness in the party when the two producers Gold and Goldberg try to escape from a conversation with the aging performer Dolores, and out of the blue Queenie screams out and *faux*-faints. When all try to revive her and ask what she needs, she feigns weakness, and then gasps, "I need to do the Black Bottom!"[25] She jumps up and begins to dance and shake and shimmy, drawing the fourteen-year-old Nadine in, "Gotcha! Come on […] it's time to get nasty!"[26] This set up names the social dance, separating it from the Charleston. How does the transition into the mid-1920s and the evolution of the Black Bottom help explain the complexities of the Jazz Age?

For some, the thrills and highs of the 1920s were getting harder and harder to attain as the decade progressed. This is in part due to a desensitization to the wildness of the behavior and white patrons becoming immune to what had previously thrilled them.[27] The apparent risqué nature of the Black Bottom helped to embody the growing desperation for continued desire and pleasure – a void the Charleston was no longer filling. Investigating the transition from the Charleston into the Black Bottom also troubles the continued transformation of Black dances into white performance styles and shifts in social culture as the decade progressed.[28] Fitzgerald describes how the second half of the decade was:

> like a children's party taken over by the elders, leaving the children puzzled … rather taken aback. By 1923 their elders, tired of watching the carnival with ill-concealed envy, had discovered that young liquor will take the place of young blood, and with a whoop the orgy began.[29]

The world-weary, self-destructive and indulgent behaviors of the more "adult" generation proliferate in *The Wild Party*. So, what exactly separates one dance from the other? How do foundational roots differ?

Many connect the Black Bottom with other dances that occurred at the jook house. However, while it was performed there, and part of the jook experience, the Black Bottom is not derived from the rural or backwoods setting of the jook house. Zora Neale Hurston explains the Black Bottom "really originated in the Jook section of Nashville, Tennessee, around Fourth Avenue. This is a tough neighbourhood known as Black Bottom – hence the name."[30] The Black Bottom emerged as part of the general fluidity of Black social dance forms, and also in part as a transition out of the Charleston, which was being quickly taken up by white performers. In Lynne Emery's *Black Dancing in the United States 1619–1970*, Lester A. Walton describes the need Black communities had to continually create dances that were from and championed their own social milieu:

> These Negro dances invariably became the rage with white people months and sometimes years, after colored people have waxed enthusiastic

over them. When the Charleston becomes a fad with the white public, colored folk were hoofing the Black Bottom.[31]

The Black Bottom became popular as a way of tuning into and embodying something that insinuates greater sensuality than the Charleston. While this indirect intimation was embodied by the liberation of the body in the Charleston, there is something more complex and daring about the Black Bottom, particularly as it was generally more popular with women. Further, the Black Bottom was less connected to high society than the Charleston, and that class distinction made it attractive to mass culture, particularly in the second half of the 1920s, when it overtook the Charleston in popularity.

Like the Charleston, the Black Bottom dispersed to the broader public through a performance on Broadway. "The Original Black Bottom Dance" was part of the 1923 musical *Dinah* with music and lyrics by Tim Brymn and Sidney Bechet. Additionally, white film actress Ann Pennington performed the dance in George White's *Scandals of 1926*. [32] Much like the Charleston, dancing masters refined the original form of the Black Bottom to make it more "suitable for the ballroom."[33] As the dance passed from bodies of Black dancers to white, in such instances both on stage and off, notions of authorship and authenticity emerged in the transformation. One of the interesting elements of this tension in the dance extends beyond a sense of artistic credit, but circulates more around the subjecthood of those who are doing the dance and the "power dynamics inherent to choreographic authorship."[34] Anthea Kraut unravels this complex issue, explaining, "choreographic copyright, in other words, has been a key site for all kinds of dancers' negotiations of subjecthood, including and especially their status as raced and gendered subjects (always cross-cut by class)."[35] Given the body is a prime site in which to examine historical agency and ownership of cultural mores, one's bodily identification can often be seen through the movement they take on, an identification of which is put forth in *The Wild Party*, particularly in Queenie's decry of the dance. While Queenie neither owns or authors the dance, she uses it as an apparatus to define her identity and status at that moment. The dance, in this case, shows her as one who has greater daring than those at the party, and that willingness to risk is a commodity in that moment of the party, and at the moment of the Jazz Age.

What is unique about the Black Bottom is that there was not necessarily a connection to a partner from the start. While the Charleston began this separation, with "breakaways" and moments of individuality, the Black Bottom took the next step, and brought the dance out of the partnered style.[36] Barbara Cohen-Stratyner explains the Black Bottom did not develop into a couple dance, but "remained a frontal performance."[37] This development decreases the level of transformation of the dance to the stage, as it has a built-in presentational quality. Dancers, mostly women, would face a preferred front, generally seeking a specific gaze from someone watching. Though there is an objectification of the female body, the dance salutes the individual performer, granting Queenie, for example, a sense of autonomy as the center of attention.

Description of the Black Bottom

The Black Bottom is a combination of "Jay Bird" steps, as in the Charleston, with knees pumping up and down, however when knees retract (and legs straighten) buttocks push out backwards, almost as if one is trying to close a door with their backside. There is often a retreating motion to the step with slides or slips going backwards, where the motivation for the movement comes from behind. Most apparent in the various footage of the dance are the influence of previous dances, mostly the Charleston, but also the Shimmy, the Bunny Hop, the Turkey Trot etc. The original Black Bottom involved the slapping of hands on the body and "chugging" hips forward and back.[38] The torso would lean back lower and lower to the floor, accompanied by hip swivelling and circling, a sort of "stirring" of the pelvis in a sensual manner.[39] Pointedly, the dance was often so modified that Black Americans did not recognize the whitened versions seen on stage.[40] The distinguishing feature of the Black Bottom that threads through video clips and descriptions is the slapping of the buttocks with hands in some manner or another.

Demystifying Indulgence Through Nostalgia

To start, the nostalgia in *The Wild Party* is initiated by the creation of the burlesque world of vaudeville on stage. LaChiusa and Wolfe, who collaborated on the book of the musical describe the mood of March's piece in their opening stage directions,

> "*A line of CHORINES enters, QUEENIE among them. SHE is a piece of work. Not young, not old. Sexy, but not because of her costume. Her face is powdered white. QUEENIE and the CHORINES strut their stuff. It's a nasty routine*".[41]

The choice to have vaudeville-style numbers or pastiches is not uncommon in musical theatre, but in this backwards glance to the Jazz Age in *The Wild Party* there is a realization that amongst the decadence and indulgence of the period there also grew a deep-seated obsession, nastiness, paranoia, and mistrust.[42] By beginning the nostalgic journey back to the twenties in *The Wild Party* with a vulgar vaudeville routine, a more complex and disturbing image of the era emerges allowing for reflection that works in opposition to the perky "flapper" that opens *Thoroughly Modern Millie*. This less-than-rose-colored nostalgia is derived from observing the self-destruction, obliviousness, and instability that infiltrates all the characters in *The Wild Party*.

Queenie calls out the Black Bottom as *the* dance she "needs" to do, when the effect of previous vices have worn out or no longer provide the meaning they once did. She sings of what she finds the Black Bottom does for her, the ultimate physicality of something new and novel: "Queenie needs some newer skin, Newer sex and newer sin […] Everybody watch Queenie go wild, Gotta get high, Gotta get thrilled, Gotta get fizzed gotta get filled."[43] Queenie believes that somehow indulgence can lead to fulfillment. This risky mindset is mixed with a misplaced sense of nostalgia for times when one was able to turn inhibitions off and explores the sense of freedom, excitement and extravagance that is celebrated in common images of the 1920s. The glories of indulgence, while celebrated in *Millie*, are starkly demystified in *The Wild Party*, while also exposing the violence that keeps racial and sexual hierarchies in place. A closer look at the choreography and its gestural extravagance explains how nostalgia for this sense of excess is activated and the damaging implications of this longing.[44]

Choreography in *The Wild Party*

Choreographer Joey McKneely began as a dancer on Broadway in *Carrie* (1988), *Jerome Robbins' Broadway* (1989), and *She Loves Me* (1993). He received his first opportunity to choreograph for Broadway and his first Tony Award nomination for choreography for *Smokey Joe's Café* (1995), followed by *The Life* (1997). He has explained one of his most remarkable experiences was working with Jerome Robbins in *Jerome Robbins' Broadway*. McKneely first learned the choreography for *West Side Story* from Jerome Robbins himself. He explains the unique experience with Robbins: "It was during these months of rehearsal that I remember watching Mr. Robbins: how his choreography always fit the situation and character. How simplicity of movement can convey more than words."[45] This experience helps in part to explain McKneely's keen awareness of movement intentions and engagement with the layering of meaning behind the dance, which extends to his use social dance as seen in the Black Bottom in *The Wild Party*.[46]

Because of the pastiche nature of LaChiusa's score for *The Wild Party*, McKneely created movement that imitates the original dances of the era, but also found embodied meaning identifiable in the twenty-first century. McKneely accomplishes two main feats with his choreography. First, he sets tone with his sexualized opening burlesque striptease. Second, he exposes any utopic or naive ideas about the joy of the Jazz Age with his crudely spectacularized Black Bottom. The nastiness of the opening burlesque, made particularly cutting by the sultry Collette and the trashy postures of the chorines, clearly establish the dark nature of the show.

The Black Bottom occurs in the story when Queenie goes on full tilt and becomes untamable by those around her. The stage directions describe the moment: "*QUEENIE dances, throwing herself at everyone, downing drinks, but nothing seems to lift her as high as she wants to go.*"[47] How this mix of the desire to be loved and to escape the self is interpreted becomes key. McKneely positions his social dance-based choreography in an overtly sexualized vein by having Queenie stand flat front, lick one hand and place it on her right back side and step forward, then lick the other and repeat on her left side. She bends over with legs splayed and hits her hands on the floor, then thrusts her hips forward with a forceful thrust of her pelvis. McKneely cuts straight to the risqué essence of the Black Bottom. There is no build up through the Charleston, or gentle introduction. The two D'Armano brothers repeat the same "lick and slap" choreography and immediately flank Queenie's side. The trio executes a double contraction of the core, as if shot twice in the stomach. At the same time, they throw their arms overhead and add an accented shout that emphasizes the aggressiveness of the pelvic thrust. The dance begins very forcefully, lacking any light or carefree tone; the movement is dirty and sensuous and performed only by those who have been singled out as leading a more sexually ambitious life style.[48] The Brothers continue the movement behind Queenie as she moves side to side in a grapevine style and starts singing. In an instrumental dance break the trio breaks into a choreography section with arms doing a lasso-like gesture overhead, while one foot pumps up and down acting as a pivot for the hips and buttocks to swing around; sharp hits of the arms side to side punctuate the movement and pick up the musical accents. Queenie is hoisted up by one of the partygoers and tossed onto the bed where she continues to squirm and writhe, all in service to her very self-aware and self-indulgent performance in front of the other party goers.

The other patrons join in the dance generally improvising along as the party and space become overtly sexualized.[49] Burrs jumps onto the bed and begins to do a very lewd version of the Black Bottom where he slowly licks his hand and wipes it on his lower body with a pronounced thrust of his pelvis back and forth. He continues this action with the other hand, standing high on the bed, center stage. Although the orgy occurs later in the show, the interpretation by Queenie and Burrs of the Black Bottom, in the context of *The Wild Party*, opens the door to the possibility of the ultimate group debauchery and decadence. The Black Bottom, in spite of its enhanced vulgarity and sexuality (added by McKneely), is in effect the beginning of the end for Queenie. The Black Bottom is the catalyst of the self-destruction that occurs in the musical. The dance pulls the pin that unfurls the dark and all-consuming indulgence in vice. Given how wrong the orgy goes – fourteen-year-old Nadine's cocaine infused rape, Queenie having sex with Black, and Burr's death – the dance functions to demystify any sentimentalism one might have for this level of indulgence.

Transferring the Black Bottom to the stage loses some of its origins from the street and private venues, as with the Slow Drag. However, the Black Bottom in its physicality already has a very bold and audacious style to it. Queenie's declaration of the dance (which is not in the poem) is a way to understand masculine aggressiveness through dance, set against Queenie's desire for attention. While the Black Bottom may be seen as a way for women to exert or demonstrate an empowerment over their sexuality, by having Burrs pick up on the gestures of the dance, a physicalized knowledge is gained as to how combative and aggressive Queenie and Burrs's relationship is. The blatant forcefulness of Burrs's need to be in control makes his killing of Black for having sex with Queenie believable. The Black Bottom, as interpreted by McKneely, offers a way into the sexual that is understood at a visceral level outside of words. Queenie's (and thus McKneely's) overt over-emphasis on the dance, however, is also telling of her insecurities, and perhaps Wolfe's schematics shine a light on the formal consequences of cultural theft. As the only woman to do the dance, Queenie's whiteness, accentuated by her white negligee, is obvious. Her vulgar, yet desperate movements are a reminder of the obliviousness with which white dancers took up Black dances. At the peak of the number, Queenie has abandoned any formal choreography and is sandwiched between the Brothers writhing forward and back. In this moment there is an interesting commingling of bodies between the Black brothers and Queenie, making clear the racialized nature of the dance.[50]

In a sharp beat, Queenie grimaces and she stops short stung by the realization Burrs is not dancing with her. She calls out for him and looks around for help, only to be interrupted by the grand arrival of her best friend and nemesis – the beautiful Kate and her handsome new beau, Mr. Black. Kate steals the spotlight and all attention from Queenie. Kate, as played by Black actress Tonya Pinkins, takes command of the show ("Best Friends") and reabsorbs the Blackness of the music and dance with expert skill and a professional nonchalance. The guests, including the young Nadine, gush over Kate's beauty and talent, as she is the one with a famous performing career, not Queenie. Kate stakes a claim for Black cultural ownership and power in the piece and recuperates a moment of dignity that had been shattered by Burrs's opening blackface routine. Kate's Black presence disrupts Queenie's white fantasy. Queenie is left abandoned, bitter, and physically destitute – a substantial contrast from only moments earlier. A sort of anti-nostalgia seeps into the musical, a not-so-subtle censure by Wolfe of the often-unashamed enjoyment of anything from the Jazz Age by Broadway audiences. The darker, more disturbing depictions of the Jazz Age work against the nostalgia some may have expected to experience at the outset of the show. By slowly dismantling the dynamic and titillating structure of the show, Wolfe puts forth a more nuanced and reflective consideration of the Jazz Age and its layered history.

Critical Reception

Critics overall were not very receptive of McKneely's looser choreography, found to be lacking in the tight formations and synchronicity expected in Broadway shows. Elyse Sommers states, "their go-go dancing and singing more frenetic than genuinely joyous," indicating an era specific misfire in terms dance.[51] While Sommers finds the dance on the hyper side, Ben Brantley describes the dance as much less: "There is minimal dancing at the party, which has been negligibly choreographed by Joey McKneely."[52] The question of whether McKneely's choreography is insignificant is an interesting one to unfold. Brantley is correct that there is minimal dancing at the party, though at the same time the party is always in motion and bodies are coming together and drifting apart throughout. This continued motion may be the frantic energy Sommer suggests, however, a more specific, synchronized dance sequence in the manner of Ashford's Charleston-based choreography in *Millie* would emphatically not have fit in dramaturgically. McKneely's physical shaping and modulation of dance styles of the 1920s embodies the indulgence of the party in two ways. Firstly, he establishes how hyper-sexual Queenie is in the opening burlesque, and secondly, he captures how reckless and in dire need of attention she is in her "spectacularized" licking and sexualization of the Brothers D'Armano in the Black Bottom song. Further, the vicious way Burrs takes on the movement signature, if not the extended choreography, helps situate him as the violent, jealous, and irrational vaudevillian monster he is. His vulgar Black Bottom demonstration works to support his behavior later when he and Mr. Black fight. The fact that the only people to be officially choreographed by McKneely into the Black Bottom are Queenie, the sexually risqué brothers, and the sexually abusive Burrs helps to assign the dance to those who have a desire to perform their sexuality for and at others. At a broader scale this overt performance of the self, particularly the racial impersonation, is how the Black Bottom is emblematic of the end of the Jazz Age.

Charles Isherwood describes in great detail the music, lighting, and set of the show, using very active descriptors, though there is little mention of bodies in motion:

> Vestiges of former grandeur cling to tattered, grimy wallpaper and peer gloomily through huge, broken windows. The haunting, delicately calibrated lighting … turns the room into a ghoulish canvas for the revelers' flickering silhouettes, which leap and dance in frenzied patterns against the walls.[53]

Bodies do cling, eyes peer around lovers, and partygoers leap and dance in frenzied patterns, though Isherwood prefers to assign these moves to the lighting design. It is the bodies in motion and the music that create the world of the poem amongst the minimal set, however, critics struggle to describe the sultry and provocative movement. Isherwood does describe the score as "firmly grounded in the music of the period in which the show is set," with melodies that "tickle the ear with pleasing, time-tested, riffs full of rumbling piano runs and scorching horn bursts," recognizing that LaChiusa succeeds musically in bringing March's Jazz Age poem to life.[54]

While critics overall disregard the choreography as an impactful factor in the show, the contrast between the over-active, hyper-sexual Queenie in most of the play and her stilled body at the end does much to emphasize how eagerly and intensely the behaviors of the 1920s were consumed. *The Wild Party* illustrates a party as an organism in itself that pulses and pushes along, consuming guests into its chaos as it goes. By the end, like the end of 1920s, all is lost. The obliviousness of the outside world and an over-confidence in veritably every aspect of life led to greater risk-taking, and the "flimsy structure" of the Jazz Age crashed to the ground.[55] Fitzgerald explains the end of the heady days of wild expectations and ideals that no one considered could come to an end: "But it was not to be. Somebody had blundered and the most expensive orgy in history was over."[56] LaChiusa, Wolfe, and McKneely work together to problematize the shiny stereotypes and cultural appropriations of the 1920s. They trouble the nostalgia that surrounds the era by offering a glimpse into a party gone too far and question the possibilities of reconciling the effects of indulgent behaviors then and now.

Towards the end of the musical, Dolores has a stark moment of honesty that foreshadows the shooting of Burrs. Her torch song holds in it a double meaning of the looming consequences of the "Second Gilded Age"[57] begun in the 1990s and the here and now: "I can tell you no party lasts forever [...] So you better hope to Jesus or Mohammad, Or whatever, That you got the right stuff, When in ends."[58] The purposeful infelicitous generation of a sentimentalized or restorative nostalgia by Wolfe towards the end of the production creates "not a reactionary desire for the past but a coherent critique of the present and a call for a different future."[59] In continuance with Wolfe's practice of recovery as resistance, as seen in *Shuffle Along* (2016), he both uses nostalgia and takes a stand against it as he unfolds the tale of the deeply flawed characters of March's poem. The demystification of nostalgia in *The Wild Party* allows for a contemplation of cultural theft, the cultural body, and an overall sense of presentness in the modern moment.

Notes

1 "When It Ends," *The Wild* Party, music and lyrics Michael John LaChiusa, 2000 in *The New American Musical: An Anthology From the End of The Century*, ed. by Wiley Hausum (New York: Theatre Communication Group, 2003), (citations of dialogue or stage directions in parenthesis).
2 LaChiusa, "Queenie Was a Blonde," 2000.
3 Ibid.
4 Ibid.
5 Peggy Downing, "This Wild Party," *Global Dispatches: Expert Commentary and Analysis*, October 13, 2015, http://www.theglobaldispatches.com/articles/the-wild-party. Downing further explains of the poem (and March's other book-length poem about the Jazz Age, *The Set-Up*): "The poems went in and out of fashion and both have been made into films: Robert Wise, in 1949 filmed The Set-Up and there was a Merchant Ivory Productions in 1975 version of The Wild Party."
6 Joseph Moncure March, *The Wild Party*, 2nd Edition (New York, NY: Covici, Friede Publishers, 1928), 9.
7 Downing, "This Wild Party".
8 March, *The Wild Party*, 62. The challenge to put sound to a poem that describes the music so expressively may explain part of the desire people have had to turn the poem into a musical or movie with music.
9 LaChiusa, "Wild Party," 2000.
10 March, *The Wild Party*.

11 LaChiusa, "This Is What It Is," 2000.

12 Ibid.

13 *The Wild* Party, book by George C. Wolfe, music and lyrics Michael John LaChiusa, 2000 in *The New American Musical: An Anthology From the End of The Century*, ed. by Wiley Hausam (New York: Theatre Communication Group, 2003), 444, (further citations of dialogue or stage directions in parenthesis).

14 John Heilpern, "Welcome to The Wild Party! Dangerous, Seedy … Fantastic," *The Observer,* April 24, 2000, http://observer.com/2000/04/welcome-to-the-wild-party-dangerous-seedy-fantastic/, accessed April 28, 2018.

15 For an interview with Spiegelman about *The Wild Party* and images of his graphic drawings see: https://web.archive.org/web/20190314171723/https://musicalstagecompany.com/musical-notes/art-spiegelman-talks-the-wild-party/.

16 Both Andrew Lippa and Michael John LaChiusa were inspired by the 1994 re-release of the poem with 75 drawings by Art Spiegelman in *The Wild* Party, based on Joseph Moncure March's *The Wild Party* New York, NY: Covici, Friede Publishers, 1928 (New York: NY: Pantheon Books, 1994). While the base material and characters for both musicals are the same. The Lippa version focuses more on the "love" triangle between Queenie, Burrs, and Black. LaChiusa focuses on the experience of the partygoers and social culture at the end of the Jazz Age and the relationships between the characters, and is therefore of more interest to this exploration.

17 Kenneth Jones, "LaChiusa's *Wild Party* Seen in NYC Sneak Peek; Wolfe Embraces Jazz Age," *Playbill,* February 17, 2000, https://playbill.com/article/lachiusas-wild-party-seen-in-nyc-sneak-peek-wolfe-embraces-jazz-age-com-87211Mervyn

18 Rothstein, "When Worlds Collide: LaChiusa and Wolfe's *The Wild Party* Reaches Broadway," *Playbill,* March 10, 2000, https://playbill.com/article/when-worlds-collide-lachiusa-and-wolfes-the-wild-party-reaches-broadway-com-101412.

19 Ibid.

20 John Heilpern at *The Observer,* who describes the show as "thrillingly wayward and risky, creating its own pocket of resistance," "Welcome to The Wild Party! Dangerous, Seedy … Fantastic," *The Observer,* April 24, 2000, http://observer.com/2000/04/welcome-to-the-wild-party-dangerous-seedy-fantastic/.

21 Burrs' whiteness, privilege, and offensiveness are the main issue here. Furthermore, the fact that Jolson and Patinkin are Jewish, and Patinkin has performed and recorded a lot of Jewish music, there is a secondary nod to how assimilated Jewish immigrants are into American culture today, which is not the case for Black Americans. Andrea Most explains that though various Jewish artists such as Al Jolson and Sophie Tucker "seemed closely aligned with the black artists … the structure and content of the plays they wrote and performed revealed their ambivalence toward racial issues." Andrea Most, *Making Americans: Jews and the Broadway Musical* (MA: Harvard University Press, 2004), 26. Wolfe may be being more generalised and is pointing at white America and whiteness, rather than Jewish actors specifically, however the "fraught relationship" between Jewish and Black Americans, "with its episodes of cooperation, compassion, suspicion, and betrayal, forms a significant and turbulent backdrop to the story of American Jews in the theatre," is not to be overlooked. Ibid., 26.

22 Heilpern, "Welcome to The Wild Party!", 2000.

23 Ibid. The blackface was an addition made by Wolfe. The poem reads: "She lived at present with a man named Burrs, whose act came on just after hers. A clown, of renown: Three-sheeted all over town." March, 10.

24 LaChiusa, "Wild Party," 2000.

25 Michael John LaChiusa and George C. Wolfe. The Wild Party. In The New American Musical: An Anthology From the End of The Century, ed. by Wiley Hausam (New York: Theatre Communication Group, 2003), 391.

26 Ibid.
27 Lisa Doolittle, "The Trianon and On: Reading Mass Social Dancing in the 1930s and 1940s in Alberta, Canada in *Ballroom, Boogie, Shimmy Sham, Shake: A Social and Popular Dance Reader,* ed. Julie Malnig (Chicago: University of Illinois Press, 2009), 119.
28 Jayna Brown observes how dance was used as a platform to work out frustrations, "white people used Black dance to restore their bodies with the spontaneity and exhilaration promised by the dream of a new democracy." Brown, *Babylon Girls: Black Women Performers and the Shaping of the Modern* (Durham, NC: Duke University Press, 2008), 175.
29 F. Scott Fitzgerald, *Echoes of the Jazz Age (1931).* Accessed March 13, 2018, http s://pdcrodas.webs.ull.es/anglo/ScottFitzgeraldEchoesOfTheJazzAge.pdf, 3.
30 Zora Neale Hurston, "Mimicry" in Nancy Cunard's *Negro Anthology* (London, UK: Wishart & Company, 1934), 44. The Stearnses explain as well that the name also derived from the song "Jacksonville Rounders," though the song title was not as popular as the Black Bottom as the word "rounders" was a stand in for "pimp." Marshall and Jean Stearns. *Jazz Dance: The Story of American Vernacular Dance* (New York: Da Capo Press, 1994), 110.
31 Lester A. Walton, "Lucky Roberts Autographs Songs for the Prince" (no publica-tion given), Dance clipping file, Dance Collection, Lincoln Center of the Per-forming Art, New York, October 17, 1926, quoted in Lynne Fauley Emery's *Black Dancing in the United States 1619–1970* (Palo Alto, CA: National Press Books, 1972), 223.
32 Stearns and Stearns, *Jazz Dance*, 110. Anthea Kraut in *Choreographing Copyright: Race, Gender, and Intellectual Property Rights in American Dance* (Oxford, UK: Oxford University Press, 2016) explores Alberta Hunter's claim to the Black Bottom as being one of the first attempts at copyrighting a dance. Kraut explains the compli-cations to Hunter's claim as in fact it was verbal, made in front of white audiences in 1925. Kraut describes the lack of paperwork, "it is possible that Hunter's claim was only rhetorical, that telling a newspaper reporter that she had the dance copy-righted was as official as she needed to be" Ibid., 145. Kraut further explains that when *George White's Scandals* began in 1926, they claimed to have invented the dance, wiping out the history that the Stearnses and others claimed went back to at least 1919. It is interesting also to note that, "as a social dance with no single author, the Black Bottom is precisely the kind of dance the law has consistently barred from copyright protection." Ibid., 143. See pages 142–150 in Kraut's *Chor-eographing Copyright* for full description of Hunter's claim and further complications.
33 The Stearnses explain the refinement of the Black Bottom, "The chief gesture that survived on the ballroom floor was a genteel slapping of the backside, along with a few hops forward and back." Stearns and Stearns, *Jazz Dance*, 111.
34 Kraut, *Choreographing Copyright*, x.
35 Ibid., xiv.
36 Breakaway means to pull away from one's partner numerous times in a dance to complete one's own steps, alterations, or showing individualized physical acrobatics or tricks.
37 Barbara Cohen-Stratyner, "A Thousand Raggy, Draggy Dances: Social Dance in Broadway Musical Comedy in the 1920s." In *Ballroom, Boogie, Shimmy Sham, Shake: A Social and Popular Dance Reader*, edited by Julie Malnig, (Chicago: University of Illinois Press, 2009), 223.
38 Chugging is a hop forward with two feet without the soles or heels of the foot leaving the floor, giving a very low to the ground appearance of shifting forward in the space.
39 Interpretations of the Black Bottom are varied. These descriptions have come from YouTube videos of the dance, "The 'Real' Black Bottom (1927)," https://www.

youtube.com/watch?v=rQ9qapVmWi4, accessed April 4, 2018; "The Black Bottom 1926, and the Black Bottom Dance," https://www.youtube.com/watch?v=jTR6xBeC2xA, accessed April 4, 2018. There is also a "Black Bottom Dance" in the film 1956 *All Things in Life Are Free*.

40 In Lynne Fauley Emery's *Black Dancing in the United States 1619–1970* (Palo Alto, CA: National Press Books, 1972) page 228, Emery refers to an anecdote from Zora Neale Hurston's section on "Mimicry" in Nancy Cunard's *Negro Anthology*, "when the Negroes who knew the Black Bottom in its cradle [Nashville] saw the Broadway Version they asked each other, 'Is you learnt dat NEW Black Bottom yet?'" Zora Neale Hurston in Jane Cunard's *Negro Anthology* (London, UK: Wishart & Company, 1934), 46.

41 LaChiusa and Wolfe, "The Wild Party".

42 Some musicals with vaudeville -styled numbers include the 1959 musical *Gypsy* with music and lyrics by Jule Styne and Stephen Sondheim, and book by Arthur Laurent, as well as the 2013 play *The Nance* by Douglas Carter Beane. A strong example of pastiche-like structures in a musical is the "Love-land" section in Stephen Sondheim's *Follies*.

43 LaChiusa, "Black Bottom," 2000.

44 "Gestural" in this context refers to the use of movement actions that have a universally understood meaning, particularly in a sensual way. It should be mentioned that a Brechtian-style is established from the beginning of *The Wild Party* using placards on easels with titles for each section. Further, there is a sense at times of performers "adopt[ing] a 'gestural' style which literally points to the artificiality of what they are doing," as in the opening burlesque routine. Additionally, the rhythmic nature of the poem on which the story is based gives the production a fable-like quality, adding a heightened sense of artificiality to the piece. Bertolt Brecht, "A Short Organum for the Theatre (1948)," in *Brecht on Theatre: The Development of an Aesthetic*, 1st ed. Edited by Bertolt Brecht and John Willet, 233–246. (New York: Hill and Wang, 1964), 233–246.

45 Joey McKneely, "Choreographer Joey McKneely Chronicles His 20-Year Rumble with *West Side Story*," *Broadway.com*, November 15, 2013, https://vancouver.broadway.com/buzz/173113/choreographer-joey-mckneely-chronicles-his-20-year-rumble-with-west-side-story/ accessed April 4, 2018.

46 McKneely was then tapped by Arthur Laurents to help update the choreography of *West Side Story* for the 2013 Broadway revival. Laurents, the original book writer and only surviving member of the original creative team wanted the show to be "Grittier. More realistic." McKneely combed through the choreography, tweaking small movements here and gestures there – the challenge being to not change or adapt the choreography, but to decide what embodied features felt dated. McKneely on the changes: "Most people would never notice the changes, for we have worked hard to make them organic to each moment. Those who know the show more intimately might see the differences; however, the choreographic elements are always Robbins." Ibid.

47 LaChiusa and Wolfe, "The Wild Party".

48 In parts of the dialogue and songs the brothers, Oscar and Phil, sing in the musical, there is an overt implication of their homosexuality and a suggestion of an incestuous relationship. March describes the relationship between the brothers, Oscar and Phil, though does not expand on the term "Brothers," as to whether it is literal or a stage name. There is one moment where Jack kisses Phil: "'You kissed him! I saw you – you nasty sneak!' Phil raised his eyebrow: 'Well – what if I did?' A groan from Oscar. He sank down." March, *The Wild Party*, 59. There is a hint in these stanzas that a protest from Oscar would have been unjust in an incestuous situation.

49 The improvised nature of the dance towards the end stands in contrast to more articulated moves that McKeely does. The choreography falls away and the

performers improvise in their own manner and physicality. This brings up a point, that requires further examination beyond the scope of this project, as to those in a cast with extensive knowledge of a social dance or style adding to the choreography. This concept is briefly explored in chapter nine in regards to those with knowledge and experience in Japanese traditional dance who help support the choreographer's work. For an extended conversation about recognition of choreography and co-choreography of musical theatre see chapter five of Liza Gennaro's *Making Broadway Dance* where she discusses Peter Gennaro's choreographing the Shark's dance sequences. Liza Gennaro, *Making Broadway Dance* (Oxford University Press, 2021), 122–125.

50 Of note, Black actress Vanessa Williams was originally cast in the role of Queenie however had to withdraw due to pregnancy. The dynamics of a Black Queenie would have shifted the interpretation of the piece and the movement therein. LaChiusa originally wrote the show with her in mind, and explains, "I don't think of it as something that was lost in the piece, but it would have been fascinating to see how an audience responded to a black Queenie. The show is all about masks that we wear culturally and the removal of those masks over the course of the party." Jonathan Frank, "Interview with Michael John LaChiusa," *Talkin' Broadway,* talkinbroadway.com, https://www.talkinbroadway.com/cabaret/lachiusa.html, accessed 13 September, 2022.

51 Elyse Sommer, "The Wild Party" *Curtain Up,* 2000, accessed 13 September, 2022, http://www.curtainup.com/wildparty2.html.

52 Ben Brantley, "Having Fun Yet Jazz Babies?" *New York Times,* April 14, 2000, https://www.nytimes.com/2000/04/14/movies/theater-review-having-fun-yet-jazz-babies.html.

53 Charles, Isherwood, "The Wild Party," *Variety,* April 14, 2000, http://variety.com/2000/legit/reviews/the-wild-party-4-1200461750/.

54 Ibid.

55 Fitzgerald, *Echoes of the Jazz Age,* 8.

56 Ibid.

57 The term "Second Gilded Age" was coined in the early 1990s to describe the growing income inequality reminiscent of the "robber barons" of the nineteenth century. Edward T. O'Donnell, "Are We Living in the Gilded age 2.0?" June 15, 2018, https://www.history.com/news/second-gilded-age-income-inequality.

58 LaChiusa, "When It Ends," 2000.

59 Tom Lutz, "Coda: Nostalgia," *Iowa Journal of Cultural Studies*, no. 5 (2004): 112.

References

Brantley, Ben. "Having Fun Yet Jazz Babies?" *New York Times*, April 14, 2000. https://www.nytimes.com/2000/04/14/movies/theater-review-having-fun-yet-jazz-babies.html.

Brecht, Bertolt. "A Short Organum for the Theatre (1948)." In *Brecht on Theatre: The Development of an Aesthetic.* 1st ed. Edited by Bertolt Brecht and John Willet, 233–246. New York: Hill and Wang, 1964.

Brown, Jayna. *Babylon Girls: Black Women Performers and the Shaping of the Modern.* Durham, NC: Duke University Press, 2008.

Cohen-Stratyner, Barbara. "A Thousand Raggy, Draggy Dances: Social Dance in Broadway Musical Comedy in the 1920s." In *Ballroom, Boogie, Shimmy Sham, Shake: A Social and Popular Dance Reader,* edited by Julie Malnig, 217–233. Chicago: University of Illinois Press, 2009.

Doolittle, Lisa. "The Trianon and On: Reading Mass Social Dancing in the 1930s and 1940s in Alberta, Canada." In *Ballroom, Boogie, Shimmy Sham, Shake: A Social and*

Popular Dance Reader, edited by Julie Malnig, 109–125, Chicago: University of Illinois Press, 2009.

Downing, Peggy. "This Wild Party." *Global Dispatches: Expert Commentary and Analysis*, October 13, 2015. http://www.theglobaldispatches.com/articles/the-wild-party.

Emery, Lynne Fauley. *Black Dancing in the United States 1619–1970*. Palo Alto, CA: National Press Books, 1972.

Frank, Jonathan "Interview with Michael John LaChiusa," *Talkin' Broadway*, talkinbroadway.com, https://www.talkinbroadway.com/cabaret/lachiusa.html, accessed 13 September, 2022.

Gennaro, Liza. *Making Broadway Dance*. Oxford: Oxford University Press, 2021.

Heilpern, John. "Welcome to The Wild Party! Dangerous, Seedy … Fantastic." *The Observer*, April 24, 2000, http://observer.com/2000/04/welcome-to-the-wild-party-dangerous-seedy-fantastic/.

Hurston, Zora Neale. "Characteristics of Negro Expressions." In *Negro Anthology*, edited by Nancy Cunard, 28–29. London, UK: Wishart & Company, 1959.

Isherwood, Charles. "The Wild Party." *Variety*, April 14, 2000. http://variety.com/2000/legit/reviews/the-wild-party-4-1200461750/.

Kraut, Anthea. *Choreographing Copyright: Race, Gender, and Intellectual Property Rights in American Dance*. Oxford, UK: Oxford University Press, 2016.

LaChiusa, Michael John, and George C.Wolfe. The Wild Party. In *The New American Musical: An Anthology From the End of The Century*, ed. by Wiley Hausam (New York: Theatre Communication Group, 2003), 350–448.

LaChiusa, Michael John. *The Wild Party*. Vocal Selections. Van Nuys, CA: Alfred Publishing, 2009.

Lutz, Tom. "Coda: Nostalgia." *Iowa Journal of Cultural Studies*, no. 5 (2004): 110–112.

McKneely, Joey. "Choreographer Joey McKneely Chronicles His 20-Year Rumble with *West Side Story*." *Broadway.com*, November 15, 2013. https://vancouver.broadway.com/buzz/173113/choreographer-joey-mckneely-chronicles-his-20-year-rumble-with-west-side-story/.

March, Joseph Moncure. *The Wild Party*, 2nd ed. New York, NY: Covici, Friede Publishers, 1928.

Moncure March, Joseph. *The Wild Party: The Lost Classic*, illustrations by Art Spiegelman. New York: Pantheon (1994).

Most, Andrea. *Making Americans: Jews and the Broadway Musical*. MA: Harvard University Press, 2004.

O'Donnell, Edward T. "Are We Living in the Gilded age 2.0?" *History.com*, June 15, 2018. https://www.history.com/news/second-gilded-age-income-inequality.

Sommer, Elyse. "The Wild Party" *Curtain Up*, 2000, accessed 13 September, 2022, http://www.curtainup.com/wildparty2.html.

Stearns, Marshall, and Jean Stearns. *Jazz Dance: The Story of American Vernacular Dance*. New York: Da Capo Press, 1994.

Walton, Lester A. "Lucky Roberts Autographs Songs for the Prince." (No publication given), dance clipping file, Dance Collection, Lincoln Center of the Performing Art, New York, October 17, 1926, in Lynne Fauley Emery's *Black Dancing in the United States 1619–1970*. Palo Alto, CA: National Press Books, 1972.

6 "I Don't Want To Show Off No More"

Parody and Nostalgia Go Toe to Toe in *The Drowsy Chaperone*

Man in Chair leans forward and speaks directly to the audience, "I hate thea-tre. Well, it's so disappointing isn't it? ... You know there was a time when people sat in a darkened theatre and thought to themselves, 'what have George and Ira got for me tonight?' or 'Can Cole Porter pull it off again? Can you imagine?'"[1] He sits contemplatively and then explains one of his favorite musicals from the 1920s is *The Drowsy Chaperone*. He sets up the record player to play the cast recording and looks to the audience, "Would you ... would you indulge me?"[2]

As he places the needle he asks, "Hear that static? I love that sound. To me, it's the sound of a time machine starting up".[3] He pours himself a cup of tea and explains overtures are no longer in fashion anymore, and he misses their welcoming feel, "That's what an overture is, a musical appetizer. A Pu-Pu platter of tunes if you will".[4] The overture concludes and so begins the parade of characters on the stage beside him. Through the exaggerated and comical characters, whether they are the "drowsy" Chaperone herself, who drinks non-stop, or the buffoon-like Latin lover Adolpho, the colorful world of the fictional musical is brought to life, primed to sweep the audience away, if only for a few hours, from their everyday lives. When Man in Chair lifts the record needle and stops the music, the performers freeze in time; a still image of the story (and the genre) solidifies in front of us for contemplation. *The Drowsy Chaperone* – the 2006 Broadway musical, not the fictional show Man in Chair describes – is a typical and atypical musical, a complex and layered love letter to all that is musical theatre, from charming characters and peppy tunes to big show-stopping dance numbers and 11 o'clock torch songs.

Dramaturgical Strategies

The Drowsy Chaperone was created as a comical "spoof of an old time musical" in 1999 at the stag party for Canadian actor Bob Martin prior to his wedding to real life actor Janet Van De Graaf.[5] Martin, who originated the role of Man in Chair, helped write the book with Don McKellar and composer/lyricist team Lisa Lambert and Greg Morrison.[6] The show was produced in Toronto in 2001 and debuted on Broadway five years later. Bob Martin quickly became

DOI: 10.4324/9781003163688-9

a beloved hero of the show and was nominated for a Tony Award for his performance of the quirky main character.

Man in Chair is a self-deprecating, overtly sincere, yet cynical host who talks directly to the audience throughout the one-hundred-minute show. He uses a combination of dry humor and comical wit to explain how meaningful musical theatre can be to an individual and how important it is to him. He explains what a musical does, "It takes you to another world. And it gives you a little tune to carry with in your head, you know? A little something to help you escape the dreary horrors of the real world".[7] Man in Chair's gushing over the genre and memorization of famous shows lines, songs, and character foibles demonstrate his affection for and near obsession with musicals. By the same token, Man in Chair peppers his dialogue with various quips about the present world:

> Alright now, let's visualize. Imagine if you will, it's November 1928. You've just arrived at the doors of the Morosco Theatre in New York. It's very cold – remember when it used to be cold in November? Not anymore. November's the new August now. It's global warming – we're all doomed – anyway ...[8]

Two dramaturgical strategies are woven into the plethora of jokes and mischievous sarcasm that Man in Chair uses to re-play the fictional show. As will be shown, one is pedagogical and one is more emotionally motivated. Both, however, are made accessible and sustainable through a gentle use of parody initiated in the text and supported by the movement signature.

In the first strategy, there is a concentrated effort for Man in Chair to provide an informed lesson in the structure and style of early musical comedy and musical theatre. Man in Chair is well informed in the conventions of the form and shares his keen knowledge (and opinions) with the audience as he plays his double-album record of the fictional 1928 musical. Man in Chair sits in his favorite chair by his record player side-stage and sets up each scene for the audience of the chaotic and clichéd story of two soon-to-be-married young lovers and the various blocking agents that get in the way of their wedding. Before placing the needle on the record for a song, he explains what to watch for in the scene, highlights of the original production, and tidbits of gossip about particular actors: "Adolpho is played by former silent film star and world-class alcoholic Roman Bartelli".[9] The setup from a savvy commentator and ardent fan is a clever choice that establishes a framework for a dialogue about the challenges and potential of musical theatre, explained through elaborate examples from the fictional show. With this intention, the various elements of the relatively thin plots of early musicals are easily identified in performance, from the comedy duo of rag-tag gangsters, to the squeaky-voiced chorus girl, to the four weddings at the end. *The Drowsy Chaperone* is a show that makes fun of itself and in this self-reflection, there is a clever imparting of knowledge on and celebration of musical theatre. This fun-making is couched in a light parodic style that lovingly mocks the conventions of the form, as well as theatre at a broader scale. As an illustration, a clever joke about theatre etiquette unfolds early on when Man in Chair's answering machine interrupts the show:

> Oh, Well, that's it. The moment is ruined. Thank you. Thank you life. It's like a cell phone goes off in a theatre [...] "Hello? What are you doing?" "Oh I'm at the theatre ruining the moment. How about you?" "Oh, I couldn't get out tonight so I thought I'd ruin the moment by proxy."[10]

His takedown of an all too often and annoying occurrence in the theatre brings the audience into the fold.

The second strategy explores how individual and collective emotional connections to musical theatre constitute a nostalgic impulse inherent in the form in general. This characteristic of the form grows out of the shared memories and emotions that musicals regularly tap into, and *The Drowsy Chaperone* makes this tendency one its main themes. Man in Chair's self-confessed love and nostalgia for the genre of musical theatre is brought to life through his sharing and light-hearted parody of his personal experiences with musical theatre. The often complex relationship people have with the genre is interrogated in this teasing manner to allow us to feel safe to join in reminiscing about our relationship with musicals. His storytelling-style works in a variety of ways. For one, Man in Chair explicitly points out bad, awful, or loathsome conventions of the form, in a sense diluting the nostalgic reflection, yet in so doing also notes, with a wink, that the form is regularly drenched in nostalgia. He admits from the start "I hate theatre. Well it is so disappointing isn't it?",[11] signalling he is not looking at the form through rose-colored glasses (in the restorative nostalgia manner) but in a more informed backwards glance (in the reflective nostalgia manner) as a way of explaining why musical theatre is meaningful to him, and by association – us. Equally important, as opposed to the parody using Orientalist stereotypes in *Thoroughly Modern Millie*, we are in on the joke. Though *The Drowsy Chaperone* is not an outright modern parody of musical theatre, self-reflexivity and a "playful, genial mockery of codified forms" are used by Man in Chair to move between his personal relationship to musical theatre and to "pay homage" to the conventions of the form.[12]

To that end, Man in a Chair helps diffuse the distaste some have for musical theatre by recognizing its slapstick and vaudeville influence. For example, he groans at and apologizes for the awful, drawn out "spitting-in-the-face" bit of stage-business that often could not be resisted in some earlier musical comedies, which he regrettably admits happens in *The Drowsy Chaperone*. Though Man in Chair warns the audience how awful this section is, when he tries to stop the ridiculous scene from taking place beside him, the record skips and the two actors repeatedly spit on each other over and over, bringing the very humor of the overdone slapstick into the plot. He does not deny these things happen in musical theatre, but mentions they are part of the form for better or worse. This overdone "spit take" allows us to laugh at the ridiculousness of early conventions and be part of the collective "groan" for those antiquated bits of business that, like it or not, are part of the history of the form, and seem to creep back in from time to time. Mostly, Man in Chair eagerly points to his favorite parts of the musical, visibly displaying an embodied happiness as he jumps in behind characters or tries to join in on the dance numbers. This differs from his opening statement on theatre, which happens in the pitch-black opening of the show, when the audience hears only his voice and his disappointment in theatre.

The Drowsy Chaperone is also about turning away from the present reality and escaping, if only for a moment, into the world of fantasy. In this escape there is a sort of contemplative nostalgia for all shows past and how those shows made you feel, and importantly, how that feeling helped shape who you are and worked as a copy mechanism along the way. Man in Chair, his lack of a specific name suggesting an Everyman, draws out and deepens this feeling in the audience very slowly through a string of clever jokes, antidotes, and general shenanigans that give us license to take pleasure in the silliness. In this layered interpretation between individual and collective memories and experiences Man in Chair constructs a representation of nostalgia that produces its own nostalgia. Considering nostalgia is often derived from collective memories, Man in Chair sets out to create a collective past for himself and the audience.[13] He is continually adding in fictional facts about actors or situations asking the audience on numerous occasions, "remember?" as if they were there in the past enjoying the moment along with him. The idea that nostalgia, as explained by Susan Bennett, "leans on an imagined and imaginary past which is more and better than the present," makes it a prime emotion to coax audience members into.[14] The constant calling back to a fictional moment or movement cultivates a shared memory, no matter how false it is.

This complex and clever framework is further explained through the analysis of key moments in the show, particularly in regards to the movement and choreography. As Man in Chair is in the driver's seat of the musical, our longing to see more of the show is produced (and controlled) by his desire to tell us more. Furthermore, his disclaimers about the show and self-deprecation, often expressed by poking fun at the form or a character, make the nostalgia safe, even attractive. The show is careful not to get too sentimental, and keeps the wry humor and self-awareness at the forefront. For example, Man in Chair takes on the bothersome issue of the classic gratuitous song or scene in front of the curtain that seems to have no place in the plot. He explains that in earlier musical theatre before more sophisticated stagecraft, there was the need for filler scenes or songs to allow for costume and set changes before a big flashy production number. He chooses to use the loose or banal narratives in pornography as an example:

> In pornography the story is simplistic – "how do I pay for this pizza?" […]
> My point is, as in a musical, the story exists only to connect the longer,

more engaging ... production numbers. What? Well, what kind of a society do we live in if we can't discuss the similarities between pornography and musical theatre?[15]

The connection between musical theatre and pornography makes for an excellent comedic moment that allows one to be both delighted and bewildered by the link this apparently conservative man made between the "mechanics" of both forms. That pornography would be the example he chooses plays into the outlandish nature of parody, and continues to allow the audience to enjoy this increasingly spirited theatrical journey.

The confession of Man in Chair toward the end of the live show that in fact he had never seen the show, but that his mother had given him the record when his father had left, brings a profound meaning to the show that had not been there before.[16] The genre and conventions of musical theatre as he sees them seem to function in some way to restore the loss of his father, or at very least help towards healing the emotional wound. In the two-fold dramaturgical structure of the piece, imagination and memory are celebrated as both a personalized coping mechanism and a crucible of creative inspiration. Taking the audience into his sanctuary and using the songs he has listened to over and over; Man in Chair imagines the entire world of the fictional show for them.

A nutty obsession with an old-time musical is soon expanded to show it is not only the plots in the show that are absurd, but also that life itself aligns with a Sisyphean-like cycle, and that reminiscence, memory, and nostalgia can be an important survival tool. The embodied component of the show provides a way in towards an understanding of the emotional and visceral connection many have to musical theatre.

Choreography and *The Drowsy Chaperone*

Casey Nicholaw directed and choreographed *The Drowsy Chaperone*; his second Broadway show after *Spamalot* in 2005. Nicholaw uses nearly every possible dance convention of the 1920s era drawing from vaudeville idioms, early revue dances from the nineteen-teens, and the Charleston. He employs multiple variations on the Charleston as well as other recognizable dance styles such as "Ballin' the Jack," where the performer bounces their hips around in a circle while popping their heels up and down.[17] He also includes elements of the Black Bottom, the shimmy, and tap dance. Pointedly, because of the celebration and playful parody of the conventions of musical theatre, all dances are exaggerated and overtly "spectacularized" for comedic effect as well as to serve the above-mentioned dramaturgical strategies. Scott Taylor, a close associate of Nicholaw explains, "In *Drowsy*, I know Casey gave attention to nostalgia, not only because of the type of musical he wanted to create, but by the nostalgia and type of dance that he knew people would expect to see for this time period and from these overdrawn but honest characters."[18] Nicholaw's embellished movement signature is created from the beginning of the show using iconic moves from the era upon which he expands through to the end; movements increase in intensity and extravagence along with the plot.

After the prologue discussing the ups and down of theatrical experiences, Man in Chair announces it is time to start and settles in with his tea saying, "you're only seconds away from being transported".[19] The set contributes to the feat of transformation as Man in Chair's worn out apartment morphs into the 1928 New York City setting. Characters at the top of the show enter through the two doors of his aged refrigerator, which once opened appear as French doors from the inside. In the opening number ("Fancy Dress"), all the characters are introduced, except for Janet, and all sing of the "wedding bells [that] will ring," an expected exposition-type song for the opening of a show.[20] The entire cast enthusiastically bounces up and down with elbows out to the side. This movement helps to get the one-step beat of the Jazz Age-styled music in the body and set toes tapping in the audience. Man in Chair joins in, ridiculously trying to imitate the choreography, something one often does only in the privacy of one's home, which works as part of the conceit of the show – he is in his home. The point of this opening allows all to feel the energy and gaiety of the 1920s in a visceral manner and enjoy the excess of excess. Each convention of the form, including the dance, draws attention to itself and is part of the imitation of the stylization of dozens of shows in the 1920s. Because the parodic style is over the top and unreal, it gives permission to love and delight in the moves. There is a parodic bent to some of the more clichéd moves in the sense that they satisfy people's expectations of dance in musical theatre. At the same time, the exaggerated manner of the choreo-graphy subtly criticizes the stereotype that dance in musical theatre is always "jazz hands" and box steps.[21] The moves spoof the stereotypes, but also capi-talize on our relationship to those stereotypes. Because of this pointed self-awareness of the conventions of the genre, each convention is deliberately exhibited and made available for both critique and delight from Man in Chair and the audience.

Man in Chair eases the anxiety or frustration some may have with the form by acknowledging the awkwardness of bursting into song or dance from the beginning of the show, which gives a license to let the musical in all its lunacy come to life. Described as "a delightful homage to a simpler and less cynical time," Man in Chair makes all comfortable with a form that he states in the 1920s was about entertainment for entertainment's sake, stalwartly asking – "what is wrong with that?"[22]

In fact, the enlarged, over-the-top execution of the most obvious gestures of the social dance (such as the pumping up of elbows in the Charleston for example) thrusts the role and meaning of dance in musical theatre forward for contemplation. Man in Chair's narration, applause, and love for each dance number emphasizes how much the meaning, memory, and subsequent embodied nostalgia mean to him, and by association, us.

Man in Chair admits the plot is "flimsy": basically, a case of mistaken iden-tity that revolves around the bride and groom not being allowed to see each other before the wedding. He admits all the characters are two-dimensional from the start, and not to be overly concerned by the "well-worn" narrative structure of the fictional show. He explains the "B" plot is equally weak involving Feldzeig, a Broadway producer, trying to replace the soon-to-be-married Janet in his show and the ditzy chorus girl who tries to get the spot. To make matters worse there are a pair of gangsters stalking the producer to resolve an unpaid debt. Man in Chair describes them:

> They were an early example of the typical Broadway gangster: full of word play and stylized movements, not really very intimidating. Unless you find dancers intimidating, which I do but for reasons which would not be appropriate to this situation.[23]

By voicing his apprehensions about dancers and dancing, Man in Chair makes an opening for any who feel the same way about the form. He recognizes the surprise or shock of people unabashedly breaking into dance moves on stage. More subtly, there is some sexual innuendo in the statement, as he hints at his desires or sexual anxieties that may not be "appropriate" to discuss. He relays to the audience an understanding of the gaze of the spectator on the often supple and sexy bodies of Broadway dancers that may hint at a certain level of voyeurism or fantasy for some – including him.

In the dance numbers of the show, the literal nature of the simple lyrics and dances are redolent of early "dance-songs" of the late teens of the twentieth century and the instructive nature of those early songs is imitated. For example, in the song "Cold Feet," the groom, Robert, and his best man, George, move so quickly in the dance (which tells of the Groom's pre-wedding nerves) that smoke comes from their feet. Their moves are so hot they are literally "smoking" – a lively pun on the title of the song. The tap dance at the beginning of the song, done only by Robert, is standard and predictable rhythm-wise with a lot of shuffle-ball-changes and heel drops that accent the off beats of the music. When George wanders in to talk to Robert he continues tap dancing through the conversation, suggesting it is just as odd to continue to dance and have a conversation as it is to stand and talk and then break into dance. Robert convinces his friend George to join in; a worn but much-loved trope in musicals and movie musicals to get a second (and sometimes third and fourth) person into the dance number and make a production out of it. The two dancers hit all the styles of "Broadway" tap dance, from a back and forth conversation with rhythms, to the repetition of small travelling steps, to more virtuoso moves. The music speeds up and that smoke swirls around their feet. This exaggeration enhances how much audiences loved a showstopper then and now. At the peak of speed and action a tap-dancing waiter comes in with a glass of water for each of them. The dancers stop, drink up, and then go back into the grand finale of the piece. As they finish the routine, Man in Chair appears between them applauding. He explains to the audience that he always pictures the actors panting and sweating after a big routine. While he speaks the performers are frozen in front of him with big smiles, panting and sweating. Man in Chair points to the beloved quirks of musical theatre that those who once performed in school musicals or have watched many, might feel a twinge of nostalgia for. Newcomers to the form are also meant to feel at ease in this nod to the ridiculous nature of those smiling and sweating final tableaux of musical numbers and that it is acceptable to point out these quirks in the form.

Perhaps one of the most memorable pieces in the musical that creates its own nostalgia is when Janet (Sutton Foster) claims she is ready to get married and is fine to end her famous performance career.[24] Janet claims she does not want to show off her skills and talent to demanding audiences anymore. What ensues is a comedy routine and dance where she indeed does show off every possible skill, from spinning plates to half a dozen cartwheels. She pokes fun at the showing off, posturing, and extended songs and dances, and their reprises that populate the form. Even the plastic grin, presentational poses, and flourishes allude to the spectacularization of the form. Feldzieg begs her, "How can you give up the footlights when you know very well you got greasepaint in your veins?",[25] Janet sings simply, "I don't want to show off no more" and then strikes a variety of poses for the many photographers.[26] The piece escalates, and Janet goes through a parade of ludicrous actions, including belly dancing and escaping from a locked box to making music by blowing on bottles. All her actions are essentially a collection of vaudeville acts. Janet teases the audience by showing her virtuosic tricks of the trade that will never be seen from her again, though we are seeing them for the first time. She states: "You'll never see this no more," then kicks a leg to her head, in effect creating a longing to never have the piece end, as each fantastic skill is only seen once.[27] With a massive build up, she puts on yet another costume, takes a deep breath, and true to the build-up of a finale of many large production numbers that end with a change of key signature to enhance the emotion using a musical half-tone step up, she states "I don't want to change keys no more, " but does.[28] The number closes with the ten ensemble members executing a dance combination of small kicks forward, bounces side to side, and backwards travelling kicks with lifted elbows followed by a turn towards Janet for a final tableaux. These Charleston-like movements done in unison function to boost the last moment of the dance with an added exuberance that Janet has been professing and expertly demonstrating. The celebration of the new woman of the 1920s is cleverly woven into this showstopper as Janet's character has it all and does it all. However, unlike the two previous chapters, the conceit itself is folded into and seen through the nostalgic remembering of Man in Chair. The choreographic strategy provides the emotional hit Man in Chair is trying to get from the number, shared with the audience. The recognizable dance moves from the realm of the Charleston help to frame the conventional number and provide the satisfaction Man in Chair has explained audiences found highly entertaining. In the collective memories of the nostalgia Man in Chair has created, this means both a fictional past and present "us." By illustrating to contemporary audiences how desires seemed so easily met through whimsy and quirky vaudeville gags there can be a longing for a time when one was readily satisfied with the style of musicals of the 1920s. The expectations for the technological phenomenons of the mega musicals were decades away; joy and belonging were felt in the conventions, as saccharine-sweet as they may have seemed. The meta-theatrical dramaturgical imperative that Man in Chair creates as tour guide to the form is made all the more poignant by his self-deprecation and honesty as he explains his love of the musical.

A second section where dance embodies nostalgia for the 1920s through the imitation and exaggeration of dance tropes is in the gangsters' comical number "Toledo Surprise." At this moment in the story the gangsters are putting the squeeze on the producer to get an overdue payment. In a bizarre set up, the gangsters, disguised as pastry chefs, couple baking with roughing up an enemy; "first you chop the nuts, then you pound the dough …"[29] Feldzieg "distracts" the gangsters from beating him up by asking them to repeat their actions, exclaiming what grace of movement they have. The gangsters are awkward at first, but within two bars of music they become master showmen.[30] The leap from the awkward Everyman into an expert mover or singer is adored in musical theatre. There is something appealing about the possibility that all can move their body with ease and that in the fantasy we too can be agile, syncopated, and stunning. Kitty, the ditzy chorus girl, stumbles in on the conversation taking the opportunity to show Feldzieg her talent. The trio and various ensemble members join in with basic Charleston moves (heel kicks, shuffle of heels, pressing of palms to the upper corner of the room while pumping knees up and down) and start building to more sophisticated moves (complex turns and kicks). Just as the big dance number really gets "cooking" Janet bursts in and announces the wedding is off. A scene ensues, and the emotional pay-off for a big production number finale is put on hold. The desire for physical and musical resolution hangs palpably in the air. In this moment, however, there is recognition of what it is we are longing for: a nonsensical dance production that we did not even know we wanted – part of how the show creates its own nostalgia. Anticipation and longing abound, strategically orchestrated by the dramaturgy of the show to create love for the genre. Feldzieg is delighted Janet will now be available for his show and he surprisingly takes the reins of the number, starting it up again with a renewed wildness and gaiety of Charleston kicks forwards and back, with accentuated shoulder shimmies, only to be stopped again by a second interruption. This "stop-and-go" formula builds to a peak, until all are madly singing and dancing about baking a cake that has no connection at all to the plot. The charm of the music and the delight of the Charleston-like dance moves from the 1920s becomes justification enough for the grand production number. In the final chorus all engage in the very clear choreography (side heel kicks: one right, one left, then two to the right) and the cast, in their tight and synchronous movement much like in *Thoroughly Modern Millie*, use the precise and energetic moves of the dance to bring the number to a higher and higher peak. This production excitement is typical and often expected in the Broadway musical, however, drawing attention to it with the stops and starts helps to substantiate just how important and effective movement and choreography is to the genre. In order to tease out (even further) the emphasis on such exhilarating and extensive choreography audiences have come to expect – the record skips. All the performers keep repeating the same double kick on the right, three or four times, until Man in Chair, who has been dancing in the second row of the ensemble, is able to get over to the record player and stop the skip. He drops the needle, and the cast finishes the number with rousing shoulder high Charleston kicks and then low to the ground lunges in canon to close the number with a much waited for, and unmistakeably spectacular, bang.

In terms of choreographic choices, determining the steps that grow out of the Charleston, build toward the finale, and maintain the comedic timing of the piece is no easy task. Particularly as the choice of steps and the scaffolded structure allows the theatrical jokes to come to full fruition. With the Charleston, the first kick comes forward with the arms and then both arm and leg retract backward. In this maneuver there is a delightful titillation in the kick forward but a coyness when that foot then touches back. By interrupting the Charleston half way through on several occasions there is not a resolution to the flirting or teasing and the anticipation builds. Nicholaw expertly harnesses the movement to help capture the theatrical joke of the moment. With each round of repetition, arms and legs adjust higher and higher building towards the grand finale. The skipping of the record welcomes the audience into the ridiculousness of it all.

This massive spectacularization of the Charleston at this moment of high physical exertion adds that final tier of engagement and unabashed admittance that this dazzling and thrilling part of musical theatre is highly desired and part of the nostalgia people have for the form. If one was not nostalgic for big production numbers at the beginning of this section, one may be more likely to be now. Like the creating of false collective memories by asking "Remember?" of fictional happenings, the constant repetition of the movement coerces the audience into a collective desire for the grandest of act one finales. The number is finished and Man in Chair staggers back to his seat. A small reprise accompanies the exiting chorus. Janet turns and asks, "Why are we dancing, our dreams are in tatters?" pointing to the outrageousness of the number at its most effective. The groom replies, "Yes. Yes…But the tone is so infectious!".[31] This gentle mockery at the end of the piece affirms that singing and dancing on and off stage can and should be a guiltless pleasure.

The first act ends and Man in Chair explains, "The curtain falls, and it's time for the intermission. At least it would be, if we were […] sitting in the Morosco Theatre watching The Drowsy Chaperone, which of course, we are not".[32] He, however, takes an intermission break. The curtain lowers behind him and he takes out a power bar and sits in his chair and eats it as the audience waits. He explains, "I have a bit of a blood sugar issue. I have to eat small meals all day long or I get jittery. I know it's rude but you wouldn't like the alternative, believe you me".[33] The detailed analysis of the fictional *Drowsy Chaperone* and subsequent holistic view of the genre (the narrator himself taking a break) gives the musical space to breathe. Unlike some sung-through musicals that exist in a sort of middle ground of dramatic impulse, the production's show-within-a-show structure (one of which breaks the fourth wall) allows what Scott McMillin calls the "crackle of difference" to emerge.[34] McMillin explains "the smoothness of unity" is not the indicator of success of a musical, rather the differences in a musical bring meaning and interest.[35] The creative team have created a structure that allows a space for nostalgia and meaning to be created and re-created. Casey Nicholaw, as both the director and choreographer, sets up an environment where Man in Chair can easily move between both shows. This Brechtian-styled choice of a narrator talking directly to the audience, effectively keeps the audience engaged by focusing in on both the micro and macro elements of the musical and works to avoid any sense of complacency.

When Man in Chair returns from his "intermission," he puts on the second record. He leaves to use the washroom, explaining that the audience can listen to the overture to the second act. He accidently puts on a record for another fictional musical, *The Enchanted Nightingale*. A complete Orientalist spectacle at an Asian palace takes place with an ensemble singing and dancing in exoticized red and gold costumes. Performers hands are flicked upwards with splayed fingers, wrists circle, and hips swivel in Salomé styled movements.[36] Man in Chair rushes back in to stop the record. The huge effort put into this small bit of comedy helps reference the various growing pains the Broadway musical has had over the years in terms of exoticizing locales and cultures. Through the playful parody he comments on and admits to some of the past problems with the genre. In his apology to the audience for the mishap, he describes *The Enchanted Nightingale*:

> A degrading piece of Chinoiserie … A slap in the face to four thousand years of Chinese history. But it had some wonderful tunes … and did you recognize Roman Bartelli as the Emperor? Yes, he was a man of a thousand accents – all of them insulting.[37]

This over the top interlude of a completely new fictionalized show, lavish set, and bedazzled costumes gives us permission to laugh at the stereotypes and in that experience acknowledge the less than politically correct history of the form. Markedly, the inclusion of this moment also reminds that this kind of exoticism and Orientalism is offensive and should be called out, as Man in Chair does.

As the narrative of the fictional musical is devolving into mayhem, Man in Chair questions,

> What a mess! Will it all work out in the end? Of course it will! It's not real! It's a musical! Everything always works out in a musical. In the real

world nothing ever works out and the only people who burst into song are the hopelessly deranged!.[38]

This sobering thought stalls the nostalgic flow, though supports a critical reflection on how important memory and imagination is to everyday functioning and finding one's way in the world.

When the illusion of the show is broken two beats before the final note of the fictional show by a power outage, the intrusion of the superintendent to fix the fuse reminds of the theatricality of the situation. The "magic" is shattered and it is difficult to imagine how to bring back and rebuild all Man in Chair has created. This effect reminds how fanciful the show Man in Chair describes is (and the one we are watching), reinforcing that one of the key values of musical theatre is to provide this escape and emotional safe-place, as a way of managing the realities of life. As the characters freeze, while the superintendent snoops around for the fuse box, there is a sense of intrusion from a parent at a teenager's party, an awkward embarrassment of letting loose or being one's self. After the superintendent leaves Man in Chair sits back down and hums a tune from the show. Surprisingly, there is not a restoration to the status quo for Man in Chair, the narrative goes the opposite direction. The characters break their tableaux and wander over to him and invite him into the finale of the fictional show. He brings the show album with him and rides off on a giant airplane (an over-the-top *deus ex machina* that ends the show) – a closing ode to escapism, theatricalization, and theatre in general. By merging the two story lines of the show-within-a-show structure the sheer fantasy of an ending works, while also acknowledging the aggrandizing of the happy ending common to musical theatre. What one may have originally thought of as misplaced nostalgia for a show Man in Chair has never seen becomes a moot point, and the show, moreover, becomes about how one uses nostalgia and memory to find meaning and comfort in life.

A complexity is achieved in *The Drowsy Chaperone* that is a tribute to a very strategic dramaturgy that uses parody and a cultivation of nostalgia to trouble one's relationship to musical theatre and society on a broader level. The production problematizes the genre and tropes of the 1920s using a skillful manipulation of parody that circumnavigates the overt commercialization of genre and makes us question why performance, and musical theatre in particular, is meaningful to us. Helmutt Illbruk explains nostalgia can be "consolatory and self protective," which is how Man in Chair starts out, however, as the show progresses and through the embodied performance of the fictional show "conducted" by Man in Chair the nostalgia becomes also about interrogating fundamental aspects of the self and one's place in the world.[39] The questions to the audience, the pauses at moments of heightened physical action to reflect on the genre, and the encouragement of self-reflexivity, all contribute to this.[40] Svetlana Boym explains there are "fewer and fewer venues for exploring nostalgia," but when a creative use of nostalgia occurs such as that in *The Drowsy Chaperone* it "reveals the fantasies of the age and it is in those fantasies and potentialities that the future is born."[41]

This section has shown how three musicals use the bodily essences of the 1920s and social dance frameworks as dramaturgical material in order to construct a sense of contemplation of the apparent liberties and freedom of the era – for better or worse. The case studies investigated in this section demonstrated how choreographers build on the social dances as a way of meaning making in the contemporary moment and how the values and desires of the everyday world of social dance are amplified through the spectacularization of the body, the female body in particular, on stage. In the following chapter, the re-emergence of social dances after the stock market crash and building up to World War II is interrogated to show how bodies in motion help rebuild social and economic momentum. In that physicalized survival mechanism much is learned about social situations and American identity. The shift in the emotional connection to movement from a sense of obliviousness and wildness in the 1920s to how social dance helps foster a new national confidence is key. Through social dance in the 1930s and 40s, I investigate how the body is created as "American" on stage.

Notes

1 *The Drowsy Chaperone,* book by Bob Martin and Don McKellar, music and lyrics by Lisa Lambert and Greg Morrison, 2006, 1, https://web.archive.org/web/20190314151809/http://currentplayers.weebly.com/uploads/1/3/5/0/13500082/drowsy_act_1.pdf, https://web.archive.org/web/20190314152051/http://currentplayers.weebly.com/uploads/1/3/5/0/13500082/drowsy_act_2.pdf.

2 Ibid., 2.

3 Ibid.

4 Ibid.

5 "*The Drowsy Chaperone*: Study Guide," Vancouver Playhouse Theatre Company, 2008. http://artsalive.ca/pdf/eth/activities/drowsychaperone.pdf, accessed April 15, 2018. Janet van de Graaff (with the added "f") is also the name of the bride-to-be in the show.

6 Soon after the stag party, Martin joined his friends to workshop the musical for the Toronto Fringe Festival. The show went on to a main stage premiere at Toronto's Winter Garden Theatre in 2001 produced by David Mirvish. Broadway producers then supported a run at the Ahmanson Theatre in Los Angeles in 2005. In 2006 the show transferred to Broadway and ran for 674 shows and 32 previews. *The Drowsy Chaperone* was nominated for thirteen Tony Awards and won five, including best musical and best score. Unlike the previous case studies *The Drowsy Chaperone* is not based on previous source material. Ibid.

7 *The Drowsy Chaperone*, 75.

8 Ibid., 2.

9 Ibid., 24.

10 Ibid., 17.

11 Ibid., 2.

12 Linda Hutcheon, *A Theory of Parody: The Teachings of Twentieth-Century Art Forms* (Urbana, IL: Chicago University Press, 2000), 46. Hutcheon further explains that parody can be many things including a more playful mockery and does not need to be malicious. *The Drowsy Chaperone*, however, does not have the critical dimension and ironic inversion that Hutcheon explains is necessary to be called modern parody. Markedly, the creators of the show do not call the show a parody, stating,

"It is an homage to old-fashioned shows that is aimed at … people who love musicals and people who are suspicious of them," Kenneth Jones, "Drowsy Chaperone is a Sweet Musical Valentine – With Salty Colored Commentary," *Playbill*, March 16, 2006, http://www.playbill.com/article/drowsy-chaperone-is-a-sweet-m usical-valentine-with-salty-color-commentary-com-131406.

13 Maurice Halbwachs, *On Collective Memory*, edited and translated by Lewis A. Coser (Chicago: University of Chicago Press, 1992), 25.

14 Susan Bennett, *Performing Nostalgia: Shifting Shakespeare and the Contemporary Past* (London: UK, Routledge, 1995), 5.

15 *The Drowsy Chaperone*, 30.

16 Long forgotten (due to the lively story-telling) is Man in Chair's confession early on when the lights first come up, "Hello. How are we today? I'm feeling a little blue myself. You know, a little anxious for no particular reason, a little sad that I should feel anxious at my age, you know, a little self-conscious anxiety resulting in non-specific sadness; a state I like to call 'blue'" (Ibid., 1).

17 Marshall and Jean Stearns, *Jazz Dance: The Story of American Vernacular Dance* (New York: Da Capo Press, 1994), 107.

18 Interview with author, May 11, 2018. Scott Taylor has been the associate choreo-grapher for several Broadway shows (*Aladdin, On a Clear Day You Can See Forever*) as well as dance captain for *Spamalot, Contact, Steel Pier*, and a dancer in *Showboat, Crazy for You*, and *Cats*.

19 *The Drowsy Chaperone*, 2.

20 "Fancy Dress," Music and Lyrics by Lisa Lambert and Greg Morrison, 2004.

21 Box steps, or a jazz square, involve a crossing over of the feet in a square fashion to keeps the performer in the same spot though moving with much energy. Jazz hands are explained in chapter one, note 43.

22 "*The Drowsy Chaperone*: Study Guide," 2008.

23 *The Drowsy Chaperone*, 13.

24 Foster's portrayal of Millie Dillmount four years previously in *Thoroughly Modern Millie* would also create a sense of "ghosting" particularly as both shows are set in the 1920s. Marvin Carlson speaks of this *theatrical memory* suggesting, "the dynamics of theatrical memory conjures ghosts of some sort in every new production." Carlson, *10,000 Nights at the Theatre: Highlights from 50 Years of Theatre-Going*, (Ann Arbor, MI: University of Michigan Press, 2017), 263. Foster's characterization of Millie is embodied in her portrayal of Janet van der Graaff. Carlson mentions the degree to which the audience is conscious of this ghosting varies, but given the nostalgic propulsions already operating in *The Drowsy Chaperone*, there is a certain level of the uncanny in Foster's inclusion in the show that would likely invoke memories of *Millie* adding to the nostalgic impulse in the form. Carlson, *10,000 Nights at the Theatre*, 263.

25 *The Drowsy Chaperone*, 19.

26 Lambert and Morrison, "Show Off," 2004.

27 Ibid.

28 Ibid.

29 Lambert and Morrison, "Toledo Surprise," 2004.

30 There is perhaps a reference here to the gangsters who intrude on the performance of the show-within-a-show in *Kiss Me Kate* (1948). This connection continues the homage to the form that *The Drowsy Chaperone* takes on, as *Kiss Me Kate* (music and lyrics by Cole Porter) remains a beloved and sophisticated example of the musical theatre genre. As a case in point, Man in Chair's opening monologue has him wondering how much audiences would anticipate what Cole Porter would come up with next.

31 *The Drowsy Chaperone*, 49.

32 Ibid., 51.

33 Ibid.
34 Scott McMillin, *The Musical as Drama* (Princeton, NJ: Princeton University Press, 2006), 2.
35 Ibid.
36 See Chapter 4 for further description of Salomé dances.
37 *The Drowsy Chaperone*, 54.
38 Ibid., 41.
39 Illbruck, Helmut. *Nostalgia: Origins and Ends of an Unenlightened Disease* (Evanston, IL: Northwestern University Press, 2012), 8.
40 This sense of reflection is further focused in on towards the end of the musical when there is a garbled final phrase uttered by the chaperone to an unsure Janet. Man in Chair has never been able to make out the phrase. The chaperone says "L-ve while you can." He is not sure if she says "live while you can," or "leave while you can" (*The Drowsy Chaperone*, 61). The moral of the fictional musical remains undelivered. He relates to the message himself and reflects on his broken marriage and concludes, "But still, in the larger sense, its better to have lived than left, right? (Ibid.). Man in Chair puts the questions over to us.
41 Svetlana Boym, *The Future of Nostalgia* (New York: Basic Books, 2001,) 351.

References

Bennett, Susan. *Performing Nostalgia: Shifting Shakespeare and the Contemporary Past.* London, UK: Routledge, 1995.

Boym, Svetlana. *The Future of Nostalgia.* New York: Basic Books, 2001.

Carlson, Marvin. *10,000 Nights at the Theatre: Highlights from 50 Years of Theatre-Going.* Ann Arbor: University of Michigan Press, 2017.

"The Drowsy Chaperone – Study Guide." Created by the Vancouver Playhouse Theatre Company, 2008. http://artsalive.ca/pdf/eth/activities/drowsychaperone.pdf, accessed April 15, 2018.

Lambert, Lisa, and Greg Morrison. *The Drowsy Chaperone.* Vocal Score. Milwaukee, WI: Hal Leonard Corporation, 2004.

Halbwachs, Maurice. *On Collective Memory.* Edited and translated by Lewis A. Coser. Chicago: University of Chicago Press, 1992.

Hutcheon, Linda. *A Theory of Parody: The Teachings of Twentieth-Century Art Forms.* Urbana, IL: Chicago University Press, 2000.

Illbruck, Helmut. *Nostalgia: Origins and Ends of an Unenlightened Disease.* Evanston, IL: Northwestern University Press, 2012.

Jones, Kenneth. "'Drowsy Chaperone is a Sweet Musical Valentine—With Salty Colored Commentary." *Playbill*, March 16, 2006. http://www.playbill.com/article/drowsy-chaperone-is-a-sweet-musical-valentine-with-salty-color-commentary-com-131406.

McMillin, Scott. *The Musical as Drama.* Princeton: Princeton University Press, 2006.

Stearns, Marshall, and Jean Stearns. *Jazz Dance: The Story of American Vernacular Dance.* New York: Da Capo Press, 1994.

Part III

Swing Dance – Rally and Rebound

After the stock market crash of 1929, the economic, political, and cultural life of the U.S. profoundly changed. The expansive world of leisure activities that had flourished in the 1910s and developed into the hedonistic pursuits of the 1920s ran out of steam (and money). The time of the indulgences of the 1920s was over, and in large urban cities poverty and economic strife characterized everyday life. Engaging in social dance was how many individuals coped, vented frustrations, and found solace and belonging, no matter how makeshift the venue or how temporary the company. In this final section, I consider how social dance is used and interpreted in three musicals set between 1930 and 1945. The case studies each explore how imagined communities are created in the face of precarity, whether in response to actions in the narrative of the musical or to sociopolitical circumstances at the time of production. I argue the shows' social dance-based choreographies work both to build communities and to express the subtext of the story, and the embodied nostalgia therein becomes the element that brings the performances' social and political meanings to light. I claim the nostalgia embodied by swing dance "opens the door for the audience to be in the community" and creates a space or undercurrent to consider deeper economic and political implications perhaps not voiced by the show or overlooked in the larger quest to fulfill the theatrical expectations of a Broadway musical.[1]

I begin with a consideration of *Wonderful Town* (1953) in order to introduce swing dance and the physical expressions of the era.[2] The comedic structure of the musical about two sisters moving to the New York City helps bridge the case studies of the previous chapter, moving from the 1920s into the 1930s in its setting. Much like *Thoroughly Modern Millie*, *Wonderful Town* is a comedy that uses pastiche combined with a light-hearted social satire to achieve its backwards glance. The opening of the show at the height of the Red Scare, however, complicates the high-spirited show and sets the stage for subtle but critical undercurrents. The following chapter considers the musical *Steel Pier* (1997) and takes on the complex task of understanding, navigating, and surviving the Great Depression using the microcosm of dance marathons and the social and economic meaning rooted within them.[3] The final chapter investigates the musical *Allegiance* (2015) and explores the specific cultural and

DOI: 10.4324/9781003163688-10

political urgencies surrounding Japanese internment in the U.S. during and after World War II through the experiences of one family.[4] Despite markedly different plots and locations (New York; Atlantic City; Heart Mountain, Wyoming) all three shows in this section use nostalgia in an embodied manner to vitalize communities that had been suppressed, deprived, or constricted.

I explore the three case studies in order of the increasing precarity of the community and characters involved in the story as a way to chart how pressing the implications of nostalgia become when the tension between self-expression and geopolitics increases. In these dynamics, the dancer is brought forth on stage as a site of embodied history and cultural memory. The investigation of how choreographers build on that physicality helps to conceptualize how the body is created as "American" on stage and the meaning of that move. I investigate the tension that arises from the intrusion of national and international affairs on self-expression and attempt to demonstrate that the greater the tension between individual freedoms and nationalistic agendas the more key the dancing body on stage and embodied nostalgia become in determining identity and integrity in the United States.

In order to understand the physicalization of community memories, longings, and historical meaning, the following section explores the transformations of the socio-political climate between 1930–1945. I briefly trace the history and foundations of swing dance and how it becomes the movement vernacular of this time in relation to shifting senses of communities and formations of national identity.

Moving Forward in a Turbulent Decade – the 1930s

The seeming suddenness of the financial crisis at the turn of the decade led to a culture of anxiety, paranoia and frustration.[5] Desperate for tax revenue, the U. S. government lifted the prohibition on alcohol in 1933. The world of the clandestine and spectacular speakeasies was emphatically over. The first glimmer of hope for a financially paralyzed population did not come until Franklin D. Roosevelt's New Deal was implemented in 1933. Despite the variety of public works programs the New Deal enacted, the Depression did not end until the U.S.'s entrance into World War II nearly a decade later.

The eventual economic recovery, as explained by sociologist David Walsh and culture and social studies scholar Len Platt, was achieved largely through Roosevelt's "revitalizing America's capitalist economic order to promote and increase the forward movement of the processes of American modernization."[6] This progressive emphasis "uniting business and labor in its organization of the economy and society," however, left the working class to fend for themselves in navigating how the vision and workings of the New Deal could offer immediate help.[7] In essence, the varied working class communities in the 1930s were caught between "their own perceived sense of failure and their desire to work."[8] This complex transition from the despair of the depression to the supposed possibilities of the New Deal, capped off with the entrance into a world war, was reflected in the social dance styles that developed alongside the burgeoning social, political, and economic agitations of the era.

Notably, the Swing Era cannot be viewed as a monolithic period; there were various sub-periods within the fifteen-year time span.[9] Concepts of community, and thus social dance, shifted with the political and economic changes of the 1930s and early 1940s. In *Swing! That Modern Sound*, historian Kenneth J. Bindas explains the transformation in social dance beginning in the 1930s: "swing and the depression era are inseparable. The crisis itself helped create a rediscovery of America, a rediscovery that involved all aspects of society" including music and dance.[10] In the 1930s, as part of recovery efforts from the economic crisis there was, in time, a political shift from a focus on individualism to an emphasis on the collective. In this U.S.-styled form of socialism (or the closest the U.S. ever got to socialism) Roosevelt "suggested that a new America could be seen on the horizon that promised a fair share for all people."[11] Swing dance, with its emphasis on belonging and increasing equality between dance partners, grew out of the working class, where many of these ideological changes were felt strongest.[12] Bindas explains, "The 1930s legitimized the worker experience and made it part of the American experience. Swing music played a central role in this transformation," and to the extent that social dance emerged as "the lifeblood of the community," swing culture readily dovetailed with the communal aspects of the New Deal.[13]

As will be demonstrated in the case studies of this section, the transitions from the Depression to the New Deal to World War II generated very different concepts of community. In the early years of the Depression, swing music and dance were embraced as a survival method to escape the gloom and despair. By mid-decade dance styles increasingly were also about inclusion, commonality, and engaging in social causes. Towards the end of 1930s, as the effects of the Depression spread out globally, and continuing on towards the 1940s with the U.S. involvement in World War II, social dances also developed an increasingly outward and global manifestation. With soldiers bringing home their experience from outside the U.S., and people's attentions turned to loved ones fighting overseas, swing dancing thus became about the effect of the world on the body.

Brief Background of Swing Culture

Swing dance came to life in the ballrooms and dance halls of Harlem, the most popular and famous being the Savoy.[14] The diverse cultural make up of Harlem at the turn of the twentieth century brought many different music and dance styles together, an amalgamation which eventually led to the development of swing dance in the 1930s. Importantly, swing dance "developed concurrently with the swing style of jazz music."[15] Swing music, performed by large orchestras, generally has a fast tempo with a pulse and syncopation that promoted dancing. Howard Spring explains swing music "is characterized by four-to-the-bar rhythms, guitar and pizzicato double bass in the rhythm section, riff-based arrangements, and assertive drumming."[16] A symbiotic sort of relationship developed between musicians and dancers in the 1930s as both pushed against the established beats and rhythms, helping to develop a new style and manner of sound and movement.[17] The basic physicality of swing dance involves a rocking side to side (or step and touch to right and then the left) followed by a ball-change (or swinging of the body and transferring of weight from one foot to the other) backwards, or outwards, while opening up the dance position (letting go of one of your partner's hands) for a spin or breakaway.[18]

As more Black Americans moved into Harlem in the late 1920s and early 1930s, the Irish, German, Italian, and Jewish communities eventually left. This shift in demographics involved a transition from substantially Jewish and Italian communities in East Harlem to a majority of Black Americans, along with an influx of Puerto Ricans.[19] As this transition progressed, the various Black communities began to work out social status and hierarchies through cultural practices.[20] In particular, the establishment of more specific groups within the communities and territorial behavior happened on the dance floor. The ongoing developments and articulations of the Lindy Hop were in part how social power dynamics were established in the community. The generally friendly competition and posturing on the dance floor resulted in several groups of dancers that ruled the numerous clubs, the most famous being "Whitey's Lindy Hoppers" at the Savoy. There was a sense of inclusivity to the different groups, and Herbert White (the namesake of the group at the Savoy) was definitely *the* man in charge of the dance culture at the Savoy. White set rules of conduct and dismissed anyone from the group or inner circle who went against him. Between the different community factions, the protocols, and the social-politics, dancers were primed to blow off some steam. The Stearnses observe how the area developed into

> a fiercely competitive jungle, and the Savoy Ballroom syphoned off much of the nervous energy this constant pressure generated among the lucky few who became deeply interested in dancing. In turn this emotional climate was reflected in the tireless vigor and daring intervention of the Lindy, or Jitterbug.[21]

And so it was in this environment that dances were created, tested out and added to. There was always an increased opportunity in swing dances for individual expression or improvisation because of the perpetual breakaway action. This improvisatory concept has been shown to be common with dances such as the Charleston, but with swing dance the breakaway becomes highly anticipated by spectators. When a dancer would "breakaway," they would pull away from their partner and showcase their ingenuity and daring in front of their fellow dancers and audience members before joining back together with their partner, all while keeping in time with the music. In this sort of showing off, there was an unspoken competition around who could invent the wildest and boldest steps and stay within the swing rhythm. The lifts and throws common to swing dances grew out of this experimentation and rivalry. Rules were understood in the ballroom: one did not steal or "bite" someone's dance step. Despite the competition and constant one-upmanship, "Nobody copied anybody else or did somebody else's specialty."[22] This code of conduct, which led to a rich variety of movements in the swing repertoire, was enforced by the likes of White or other leader-types of the different ballrooms and dance groups. Building on the basic movement structure of the dance, performers could add in many secondary options to show flair and ingenuity.

This broad spectrum of possibilities was part of the popularity of the dance. The improvisational and creative impulses produce the swing dance body as one with subjectivity and self-confidence – qualities that helped to pull one out of the gloom of the depression. In the world of the energetic and constantly evolving swing dances, the body is empowered, celebrated, and "physicalizes the social cues" of the dance hall.[23]

The exact genesis of the name "Lindy Hop" is often misunderstood as being named after the aviator Charles Lindbergh who flew (or hopped) solo across the Atlantic in 1937. In fact, many were calling the swing style of dance the "hop" years before that time. Though once the connection was made to Lindbergh and the publicity around that event, the Lindy seemed to gain in momentum across the nation. In general, the swing dance styles, whether appended with other variations or names, continued on through the Swing Era. The Stearnses explain that vernacular dances "survived and prospered through innumerable variations, reinterpretations, revisions, and revivals," and that this was independent of what culture was performing the dance.[24] Importantly, the main impact of the formations of the dance was that it moved away from rules and hierarchies. Dance historian Terry Monaghan asserts: "the driving reciprocal dynamic of both partners characterized the essential vitality of the dance that paid minimal deference to the ballroom conventions of leaders and followers."[25] The opportunity for self-expression and equality within a duo was appealing to the general populace. The popularity of the swing music and dance spread across the nation and white audiences and dancers readily took it up as their own. The improvisatory nature of the dance opened up space for a whitening of the dance, transforming the dance into what became known as the Jitterbug. White dancers kept a straight back while doing the dance as they had done with the Charleston.

They developed a bouncier style as they were not as daring with acrobatics or moves that took them close to the floor, Black dancers dubbed the characterization the "jitterbug" to describe white dancer's jittery execution of the dance and the name stuck. To call the dance the Lindy today keeps a sense of ownership of the dance to Black Americans. In the 1930s and 1940s the overwhelming popularity of white orchestras, singers, and dancers (even in their jittery style) made swing dance a national craze, appropriately earning the title the "Swing Era."

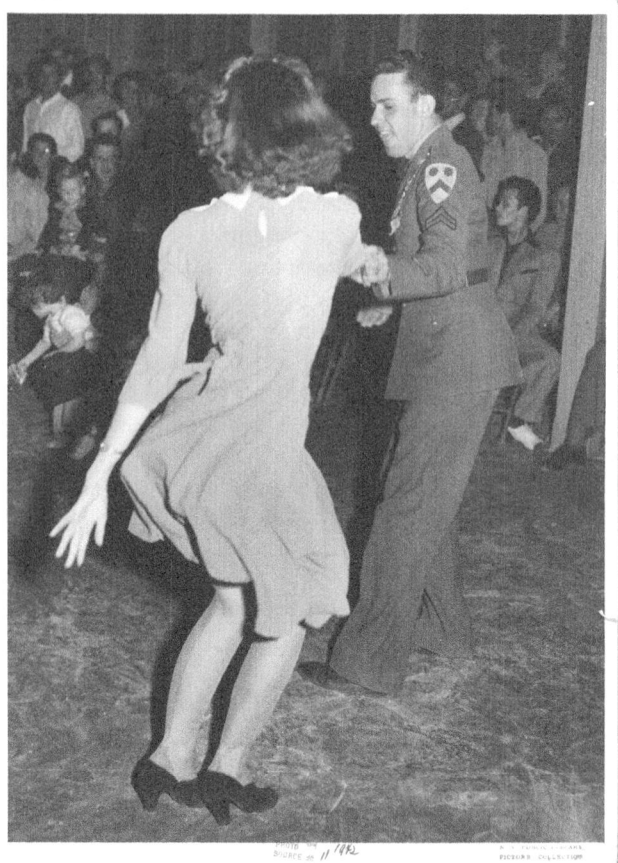

Figure III.1 "Jitterbug contest" The Miriam and Ira D. Wallach Division of Art, Prints and Photographs: Photography Collection, The New York Public Library
Source: New York Public Library Digital Collections. Accessed September 14, 2022. https://digitalcollections.nypl.org/items/1f2b7800-b56c-0137-30d6-295ccba5e65f.

Swing Dance, World War II, and National Identity

Though there were many styles of swing-styled jazz music circulating due to the numerous bands touring and crisscrossing the United States, swing music and dance culture rose to the top of the popular lexicon in part because the moves and music were synonymous with popular cinema of the time, such as *Swing Time* (1936), *Hollywood Hotel* (1937), and *Hellzapoppin'* (1941).[26] Sherrie Tucker explains in *Dance Floor Democracy: The Social Geography of Memory at the Hollywood Canteen*, "By the late 1930s, mainstream swing success required entrée to West Coast mechanisms of the culture industry, which had already gone west with the movies."[27] The novelty and popularity of cinema bolstered the excitement surrounding the dance. Though racial appropriation is not an emphasis in this section, it is important to remember that it was ongoing through the Jazz Age. Monaghan observes, "Broadway and Hollywood productions that incorporated the Lindy Hop in the 1930s and 1940s projected the dance form around the world, even though the key dance motif was reinterpreted according to the largely racist practices of those industries."[28] Despite "new white and black generations, with a pronounced interest in integration" and a greater sense of inclusion in the mid-1930s, there was still much to be done before ownership and contributions of Black music and dance styles was rightly recognized.[29]

After the attacks on Pearl Harbor in 1941 and the U.S declaration of war on Japan on December 8, 1941, the idioms of swing culture were steadily taken up as iconography of America for the shaping and promotion of national pride.[30] For instance, the image of the swing dancer, particularly the handsome soldier with a pretty female partner, was used to garner national support and applaud expressions of patriotic duty. Through music and dance venues, such as the Hollywood Canteen, VSO shows, and acclaimed dancehalls, swing dancing, as will be investigated in *Allegiance,* became a social emblem of being involved and generally supportive of the war.

In the three musicals of this section the moments of swing dance happen diegetically as part of the plot. Each of the particular narratives (two of which are set pre-World War II) has its own set of social and political issues that, to a varying degree, create tensions between self-expression and national conformity that are worked out on the dance floor. The social dances themselves, performed essentially on "the dance floor of the nation," come to define different historical and political moments and impacts of the decades.[31] From 1941 forward, when the inflated mythologies of swing dance and the war are considered alongside formations of national identity and nationhood, the dance becomes a complex set of negotiations surrounding meaning and bodily identity. Studying the complexities of that intersection exposes some of the biases the nation holds and demonstrates how in the U.S, according to Tucker, "World War II is remembered and memorialized," particularly in the manner "official memories are recruited to justify actions globally."[32] Attaching swing dancing to images of World War II, strategically harnesses the ideas of inclusion, friendly competition, and excitement of the dance floor for the purpose of national pride. The idea of soldiers shipping out in the morning and asking for one last dance before they go, or the soldier returning from the war to dance and celebrate with his sweetheart, has become such a part of the mythology and iconography of the United States that when a show comes along that challenges this scenario such as *Allegiance,* where Japanese American bodies performing swing dance are somehow not thought of as American by U.S. authorities, there is a rupture in that national narrative. That break problematizes U.S. consciousness that sees itself as a melting pot nation and points to the tension between the personal and the political, and the private and the public.

The eventual "nationalizing of swing culture" in the early 1940s co-opts the music, dance, celebration of self-expression, and community belonging as patriotic actions.[33] However, *Wonderful Town*, *Steel Pier*, and *Allegiance* trouble the connection between swing dance and pure patriotism, demonstrating how the dance can work in more complex or subversive ways. Each of the following chapters illustrate via the aforementioned case studies, that people were often identified, whether deliberately or more inconspicuously, based on how their bodies responded to developments around them as seen in moments of social dance.

Notes

1 Author interview with director/choreographer Andy Blankenbuehler, September 17, 2017.
2 *Wonderful Town*, book by Joseph A. Fields and Jerome Chodorov, lyrics by Betty Comden and Adolph Green, and music by Leonard Bernstein, 1953. The only available recording of *Wonderful Town* is the 1958 CBS Television live telecast of the stage musical (available in consecutive scenes on YouTube at: https://www.youtube.com/watch?v=_pCfW8nX1ZU, accessed July 23, 2018) and in its entirety at Museum of Television and Radio, New York.
3 *Steel Pier*, book by David Thompson, lyrics by Fred Ebb, music by John Kander, 1997. *Steel Pier* has been viewed at the New York Public Library's Theatre on Film.
4 *Allegiance*, book by Marc Acito, music and lyrics by Jay Kuo and book by Marc Acito, Kuo and Lorenzo Thione, 2015. *Allegiance* has been viewed at the New York Public Library's Theatre on Film and seen live.
5 While coming as a shock to so many, the stock market crash was a result of various factors developing over the decade. In the early 1920s, post-World War I optimism led to an increase in production and employment resulting in a prosperous economy. Beginning around 1924 stock market securities began to rise at a very quick rate resulting in a stock market boom over the next few years. The vision amongst many was that there was no end in sight for the prosperous time and people "proceeded to build a world of speculative make-believe." Though signs of the economic lessening (decrease in production and construction) began as early as 1925, with the low lending rates, people continued to build debt. Despite erratic behavior of the stock market toward the end of the decade, it always seemed to recover (and then some). Small indications, and mini crashes several months before the ultimate crash largely went unnoticed. As stocks began to fall at the end of 1929 panic ensued and the market bottomed out – not to recover for over a decade. John Kenneth Galbraith, *The Great Crash of 1929* (Boston, MA: Mariner Books, 1954), 3,7.
6 David Walsh and Len Platt, *Musical Theatre and American Culture* (Westport, CT: Greenwood, 2003), 84.
7 Ibid., 97.
8 Kenneth J. Bindas, *Swing! That Modern Sound* (Jackson: University Press of Mississippi, 2001), 99.
9 Howard Spring explains the Swing Era is generally considered between 1930–1945: "Swing began to take shape around 1928 and was well established by 1932... It became a national fad in 1935 when Benny Goodman's band brought a particular brand of swing to white teenagers, one that combined the performance practices of the great African American bands, such as those led by Henderson and Chick Webb, with modern arrangements of current pop songs." Spring, "Swing," *Grove Music Online*, January 31, 2014, https://doi-org.ezproxy.gc.cuny.edu/10.1093/gmo/9781561592630.article.A2258226.
10 Bindas, *Swing!* 99.

11 Ibid.

12 Ibid.

13 Julie Malnig, "Introduction," *Ballroom, Boogie, Shimmy Sham, Shake: A Social and Popular Dance Reader* (Chicago: University of Illinois Press, 2009), 12.

14 Other notable ballrooms in Harlem the 1930s include the New Star Casino and the Alhambra. Marshall, and Jean Stearns. *Jazz Dance: The Story of American Vernacular Dance* (New York: Da Capo Press, 1994), 317.

15 Claude Conyers, "Swing Dance," *Grove Music Online,* February 23, 2011, https://doi-org.ezproxy.gc.cuny.edu/10.1093/gmo/9781561592630.article.A2092734.

16 Spring further describes how the emphasis on the syncopation and pulse of the music can vary depending on the musician, which helps to explain the many varieties of swing music. Additionally, the size of the band increased in size (approximately ten musicians increasing to seventeen or more) to include full sections of instruments such as brass or saxophones. "Swing," *Grove Music Online,* January 31, 2014, https://doi-org.ezproxy.gc.cuny.edu/10.1093/gmo/9781561592630.article.A2258226.

17 Julie Malnig reminds that music and dance chronologies, "historically have been inextricable linked," however, this creative link is often de-emphasized from both disciplines in the academy. Even so, there was very much a connection between the passions and actions of both the dancers and musicians and orchestra leaders, particularly involving tempo. Malnig, *Ballroom, Boogie, Shimmy Sham, Shake*, 3.

18 The one dance that can be most connected with the athleticism of swing dance is the Texas Tommy. Claude Conyers explains the Texas Tommy: "A vigorous social dance for couples, arguably the first swing dance. The argument is that it was the first social dance using the basic 8-count rhythm of swing dance to include a breakaway step from the closed position of other couple dances of the time (1909–10). It was one of many dances that originated in the dance halls of the Barbary Coast red light district of San Francisco. It was not long before the Texas Tommy was danced on Broadway, in *Ziegfeld Follies of 1911,*" "Texas Tommy," *Grove Music Online,* February 23, 2011, http://www.oxfordmusiconline.com.ezproxy.gc.cuny.edu/grovemusic/view/10.1093.

19 In 1910 ten percent of the population in Harlem were Black, in 1920 it rose to thirty-two percent and by 1930 it would reach seventy percent. "An Affluent White Harlem?" Andy A. Beveridge, August 27, 2008, *The Gotham Gazette,*http://www.gothamgazette.com/index.php/demographics/4062-an-affluent-white-harlem.

20 Stearns and Stearns, *Jazz Dance*, 317.

21 Ibid., 320.

22 Ibid., 323. This law of conduct continues today, particularly in regards to hip-hop and tap, where there is often a cypher, or informal circle, where artists can practice and promote their moves in a judgment free zone. There is an understanding that there is to be no insulting of each other (as there may be in a rap-battle) and that one does not copy or another dancer's moves. While hip-hop is outside the era investigated in this project, a future investigation of how it is theatricalized and reconfigured for the stage would be beneficial to the study of social dance in performance.

23 I draw on the scholarship of Elizabeth Grosz here when she discusses the unfinished nature of the body, one that is constantly being shaped and formed by the world around it. Elizabeth Grosz, *Volatile Bodies: Toward a Corporeal Feminism* (Bloomington: Indiana University Press, 1994), x. Grosz, *Volatile Bodies*, x.

24 Stearns and Stearns, *Jazz Dance*, 114.

25 Karen Hubbard and Terry Monaghan, "Negotiating Compromise on a Burnished Floor: Social Dancing at The Savoy." In *Ballroom, Boogie, Shimmy Sham, Shake: A Social and Popular Dance Reader*, edited by Julie Malnig (Chicago: University of Illinois Press, 2009), 133.

26 David W. Stowe explains this connection: "Most of the swing era's most popular songs came from movies. Because many studios were in partnership with New

York music publishers, they profited from royalties from air play and sheet music sales at the same time the latter helped promote the movies from which they were drawn." Stowe, *Swing Changes: Big-band Jazz in New Deal America* (Cambridge: Harvard University Press, 1994), 132.

27 Sherrie Tucker, *Dance Floor Democracy: The Social Geography of Memory at the Hollywood Canteen* (Durham, NC: Duke University Press, 2014), 26.

28 Terry Monaghan, "Why Study the Lindy Hop?" *Dance Research Journal* 33, no. 2 (Winter 2001): 126.

29 Hubbard and Monaghan, "Negotiating Compromise," 135.

30 After the U.S. declared war on Japan, the Germans declared war on the U.S., prompting reciprocation from the U.S. While the U.S. entry into the war in Asia was different, ultimately the U.S went to war with the Allies against the Axis powers.

31 Tucker, *Dance Floor Democracy*, xix.

32 Ibid..

33 Ibid., 30.

References

Beveridge, Andy A. "An Affluent White Harlem?" *The Gotham Gazette*, August 27, 2008. http://www.gothamgazette.com/index.php/demographics/4062-an-affluent-white-harlem.

Bindas, Kenneth J. *Swing! That Modern Sound.* Jackson: University Press of Mississippi, 2001.

Bindas, Kenneth J. "Texas Tommy." *Grove Music Online*, February 23, 2011. http://www.oxfordmusiconline.com.ezproxy.gc.cuny.edu/grovemusic/view/10.1093.

Blankenbuehler, Andy. Personal Interview, New York City, September 12, 2017.

Conyers, Claude. "Swing Dance." *Grove Music Online*, February 23, 2011. https://doi-org.ezproxy.gc.cuny.edu/10.1093/gmo/9781561592630.article.A2092734.

Galbraith, Kenneth John. *The Great Crash of 1929.* Boston, MA: Mariner Books, 1954.

Grosz, Elizabeth. *Volatile Bodies: Toward a Corporeal Feminism.* Bloomington: Indiana University Press, 1994.

Hubbard, Karen, and Terry Monaghan. "Negotiating Compromise on a Burnished Floor: Social Dancing at The Savoy." In *Ballroom, Boogie, Shimmy Sham, Shake: A Social and Popular Dance Reader,* edited by Julie Malnig, 126–245. Chicago: University of Illinois Press, 2009.

Malnig, Julie, ed. *Ballroom, Boogie, Shimmy Sham, Shake: A Social and Popular Dance Reader.* Chicago: University of Illinois Press, 2009.

Monaghan, Terry. "Why Study the Lindy Hop?" *Dance Research Journal* 33, no. 2 (Winter 2001), 124–127.

Spring, Howard. "Swing," *Grove Music Online*, January 31, 2014. https://doi-org.ezproxy.gc.cuny.edu/10.1093/gmo/9781561592630.article.A2258226.

Stearns, Marshall, and Jean Stearns. *Jazz Dance: The Story of American Vernacular Dance.* New York: Da Capo Press, 1994.

Stowe, David W. *Swing Changes: Big-band Jazz in New Deal America.* Cambridge: Harvard University Press, 1994.

Tucker, Sherrie. *Dance Floor Democracy: The Social Geography of Memory at the Hollywood Canteen.* Durham, NC: Duke University Press, 2014.

Walsh, David, and Len Platt. *Musical Theater and American Culture.* Westport, CT: Greenwood, 2003.

7 "Good neighbors – Good neighbors"

Wonderful Town and Nostalgia for Lost Communities

In the 1958 CBS Television live telecast of *Wonderful Town,* two sisters from Ohio, Ruth (Rosalind Russell) and Eileen (Jacquelyn McKeever), arrive midday in Greenwich Village in 1935 to a street scene of carefree bohemian life in action.[1] A guide describes the seen for his tourist group, "Ever since eighteen-seventy Greenwich Village has been the Bohemian cradle of painters, writers, actors, etc., who've gone on to fame and fortune. Today in nineteen-thirty-five, who knows what future greats live in these twisting alleys? Come along!"[2] The delightful community of eccentric characters going about their daily lives sets a near instant time-machine effect in motion, drawing the audience back to an era of abundant self-expression and the passionate pursuit of artistic whims. Greenwich Village of the mid-1930s: Abstract Expressionist painter Hans Hoffman's art school was attracting avant-garde artists from around the world; the legacy of the Provincetown Players, who had lived in the village a decade earlier, continued to appeal to emerging writers and young actors set on the exploration of their craft; and the opening of the first racially integrated night club "Café Society" was only a few years away.[3] Not only are the television audiences of 1958 drawn back to the bohemian spirit of the Village in 1935, but they could also relish in seeing the near same cast and production of the beloved 1953 Broadway musical that occurred five years earlier.[4]

And so, the enthusiastic tour guide gathers the tourists at the upstage side-walk at the edge of the stage. They exclaim in amazement: "Look! Look! Poets! Actors! Dancers! Writers!".[5] Three women dressed in long-sleeved black body suits and flowing skirts enter in a triangular formation from stage right. The influence of original choreographer Donald Saddler's ballet background is readily visible in the pointed toes and turned-out legs of the dancers; the inclusion of numerous iconic modern dance moves allows for a playful imitation of the modern style. For instance, as each dancer maneuvers around an artist and his easel, they curve their upper body into a spiral shape while a bent leg with flexed foot reaches towards their cupped hands. The angularity and abstract gestures suggest the modernist avant-garde, perhaps they are Martha Graham dancers drilling themselves in the moves of their renowned leader? While the dancers stand out amongst the other performers in the

DOI: 10.4324/9781003163688-11

telecast, in their uniqueness, they also fit in perfectly amongst the bohemian group of artists, musicians, writers, and poets going about their lives in the same absorbed manner. The glories of the 1930s are felt in the sense of *bon vivance* that permeates the neighborhood. After a final build of a cacophony of individual artistic practices, wildly gesturing bodies, all crowding towards each other in a *"mad dance of self-expression"* (as described in the stage directions) the tourists are led off to the next stop on the tour – "Now we will see MacDougal Alley".[6]

By a turn of good fortune, the sisters find themselves renting a tango instructor's basement level apartment with one long street level window. Tucked in their new *pied à terre*, they realize they are being watched from outside by two strange men. The ogling men are half-heartedly chased away by a police officer. Despite the adventure and excitement amongst the carefree residents of the village, the third rumble of explosives cutting the new down-town subway line prompts the sisters to wonder, "Why-o-Why-o [...] did we ever leave Ohio?"[7] The beautiful ballad by composer Leonard Bernstein, with its simple harmonies in thirds and small musical range (both to accommodate Russell's limited vocal ability), is structured perfectly for the two female voices.[8] The chaos of the village and tinge of fear caused by the peeping Toms is juxtaposed with the clean and simple ballad. As Ruth and Eileen sing out about their beloved home state, our love and longing for home, or at least a relief from city life, burgeons as well. By a swift and clever sleight of hand the experienced production team make Americana palpable and strangely welcome.

Overall, the vivacity of the 1930s set up at the beginning of the production allows for a sweet contentedness to form around Depression-era Manhattan.[9] *Wonderful Town* can be broadly interpreted as a nostalgic romp through Greenwich Village in the 1930s, however, investigating how that nostalgia functions in a show that opened "at the height of the McCarthy and HUAC hearings, during a period when many of Bernstein's colleagues were under siege" helps depict a progressive undercurrent within the show.[10] To start, the leering action of the men crouching by the sisters' window hints at the anxieties surrounding surveillance in the 1950s in the entertainment industry and beyond. The sense of one's actions being watched or spied on at the time led to an incredible amount of paranoia and fearfulness. Positioning much of the musical inside the sister's apartment, always with the street window above them, expresses a continued sense of close observation, and the leering men draw attention to this. Comparatively, the 2003 revival of the show on Broadway in a post-9/11 period of heightened social and political tension supports the nostalgic power of the show to provide both escape and consideration of community in the U.S.[11] Interrogating how this purposeful nostalgia is embodied helps clarify what social dance is *doing* in *Wonderful Town* beyond celebrating the era. I trace how the vernacular movements from the 1930s are intertwined with some movement styles of the 1950s, creating an embodied association with both past and present styles. This temporal blending helps signal how nostalgia can be understood, as described by literary scholar Patricia Rae as a "renewed commitment not to the past but to a future of significant social change."[12] Embodying past moments and the emotions that surround them can help articulate what is missing in the present and actuate prospective introspection.

Significantly, by political design, everyday social structures in the 1950s had become more about the atomization and oppression of society. The fear of accusation, persecution, and damage to one's reputation as a result of an allegiance to various communities, opinions, and self-expressive activities was real. The House Un-American Activities Committee (HUAC) had begun investigations in 1945, and by the mid-1950s, many entertainers had been deported or arrested.[13] In a move that can be considered a massive abuse of power on the part of U.S. Senator Joseph McCarthy, artists had no choice but to censor their work for fear of being called out. Some adhered to these rules or found ways to work around them. *Wonderful Town* lyricists Betty Comden and Adolph Green insert subtle political undertones – to be explored in this chapter – while playwright Arthur Miller is more forceful. In fact, Miller's play *The Crucible* had been running for a month on Broadway before *Wonderful Town* opened, and the two productions ran concurrently on Broadway for a large part of the year. Though *Wonderful Town* is not political in the way *The Crucible* is (using the Salem Witch trials of 1692 as a metaphor for HUAC activities and accusations), there is an undercurrent of liberal thought to *Wonderful Town*. Notably, as is shown in the first few scenes of *Wonderful Town*, Ruth and Eileen quickly make a community for themselves and create a sense of belonging within a group in Greenwich Village that is shown to be liberal and open-minded. As will be explored, the movement in *Wonderful Town* enhances the communal aspect of the 1930s society and creates an embodied nostalgia for these modes of expression, particularly given government intolerance for such liberal activities in the 1950s. In this structure there is a tension set up between competing ideas of community: the cosmopolitan mixing of the 1930s versus the republican desire for a conservative, less inclusive community structure of the 1950s.

Background of *Wonderful Town*

Comden and Green were part of an accomplished creative team; Joseph A. Fields and Jerome Chodorov wrote the book and Leonard Bernstein composed the music. The musical is based on Fields and Chodorov's 1940 play *My Sister Eileen*, drawn from the short stories of aspiring "proletarian writer" Ruth McKenny.[14] *Wonderful Town* is composed of dramatically linked vignettes, essentially created as a vehicle for the vast comedic talent of Rosalind Russell, who had starred in the 1942 film of the play. Following the shenanigans that occur during the sisters' numerous adventures, which for Ruth ends by finding both a job in journalism and love, and fame for Eileen, the show celebrates the uniqueness of Greenwich Village.

Of the case studies in this project, *Wonderful Town* was produced closest to the era in which it is set and during an era of musical theatre where mythologies of what it meant to be American flourished on stage.[15] *Wonderful Town* comes from an era of musical theatre when Richard Rogers and Oscar Hammerstein II's shows played regularly.[16] Elizabeth L. Wollman explains popular musicals at the time, such as *The King and I* (1951) and *South Pacific* (1949), "played simultaneously on America's collective healing from and nostalgia for the Good War," while also "touch[ing] on a number of contemporary issues and concerns, including shifting gender roles and the country's new status as a global super power."[17] *Wonderful Town*, with an independent woman as the lead role, aligns more closely with *Guys and Dolls* (which opened in 1950, and was still running when *Wonderful Town* opened in 1953) than the works of Rodgers and Hammerstein.[18] Both *Guys and Dolls* and *Wonderful Town* follow stories of New York life in the 1930s and essentially appear as "American fairytales" of life in the city where people from all walks of life find ways to live together in harmony.[19] The theme of New Yorkers getting along despite differences and celebrating self-expression avoids overt attempts at education or moral lessons (which characterized various Rodgers and Hammerstein shows) and sets the shows apart from the duos' substantial oeuvre of work.[20]

As a matter of involvement in social issues, Bernstein, Comden, and Green had been part of a community of artists in the 1930s that were socially conscious and together made up the "cultural front." American studies scholar Michael Denning in *The Cultural Front: The Laboring of American Culture in the Twentieth Century* explains, "The 'cultural front' referred to both the cultural industries and apparatuses – a 'front' or terrain of cultural struggle – and the allegiance of radical artists and intellectuals who made up the 'cultural' part of the Popular Front."[21] The Popular Front was an "insurgent" social-democratic movement created out of the political turmoil in the 1930s that aimed to "unit[e] industrial unionists, Communists, independent socialists, community activists, and émigré anti-fascists around laborist social democracy, anti-fascism, and anti-lynching."[22] As part of the cultural front, Bernstein, Comden, and Green "sought in particular to create distinctly American art forms that did not erase ethnicity."[23] This can be seen in the team's earlier musical *On the Town* (1944) that, along with various choices to include immigrants and a variety of ethnicities in the ensemble and crew, cast the Japanese-American dancer Sono Asato in a lead role even though the U.S. was at war with Japan.[24] These kinds of political overtures were *de rigeur* in the musicals of the 1930s and not uncommon in the early 1940s, however, by the 1950s when *Wonderful Town* was produced these sorts of provocations would be all but eliminated by a general fear of being persecuted for communist or Liberal activity. Conceivably, turning away from more overt political connections on the surface was necessary to protect from HUAC attention. Despite the risks, there are indicators in *Wonderful Town* of the creators' other interests and values threaded through the play that work to create a nostalgic imperative for the radical intentions of the 1930s, which stands in stark contrast to the witch-hunts that had begun the same year the show debuted on Broadway.

For instance, by putting forth a positive image of female independence in New York in the characters of Ruth and Eileen and an appreciation of self-expression, as seen in the Villagers, *Wonderful Town* identifies with a liberal and public-spirited style associated with the left. As will be explored, Comden and Green's lyrics, in collaboration with Bernstein pastiche-styled score, weave together a sentimental nostalgia for bohemian Greenwich Village and witty musical comedies, with a reflective nostalgia that allows for contemplation of how displaced one feels in the present world. Daniel Gundlach points out this duality in "Maybe I'd Better Go Home: Nostalgia in *Wonderful Town*":

> *Wonderful Town* embodies nostalgia for two contradictory things: small-town America (Ohio) and the New York of the mid-1930s when one could safely be a communist, legitimately envisioning and working for a communitarian and egalitarian nation, something Bernstein and Comden and Green (and McKenney herself) strove for throughout their lives.[25]

It is important to note that the entire score and lyrics to the show were pulled together in under a month. As such, it is difficult to surmise how much these greater complexities are strategically layered into the show.[26] According to Carol Oja, in the rush to finish the score before the contract with Rosalind Russell wore out, the more political or satirical layers were not fleshed out.[27] Oja found early drafts of the score were more cutting edge, and later drafts "show a process of rounding off political edges."[28] Any radical or subversive intentions are to be experienced and interpreted through the nostalgic power of the piece that has the potential for audiences to reflect on an era where self-expression was supported and working classes rallied for equality and fair rights.

Strategies, Structure, and Layers of Meaning

The use of a narrative style characterized by episodes and multiple locations to express the hustle and bustle of New York City can be seen on Broadway from the nineteenth century in shows such as Benjamin Baker's *A Glance at New York* (1848) or *The Greenwich Village Follies* (1919) with music by Irving Berlin. The *Follies* in particular celebrated the avant-garde and all things experimental and modern in New York. Impressively, the *Follies* included three dances performed by Martha Graham herself. *On the Town* also shares numerous similarities to this episodic style of narrative.[29] One of the main differences between *On the Town* and *Wonderful Town*, however, is the temporal distance between when the show is set and its production. *On the Town* was essentially set in its present day and "aim[ed] to capture the city's street life and its potential for a devil-may-care fling during a reprieve from battles on land and sea."[30] There is a sense in *On the Town* of investigating the New

York City right outside the doors of the theatre. Conversely, *Wonderful Town* is taking a backwards glance of nearly twenty years, and this colors the show differently. Furthermore, there was already a popular precedent set by *Guys and Dolls* for a playful look back to the 1930s. Likewise, given the bleaker economic circumstances for shows on Broadway in the 1950s, engaging with nostalgia for the 1930s would prove to be a smart marketing in consideration of increasing production costs.[31]

The structure of the show is quite clear, it is a two-act musical with ten songs. It is a musical comedy with a stellar cast and Bernstein's modern music filled with theatrical potential. However, more specifically, as articulated by Brooks Atkinson in his 1953 review, *Wonderful Town* is about a point of view: "The satire of Eileen and of the Village is affectionate. Even the charlatans and delinquents are likable characters."[32] The friendly satire uses wit, gentle mockery, and plenty of exaggeration to poke fun at people's behavior, foolishness, and vices. The musical showcases a breadth of tolerance and acceptance of people's oddities and idiosyncrasies, while also tracing the journey of two women stepping out of expected family roles for women at the time.

Though the women's struggles to find jobs at the beginning is quite playful, Ruth does not accept her expected role of pursuing female designated jobs such a being part of a secretarial pool. Rather, as Elizabeth L. Keathley observes, Ruth "struggles to be taken seriously and repeatedly encounters conflicts between her professional goals and her personal relationships in ways that are specific to the situation of working women."[33] After World War II and continuing into the 1950s, women's roles were redefined to be in the home as caretaker of the family and household. Keathley explains this backwards step from earlier decades; "by mid-century 'modernity' was translated into 'New Look' dresses, helpful household appliances, and devotion to housewifery and motherhood."[34] The character of Ruth stands in stark contrast to these new designations. Ruth is a writer who seeks out opportunities to sell her stories, en route to becoming a legitimate journalist. Not only do her forays for work fail, so do her attempts at getting a date. Her self-mockery of her inability to attract a man in the song "One Hundred Easy Ways" is a lament of her lack of male companionship in the narrative, along with a supportive wink at women's liberation and female empowerment. Comden and Green's lyrics uphold women's abilities to succeed on their own and champion female mastery of masculine jobs. Ruth sings: "You've met a charming fellow and you're out for a spin [...] Don't bat your eyes and say, "What a romantic spot we're in," Just get out, crawl under the car, tell him it's the gasket and fix it in two seconds flat with a bobby pin".[35]

Strategically, in a Brechtian-styled move, as the show is set in the mid-1930s when women were becoming part of the work-force, Ruth's behavior would fit in. Keathley explains the necessary distancing needed; "Ruth Sherwood could appear in a period piece set in the 1930s, but she could not represent the concerns of women in the postwar era."[36] As an additional safeguard, Russell played Ruth in the 1942 film, establishing her comedic talent and the character's independent streak, while also associating her with the role early on. In

1942, women were still filling the jobs of absent men who had become soldiers, so some of that "radical" behavior could be carried through to the 1953 musical. Regardless as to whether purposeful critical moves were noticed by audiences or critics, these tactics, as in the lyrics of "One Hundred Easy Ways," still would have been seen as somewhat precarious as "all liberationist movements were bracketed together as anti-American."[37] The freedom of expression of the 1930s, as seen in the opening of *Wonderful Town,* was a thing of the past in the 1950s. Keathley explains, "Postwar America was a place quite different from 1930s New York, for the radical culture of the Popular Front had been decimated by the Cold War fear of communism and all that was associated with it."[38] By and large *Wonderful Town* is part homage to the 1930s and part a petition to not forget the way life used to be, a nostalgic turn that is both sentimental and political.[39]

One of the main shifts the creative team made from the 1940 play that brings greater social impact to the production was to move Ruth and Eileen outside into the world of Greenwich Village and beyond. The play took place entirely in the sisters' apartment and only referred to outside experiences. By putting Ruth and Eileen in the apartment and around the city, a more palpable construct between the rural and the city, the personal and the public, and individualism and nationalism is able to percolate to greater or lesser extent throughout the show. Further, by taking the story "to the streets" the sense of community makes the scene more relatable for the audience coming into the theater from the streets of the city.

Putting to one side where audiences may have come into the theatre from, there is very much a mixing of different groups in *Wonderful Town.* There is a utopian wish in *Wonderful Town* that despite political, social, religious, or sexual differences and individual foibles we can find a way of living together with love and laughter. The opening resonates with hopefulness sung by the quirky denizens of the Village, "Here we live, Here we love […] Life is mad, Life is sweet, Interesting people live on Christopher Street!" [40] At the same time, it is important to mention that there was a subculture in the 1950s that was striving to remove itself from societal control and expected roles. The Beat generation of the 1950s was renowned as anti-conformists, left wing, and anti-war. Bernstein, Comden, and Green use some of the lighter sensibilities and stereotypes of the more popular branch of that generation – the aptly named "Beatniks" – in *Wonderful Town.* As we will see in "Swing!" and to some extent in the opening, various affectations of youth culture in the 1950s, including long hair, Bebop jazz, and a variety of fashion affectations, are used in the musical that draw attention to ongoing grassroots social movements going on amidst the political brinkmanship and paranoia of the 1950s.

Modern Moves: Choreographic Strategies and Imagined Communities

Brooks Atkinson applauds the contributions of what he calls "ballets" by "dance arranger" Donald Saddler for "the skill with which they help portray the rag-tag and bobtail street life of the old Village and satirize the bizarre forms of revelry that manage to destroy the sobriety of Manhattan."[41] Saddler (1918–2014) was a soloist with American Ballet Theatre for many years but often returned to musicals, with which he had experience through Hollywood movies as a teen.[42] Though he had been involved with various shows as an assistant, his first credit as a Broadway choreographer was *Wonderful Town*. Saddler was highly respected by dancers, and as the original program to *Wonderful Town* states, "a favorite with balletomanes."[43] His ballet background is very apparent in his choreography, and he borrowed dancers from the ballet world for the production. Even in the small amount of footage of the original, a lifted (or upright) balletic style is apparent. As can be seen in the telecast, however, Saddler shows the eclectic group of community residents through his playful choreography that uses small group choreography within the larger choreographic presentation that thread together to create a sense of community.

Creating the tapestry of movement styles in *Wonderful Town* was not an easy feat for Saddler as a myriad of lifestyle choices and thus movement styles defined the modern moment of the story in Greenwich Village. This eclectic mélange was a different mode of performance from the storybook characters and narratives common in ballet. As such, though Saddler is credited as the choreographer and received the Tony Award for Best Choreography, there are several accounts of Jerome Robbins helping out. Humphrey Burton explains, "Jerome Robbins was brought in – uncredited at his request – to 'show-doctor' the dance routines, reportedly after Miss Russell was accidently dropped by a male dancer at a performance in Boston."[44] Despite the fact Saddler had performed in a variety of energetic Hollywood musicals and was used to social dance and jazz movement, because *Wonderful Town* was such an "acrobatic production," particularly "Conga!," with the many lifts and throws of Russell some advice and assistance from Robbins added some reassurance to the star.[45] Robbins did not take over the show or drastically alter the dancing, though credit is sometimes wrongly assigned to him. In *There's a Place for Us: The Musical Theatre Works of Leonard Bernstein*, Helen Smith affirms Robbins's absence in *Wonderful Town* as she finds the dancing "all spectacle rather than narrative."[46] Robbins's style had always been to forward the plot using dance as in *West Side Story* (1957) or *Fiddler on the Roof* (1964), and as Smith indicates, the dances in *Wonderful Town* are more distinct production numbers keeping Saddler's movement signature generally intact.

While Saddler did not use dance emphatically as a plot device, the musical is always physically in motion, an effect that helps to envision the vibrancy of the community. There are two main instances in the musical that best demonstrate this momentum as well as a physical connection to collective memory that readily creates a sense of embodied nostalgia: the opening introduction of Greenwich Village and its denizens as described earlier, and "Swing!" in the second act. These production moments show popular ways of moving and how the "life blood of the community" flowed in 1935.[47] Ruth's engagement with the Brazilian navy cadets in "Conga!" adds a comical bent to the challenges of trying to get an interview, as well as some subtle political undercurrents to be discussed at the close of this chapter.

As described, the opening number introduces the cacophony of sounds, people, and movements of the city. There is a sense of contrast between the rural or Midwest United States, represented by Ruth and Eileen, and the capitalist metropolis of New York shown in the opportunist hustlers and bustlers of the city. Within that difference there is also a polarity between the conservative values of a small town and the more liberal ways of New York displayed through movement and body language. Eileen and Ruth stand stiffly with their arms close to their bodies and suitcases held tight. They move around the stage in small tentative steps, staying clear of any engagement with strangers. Residents of the village, conversely, move broadly around the stage with swooping strides and grand arm gestures that denote their profession, whether a painter or a restaurant owner etc. The modern dancers bring the grandest moves to the repertoire of movement, their overt seriousness part of the comical structure of the musical. The stiffness of Ruth and Eileen, as travelers from Ohio, would have been apropos to the 1950s as their posture at the beginning of the show embodies conservativeness. The local residents express the bohemian flair of the village in their freedom of movement, sparking a sense of nostalgia for a more open-minded way of life. In both cases bodies are shown to be "inscribed, marked, engraved, by social pressures external to them," influencing how they move through the world of the musical.[48]

The "Swing!" section is of interest in this case study because of its upfront interpretation of and poking fun at the music and social dance of the time, blended with some aesthetic sensibilities of "Beatniks." The scene explores how the body takes on the physical expressions of the era: liberated movement, social gatherings, and expressed sexuality. This is an area where the blending of past and present styles, as seen in the body, points towards a sense of social change. For instance, there is a teaching or persuasive quality to the piece as the Villagers instruct Ruth (and the audience) how to feel the groove of swing and get "hep."[49] Getting "hep" can be seen also as a wish for an open, aware, socially progressive attitude moving forward. In this structure there is a signal to how much current conservatives could use a lesson as well. The scene involves Ruth's reluctant employment experience as a street promoter for the new jazz club The Village Vortex. She must go about the Village wearing a large belt that flashes "VORTEX." The street location of the song sets forth swing dance as a more working class or community dance. When Ruth runs into Bill (her connection to the publishing world and eventual love interest), she is embarrassed to be found out having abandoned her writing pursuits and tries to convince him she is headed to the opera. The club promoter barges in to tell her to get back to work and tosses a pamphlet at her to read. Ruth begins to read the pamphlet with much hesitation: "Get hep, Step up, Step up".[50] On the second try she gains more confidence and rhythm and a drumbeat underscores her patter. As she begins to sing, a female dancer in cigarette pants moves in behind her, shuffling her feet in time to the music with her hips pushed forward.[51] Two other dancers, in the same streamlined silhouettes come in hunched over with fingers snapping and heads bent down. They pivot, low to the ground with hips swiveling as others join in. All are obviously trained ballet dancers, visible in the turn out of their legs and hips as they walk.[52] The movement qualities of swing dancing, particularly the lower sense of gravity, stand in contrast to the lifted more ethereal emphasis in ballet training. However, the parody of the dance in "Swing!" and thus the under-lying subtext, points to how not "hep" the white dancers are particularly in contrast to the Black founders of the dance, who are nowhere to be seen. In this consideration, the swing dance styles presented are so exaggerated that the effect is comical.[53] The parody continues as a train of four dancers enters from between two buildings in the same hunched over pulsing step and arrive at Ruth's spot. They roll up to a straight standing position waiting for her next line. As Atkinson observes, Saddler's greatest contribution is that "he satirize[s] the bizarre forms of revelry" that functions to disrupt the sense of alienation and paranoia that was taking over society in 1953.[54] Indeed, the movement gets more playful and ridiculous in its interpretation as the song progresses. The dance begins to take on more affectations of the 1950s Beatnik style (hunched over, disaffected expressions, low swinging arms, and finger snaps) that works to imagine a connection between the progressive groups of the 1930s and those of the 1950s.[55]

Ruth tries to move a little in the swing style, with which she is obviously unfamiliar. The Villagers are unimpressed and wander off, but linger back as she continues to sing with more gusto. They turn with arms high and fingers splayed primed to show her how the dance is done. The Villagers break into a jazz square sharply accentuating the first beat and then swinging their hips around in a square to come back and hit the down beat again. They repeat this action several times, using their bodies to get Ruth into the groove. In this way, the only way to get "hep" to the music is to feel it in the movements of the body. Musically the "Swing!" number is different from anything else in the show. Smith finds the mixture of musical styles and genres in *Wonderful Town* "creates the effect of a vaudeville show," which fits into the pastiche style of the musical.[56] Bernstein was recycling or adapting various unused pieces from his past, which is understandable in the rushed time frame of production. Smith observes that with "Swing!" the main point of the number is a lively communal spectacle, and though the time marker of 1935 does not specifically fit the song, small historical inaccuracies are "unimportant when the visual and musical impact of the number is considered."[57]

Once Ruth gets the movements, she is able to improve on her jazz-styled vocals. The stage directions describe how she is to sing to the Villagers: "*Answering in Cab Calloway fashion*" to improvise some scat. The stage direc-tions then describe, "*By this time Ruth is in a glaze-eyed hypnotic trance … she delivers patter in a husky dreamlike monotone*".[58] She begins, "Well, yes, yes, baby,

I know! That old man Mose kicked the bucket, The old oaken bucket that hung in the well – Well, well, well, baby I know".[59] She improvises on these lyrics and her performance gets more and more distorted the deeper she gets into it. Her scat in the style of Cab Calloway, particularly at she takes a masculine posture as she does it, adds a bizarre twist to the number. Importantly, there is a signal in the comical parody of her scatting to the cultural theft by white musicians, dancers, and orchestra leaders of Black cultural forms, which by 1953 (and even more so in 1958) was quite common.[60] Katherine Baber takes on the racial and gender issues in *Wonderful Town* and *On the Town*, which both use jazz music and dance as a uniformed "American" creation. She explains, "deploying what was still essentially black musical style for a white female performer also aligns *On the Town* (and eventually *Wonderful Town*) with other manipulations of gender within the Broadway tradition."[61] The teaching aspect to the number, of the Villagers (played by a mostly white cast) transferring knowledge to the white woman from Ohio, stands as an example of how these music and dance appropriations are transmitted and circulated. *Wonderful Town,* as seen in the 1958 telecast, displays this kind of absorption of Black styles. In analyzing the chronology of swing music, Smith explains the "Swing!" number "can also be seen as derived from the music of white bandleaders, despite the Calloway call-and-response section."[62] This taking on or racial impersonation was part of how the younger generation moved through the world, claiming that which is "hep" as their own. Norman Mailer, in his renowned 1957 essay "The White Negro: Superficial Reflections on the Hipster," finds this grandiosity so astonishing because of the absence of self-recognition (or "narcissistic detachment") of their actions.[63] Mailer muses on this shift in the younger generation, "So there was a new breed of adventurers, urban adventurers who drifted out at night looking for action with a black man's code to fit their facts."[64] It is hard to ignore the racial impersonation, except to explain that in the effort to illustrate Greenwich Village as a community obsessed by jazz culture, the exaggerated parody is meant to be light-hearted and affectionate. Musically, "Bernstein's aim was not to create an exact imitation of a swing piece but to suggest the genre."[65] The show's motive was not to tell of the social and cultural history building up to 1935 in the village but rather to show a whimsical snapshot of the time, aimed to both entertain, amuse, and to jog people's memories back to a time of self-expression and a buoyant sense of community, however imagined it may be. Still, "Swing!" reminds of the genuine thrill of the Black music and dance without acknowledging its roots or referring to Harlem, except the Cab Calloway reference. A case could be made that "Swing!" conceivably points to the government whitewashing the complexity of civil rights issues and equality by HUAC, as with the mostly white original cast there is a marked absence of Black performers on stage, though casts were hardly diverse on Broadway in the 1950s.[66] On the whole, "Swing!" is not so much about racial appropriation but uses exaggeration and parody to make one consider the broad assumptions of those who would condemn communities of artists and freethinkers. Notably by the end of the number there is a celebration of those who get "hep" and "Dig the message," learning to embody rhythm and groove, essentially supporting diversity in cultural contributions. This message to "step up" stands in stark contrast to the conservative voices sowing paranoia and fear across America in 1950s.

There is also a practical explanation behind the instructive, and thus imitative nature of the piece that may help to understand the way of learning the aesthetics of jazz in the show. Saddler explains that when he was first working with the creative team, Russell, a renowned film actress at the time, confided in him that she was quite insecure about her dancing, and confessed she was not as talented dance-wise as the others. She asked Saddler if he could create movement scenarios for her that allowed her to follow.[67] In this manner, the dancers "teach" her in the rhythm and ways of swing. This choreographic strategy helps to explain the structure of the piece and how the more the moves increase in difficulty the more Russell is coaxed into place by the ensemble. The dancers pace around Ruth in low, close to the ground crouches with knees deeply bent. She quickly picks the style up encouraged by the dancers who chant "you gettin' hep." Through this instructive style of social dance-based choreography where the dancers lead her on with the latest moves, she figures out how to get "hep" (much like the two gangsters encouraged to dance in *The Drowsy Chaperone*). There is a sense that the audience too could learn to get "hep," through taking on music, singing, and dancing styles.

Good Neighbors, the Conga, and Female Independence

In line with the creative team's purposes, the narrative grows in excitement as Ruth and Eileen come to take control of those around them and help each other to achieve their goals. Their body language shifts from the earlier stiffness to a more supple and confident movement dynamic and posture. In 1953, there is potential for an embodied nostalgia to emerge in consideration of prospects for women at that time which was much different than in 1935 and the backwards step female empowerment was faced with. Keathley describes when men came back from the war, "Women were offere[ed] domestic activities to replace their productive wartime roles, bequeathing those 'masculine roles to returning veterans'."[68] Men came back to the U.S., and many women returned to the home and were expected to take on the role of homemaker. Keathley explains while around the world women were becoming more and more independent, "the United States seemed intent on turning back the hands of time."[69] Baber explains the showcasing of Ruth's independence in the musical stands at the crosshairs of "a portrayal of feminine independence in tension with postwar 'American family values."[70] Nonetheless, female bodies in *Wonderful Town* are produced as determined and filled with agency and a reminder of a time when female agency was a more tangible and attainable concept.

Perhaps the gutsiest move by Ruth in *Wonderful Town* is her dedication to pursuing a career in journalism that takes her to the docks to interview Brazilian navy cadets. The "Conga!" section celebrates the thrill of dance and physical engagement in 1935 while also allowing Ruth, acting as a journalist, to question the foreigners about what they think about the United States. The interview of newly arrived Brazilian navy cadets is thought up by Chick Clark, a sleazy newspaper employee, to get Ruth out of the picture while he makes moves on Eileen. Ruth gives her best attempt to interview the cadets, who only want to dance the "American Conga." Ruth reluctantly agrees to show the sailors the Conga in exchange for their answering of her questions. She starts with, "What do you think of the USA...the NRA...TVA?".[71] They never answer, however Ruth persists: "What's your opinion of women's clothes, Major Bowes, Steinbeck's prose, How do you feel about Broadway Rose?".[72] As Humphrey Burton explains, the time-marker questions "illustrate the collaborators encyclopedic knowledge of the thirties."[73] The number also uniquely functions to showcase Ruth's spunk and come-what-may attitude and, importantly, provide an outrageous act one finale.

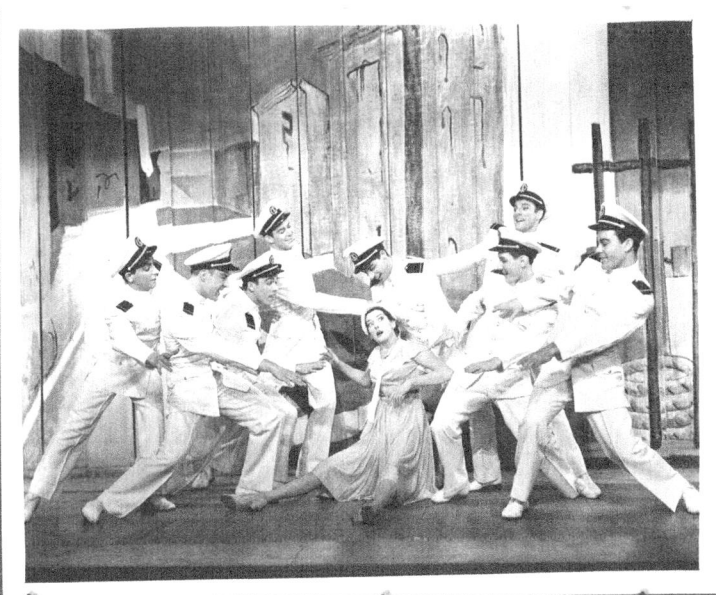

Figure 7.1 Rosalind Russell and chorus boys dressed as Brazilian cadets in "Wonderful Town" 1952, *Wonderful Town,* Billy Rose Theatre Division, The New York Public Library

Source: Billy Rose Theatre Division, The New York Public Library, "Rosalind Russell and chorus boys dressed as Brazilian cadets in Wonderful Town" New York Public Library Digital Collections, accessed September 14, 2018. http://digitalcollections.nypl.org/items/5e66b3e8-dc47-d471-e040-e00a180654d7.

The switch over to the Cuban beats of the conga is also a clever way Bernstein can play with a variety of music styles, a "trademark eclecticism" that comes to full fruition in *West Side Story*. [74] A slightly troubling aspect of the dance is how much the Brazilian sailors "man handle" Ruth. [75] Also of concern is the appropriation and inaccurate portrayal of Cuban and Brazilian culture to be expanded on shortly. To start, as the number becomes more physical, Ruth makes a plea to the sailors: "Good Neighbors [...] Remember our policy, Good neighbors – I'll help you, If you'll just help me". [76] An innocent enough request, there exists deeper meaning in the lyrics, particularly in the hail "Good Neighbors," which is repeated three times in the song. Franklin Delano Roosevelt introduced the Good Neighbor Policy during his tenure as president (1933–1945). As Brian Herrera explains in *Latin Numbers,* the policy was aimed "toward Latin America and to encourage 'friendly' commercial, cultural, and military relations among neighboring American republics." [77] By 1953 however, this policy had generally dissolved and was "redeployed in the postwar era away from Pan-American collaborations toward proto-Cold War engagements." [78] Ruth's reference to the policy would be correct for the 1930s. Her repetition of the phrase adds emphasis to the terminology, evoking a reflective nostalgia for a policy that would seem quite distant in 1953. Herrera explains, "Ruth's admonition to 'remember our policy' also reanimates inter-American rhetoric in a nostalgic register, evoking the Good Neighbor ethos as a quaint policy of the past." [79] Comden and Green cleverly insert the motto as a way to intimate the issue and the shifts therein.

At the forefront of this humorous and entertaining number, however, is how far Ruth will go and how much she will endure to get a story. In continuance of Russell requesting movement scenarios that allow her to follow others, the "Conga!" functions similarly as the cadets "move" her around in their exuberance for the dance. [80] Historically, the conga was "an adaptation of a long-standing Cuban *carnaval* tradition, 'conga line' performances had been seen in commercial venues in the United States and United Kingdom since at least 1935." [81] As opposed to a coupled social dance, the Conga features an entire line, often made up of dozens of participants, physically linked together doing the same moves. The kinesthetic connection between dancers extends from the start of the line all the way down to the end. Each participant holds the shoulders or waist of the person in front of them as the line surges forward. The thrill of the Conga comes from the leader snaking in and around the space leading the participants in unexpected ways. In *Wonderful Town* the Conga line does just this. As Ruth attempts to detach herself from the group, she inadvertently leads the sailors back to the Village. Community members join in bumping and jostling through the neighborhood, creating such mayhem that the police come in and arrest Eileen, who Ruth – in desperate need of a break – forced to take her place leading the group around. The dance works as a plot forwarding device as it lands Eileen in jail, where her notoriety on the front page of the newspaper the next day is noticed by a club owner who gives her a shot on stage. The collective nature of the dance functions to uphold a sense of community. The uniformity suggests a sense of togetherness that all are willing to join in the "foreign" dance, while also parodying the dance and the inability of Ruth and Eileen to stop it from multiplying in intensity and size. The joy over the collective physical action from the sailors and the community members who join in sits in contrast to the desperate attempt from Ruth and Eileen to escape the Conga line. The boisterous song and dance number by way of its many repetitions of lyrics and movements does allow a hint of the political to creep in. The situation sets up a physical tension between self-expression and collective action that leans towards a demonstration of collective behavior and how quickly it can happen. Joining in on community activity is celebrated, but with a slight tinge of the perils of coercion into a cause or more acutely, an ideology, such as McCarthyism. Though, in the farcical nature of the piece we are encouraged to enjoy the silliness and the music. In the narrative, the "Conga!" episode and Eileen's newfound notoriety firmly establish that Ruth and Eileen cannot return home now.[82]

Critical Reception

Because of its "natural blend of friendliness and satire," critics generally adored *Wonderful Town*. [83] Brooks Atkinson recognized the charm that Bernstein, Comden and Green tried to bring to the show; "They made the Greenwich Village of the 1930s look crack brained without being unsociable."[84] Political undercurrents or social meanings are not mentioned by critics, nor are the Good Neighbor references; most reviews understandably focus on Russell. Walter Kerr describes how she embodies her performance, "instead of attacking a song, she inhabits one, moving around in it, with such confidence and grace and honest exuberance as to make it entirely her own."[85] Kerr briefly mentions Comden and Green "have remembered their own village pasts with enough ardor and irony to supply some accurate and inventive lyric ideas."[86] *Time* went so far as to put Russell on the cover of their March 1953 issue, stating her performance "represents the triumph of personality over technique: she communicates to her audience all the rewarding warmth and humor of shared experience."[87]

In regards to the choreography, Donald Saddler's dance numbers are thought to "[c]apture perfectly the raffish individualism in village life."[88] Though Saddler's "ballets" can stand on their own, they are recognized for the way they each show the flavors of the people of the village and a sense of community.[89] Atkinson finds each one stirs up a sense of nostalgia for the music, the moves and the moment – "A colorful phantasmagoria of village scenes."[90] Kerr states Saddler "tells a dance story with verve, clarity, and high good humor."[91] Looking at numerous reviews of productions over the last few decades, there is no mention of political subtext, though that does not mean it is not there. The lasting power of the show is in its unabashed and joyous portrayal of New York City. Ben Brantley responds to the 2003 Broadway revival, "And no matter how long you've lived in New York City, you start to see it with the eyes of a new arrival who believes anything is possible here."[92] While Brantley finds the revival (directed and choreographed by Kathleen Marshall) "unfinished" and not "an obvious candidate for the minimalist approach," the show itself has lasting quality because it "melds urban jitters and jive with a wistful melodic romanticism," supporting the nostalgic power of the piece to imagine 1930s Greenwich Village.[93]

In all, *Wonderful Town* illustrates the "foibles" of Manhattan life, and this becomes an attractive subject matter because of the very nature of audiences. Whether audiences are residents of New York, or tourists, the show offers a glance into the life of residents in 1935 New York City. The physicality of the show does much to recognize how 1935 was about movement, action, and expressing oneself socially and politically through the body, which stands in contrast to overall conservatism in the 1950s. By the time of the production of *Wonderful Town*, geopolitical tensions were increasing and McCarthyism was all around, however, the Americanness of "Swing!" or the intensity of "Conga!" draws attention to female ingenuity and resilience. *Wonderful Town*, using entertaining and clever social satire filled with comedic momentum, allows us to enjoy, but also reflect on, a different time with greater freedom of expression and movement. The collaborators use nostalgia for the 1930s to imagine a community in the face of precarity, reminding through subtle hints that self-expression and community involvement had the potential to instigate change and could again. Being part of the choreography in *Wonderful Town* is to be part of a progressive undertone that circulates throughout the show. The embodiment of the adventurous and spirited lifestyle of Greenwich Village in the 1930s marks the body as self-expressive and open to ideas. Conversely, the continued weaving in of the melodies and softness of "Ohio" keep a memory of the charm of small-town life and simple living imprinted in the body of the singers, if only for the duration of the song.[94] These two embodied manifestations create nostalgia for a time where people were not using fear and intimidation for political advantage. As has been demonstrated, the embodied nostalgia in *Wonderful Town* becomes the subversive element that brings the performances' social and political meanings to light. In the next chapter, dancers feel a more visceral desperation in their situation, breaking their bodies and souls for a chance at prize money at dance marathons in Depression-era Atlantic City.

Notes

1 The original 1953 Broadway production of *Wonderful Town* was not filmed in its entirety, only a few very short excerpts exist. The descriptions of *Wonderful Town* in the following passages come from viewing the 1958 CBS Television live telecast of the stage musical (available in consecutive scenes on YouTube at: https://www.youtube.com/watch?v=_pCfW8nX1ZU, accessed July 23, 2018) and in its entirety at Museum of Television and Radio, New York. In *Forever Mame: The Life of Rosalind Russell,* Bernard F. Dick claims, "The closest approximation of Rosalind's

opening night performance is the kinescope of the two-hour live telecast of *Wonderful Town*." He explains, "Rosalind admitted that she could never top the performance she gave on opening night, 25 February 1953. Subsequent performances were never less than professional but never equaled the evening of the premiere." *Forever Mam,* (Jackson, MI: University Press of Mississippi, 2006), 160. There is a two-minute silent excerpt filmed by a family member of Rosalind Russell in 8mm from the 1953 Broadway production, which gives a general sense of the show and shows the similarities between the telecast and the stage version. Available at: http s://www.youtube.com/watch?v=2G7zdKyQm7U, accessed October 29, 2018.

2 Guide, Act 1, scene 1 *Wonderful Town,* Joseph A. Fields, Jerome Chodorov, Betty Comden and Adolph Green (New York, NY: Random House Publishing, 1953), 8.
3 Michael Denning, *The Cultural Front: The Laboring of American Culture in the Twentieth Century* (New York: Verso, 1997), 339.
4 In the 1958 telecast Rosalind Russell reprised her Broadway role with most of the same cast except Jacquelyn McKeever played Eileen (originally Edie Adams) and Sydney Chaplin played Robert Baker (originally George Gaynes). Ralph Beaumont helped adapt Donald Saddler's choreography for the telecast, which has been filmed as if on a stage.
5 *Wonderful Town,* 8.
6 Ibid., 9.
7 Betty Comden and Adolph Green, "Ohio," 1953.
8 Bernard F. Dick explains, "Bernstein realized [Russell] had a limited range with four good notes that he used brilliantly in Ruth's duet with Eileen." Dick further states, "the middle section of 'Ohio' was much easier for Rosalind since it required what Comden correctly called 'speech song,' in which the lyrics had to be musically inflected rather than sung full voice." Dick, *Forever Mame,* 158.
9 Book writers Joseph Fields and Jerome Chodorov originally set the play specifically in 1935, but in 1953 were vaguer about the date stating the show takes place "*in Greenwich Village in the 1930s,*" which allowed for more variation in the pastiche nature of the score. There are, however, several references in the libretto to 1935 specifically: the tour guide announces the year at the beginning of his tour and signs for an art contest in 1935 are requested in the stage directions for "Christopher Street." For a thorough analysis of the specific musical "time-markers" used by composer Leonard Bernstein see Helen Smith's *There's a Place for Us: The Musical Theatre Works of Leonard Bernstein* (Farnham, UK: Ashgate Publishing, 2011).
10 Carol J. Oja, "Bernstein's *Wonderful Town* and McCarthy-Era Politics," *Prelude, Fugue and Riffs* (Spring/Summer 2007): 8.
11 The 2003 Broadway revival of *Wonderful Town* was directed and choreographed by Kathleen Marshall and starred Donna Murphy in the role of Ruth. The case could be made that given the musical is still set in the sister's apartment (for the most, not all of the show) there is still a sense of observation or bird's eye view that could connect to the heighted surveillance by Homeland Security post-9/11.
12 Patricia Rae, "Radical Nostalgia in George Orwell's *Coming up for Air*" in *Modernism and Nostalgia: Bodies, Locations, Aesthetics* ed. Tammy Clewell (Basingstoke, UK: Palgrave Macmillan, 2013), 149.
13 Carol Oja describes the build up to this moment: "Two years earlier the famous 'Hollywood Ten' had appeared before the House Un-American Activities Committee, charged with Communist affiliations, and they had refused to answer questions resulting in prison sentences for contempt of congress and subsequent blacklisting by the Hollywood studios. Oja, *Bernstein Meets Broadway: Collaborative Art in a Time of War* (New York: Oxford University Press, 2014), 114.
14 Elizabeth L. Keathley, "Postwar Modernity and the Wife's Subjectivity: Bernstein's *Trouble in Tahiti,*" *American Music* 23, no. 2 (Summer 2005): 249. Though overt political underpinnings faded from the narrative or were edited out from earlier drafts

by the time *Wonderful Town* is produced in 1953, McKenney's stories, published in 1938, were "the autobiographical tale of a left-wing feminist," and created a subtle political residue that lingers in future iterations, including the play, the 1942 film, and the musical. Keathley, "Postwar Modernity and the Wife's Subjectivity," 246.

15 Notably, *Wonderful Town* is a much earlier musical in contrast to the other case studies of this project and works to demonstrate that a long temporal distance is not needed for the operation of nostalgia.

16 There had only been six rounds of Tony Awards by 1953. In 1949, *Kiss Me Kate* won the first Tony award for Best Musical followed by *South Pacific* in 1950 and *Guys and Dolls* in 1951. Rodgers and Hammerstein's *The King and I* won the Tony for Best Musical the previous year in 1952. *Wonderful Town* won best musical in 1953, along with Best Actress for Russell. *Tony Awards,*https://www.tonyawards. com/en_US/history/pastwinners/tonys_results, accessed Sept. 19, 2018.

17 Elizabeth L. Wollman, *A Critical Companion to The American Stage Musical* (London, UK: Bloomsbury Publishing, Plc, 2017), 126.

18 *Guys and Dolls,* music and lyrics Frank by Loesser, book by Jo Swerling and Abe Burrows, 1950.

19 Wollman, *A Critical Companion*, 131.

20 The song "You have to be carefully taught" from *South Pacific* is the most evident example of this educational emphasis in Rodgers and Hammerstein's musicals. John Bush Jones explains of Hammerstein's educational interests that began with *Oklahoma!* "it was then that Hammerstein first expressed on the musical stage his liberal and humanitarian interest in the eradication of prejudice and the need for acceptance and tolerance, however obliquely in his analogy of 'the farmer and the cowman.'" Jones further explains how this didactic interest stayed throughout the rest of his work with Rodgers. Jones, *Our Musicals, Ourselves: A Social History of the American Musical Theatre* (Waltham, MA: Brandeis University Press, 2004), 160.

21 Michael Denning, *The Cultural Front*, xix.

22 Ibid., 4. Keathley further summarizes Denning's groups as: "antifacist émigrés, such as Kurt Weill and Bertolt Brecht; disaffected modernists, such as Aaron Copeland and Marc Blitzstein; or ethnic, second-generation Americans born between 1904 and 1923, who were raised during the Depression by working class immigrant parents," "Postwar Modernity and the Wife's Subjectivity," 246.

23 Ibid., 26.

24 For more on casting practices and political strategies in *On the Town* including the details of casting Japanese American actress Sono Osato in the role of Ivy Smith and her experience in the show see chapter four of Carol Oja's *Bernstein Meets Broadway: Collaborative Art in a Time of War*, 2014.

25 Daniel Gundlach, "Maybe I'd Better Go Home: Nostalgia in *Wonderful Town*," … *wie die Stadt schön wird' Leonard Bernstein: Wonderful Town: Eine Werkmonographie in Texten und Dokumenten*, edited and translated by Heiko Cullman, Michael Heinemann, Andreas Eichhorn (Dresden: Thelman, 2017), 2.

26 One of the main reasons for the rush was Bernstein, Comden, and Green were pulled in at the last minute after the original composer and lyricist, Leroy Anderson and Arnold Horwitt were let go.

27 Oja, "Bernstein's *Wonderful Town* and McCarthy-Era Politics," 8.

28 Ibid.

29 *On the Town* (1944) follows the story of three intrepid sailors on a twenty-four-hour shore leave and their experiences in the city. The musical was based on Jerome Robbins's ballet *Fancy Free*. The show has been revived numerous times, most recently in 2014, *IBDB Internet Broadway Database,*https://www.ibdb.com/broadway-production/on-the-town-497107, accessed September 19, 2018.

30 Oja, *Bernstein Meets Broadway*, 4. Oja explains this currentness was the mission of the ballet *Fancy Free*, the inspiration for *On the Town*. In regards to the realism or

believability of the storyline of *On the* Town, in 1944 sailors would have been in town for shore leaves, and women would be filling jobs such as taxi drivers (as the character Hildy does in the show). Additionally, there was a real Miss Turnstiles competition called Miss Subways that happened between 1941 and 1976. The winners would have their photos and biographies framed in the subway cars and stations. Andrew Savulich, "Miss Subways through the years: The iconic NYC subway queens then and now," *New York Daily News*, May 25, 2018, http://www.nydaily news.com/new-york/subways-nyc-iconic-beauty-queens-gallery-1.1311904.

31 As Raymond Knapp explains of *Guys and Dolls,* and I find true of *Wonderful Town,* "only a startling lack of *joie de vivre,* and an utter refusal to accept American culture, could lead to a total rejection of Guys and Dolls, although it makes an equal investment in Americana." Knapp, *The American Musical and the Formation of National Identity* (Princeton University Press, 2005), 110. Regarding economic conditions and financial risks of putting on a show in the 1950s Wollman explains, "During the first fifteen years of the postwar era, the cost of production of Broadway increased sharply, especially for musicals, which often demand more than straight plays in terms of casting, costuming, scenery, technology, orchestral accompaniment, and crew;" additionally, in the 1950s, "ticket prices on Broadway doubled." Wollman, *A Critical Companion*, 125.

32 Brooks Atkinson, "*Wonderful Town*: Rosalind Russell as the Head Clown in A Big Broadway Musical Show," *New York Times,* March 8, 1953, https://search-p roquest-com.ezproxy.gc.cuny.edu/hnpnewyorktimes/docview/112591993/fulltext PDF/CB1C40C850394234PQ/1?accountid=7287.

33 Keathley, "Postwar Modernity and the Wife's Subjectivity," 249.

34 Ibid., 222.

35 *Wonderful Town*, 37.

36 Keathley, "Postwar Modernity and the Wife's Subjectivity," 250.

37 Ibid., 221.

38 Ibid., 250.

39 Ibid.

40 *Wonderful Town*, 9.

41 Atkinson, "*Wonderful Town*,".

42 Saddler was in the chorus of numerous MGM musicals, *The Great Ziegfeld* (1936), *The Wizard of Oz* (1939), *Babes in Arms* (1939), *Lady Be Good* (1941), and dozens of others. He went on to be a very successful choreographer of television musicals and specials including the Tony Awards in 1983 and *Alice in Wonderland* in the same year.

43 Donald Saddler Production File, *Wonderful Town*. Box 68.5. Donald Saddler Papers. Jerome Robbins Dance Division, The New York Public Library.

44 Humphrey Burton, *Leonard Bernstein* (London, UK: Faber & Faber, 1994), 225. Gundlach also reports in "Maybe I'd Better Go Home: Nostalgia in *Wonderful Town*," that Carol Oja "cites documentary evidence that Robbins was called in to "essentially take over" the choreography of "Christopher Street" in particular, 10.

45 Burton, *Leonard Bernstein*, 225. Saddler speaks briefly about his friendship with Robbins and choreographing for Rosalind Russell in a 2002 interview conversation with Camille Hardy and Barbara Palfy. Jerome Robbins Dance Division, The New York Public Library. "Interview with Donald Saddler" New York Public Library Digital Collections. Accessed September 17, 2022. https://digitalcollections.nypl. org/items/a770cf80-f871-0130-05ce-3c075448cc4b.

46 Helen Smith, *There's a Place for Us: The Musical Theatre Works of Leonard Bernstein* (Farnham, UK: Ashgate Publishing, 2011), 78.

47 Julie Malnig, "Introduction" *Ballroom, Boogie, Shimmy Sham, Shake: A Social and Popular Dance Reader* (Chicago: University of Illinois Press, 2009), 4.

48 Elizabeth Grosz, *Volatile Bodies: Toward a Corporeal Feminism* (Bloomington: Indiana University Press, 1994), x.

49 The term "hep" was first coined by Cab Calloway meaning "hip" or "cool." Calloway used the term as in "are you hep to the jive?" The term also refers to being up to date with the latest trends and happenings. *Urban Dictionary*, https://www.urbandictionary.com/define.php?term=hep, accessed September 4, 2018. This sort of play on language was also a characteristic of the socially and self-declared modish Beatniks.

50 *Wonderful Town*, 140.

51 These descriptions are from the 1958 CBS telecast of *Wonderful Town*.

52 These stylized movements in 1953 production (bent over, snapping etc.) would precede Jerome Robbins's work in *West Side Story* (1957). Though, with the live telecast in 1958, some aesthetics of the movement may have been influenced by the opening of *West Side Story* a year earlier and adapted by the arranger of the dances for the telecast, Ralph Beaumont.

53 An excellent example of the lower center of gravity and bent knees that are key to the style can be seen in the 1941 film *Hellzapoppin*. A link to where they specifically do the Lindy hop can be viewed here: https://www.youtube.com/watch?v=qkthxBsIeGQ.

54 Atkinson, "*Wonderful Town*".

55 Some similarities can be seen between the style of the swing dancers and Audrey Hepburn's "Beatnik Dance" choreographed by Eugene Loring for the 1957 film *Funny Face*. Hepburn's Beatnik style may have influenced the changing of costumes from dresses in 1953 to cigarette pants for the women in 1958.

56 Smith, *There's a Place for Us*, 89.

57 Ibid., 87.

58 *Wonderful Town*, 143.

59 Ibid.

60 Much like in *Millie* discussed in Chapter 4 and the ethnic parody Angela C. Pao describes there could be more obvious signals that this is a parody or satire.

61 Katherine Baber, "'Manhattan Women': Jazz, Blues, and Gender in *On the Town* and *Wonderful* Town," *American Music* 31, no. 1 (Spring 2013): 80.

62 Smith, *There's a Place for Us*, 84.

63 Norman Mailer, "The White Negro: Superficial Reflections on the Hipster," *Dissent Magazine,* (Summer 1957): 279. https://www.dissentmagazine.org/article/the-white-negro-superficial-reflections-on-the-hipster-2, accessed November 1, 2018.

64 Ibid., 279.

65 Smith, *There's a Place for Us*, 84.

66 The diverse cast in the 2003 revival helps dispel this notion.

67 "Interview with Donald Saddler," Jerome Robbins Dance Division, New York Public Library Digital Collections. http://digitalcollections.nypl.org/items/a770cf80-f871-0130-05ce-3c075448cc4b, accessed July 31, 2018.

68 Keathley, "Postwar Modernity and the Wife's Subjectivity," 223.

69 Ibid., 223.

70 Baber, "Manhattan Women," 83.

71 *Wonderful Town*, 108.

72 Ibid.

73 Burton, *Leonard Bernstein*, 225.

74 Brian Cockburn, "Wonderful Town (Review)," *Notes* 62, no. 3 (March 2006): 791.

75 Humphrey further explains Russell reported getting over 1000 bruises in the run of the show.

76 *Wonderful Town*, 108

77 Brian E. Herrera, *Latin Numbers: Playing Latino in Twentieth-Century U.S. Popular Performance* (Ann Arbor: University of Michigan Press, 2015), 20.

78 Herrera, *Latin Numbers,* 36.

79 Ibid., 43. Daniel Gundlach also makes this connection in "Maybe I'd Better Go Home: Nostalgia in *Wonderful Town*."

80 Barry Kernfeld and Pauline Norton explain that the Conga is "A Latin-American carnival road march that gained prominence in the USA from around 1937. The [Cuban-born] bandleader and actor Desi Arnaz was chiefly responsible for transforming it into a social dance craze, especially through his appearances in Rodgers and Hart's Broadway musical *Too Many Girls* (1939). The music for the dance is built on a repeated rhythm, which corresponds to three shuffle steps on the beat and a kick that slightly anticipates the fourth and final beat, with the torso twisting from side to side." Kernfeld and Norton further explain that Bernstein parodied the dance in *Wonderful Town*. "Conga," *Grove Music Online* January 20, 2001, http://www.oxfordmusiconline.com.ezproxy.gc.cuny.edu/grovemusic/view/10.1093.

81 Herrera, *Latin Numbers*, 19. John Storm Roberts further explains that Conga dance and music was popular towards the end of 1930s, because of Arnaz but also "the conga rhythm is more easily simplified than most Cuban rhythms and was a natural for nightclub floorshows." As such, "Conga!" in *Wonderful Town* fits within the historical timeline as a style audiences found highly entertaining. By the time *Wonderful Town* opened 1953 Latin music (particularly the mambo) continued to be fashionable and so Bernstein's take on Latin rhythms would be suitable. Roberts, *The Latin Tinge: The Impact of Latin American Music on the United States* (New York: Oxford University Press, 1979), 224.

82 The melody of "Ohio" lingers in fragments throughout the show, a sort of *leitmotif* for when things are not working as planned for Ruth and Eileen. The intermittently reoccurring theme of home in *Wonderful Town* helps to create nostalgia in the show. Whether it is a place one longs for, or when one realizes they can never really go home again, the nostalgic frame works to unite thinking across a nation that is immersed in the complicated aftermath of World War II.

83 Atkinson, "*Wonderful Town*".

84 Ibid.

85 Walter F. Kerr, "Wonderful Musical," *New York Herald Tribune,* March 8, 1953. http://ezproxy.nypl.org/login?url=https://search-proquest-com.i.ezproxy.nypl.org/docview/1313690882?accountid=35635.

86 Ibid.

87 "The Comic Spirit," *Time* 61, no.13 (1953): 42. http://search.ebscohost.com.ezproxy.gc.cuny.edu/login.aspx?direct=true&db=a9h&AN=54171563&site=ehost-live.

88 Atkinson, "*Wonderful Town*".

89 Because of Saddler's strong association with the ballet world at the time, his choreographic contributions are often called ballets, out of both respect for his previous work and to keep an association with the ballet community.

90 Atkinson, "*Wonderful Town*".

91 Kerr, "Wonderful Musical".

92 Ben Brantley, "Theatre Review; Sis, Today the Village, Tomorrow the World," *New York Times*, November 24, 2003, https://www.nytimes.com/2003/11/24/theater/theater-review-sis-today-the-village-tomorrow-the-world.html.

93 Brantley, "Theatre Review; Sis, Today the Village, Tomorrow The World," 2003.

94 Grosz, *Volatile Bodies*, x.

References

Atkinson, Brook. "*Wonderful Town*: Rosalind Russell as the Head Clown in A Big Broadway Musical Show." *New York Times*, March 8, 1953. https://search-proquest-com.ezproxy.gc.cuny.edu/hnpnewyorktimes/docview/112591993/fulltextPDF/CB1C40C850394234PQ/1?accountid=7287.

Baber, Katherine. "'Manhattan Women': Jazz, Blues, and Gender in *On the Town* and *Wonderful* Town." *American Music* 31, no. 1 (Spring 2013): 73–105.

Billy Rose Theatre Division, The New York Public Library, "Rosalind Russell and chorus boys dressed as Brazilian cadets in Wonderful Town" *New York Public Library Digital Collections*, accessed September 14, 2018. http://digitalcollections.nypl.org/items/5e66b3e8-dc47-d471-e040-e00a180654d7.

Brantley, Ben. "Sis, Today the Village, Tomorrow the World." *New York Times*, November 24, 2003. https://www.nytimes.com/2003/11/24/theater/theater-re view-sis-today-the-village-tomorrow-the-world.html.

Burton, Humphrey. *Leonard Bernstein*. London, UK: Faber & Faber, 1994.

Cockburn, Brian. "Wonderful Town (Review)." *Notes* 62, no. 3 (March 2006): 790–791.

Denning, Michael. *The Cultural Front: The Laboring of American Culture in the Twentieth Century*. New York: Verso1997.

Dick, Bernard F. *Forever Mame: The Life of Rosalind Russell*. Jackson: University Press of Mississippi, 2006.

Fields, Joseph A., Jerome Chodorov, Betty Comden, and Adolph Green. *Wonderful Town*. New York, NY: Random House Publishing, 1953.

Grosz, Elizabeth. *Volatile Bodies: Toward a Corporeal Feminism*. Bloomington: Indiana University Press, 1994.

Gundlach, Daniel. "Maybe I'd Better Go Home: Nostalgia in *Wonderful Town*." In … *wie die Stadt schön wird' Leonard Bernstein: Wonderful Town: Eine Werkmonographie in Texten und Dokumenten*, edited and translated by Heiko Cullman, Michael Heinemann, and Andreas Eichhorn. Dresden: Thelman, 2017.

Herrera, Brian E. *Latin Numbers: Playing Latino in Twentieth-Century U.S. Popular Performance*. Ann Arbor, MI: University of Michigan Press, 2015.

"Interview with Donald Saddler." Jerome Robbins Dance Division, New York Public Library Digital Collections, New York, http://digitalcollections.nypl.org/items/a 770cf80-f871-0130-05ce-3c075448cc4b, accessed July 31, 2018.

Jones, John Bush. *Our Musicals, Ourselves: A Social History of the American Musical Theatre*. Waltham, MA: Brandeis University Press, 2004.

Keathley, Elizabeth L. "Postwar Modernity and the Wife's Subjectivity: Bernstein's Trouble in Tahiti." *American Music* 23, no. 2 (Summer 2005): 220–256.

Kernfeld, Berry and Pauline Norton. "Conga." *Grove Music Online*, January 20, 2001. http://www.oxfordmusiconline.com.ezproxy.gc.cuny.edu/grovemusic/view/10.1093.

Kerr, Walter, F. "Wonderful Musical." *New York Herald Tribune*, March 8, 1953. http://ezproxy.nypl.org/login?url=https://search-proquest-com.i.ezproxy.nypl.org/docview/1313690882?accountid=35635.

Knapp, Raymond. *The American Musical and the Formation of National Identity*. Princeton: Princeton University Press, 2005.

Mailer, Norman. "The White Negro: Superficial Reflections on the Hipster." *Dissent Magazine* (Summer 1957): 279. https://www.dissentmagazine.org/article/the-white-negro-superficial-reflections-on-the-hipster-2, accessed November 1, 2018.

Malnig, Julie, ed. *Ballroom, Boogie, Shimmy Sham, Shake: A Social and Popular Dance Reader*. Chicago: University of Illinois Press, 2009.

Oja, Carol J. *Bernstein Meets Broadway: Collaborative Art in a Time of War*. New York: Oxford University Press, 2014.

Oja, Carol J. "Bernstein's Wonderful Town and McCarthy-Era Politics." *Prelude, Fugue and Riffs*, Leonard Bernstein Office Newsletter, Spring/Summer 2007.

Pao, Angela, C. "Green Glass and Emeralds: Citation, Performance, and the Dynamics of Ethnic Parody in *Thoroughly Modern Millie,*" *Multi-Ethnic Literature in the U.S.* Volume 36, no. 4 (Winter 2011): 35–60.

Rae, Patricia. "Radical Nostalgia in George Orwell's *Coming Up for Air.*" In *Modernism and Nostalgia: Bodies, Locations, Aesthetics*, edited by Tammy Clewell, 149–165. Basingstoke, UK: Palgrave Macmillan, 2013.

Roberts, John Storm. *The Latin Tinge: The Impact of Latin American Music on the United States.* New York: Oxford University Press, 1979.

Saddler, Donald Production File, Wonderful Town. Box 68.5. Donald Saddler Papers. Jerome Robbins Dance Division, The New York Public Library.

Savulich, Andrew. "Miss Subways through the years: The iconic NYC subway queens then and now." *New York Daily News*, May 25, 2018. http://www.nydailynews.com/new-york/subways-nyc-iconic-beauty-queens-gallery-1.1311904.

Smith, Helen. *There's a Place for Us: The Musical Theatre Works of Leonard Bernstein.* Farnham, UK: Ashgate Publishing, 2011.

"The Comic Spirit." *Time* 61, no.13 (1953): 42. http://search.ebscohost.com.ezproxy.gc.cuny.edu/login.aspx?direct=true&db=a9h&AN=54171563&site=ehost-live, accessed November 14, 2018.

Tony Awards. "History." Accessed September 19, 2018. https://www.tonyawards.com/en_US/history/pastwinners/tonys_results.

Urban Dictionary. "Hep." Accessed September 4, 2018. https://www.urbandictionary.com/define.php?term=hep.

Wollman, Elizabeth L. *A Critical Companion to The American Stage Musical.* London, UK: Bloomsbury Publishing, Plc, 2017.

8 When Nostalgia is Your Only Hope
Steel Pier and Dance Marathons

Ocean waves are heard crashing against the New Jersey shore. The wood slats of the pier shimmer in the early dawn. Seagulls caw above the waves. A group of intertwined dancers unfold onto the stage from upstage left. Limbs linked together, the bodies reach forward toward the pier, then are pulled backwards in an undertow that spreads them out across the upstage corner. They surge forward again, this time lunging and diving downward to recover and arch backwards. They spiral around themselves to stand upright for a breath and are drawn backward again. The ethereal opening scene is bathed in blue light that slowly expands to reveal a sandy outline of the shore. The dancers circle around with legs drawing deep compass-like circles; the shuffling of feet sound like small cascades of waves on a wet beach. The sea becomes the land and the bodies of the dancers unravel to form a long chain center stage. The dark blue light fades and the dancers in their airy garments take on an array of positions that once the morning haze drifts away comes to be seen as a line-up of ballroom dancers, frozen in various stages of partnered choreography – a woman bends back in an arching dip; a man's square shoulders form a dance position that encircles a woman pulling backwards with outstretched arms; a woman is seated on the thigh of a partner, her legs frozen mid-fan, mermaid-like washed up on the shores of her partners legs. The lacey effect of intertwined arms and legs draws the eye in. Abruptly the bodies turn towards center and the middle couple snaps into a formal and strict dance position. The other dancers connect creating an extended machine-like "factory" of dancers now methodically and diligently repeating the same waltz step over and over. The shift from the lithe ocean waves to the robot dancers is jarring, the lights darken, the sound of the waves crashing increases, a discordant waltz emerges in the music, and as quickly as they arrived, the lilting rhythm of the music pushes them off the stage leaving only the barren Steel Pier. Rita Racine stands watching the waves, swearing to herself and the audience this will be her last dance marathon.[1]

Background of *Steel Pier*

Choreographer Susan Stroman explains the original impetus for *Steel Pier* was the desire to do a show with "a great deal of dance in it."[2] Having won two

DOI: 10.4324/9781003163688-12

Tony Awards for best choreography for *Crazy for You* (1992) and *Show Boat* (1995) prior to *Steel Pier*, Stroman was clearly established an expert physical storyteller who uses innovative and unique movement signatures to create the world of the musical. When she sat down with director Scott Ellis, book writer David Thompson, and composer and lyricist team John Kander and Fred Ebb, and expressed her mission they asked, "Where is dance set? How can we do that?" Stroman points out in the group's creative process; "John Kander always looked for a darker story and tried to find light within [it]. You know whether it's a Latin prison or Nazi Germany."[3] As a result, the idea of the dance marathon occurred to the team as a captivating place to set a story that could provide a "metaphor for what people had to live for" in the time of the Depression. This worked as a narrative impetus as the dance marathon offers a scenario where stakes are extraordinarily high for the body in motion. Furthermore, it became readily apparent to the team that there was a desire to tell the generally unknown story of the exigencies and exploitations of the American phenomenon of dance marathons.

Set in 1933, *Steel Pier* revolves around Rita Racine, a star of dance marathons and part-time singer in vaudeville circuits who is promised by her marathon promoter husband this will be her last marathon. The story is set in Atlantic City on the famous Steel Pier, suspended out over the ocean on wood pilings. The impending doom of the pilings set to plunge into the water is poignant – dance marathons during the Depression were about life or death. As Rita is preparing below the pier on the beach she meets up with Bill, a stunt pilot. In an expressionistic thread to the show, we find out Bill has died in a plane crash and has been granted three weeks to live in order to cash in a coupon he got at one of Rita's shows for a dance. Rita, however, remains unaware of Bill's ephemerality until his final day, melding her recognition of his impending death with the anguish of the dance marathon. Rita's husband is eventually exposed as a fraud and cheat. Towards the close of the musical Rita realizes Bill is dead. She leaves her husband and the dance marathons behind and walks away from the sparkling marquee lights of the Steel Pier.

The 1997 musical is a haunting tale that exposes the ugly truths about the desperation of many in the years between the Depression and the build up to World War II loosely disguised as a romantic adventure. Stroman explains the structure of the show: "the marathon became a cradle to tell this love story." The dance marathon setting also provided the opportunity to show dance in a diegetic manner allowing for the social and political meaning already embodied in the dances to rise to the surface, or at least underscore the narrative. Stroman describes: "It gave us the opportunity to show dance, all different dance of the social dance forms that were in America at that time, and before that time, now in one space." Having a narrative reason to be able to put so many dances on stage (the Lindy Hop, the Grizzly Bear, the Bunny Hug, the Fox Trot, etc.) creates the opportunity to explore the nostalgia inherent in the dances and what the body can do in these situations, when the poorest and most desperate of people are clinging to survival through dance. Brought together by circumstance, the eclectic group of competitors find a fleeting sense of belonging in their shared desperation and imagined community. As some marathons lasted for weeks and months, participants had a temporary place to be, a home, a job, and a goal (cash prizes) to reach for. The marathon provided a place where one could feel they belonged to something, and no matter how fleeting or imagined the situation, it was much better than being out on the streets. In this consideration, *Steel Pier* explores how the economic, social, and personal stresses are manifested in the body in motion.

Choreographic and Dramaturgical Strategies

Part of the challenge of creating the dance marathon on stage is contending with the idea that people might look back on the marathons (often filled with Americana) with nostalgia, or at least be thrilled by the continuous dancing. Even though a film like *They Shoot Horses Don't They?* (1969) exposes the darker side to the marathon world, many may take delight in watching continued dancing all night long, especially on Broadway.[4] With only a few breakout scenes where Rita and Bill talk during short rest periods, the dancing continues the entire duration of the show. The dramaturgical strategy was to begin the marathon in quite a "jolly" manner, and then as "the show goes on the dancers get more exhausted and wounded and hurt and sad." Bodies begin to slouch, polished smiles start to fade, and fancy footwork is sacrificed for shuffling and swaying. The structure of the musical is somewhat opposite to how dance has operated in Stroman's previous productions, where it is regularly used as a plot-forwarding device or dramatic tool.[5] In *Steel Pier*, Stroman and director Scott Ellis also use the rest moments in the marathon to forward main plot points. Due to the diegetic nature of the marathon in the show, contestants can only really talk to each other during the breaks, whether it is in the women's dressing room, or outside on the pier where Rita and Bill get to know each other. The movement within the dance marathon, however, does provide the framework for the narrative arc of the show and Stroman employs several innovative strategies to achieve the embodied storytelling.

One of the most effective dramaturgical and choreographic choices Stroman and Ellis make is how they communicate the passage of time of the three-week marathon and the subsequent mental and physical breakdown of the dancers within two-and-a-half hours. To achieve the effect, every ten minutes or so the lights darken to a deep blue and the music changes from upbeat swing music to more complex, sensual, and discordant jazz rhythms. This shift provides a disturbing, near uncanny, contrast to the story of the saccharine-sweet marathon. In these moments, time is seen rushing by on a counter just below the proscenium arch and the dancers shift from presentational-styled social dance to more contemporary-styled gestural choreography. Stroman proceeds in this manner balancing the choreography between the collective and communal dances of the marathon and the internal moments of self-expression. This back and forth conveys the tension between inner expressions of humiliation and despair and an outward clinging to a remnant of the American Dream. At the intersection of these modes of being, a sense of nostalgia emerges for a time when social dancing meant socialization, not survival. To underpin the importance of achieving this duality in the choreography and in order to critically examine the social and political complexity of this experience for the participants a deeper comprehension of dance marathons is needed.

Background of Dance Marathons

The earliest dance marathon in the U.S. was recorded in 1923.[6] At first there was a novelty and charm surrounding the marathons. Young ingénues would sign up as a way to be discovered for potential film or stage work. In the wild and exuberant years of the 1920s, interest in leisure activities was paramount and the younger generation sought out physical amusements at which they could thrive and be noticed. The interest in and creation of dance marathons came from what theatre and performance studies scholar Carol Martin in *Dance Marathons: Performing American Culture in the 1920s and 1930s* describes as, "a cultural discourse in the 1920s about breaking records," and in this era she explains, "people would do anything on a dare."[7] An enthusiasm to be the best at something, or to take on an outrageous challenge, was part of American culture. This "Age of play" of the 1920s provided a release from the intensity and anxiety that had surrounded World War I.[8] Martin explains dance marathons, unlike more serious feats, were attractive, as no special skill was needed except "intemperate stamina and enthusiasm," underlining how much social dance was already part of everyday life.[9] Audiences delighted in the long nights and collection of characters that joined up, along with an interest in a battle of the sexes – could men or women last longer?[10] Psychology professor Frank M. Calabria in *Dance of the Sleep Walkers: The Dance Marathon Fad* explains why audiences were so fascinated by dance marathons, "It was as if viewing others in perpetual motion allowed spectators to vicariously release the collective anxieties and tensions of the turbulent decade following America's first global war."[11] There was a fascination for the body in motion, which is reflective of both the modernization and mechanization in the era.[12]

After the stock market crashed in 1929, the dance marathons took a much more frantic and disreputable turn, mirroring a disconnected, poorly managed, and unregulated economic system.[13] Promoters took advantage of the participants, who were increasingly desperate for the promise of food and a roof over their heads for the duration of their participation. Martin explains the system of exploitation at the heart of the marathons; "The primal dance marathons' theatricality was raw industrial capitalism operating in the midst of nostalgia for agrarian self-determination and control."[14] Individualism and self-expression get sacrificed, and thus longed for, as the dancers become cogs in the capitalist machinery of the marathon. Promoters would invent all sorts of scenarios, competitions, and false narratives around participants to fuel interest, particularly from sponsors. Competitors were pawns to be manipulated by the corrupt "officials." The commodification of the participants' suffering leads to a sense of dehumanization. Audiences, whose sense of humanity was perhaps dulled by the hardships of the time, paid to watch participants go through the humiliating activities of the promoters.

In spite of these conditions, for the participants, being part of a the marathon community dulled the reality of the economic disparity that surrounded them. Though for participants it also became about one's own crisis relative to one's place in the world, as is explored in *Steel Pier*. While the marathons did operate in "the ability to endure," the events "exploited the daily grind, exposing the economic dangers lurking in everyday life, even while celebrating the heroism and perseverance of ordinary people."[15] In this very precarious structure there is nostalgia for the return of social dance as a place of socialization and bodily expression, not humiliation and hardship. The co-opting of this nostalgia by promoters of the dance marathons becomes a very cruel manipulation of people at their very lowest, using what was once dear to them and turning it into something painful and exhausting. The "commercialization of leisure" becomes a dark and ill-intended manipulation of the general populace and popular entertainment.[16] Calabria observes marathons were a "dehumanizing spectacle accompanying hard times," as identities get lost amidst the competition.[17] Social dance, that was once about both self-expression and a sense of belonging, in the dance marathon becomes a kind of social ill infected by capitalist greed and self-interest on the part of the promoters. The nostalgic meaning within the dance becomes a survival mechanism for the dancers, and society writ large. An investigation of Stroman's choreographic strategies, movement acquisition techniques, and how she fuses movement within the context of the libretto helps to understand how dance can offer a sense of durability and endurance in a tumultuous and precarious time.

Choreographic and Narrative Strategies

Stroman explains the nostalgia inherent in social dance in the 1930s and 1940s and why it is such a poignant era to bring to life on stage: "after the Twist was invented, no one touched anywhere. No one danced together any longer, and all the dancers became separate, and they still are today in the social world." A social dance event, as Stroman observes, "was the first time a man and a woman touched romantically, and ultimately if you slow danced with the right person that night, you ended up falling in love." This romantic potential is part of the structure of *Steel Pier*. The show opens on a very rosy nostalgic note, much like *Ragtime*. The title of the show is written in bold letters across the scrim.

Inside the letters there are historical photos of social dancing with women in formal dresses and men in suits. There is a suggestion of the dance marathons, though it is all very sunny, with bold yellow bands radiating from the letters, and various amusement park fixtures in the background of the letters. To start

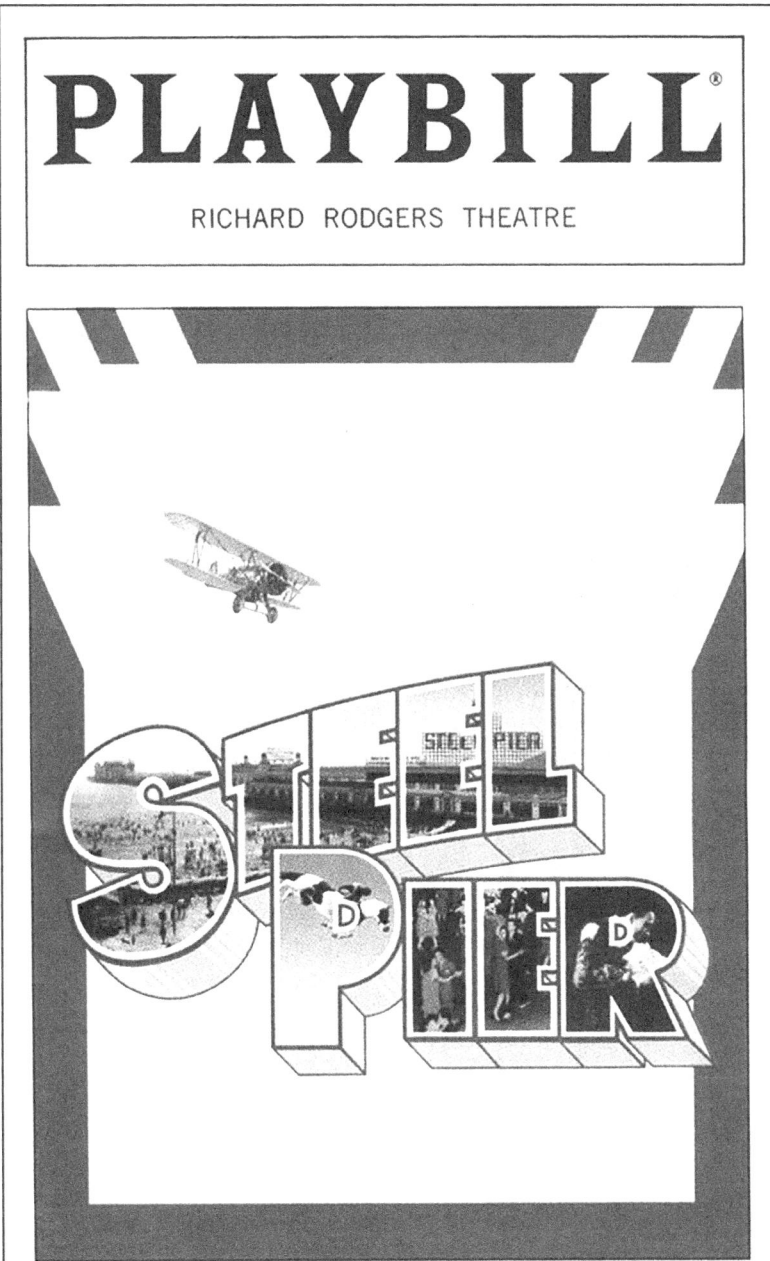

Figure 8.1 Title image projected on downstage scrim at the opening of the show and mirrored on the Playbill. Design by James Candy, 1997

Source: Used by Permission. All rights reserved, Playbill Inc.

the marathon, a spectacular façade of the entrance of the ballroom on the pier descends from the ceiling; the sparkling bulbs and ornate shapes light up the night. A build of final calls to enter the dance marathon culminate in Rita (Karen Ziemba) declaring this marathon will be her last as she signs up with Bill (Daniel McDonald).

The opening song of the marathon, "Everybody Dance," begins and couples come spinning in dancing an array of different styles. Most swing dance, some do a one-step, and all join in on the festivities, keeping in time to the rhythm of the swing-styled music. The celebration of social dance is exceptional and the desire to get noticed and win is palpable in the various added flourishes such as high kicks, lifts, and dips from couples. Mick, the host, and Rita's husband, chastises a couple for doing the Grizzly Bear, announcing it is not allowed (too sensual and non-moving), but the Bunny Hug is.[18] As the musical quickly unfolds, the operation of the marathon – its scams, fixed moments, and preferential treatment – expose the social and economic structures that created this phenomenon. A fraying of the edges of the newly assumed community created by the marathon begins for the struggling participants. Foremost, the effect of the economic depression becomes visible in the bodies of the dancers; the exasperation and despair begin to show in their slouched shoulders and heavy feet.

Despite the excruciating circumstances, there are moments of hope from various secondary characters who believe maybe it will all end and they can return to the life they had before the economic crash. This utopic desire hints at the naivety of those in the Depression Era who thought the market would realign itself soon after the economic crash. Rita mentions several times how she longs to return to her and Mick's home after the marathon. The final straw for Rita is when Mick's admits he sold their house a long time ago, that there is no going home. The knowledge spreads through the rest of the dancers as none have homes anymore. This bleak moment of recognition connects this particular marathon to the larger economic situation in the 1930s. Markedly, as the economic depression spread into Europe there was the realization that global financial and social systems needed to change and there would be no quick fixes. Governments, communities, and individuals were forced to adjust and discover new actions for survival. In *Steel Pier*, the nostalgia Rita had for her home and a simpler time is shattered, and she realizes continuing to be part of Mick's "dance" is futile. While the dance marathon is, as Stroman said, "a cradle for a love story," its pointlessness and forced collision with one's lost past forces reflection beyond the framework of a love story.

In this manner the choreographic strategy of transitioning between sections to show the passage of time, allows for an internalization of the outward experiences and contemplation of the moment. In these moments, though the dancers are still partnered, arms reach out in desperation as they circle low to the ground and even transition to the floor, as if sinking into the abyss of the internal frustration of the marathon. Stroman explains this transition effect; "It would be showing the reality, how they were feeling and really struggling and more the inner thoughts of the dance in a more abstract way." This effect sets up a profound contrast between the external community aspect to social dance and the internal dialogue of navigating this moment of competition, and the anguish and endurance. In the social dance of the marathon, there is a sense of conformity to the wills of the competition. There is a push from promoters trading on a shared desire to keep up as part of the collective community, which in this case stands in for the nation as a whole in the Depression. In the transition moments the lighting shifts to blue and the anguish is physicalized as partners push and pull against each other in individual levels of desperation. As the marathon becomes starker, there becomes less reason for Stroman to replicate the social dance, particularly as the embodied nostalgia the participants believed in begins to crumble in the face of both physical and mental exhaustion.

As a matter of explanation, Stroman trained as a ballroom dancer herself. She describes she brought the cast into the world of the dance marathons by having daily social dance classes. This was both to get them physically connected and familiar with the vocabulary of the dance and to make her and her assistant Chris Patterson's job easier. They were able to simply call out social dances for the ensemble to do at certain points. Stroman explains her strategy; "if they learned their terminology of what the entire show was about, the entire company, they're in it together and they understand it's tough. It's almost like they lived in that time period."[19]

The choreography towards the end of *Steel Pier* plunges into an exploration of the tension between self-expression and individuality, and necessity and survival. The flourishes, breakaways, and tricks of the swing dance are gone. Partners cling to each other, going through the motions, moving closer to a sense of collective survival than expressed individuality. Calabria describes the loss of humanity that comes with the dance marathon as dancers become shells of their former selves and "live the life of the automaton thereby restricting spontaneity and freedom."[20] The imagined community is a straw man, a fallacy created by the promoters as well as the participants themselves. Continuing to dance is an illusion that Rita had come to believe as a way of belonging in the world. By the end of the show, Rita realizes the reality of her situation: there is no person, or ideology, that can save her, and she is losing herself into the void of the marathon. Rita leaves before the marathon is over. In her wake, the remaining dancers, now fully distorted in their movements, collide together in a broken jumble at the archway of the ballroom on the pier. The image of the over-worked shells of human beings crashing into each other in the doorway is a very bleak closing – a broken machine serving no individual or collective purpose. A small sense of hope emerges with Rita's departure, though the overwhelming impression of a country adrift in the wake of national effort to fix the economic woes circulates in the space. Rita's break from the marathon allows for a contemplation of misplaced or misunderstood nostalgia society has for the Swing Era. The music and dance of the era was appealing and exciting on the surface and celebrated the zeitgeist of the time, however, it was also an era where self-expression was overshadowed by American modernization and the move of the U.S. towards global power.

Critical Reception

Even in a show about dance, overall there is little mention or interrogation of the choreography in the reviews. There was, however, a general consensus that Stroman was able to blend the social dances with her innovative movement signature and create appealing dance numbers. Greg Evans does briefly discuss the choreography and is quite positive regarding the talent of the collaborators stating: "choreography by Susan Stroman that cannily blends period steps with her trademark innovations, and some of Kander and Ebb's strongest writing in years overshadow whatever missteps this musical makes."[21] In essence, by keeping a semblance of the social dances in their original form they are both recognizable to the audience and retain a historical grounding. Evans explains Stroman is able to tell the numerous stories that circulate in the marathon, while at the same time "showcasing [her] vibrant choreography."[22] Evans is an astute observer of the dance commenting, "The dances range from the fox trot and tap to the Lindy Hop, and even within the constraints of the historical dance styles, Stroman works her idiosyncratic touches."[23] He refers to the scratching sounds the dancers make on the floor in the opening moments that "mimics the sound of ocean waves."[24] Evans picks up on the details that amplify the meaning of the social dance and stakes of the dance marathon. The choreographic signature of the musical, a fusion of known social dance and contemporary modulations, is the life breath of the musical. In the production bodies are constantly moving, dances are called out by the host, participants talk of the steps, their experience and yet, in the reviews, there is not a consideration of the power and impact of dance. Nor is there a mention of what dance is *doing* in the show, which is telling a story of survival and endurance. While some technical innovations and idiosyncrasies are mentioned it is the details that have been described in this chapter that illustrate what is happening through dance and works to illuminate what is disconcerting about the era and the eventual breakdown of the body in motion.

This collapse of the body is in fact one of the main challenges of the choreography. The movement still needs to be engaging yet follow a narrative that has bodies resorting to minimal repetition and eventually breaking down. Ben Brantley picks up on this downward spiral in the novelty of the dances. He finds the show to be "hypnotic in the wrong ways, there's no center of energy to grab on to."[25] This sense of being adrift for the audience, not sure of who or what to pin ones hopes, is a risk the show takes. By not offering a positive and uplifting journey, particularly with a choreographer as renowned as Stroman, exposes what audiences generally expect dance to do (thrill, titillate, and impress). Stroman is pushing against expectations and asking more of the movement; to have the movement reflect the precarity of the human condition at this particular moment in time. The aforementioned transformation in the dance, that touches on the nightmarish and casts a surrealist tinge to the piece, displays the deceitful side of the marathon and engages with the politics of memory of the Depression – effects all achieved through the choreography. Rita's flight or removal of her body from the marathon is empowering and yet Brantley finds there is no conclusion to this exploration. Brantley does concede Stroman "has provided some lovely dance numbers that find the kinetic poetry in physical exhaustion."[26] His description effectively reduces the danced-through musical to what seems like a couple of movement showcases. When Rita refuses to continue to dance the change is stark, her stillness is palpable amongst the persistently moving dancers. Unfortunately, such depth of movement was often lost or understood as repetitious or "tiresome," which is in fact what it was meant to be.[27]

Stephen Mosher is one of the few critics to explore dance and its meaning making when he mentions the "Sprints" number that closes the first act. In this moment dancers are tied together in pairs and forced to run a number of laps around pylons. The last couple to cross the finish line is eliminated. This senseless race is hyped up through much of the first act, and when Rita takes the first corner, she falls. The whole ensemble freezes mid-fall and begins to rewind. Mosher describes, "In one of the most baffling moments I have ever, ever, ever seen onstage, the music sounds like a record album being played backwards and all the runners begin moving slowly in reverse."[28] This moment in the musical begins the descent or shift of the musical into a more expressionistic style of people's inner experiences, with surrealist moments of subconsciousness as described.[29] We want Rita to get a second chance and this reversal allows her to correct her step. This rewinding fulfills a wish so many had with the economic crash, "if only" one had been more responsible or safeguarded their funds. A nostalgic reflection on past decisions and other options that might have been available is sparked in this moment of reversal.[30] The frozen dancers embody the potential of the American experiment in this moment of second chances, where there is a brief consideration of past moments of self-expression and economic freedom before returning to the collective body of the marathon. Throughout *Steel Pier* there continues to be the possibility that one might win, and this false hope encapsulates how abandoned U.S. communities felt before the promises of the New Deal began to take effect many years later.

Survival, Nostalgia, and the American Dream

Dance marathons were very much built on the concept of the American Dream – not that the promoters would let dancers achieve it – but by relying on and co-opting mythologies around the American Dream they drew people in and exploited their desperation. Dancers would cling to this longing for a home or a dream that their parents had, or that they once knew. Martin explains the manipulation of the nostalgia and myth in service to patriotism: "To be jobless and to protest was construed as anti-American behavior.

Marathon promoters wanted above all to be American. They decorated their theatres with patriotic bunting, and the masters of ceremonies proclaimed the American-as-Apple-pie virtues of the contests."[31] The marathon in *Steel Pier* creates this sense of Americana.

As marathons began to be banned in more and more states, those who continued to participate in them were seen as part of the problem and as having no self-respect.[32] It became too frightening to see these people slowly degrade in front of spectators eyes; it was too close to the "unemployed vagrants sweeping across the nation" in the 1930s.[33] Towards the end of *Steel Pier*, the marathon begins to fall apart; a husband leaves his obstinate wife; the brother of the famous brother and sister duo begins to lose his mind and is forced to leave against his will. Mick pushes on with his promotions and continually ramps up the stakes of the marathon, and those who cannot keep up leave as fellow participants shrug in their exhaustion. Martin explains the new image the marathons dancers began to take on; "The unemployed were now unpleasant reminders of the failure of the American Dream."[34] This is seen in the broken dancers who in the act of stopping to dance and stand still – slumped, exhausted, and broken – embody so much of the disappointment and damage that the Depression had caused, at first nationally, then through Europe and Asia. Rita breaks out: she stops dancing, she stops believing, she stops longing, and she steps slowly away. Stroman explains the ending: "It's almost like as she's walking away from it, it gets even uglier and uglier…and it's right that she walks away from it. There's nothing about [the marathon] she should be involved in. It has an uglier side to it." The boy does not get the girl at the end of this show; there is no conclusion to happily tie up loose ends. Rita walks away seemingly strong in her own mind, and in this way, it does not follow the regular conventions of a musical where the couple is united at the end.

Steel Pier has been shown to be a complicated example of what deeper meaning is gained when social dance is brought on stage. In a show with continuous dancing, the impact of the social pressure on the body is amplified when the body stops moving. Notably, the emotional shift for Rita comes when she stops dancing. Stroman's original impetus to seek out where dance happens as a setting for a musical becomes the struggle for the show, a contradiction to the original motivation. Indeed, some critics say the very dance marathon nature of the show slowed things down or detracted from the plot. The marathon structure also represents a different sort of structure for a musical, taking the diegetic construct to its most saturated degree; the dance is always diegetic. Stroman suspects the reason for the short run; "in fact perhaps that's why, another reason, people didn't accept it as much is because it was bucking the norm of a musical." While there are a variety of "I want" songs and certain big show-stopping numbers, the show, while appearing as a traditional musical, in fact takes on a more abstract feel without following any complex formula. The phenomenon of the dance marathons was a real and problematic development in U.S. history that cannot be overlooked. In the dance marathon, there was no way to dream away the present. It was the reality of life twenty-four hours a day, exposing the American experience in the Depression Era. Martin concludes the dance marathons were "a vibrant distorting mirror, refracting a society's desires, entertainments, working habits, scams, and brassy personalities."[35]

The friction between the individual and the system that creeps into *Steel Pier* leaves little optimism. The marathon stands in for so much more than an excuse to dance all night long at the theatre – the economic strife, the political corruption, the cultural falsities, the dismantling of nostalgia, and the exploitation of the poor. Ben Brantley picks up on the crumbling hope for humanity in *Steel Pier*, "this microcosmic world is clearly meant to be a metaphor for a sick society."[36] *Steel Pier* opened several months after the start of Bill Clinton's second term. What began as a year of hopeful promises crumbled first with a global economic crisis, and then the eventual exposing of the Monica Lewinsky scandal and subsequent impeachment trials of Clinton over the following year. There is something precarious about *Steel Pier*, similar to the house of cards that seemed primed to fall amidst the politics and economics of the time. As Stroman describes the pier, "anything could collapse, anything could go wrong. It's not even on firm ground."

When Rita is given a second chance in "The Sprints" and Bill says in the instant of frozen time, "You can't fall now" – Rita gains strength from the moment.[37] Stroman uses social dance, and the internalization that the marathon forces through its exhaustive and mind-bending journey, as a way for Rita to come to her decision. While her departure withholds any happy-ending, female resilience and integrity are shown to prevail, a nuance that is only brought to light by her refusal to continue dancing. The eventual fragmentation of the nostalgia exploited by the marathon makes this empowerment possible. While the marathon was a sort of self-imprisonment for Rita and the community of participants out of desperation and hopelessness, in *Allegiance* the confinement is very real.

Notes

1 Description and analysis based on the 1997 Broadway production as viewed at New York Public Library's The Theatre on Film and Tape Archive (TOFT), Billy Rose Theatre Division, New York Public Library for the Performing Arts.
2 Interview by author, June 22, 2018. All further interview excerpts in quotations.
3 Stroman is referring to Kander and Ebb's previous shows *Kiss of the Spider Woman* (1992) and *Cabaret* (1966) respectively. Stroman had worked with Ellis, Kander, and Ebb on *Flora the Red Menace* in 1987. The group (without Ellis) worked together on *The Scottsboro Boys* off and on between 2002 and its premiere in 2010. Fred Ebb's death in 2004 paused the project for several years.
4 *They Shoot Horses Don't They* (1969), directed by Sidney Pollack, is based on Horace McCoy's 1935 novel of the same name. The film starred Jane Fonda, Michael Sarrazin, and Susannah York, *Imdb,* accessed September 20, 2018, https://www.imdb.com/title/tt0065088/. An additional cultural reference to dance marathons is the popular television series *The Gilmore Girls* on the WB network, which

ran from 2000–2007. In the episode "They Shoot Gilmores Don't They?" a dance marathon is the main plot, *Imdb,* accessed December 8, 2018, https://m.imdb.com/title/tt0238784/.

5 Stroman's previous shows are often recognizable by how the movement is strategically woven into the plot, or make up the plot all together as in *Contact* (2000). Selections of Stroman's other shows that have highly integrated choreography include: *Crazy for You* (1992), *Show Boat* (1993), and *Oklahoma!* (2002).

6 Carol Martin, *Dance Marathons: Performing American Culture in the 1920s and 1930s* (Jackson: University Press of Mississippi, 1994), xviii. Martin is also listed as a "Dance Marathon Consultant" in the *Steel Pier* Playbill, accessed September 25, 2018, http://www.playbill.com/playbillpagegallery/inside-playbill?asset=00000150.

7 Ibid., 5.

8 Frank M. Calabria, *Dance of the Sleep Walkers: The Dance Marathon Fad* (Bowling Green, OH: State University Popular Press, 1993), 1.

9 Martin, *Dance Marathons*, 7.

10 Ibid.,10.

11 Calabria, *Dance of the Sleep Walkers*, 6.

12 See Mark Franko's The Work of Dance: Labor, Movement, and Identity in the 1930s (Middleton, CT: Wesleyan University Press, 2002) for more on how the body, particularly the female body becomes defined by the mode in which it moves and the labor it undertakes.

13 David Walsh and Len Platt, *Musical Theater and American Culture* (Westport, CT: Greenwood, 2003), 80.

14 Martin, *Dance Marathons*, 104.

15 Ibid., 53.

16 Ibid., 13.

17 Calabria, *Dance of the Sleep Walkers*, 3.

18 The Bunny Hug is a tamer, less physically connected dance than the Grizzly Bear.

19 The sheer amount of dancing in *Steel Pier* does have a certain political quality to it in the sense there would be a tremendous amount of labor going into eight shows a week. In our interview, Stroman felt Broadway dancers are so much more protected, supported, and well cared for on Broadway today than they were fifteen or twenty years years ago, suggesting perhaps working conditions were not as strictly regulated in the 1990s for dancers providing a hint of double meaning to the marathon plot.

20 Calabria, *Dance of the Sleep Walkers*, 3.

21 Greg Evans, "Steel Pier," *Variety*, May 5, 1997, https://variety.com/1997/legit/reviews/steel-pier-1200449981/.

22 Ibid.

23 Ibid.

24 Ibid.

25 Ben Brantley, "Party's Over Chum, Just Keep Dancing," April 25, 1997, *New York Times*, https://www.nytimes.com/1997/04/25/theater/party-s-over-chum-just-keep-dancing.html.

26 Ibid.

27 Elyse Sommer, "A Curtain Up Review: *Steel Pier*," 1997, *Curtain Up: The Internet Theatre Magazine of Reviews, Features, Annotated Listings*, http://www.curtainup.com/steelrev.html, accessed July 25, 2018.

28 Stephen Mosher, "Great Moment in New York Theatre: *Steel Pier*," *The Stephen Mosher Blog,* July 19, 2010, http://stephenaaronmosher.blogspot.com/2010/07/great-moments-in-new-york-theater-steel.html.

29 This moment is very clever and pre-empts *Hamilton*'s "Satisfied," by nearly twenty years. In "Satisfied" Angelica Schuyler rewinds time to where she first meets Alexander Hamilton, and reconsiders her choices.

30 Sean Scanlan, echoing Svetlana Boym (*The Future of Nostalgia* (New York: Basic Books, 2001)) explains that a reflection on the past can often be considered nostalgic not in the sense of yearning for the past, "but about provoking a secondary reaction," Introduction in *Iowa Journal of Cultural Studies* 5, (2004): 4.
31 Martin, *Dance Marathons*, 133.
32 Ibid., 134.
33 Ibid.
34 Ibid.
35 Martin, *Dance Marathons*, 146.
36 Brantley, "Party's Over Chum".
37 Kander and Ebb, "Sprints," 1997.

References

Boym, Svetlana. *The Future of Nostalgia*. New York: Basic Books, 2001.

Brantley, Ben. "Party's Over Chum, Just Keep Dancing." *New York Times*, April 25, 1997. https://www.nytimes.com/1997/04/25/theater/party-s-over-chum-just-keep-dancing.html.

Calabria, Frank M. *Dance of the Sleep Walkers: The Dance Marathon Fad*. Bowling Green, OH: State University Popular Press, 1993.

Evans, Greg. "Steel Pier." *Variety*, May 5, 1997. https://variety.com/1997/legit/reviews/steel-pier-1200449981/.

Franko, Mark. *The Work of Dance: Labor, Movement, and Identity in the 1930s*. Middletown, CT: Wesleyan University Press, 2002.

Martin, Carol. *Dance Marathons: Performing American Culture in the 1920s and 1930s*. Jackson: University Press of Mississippi, 1994.

Martin, Carol. "American Dance Marathons." In *Ballroom, Boogie, Shimmy Sham, Shake: A Social and Popular Dance Reader*, edited by Julie Malnig, 93–108. Chicago: University of Illinois Press, 2009.

Mosher, Stephen. "Great Moment in New York Theatre: *Steel Pier*." *The Stephen Mosher Blog*, July 19, 2010. http://stephenaaronmosher.blogspot.com/2010/07/great-moments-in-new-york-theater-steel.html.

Playbill. "*Steel Pier*." http://www.playbill.com/playbillpagegallery/inside-playbill?asset=00000150., accessed September 25, 2018.

Scanlan, Sean. "Introduction: Nostalgia." *Iowa Journal of Cultural Studies* 5 (2004): 3–9.

Sommer, Elyse. "A Curtain Up Review: *Steel Pier*." 1997, *Curtain Up: The Internet Theatre Magazine of Reviews, Features, Annotated Listings*, http://www.curtainup.com/steelrev.html, accessed July 25, 2018.

Stroman, Susan. Personal Interview, New York City, June 22, 2018.

Thompson, David, John Kander, Fred Ebb, Scott Ellis, and Susan Stroman. *Steel Pier*. New York, NY: Samuel French, 1998.

Walsh, David, and Len Platt. *Musical Theater and American Culture*. Westport, CT: Greenwood, 2003.

9 "Get in the game"

Destabilizing Nostalgia in the Crisis of Identity in *Allegiance*

The thorny silhouette of the internment camp fence casts a fractured shadow over the homemade banner that reads "Heart Mountain Dance." The banner is attached to a communal yard post and camp table along with homemade paper flowers that hang from the austere barracks. The haze of thick Wyoming dust lingers as the sun sets behind the barbed wire. Finally able to let off some steam, the younger residents of the Japanese American internment camp enter down stage right in a low, coiled position primed to unwind into a series of hip shaking, heel twisting "sugars."[1] The dynamics of the dance moves grow in intensity along with the build towards the chorus of the 1940s-styled swing music. Partners quickly find each other, bodies pull together, and the music, coming from a small ramshackle radio, hits the melody – horns wail and drums crack and thud, and the toe-tapping music fills the auditorium. Bodies that had been uncomfortable, resistant, and anxious in the hushed meeting of the previous scene are energetic and, for a moment, visibly content. The modest dresses of the women flare out and up as partners, encouraged by the burgeoning melody and percussive beats of the music, become more enterprising in their moves. The Japanese American internees show off their dance moves to one another as elder family members look on with pleasure. The choreography builds to a hot finale, complete with the trademark overhead throws and big breakaways of the Lindy Hop. For just a moment, if one focuses on the bodies dancing and not the structures of imprisonment surrounding them, the situation seems like any dance on a Saturday night in the U.S. in the early 1940s. The energy is palpable, couples playfully flirt, and bodies come together in a harmony of motion. Spirits seem high. After the first song, a dancer proclaims, "Welcome to our first – and hopefully not annual – Heart Mountain dance!"[2]

DOI: 10.4324/9781003163688-13

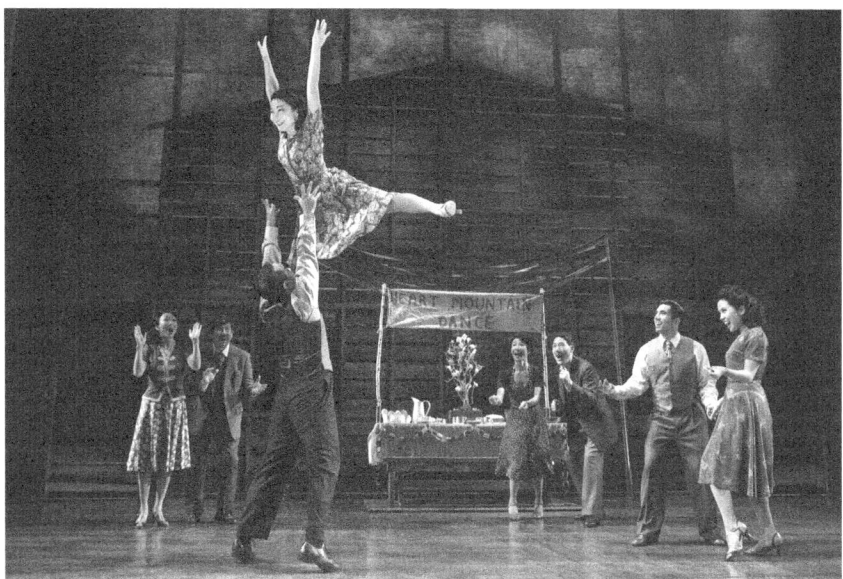

Figure 9.1 Allegiance (2015) "Heart Mountain Dance"
Source: Photo by Matthew Murphy.

In this investigation of the 2015 Broadway musical *Allegiance,* I consider how the embodied perspective brought forward by social dance moments, such as the one described above, provides a unique method towards attempting to understand, permeate, and challenge the borders between "them" and "us," and between the individual and the nation.

The day after the attacks on Pearl Harbor by the Japanese on December 7, 1941, the *New York Times* reported of the many instances of restriction of Japanese movement in the U.S.: "One of the first steps taken here last night was the round-up of Japanese Nationals by special agents of the Federal Bureau of Investigation. More than 100 FBI men fully armed were assigned to the detail."[3] Markedly, the status of Japanese-Americans changed overnight. In the heated and controversial moments of the internment of Japanese Americans that followed the bombing, national identities, personal freedoms, and outlets for self-expression were thrown into chaos as the Japanese American body was condemned as the "other," or the "enemy." The movement strategies expressed through the choreography in *Allegiance* help to define national identity and formations of the self. In particular, the swing dance sensibilities choreographer Andrew Palermo uses at the "Heart Mountain Dance" (as described above) create a mode of identity formation and communal belonging for the internees, collapsing presupposed ideas of race and "Americanness." Pointedly, jazz music and swing dance was an integral outlet for expression for the younger generation at the time and this mode of belonging and coping becomes amplified and increasingly exigent in the internment. Music studies scholar Rachel Aragaki contends, "In the camps, these genres offered musicians and dancers the opportunity to express their Americanness at a time when that aspect of their identity felt stripped away."[4] Investigating the embodied meaning of Japanese Americans swing dancing destabilizes the nostalgia inherent in the dance and helps to recover the notion that a Japanese American body is also an American body and a vital part of U.S. culture.

Background of *Allegiance*

With music and lyrics by Jay Kuo and book by Marc Acito, Kuo, and Lorenzo Thione, *Allegiance* was motivated by the experiences of actor George Takei and his parents in a Japanese American internment camp during World War II. Takei, popularly known for his role as Hikaru Sulu in the original *Star Trek* series and subsequent movies, was incarcerated as a young child at the Rohwer, Arkansas, camp and the Tule Lake, California, camp in the 1940s.

Kuo explains he ran into Takei two consecutive nights at the theatre in 2008. Kuo decided to go up to him and ask why he was crying during the show (*In the Heights*), particularly the number "Inútil" (about a father feeling useless). Kuo explains Takei's answer in an interview:

> The song had reminded him of his own father who had been unable to help their family escape the terror of the internment and had lived with that feeling of uselessness... .George told me his story of growing up in an internment camp and I was mesmerized.[5]

Takei began telling him about his past, to which Kuo suggested it would make an excellent piece of theatre and would like to send him some ideas. The creation of the musical began from there with readings followed by workshops, leading to its eventual premiere in San Diego in 2012. After various rounds of changes, the musical opened on Broadway in 2015 and ran for thirty-seven previews and 111 performances. The musical has an extensive website detailing nearly every aspect of its journey from inspiration, to creation, to premiering in California and then transferring to Broadway.[6] The website provides an "Educators Resource Guide" for teachers that discusses the history of the Japanese internment and the politics surrounding World War II.[7] An enormous amount of effort has been made to include information about the creative process, as well as the history of Japanese internment. Described as "a modern advocate for Asian-American and LGBT causes," Takei used his media platforms to bring the messages of the show to a broader audience.[8] His work on the show has augmented his continued advocacy for the awareness and reconciliation of the Japanese internment and the reparative efforts therein.[9] In tandem, Takei's development of the musical with Kuo, Acito, and Thione has made an impact on the Broadway landscape. Arts journalist and editor Diep Tran emphasizes that

It's not just the topical subject matter – immigration, xenophobia, war-time paranoia – that makes *Allegiance* an especially significant entry to the Broadway season. It also happens to be the first musical created by Asian Americans, directed by an Asian American (Stafford Arima), with a predominantly Asian cast, to grace the Broadway stage.[10]

Equally, the fictive exploration of Takei's experience offers a narrative that exposes an ordeal experienced by the Japanese American community told from a Japanese American perspective. In this aspect, *Allegiance* stands in contrast to musicals such as *The King and I* and *Miss Saigon*.

The plot of *Allegiance* follows the incarceration of the fictional Kimura family, which includes: Ojii-chan the Grandfather, Tatsuo the Father, his son Sammy, and daughter Kei. The family is taken to Heart Mountain camp in Wyoming where they hesitantly settle in amongst fellow Japanese Americans. A conflict of generations quickly arises, as Sammy wants to enlist in the Army to prove his loyalty as an American citizen, whereas his father refuses to admit an allegiance to the United States and gets sent to a work camp. Thereupon, Sammy clashes with Frankie, a fellow resident of the camp who refuses to go along with the ethics of the incarceration. Though cooperation with camp authorities would be seen (supposedly) as a sign of loyalty to the U.S. and possibly ease the difficulties of their confinement, Frankie stages continual protests and disruptions. When friends and family members clash over the "Loyalty Questionnaire," Sammy joins the 443 regiment, an all-Japanese squadron known to be sent on the most dangerous, largely suicide missions.[11] Sammy goes on to become a war hero, but in his absence his sister joins up with Frankie, both romantically and ideologically, and the two work together to help get the camps dissolved. The story ends over fifty years after the war when Sammy receives word that his sister Kei, whom he never saw again after she joined with Frankie, has died. Kei and Frankie's daughter Hana (his niece) brings him the news, and in their new relationship they start the lengthy work of personal forgiveness and recovery. The broader theme of national reparation and acknowledgement that still needs to be done around the Japanese interment in the U.S. hangs heavy in the air as the curtain falls.

The complicated story traces the question: What makes someone American? And what happens when national ideologies and security override self-expression and individualism? The musical interrogates how loyalty or allegiance is deeply imbricated in the formation of an American identity. Further, the show explores other facets of cultural formation and trustworthiness, from food to language, and demonstrates how ideologies change from generation to generation. Given the conventions of musical theatre and the propensity (and demand) to enhance emotion through song and thrill through dance, the moments of movement and music used to express "Americanness" stand out and become a pronounced measure of national identity. When self-expression through swing dancing is considered as a nationalizing force there is a cleaving of previous assumptions about America's melting pot reputation and the formation of identity in the United States.[12] Turning to the methodologies of movement development, acquisition, and fusion with the libretto helps to unpack how this complexity operates in the musical.

Choreographic Strategies in *Allegiance*

Choreographer Andrew Palermo has had an extensive performance career as a dancer on Broadway, as well as a substantial career as a choreographer in both musical theatre and concert dance.[13] He explains the draw of the show for him: "It did give me the opportunity to work in different styles across the show. There's swing, there's traditional Japanese dance, there's my gestural stuff, there's hardcore jazzy in 'Victory Swing.' For me it was fun being able to flex muscles in all the ways."[14] Palermo's choreographic strategy uses swing dance, jazz idioms, and some Japanese traditional dance to imagine a community and enable a greater understanding of how identity and nationality is shaped and embodied.

Swing dance culture in the U.S. specifically at the time of World War II was tied to one's coming of age in the U.S.; thus, it would be apropos that the youth in *Allegiance* take it up. Megan Pugh observes in *America Dancing* that, as the popularity of swing dancing spread, "observers celebrated it as a new national folk dance, proof of the American melting pot at work. When the country entered World War II, the Lindy began to seem like a sign of American grace, modernity and strength."[15] To that end, prior to the "Heart Mountain Dance" in *Allegiance*, the younger generation is shown taking on more of a leadership role amongst the internees at the camp. They gather and make a list of their demands for their time in the camp. They decide that dance was a main leisure activity prior to their internment and should continue to be. They create for themselves an imagined community in the face of precarity, and social dance is where they start. Being interned against one's will in a location far from one's home makes impossible any sense of belonging; however, swing dancing outside on a hot summer night was how these American-born internees found a sense of belonging and self-expression prior to internment, and they use it as such in the camp in order to maintain a sense of comfort and *Gaman* as encouraged by the elders.[16] The dance space is set up and the internees make their depressing circumstances bearable for at least one night through music and dance. The nostalgia inherent in the dance, established as "*the* American dance form" as early as 1937, helps them to imagine a sense of community in the internment camp and attempt a sense of normalcy.[17] The dance also provides a plot point for the beginning of Kei and Frankie's relationship.[18]

The Japanese American body swing dancing amongst the shadows of the fences and the armed watchtowers is a complex image entwined with notions of identity, memory, and nostalgia for "simpler" times on the part of the internees. The dance creates a layered image of the Asian body in the narrative as there is a juxtaposition between the characters, who are "*Nisei*" (second generation Japanese American), and the "*Issei*" (Japanese born immigrants) who are watching but do not dance. Aragaki explains, "The swing music and dance is a vehicle to view [the] different relationships, embodying the simultaneous community-building and alienation on stage."[19] In effect, the constant strain in the story between one's commitment to one's sense of self and family and an allegiance to the nation is sensed in the choreography, particularly through choices of who does it and how. For example, in the "Heart Mountain Dance" three *Nisei* couples dance in impressive unison enhancing its collective feel; there is no individuality in the breakaways, and all bodies move as close as possible in similar fashion. The choice to choreograph the dance with three couples working in precision is thrilling but also transforms the general roots of swing dance as a playful popular pastime where one could experiment with new moves and fun breakaways to a sense of collectivism as the three couples mirror each other. Individual personalities fade in the social-dance based choreography in order to give space for a sense of solidarity between community members and their legitimate claim to be citizens. The dynamic and expert execution of the swing dance by the Japanese Americans in the internment camp disrupts the accusations of "otherness" and enhances their "Americanness."

Further, the skill and ease displayed by the dancers has the potential to arouse memories of dance halls, school gyms, and patio dances and represent moments of peace and pride in the U.S. There is a sense of nostalgia for a time before the attacks on Pearl Harbor and the South Pacific. Palermo employs swing dancing in collaboration with Jay Kuo's 1940s-styled score to break down racial tropes and demonstrate how social dance can be used to indicate and inspire inclusion and understanding across cultures. The group precision and presentational style in the onstage dance amplifies these meanings. William Given describes the impact these stories had on audience members when, in a talk back with an audience of students, Paul Nakauchi who played Tatsuo Kimura explained, "his parents had been internees. There was a palpable moment, including some audible gasp, as the students realised the fictional characters they had just witnessed were so intimately connected to their own worlds."[20] When Michael K. Lee (who played Frankie, and sings and dances in the upbeat, and satirical song "Paradise") spoke to students who were just learning about internment, he encouraged "It's your responsibility to go out and search for information now." As Given states – "the conversation had begun," and this was the goal of Takei from the beginning.[21]

Japanese Bodies on Stage

The theatricalization of Asian Americans in internment camps on stage in *Allegiance* draws focus to a U.S. crisis of identity during and after World War II. Even as Asian immigrants they were already marked and with their internment the image of the U.S. as a melting pot or multicultural nation is revealed to be nothing less than a tightly held mythology. The paranoid singling out of the Other exposes the failure of America as "the good society, the epitome of enlightenment and modernity."[22] The control of the Other is constructed around visibility and how bodies look, not what they believe or actions they take, a pointedly close-minded stance. Performance Studies scholar Karen Shimakawa, in *National Abjection: The Asian American Body on Stage*, explains the "irreconcilable contradiction" in the singling out of Japanese Americans:

> Regardless of the citizenship status, and unlike (white) immigrants from other countries then at war with the United States, Japanese Americans were deemed suspect, deprived of their constitutional rights, removed from their homes, and imprisoned by the "War Relocation Authority."[23]

This contradiction to the treatment of other immigrants that have greater ease in their assimilation (able pass as American because of their whiteness) complicates how nationhood or a national citizen is formed. This bias is alluded to in the production when Sammy asks why Joe DiMaggio is not being interned despite his Italian roots. The internment calls into question how identity is defined and by whom, as well as the global implications of identifying with a particular nation. The frustration in this paradigm that *Allegiance* briefly addresses is the absurdity of the situation set against the conflict of World War II. In fact, what was being fought against overseas was happening in the U.S. Shimakawa observes, "The democratic principles ostensibly being defended abroad – freedom from racist genocide and colonial/nationalist brutalities – led directly to racist-nationalist oppression and property theft at home."[24]

The "Heart Mountain Dance" works to create a sense of home for the internees. The dance, and the various antics that follow including Frankie's parody of Mike Masaoka (the leader of the Japanese American Citizens League) in "Paradise," help to demonstrate that having fun and challenging the status quo are one's right as an American. Shimakawa proposes, "performance may be pressed into the service of, or may serve as a counter discourse to, those dominant narratives of national belonging and national exclusion," and the swing dance in *Allegiance* does just this.[25] The term "uncanny strangeness" is used by Shimakawa to describe the presence of Asian American bodies on stage that work as part of narratives outside the usual stereotypes so often pursued in the theatre.[26] It is in this realm that Asian American identities can be re-worked beyond national assumptions and move forward towards gaining greater meaning. She explains this conceptualization "offers us a 'practice field' for reimaging Asian Americanness and its relation to national abjection."[27] In this consideration the swing dance scene becomes essential in moving beyond stereotypes and potentially destructive "restorative" nostalgia toward a greater reflection of the embodied nostalgia within the Japanese American dancers swing dancing. In particular the *Nisei* hold within them an embodied and collective memory for a time of relative normalcy in the U.S. when they could work out their anxieties about life in the dance hall as part of a community along with everyone else, not interned against their will. A nostalgia for that time circulates in the "Heart Mountain Dance" underpinned by a sense of unity (however short-lived) in the unison.

The swing scene stands in contrast to an earlier movement sequence in the performance involving Japanese traditional movement practices. Prior to the internment, the younger generation performs a dance around a tree in honor of Obon, a traditional Japanese festival honoring one's ancestors. The Japanese-styled dancing used in the scene is sustained and elegant, as one would imagine for holiday protocols; a grapevine-like step with flexed hands held at chest level. This stands in contrast to the "Heart Mountain Dance," with its virtuosic display of gymnastic-styled skills needed to execute the choreography, particularly in synchronicity. There is a sense of "uncanny strangeness" seeing the same performers expertly executing both styles. This strangeness would vary between audience members depending on if one was Japanese, Japanese American, white or non-culturally aligned and what one's experience with seeing professional level swing dance and by whom.

Importantly, in regards to creating the Japanese styles dance, Palermo explains how that movement quality was brought in. He shares that one of the cast members who had done choreography in earlier iterations of the show, Rumi Oyama (who played Mrs. Tanaka), had experience doing traditional Japanese dance and consulted on the choreography. He explains, "I would choreograph and then I would say to her 'does this work? Is it authentic?' How would the hands be? She would be very helpful in that." He also explains that cast member Janelle Toyomi Dote was helpful in creating the correct gestures for the traditional dance.[28] There is no mention of Rumi Oyama's contribution in the Playbill, however Janelle Toyomi Dote is listed as the assistant dance captain.[29] At a broader level, this points to the importance of publicly acknowledging (whether in the press surrounding the show or in the program) any contributions by dancers whose bodily archive and experiences includes cultural movement styles that are brought into a musical.[30] This attention is needed, as champion by Liza Gennaro in regards to the work of her father Peter Gennaro in *West Side Story*, in order to avoid their work and identity being "erased form the creative record as a creative contributor."[31] More choreographers can and should make these acknowledgements whenever possible.

Critical Reception

The question remains – why was the show not particularly successful on Broadway and what were the dramaturgical strategies that caused the short run? There are various factors that may have influenced the limited success of the play on Broadway. First, the adaptations made from the original San Diego production, though they helped the story, may have hindered the likeability and/or depth of some of the characters. Additionally, the exaggeration of events for emotional effect and theatricality may have been too heavy-handed for some.[32] Second, various critics questioned whether the genre of musical theatre is the correct style to tell such a serious story about a very dark point in U.S. history, including David Rooney who concludes, "An important story that hasn't found its ideal form as a musical."[33] Though musical theatre as a genre has explored challenging or disturbing moments in history, the music and lyrics in *Allegiance* do not support the magnitude of such a difficult topic. Though the musical was generally well received and attended by audiences, the show lacked the musical sophistication and complexity needed to carry the emotional heft. The score lacked innovation and seemed to be too reminiscent of past musicals such as *Les Misérables* or *Miss Saigon*.[34] There was a general consensus among critics that the music and score were lacking, exemplified in phrases used in a myriad of reviews to describe the score such as, "obvious," "derivative music and pedestrian lyrics," "workmanlike score," "generic," "unmemorable," "pretty standard older style Broadway fare, not particularly innovative, nothing particularly surprising," and "doesn't make the grade."[35]

Despite prominent images of the dance moments, much like the one included at the top of this chapter, included in the reviews and promotional materials, there is little said of the choreography. Though publicity shots, are often more sensational in order to sell the show, the images overpromise a "dance musical." At very least there is an inconsistency in the reviews that add these pictures to their critique while not commenting on the movement.[36] Markedly, in over a dozen reviews of the Broadway show, few mention the dance, and only then to say it is included. There is no analysis of its use or function, save for Linda Winer, who says it "signif[ies] Americana," and Jonathan Madell, who says the numbers are "energetically choreographed."[37] Other short mentions of the choreography include Jeremy Gerard's statement: "Less successful are the staging by Stafford Arima and the dancing by Andrew Palermo, which have the virtue of avoiding Asian cliché but also fail, like the songs, to give the show wings."[38] David Finkle also suggests, "Palermo doesn't do much out of the ordinary."[39] While Jenn Fang does not mention the choreography, she provides a nuanced and detailed reading of some of the missteps in the musical drawing attention to the "shoe-horned" in relationship (and song "With You") between Sammy and Hannah the camp nurse and problematizes that choice,

> More frustrating, Hannah's character – who seems to exist largely to serve as a sympathetic character to capture the interest of White audiences – becomes a vehicle whereby White Guilt and the White Savior Complex finds bizarre and unsettling articulation; this plot point takes a disappointing turn late in the second act that almost threatens to trivialize the musical's larger lesson regarding Japanese American incarceration.[40]

Music and dance scholar Angela Yuki Proulx comes to similar conclusions stating, "A historical play about Asian American Trauma means making the subject matter palatable for main stream audiences," exampling the insertion of the romance with Nurse Hannah as one such adjustment.[41] Proulx explains that the character of

Hannah, particularly in her song, "Should I" (where she wonders if she should break established rules of engagement with prisoners) "opens herself up to a new world view, one not rooted in binaries."[42] Despite the score not generally succeeding there is a sense of growth in a song such as "Should I" – perhaps a suggestion to a mainstream audience do the same? By unpacking some of these smaller moments in the music, movement, and staging a level of complexity in the musical is brought forth. For instance, Fang refers to the haunting interpretation of the moment of the dropping of bombs on Hiroshima and Nagasaki describing it as, "a particularly powerful and evocative tribute to the emotional trauma that is otherwise typically divorced from our teaching of this unforgivable moment in global history."[43] In the corresponding song, "Itetsuita" (meaning "we are frozen") the ensemble stands in columns of distorted lights all facing different directions with arms by their sides. At the peak of the short song the ensemble take a quick step to all face front and the lights scan their bodies from foot to head tracing an arc to the ceiling. It is a chilling moment that offers, as Fang explains, "an evocative tribute" achieved through subtle movement and rich choral arrangements. Though Fang doesn't explicitly refer to the movement, she keys into the essence of that moment of physical staging.

In regards to the descriptors as put forth above by Winer and Finkle regarding the aesthetics of the show such as "Americana" and "not much out of the ordinary" they do offer up some considerations. The iconicity of swing dance and jazz music as an American invention in modern society has been built up from years of being associated with the Jazz Age, the Savoy, Harlem, New York, and America in general. Whether one agrees with or buys the sentimentalized story or music, in the discussion of how one shows their allegiance, as Tucker described earlier, swing dance is an expression of a national consensus of American patriotism.[44] If Palermo had over-choreographed the "Heart Mountain Dance" with a myriad of innovative and unfamiliar steps that only hinted at the social dance, the connection to the "ordinary" or everyday social dance would be lost. As it is, the dance has some spectacular feats and lifts, all generally out of the West Coast Swing vocabulary, that serve to show how bodies that look Japanese are also American. A notable mention is the end of "Heart Mountain Dance" which concludes with a very difficult high-flying lift that quickly transitions into a dip where the man is supporting the woman only by her neck (with one hand) in a very low plank-like position. In the dance's spectacularization and display of a highly professional level of virtuosity, there is the familiar thrill and excitement culturally associated with the moves and situation of a dance form created in the U.S.

Shifts in Dramaturgical Strategies and Historical Accuracies

The historical inaccuracies and embellishments in *Allegiance* are part of the structural changes that occurred through the various try-outs. The earliest iterations of the show seem to be more on point with a clear narrative through-line of the Kimura family's story, however, and as is common with many shows, by the time it reached Broadway the production had evolved from its simple storytelling to be more sentimental and sensational. There is an intentional increase, from the early iteration to the Broadway premiere, in the nationalistic agenda and harshness of conditions in the camps that increase tensions of the geopolitical on self-expression. Critics and scholars have pointed out that conditions in the internment camps were not as violent and forceful as they are portrayed on stage. Residents of the camps were not forced to a strip search, they were not spoken to through a loudspeaker, and soldiers with guns did not order them around. In the musical, all Japanese Americans are removed quickly from their homes at the same time and sent directly to camps. Brian Niiya explains this happened over much time and most were sent to an assembly center first.[45] While these sorts of time-based issues are generally overlooked given the short time frame of a live production, the choice to omit various details begins a cycle of exaggeration and an inflation of the tension for dramatic effect. The propagating of the nationalist agenda risks overwhelming the personal journey of the characters in the show. Frank Abe suggests the portrayal of the camps is way off: "It's laughable nonsense, as if the camps were run not by Dillon Myer and the WRA but by Hermann Göring and his Luftwaffe."[46] The suggestion from the creative team is that through exaggeration, attention is drawn to the issue and perhaps helps to begin education about the facts.

Beyond historical inaccuracies and the portrayal of the truth on stage, theatre and performance studies scholar Emily Roxworthy explores the deeper effect of the transformations and exaggerations in the show, explaining how empathy becomes key to the success of the performance. She observes, "most of the critical empathy had been stripped away by the time [*Allegiance*] was sent to Broadway," making the show a very tedious balancing act of exploring this tension.[47] In earlier iterations the ghost of Sammy and Kei's grandfather (Takei's character) haunted the show, which helped to connect the past and the present. Roxworthy observes that the removal of the ghost character "means that the ghost of the internment frames, but does not intrude on, the past unfolding on stage."[48] This choice perhaps, as Roxworthy suggests, "sanitizes the past for present day audiences," and destabilizes the reflection one might have on past decisions and actions or on present day circumstances. This avoidance of the continuous tensions between the past and the present which the ghost amplified leaves the embodied meanings and choreography to do greater narrative work.[49]

Conclusion

The numerous iterations and try-outs make it difficult for a choreographer (who is not also the director) to maintain a choreographic through-line. As such, the choreographic signature does not thread throughout the show but is broken up into parts. In particular, the moments drawn from social dance, both Japanese and American-styled, bring in considerable meaning.[50] As the complicated threads of the story unfold the realization of the difficulty in identifying what constitutes being American permeates the story. As has been previously stated there is a nostalgia that circulates around World War II of the soldier and the nurse, or the reunited lovers, as an emblem of America's experience in the War. When the "Heart Mountain Dance" begins and the empty stage fills with Asian bodies doing American Swing dance, and doing it extraordinarily well, there is an "uncanny strangeness" that destabilizes the nostalgic image many have come to embrace surrounding World War II and swing culture.[51] While the Japanese American characters' ability to move does not solve their problems, the audience is shown how "American" the internees are. This moment and the following comedy dance "Paradise," a satirical take on the absurdity of their situation sung by Frankie, function to force a rethinking of nostalgia and clarifies the substantial impact of the swing dance by contrast. In all, the swing dance in *Allegiance* deflates the restorative type of nostalgia where one is trying to patch up the past to make a perfect picture, and offers a reflective angle that forces a taking apart of ingrained notions of who knew and did swing dance in the 1940s.

Despite the short Broadway run, Takei and the creators remained determined to get the story out to America. When the reality of the shorter run seemed inevitable, Takei moved quickly to film the musical. As a result, on the seventy-fifth anniversaries of the Attack on Pearl Harbor, and the beginning of the forced internment, *Allegiance* was screened across U.S. theatres. The screenings were accompanied by lectures, provided spaces for reflection, and offered opportunities to join in human-rights activism. Markedly, several months into the 2020 Covid-19 lockdown, *Allegiance* was released for streaming for a month, with a second longer streaming window in March 2021. In the modern moment in which violence is being perpetrated against Asian Americans amidst an increasing rise in anti-Asian racism, *Allegiance* performs an important and often neglected disruption to the notion of U.S. exceptionalism, both historically and in the present. While at first there were only select screenings of the musical on key anniversary dates, thanks to Takei and his team's efforts the musical is now available on streaming platforms world-wide and continues the conversation surrounding the much-needed work of reparation and reconciliation. Theatre and performance scholar William Given explains, "The show became more than just an entertaining spectacle confined to a two-hour time frame on the stage. It became a catalyst for dialogue."[52]

In all three musicals of this section swing dance is employed by the choreographer to imagine a community in the face of precarity. Nostalgia has been shown to be the emotional spark that makes this vital and visceral communal connection possible. The study of these shows demonstrates how social dance can embody implicit meanings in a story, and how the embodied nostalgia therein can, to a greater or lesser effect, intimate greater social and political awareness. Social dance in all three musicals is shown to create a community that has the possibility, whether overtly or more covertly, to instigate, or at very least suggest, change. Significantly, the circumstances under which the concepts of community are created are very different. In *Steel Pier*, set in the early 1930s, swing dance helped a country escape, if only momentarily, from economic realities. In the Depression Era, swing music and dance were integral to enlivening the despair in everyday life, and, as seen in the dance marathon in *Steel Pier*, about collective survival itself. As the decade (and Depression) progressed and Benny Goodman became the most prominent white bandleader to employ Black musicians in his band in 1936, swing dance and music became also about cultural mixing and civil rights.[53] Though this racial integration was only a small step, the embrace of diversity and self-expression as seen in *Wonderful Town*'s "Christopher Street" brought differing communities together with a greater sense of inclusion. By the end of 1941, only a year or so before the emergence of "Bebop" styled jazz music, the Japanese attack on Pearl Harbor led to the U.S. declaring war on Japan. With the devastation of the attack and the uncertainties of being in a state of war, government officials, the entertainment industry, and communities turned to swing music and dance as a morale booster and show of patriotic support. In *Allegiance*, the one musical of this project that openly examines concepts of nationalism and geopolitics, community is created around swing music and dance as a tenet of American identity. In all, for the choreographers of the case studies, by using swing dance as a framework, the varied meanings and constructs of community embedded in the dance, and inscribed on bodies, adds to the impact and discursive development of the musical.

Though two of the three shows were a disappointment at the box office and to critics, the analysis of the social dance in them has helped to understand what the choreography is trying to do in the show and why. The less successful shows generally suffered because of an unformulated story (*Steel Pier*) or unsophisticated score (*Allegiance*), not on account of the choreography. This analysis has shown the importance of investigating choreography in musical theatre through the lens of the social dance(s) of the era in which the production is set. Svetlana Boym has found nostalgia is "coeval with modernity."[54] This can be true of the relationship between nostalgia and social dance because of continual shifts in social dance and communities over time and place. The audience may not be aware of the roots of a dance but the nostalgia that "co-evolves" with a past social dance when brought into the contemporary moment on stage brings the possibility of deeper meaning, contextualization, and understanding of that community.

What is often difficult to explain or attend to after 1945 is the falling off of social dancing throughout the U.S. As the Stearnses observe, "When the swing era faded in the forties, a blackout of about ten years intervened – from 1945–1954 – with little or no dancing."[55] There are various reasons for this, one of the main ones being a tax from the federal government on dance floors across the nation.[56] In the following conclusion, I point towards the transition into the rock'n'roll dances and what this transition means for choreographers, social dance communities, and the body in motion on stage.

Notes

1 Sugars are a common move in Charleston and swing dance where dancers keep their weight on the balls of their feet and with each step to the side the knee follows in line with the leading foot. This movement alternates left and right creating a twisting or shimmy-like action with the lower body.

2 *Allegiance*: 2015, music and lyrics by Jay Kuo and a book by Marc Acito, Kuo and Lorenzo Thione, inspired by the personal experiences of George Takei.

3 "Entire City put on War footing," *New York Times,* December 8, 1941. Accessed April 18, 2022, permalink: https://nyti.ms/3uSyDOf https://timesmachine.nytim es.com/timesmachine/1941/12/08/105167834.html?pageNumber=1.

4 Rachel Aragaki, *Swing-Power: Music, Historical Learning, and Critical Empathy in Jay Kuo's Allegiance* (California State University, Long Beach, 2021), 2.

5 Nicole Hertvik, "An Interview with Jay Kuo, Composer and lyricist of 'Allegiance,'" *DC Metro Theatre Arts,* December 7, 2016, https://dcmetrotheaterarts. com/2016/12/07/interview-jay-kuo-composer-lyricist-allegiance-film-broadway-musical-will-show-theaters/.

6 "Allegiance," http://allegiancemusical.com/#ahHdc3gocE76FSpM.97, accessed June 5, 2018.

7 There is a vast amount of information available on the *Allegiance* website including "Translating a Painful History for Broadway," "A Lesson in Hateful Politics' Consequences," "Diversity, the New Lead Role on Broadway," "What My Time in an Intern Camp Taught Me" (by Mike Honda the U.S Representative for California), and "George Takei's New York."

8 Robert Kahn, "Takei, at 78, Boldly Goes Into Painful Family History," *NBC New York,* November 8, 2015, https://www.nbcnewyork.com/entertainment/the-s cene/Review-Allegiance-George-Takei-342666812.html.

9 George Takei is one of the most followed celebrities on Twitter. Jeremy Cabalona explains, "Takei knows his audience very well. While he has expanded his following through strong involvement in the gay rights movement (his *It's Ok to be Takei* initiative, for instance) and Asian American groups (he is on the board of the Japanese American National Museum), his core fan-base consists of *Star Trek* fans who appreciate Takei for his self-aware humor." Cabalona, "How George Takei went from *Star Trek* to Social Media Superstar," *Mashable,* April 20, 2012, http s://mashable.com/2012/04/20/george-takei-social-media/#3Pbxvz26Juq4.

10 Diep Tran "Broadway's Yellow Fever: From South Pacific to Allegiance, The American Musical Has Traveled From Well-Intentioned Orientalism to Something Like Authenticity." *American Theatre* 32, no. 9 (2015): 58.

11 The War Department and the War Relocation Authority (WRA) determined whether someone was loyal to America or the Emperor of Japan. The WRA created what was casually called the "loyalty questionnaire." This form, formally known as the "Statement of United States Citizen of Japanese Ancestry," also titled Selective Service Form 304A, becomes the crux around which the conflict of the story operates. The questionnaire can be narrowed down to two main questions, number 27 and 28: would you be willing to serve the U.S? and would you be willing to swear allegiance to the U.S? In *Allegiance* Sammy declares he will answer yes to both, while his family and Frankie vehemently answer no, not because they don't consider themselves Americans but to protest the injustice of the internment. Cherston M. Lyon, "Loyalty Questionnaire," *Densho Encyclopedia,* n.d. https:// encyclopedia.densho.org/Loyalty_questionnaire/, accessed June 15, 2018.

12 This instance puts into question what Sherrie Tucker calls "the dance floor of the nation" and how in the circumstances of the Japanese Internment the government wants to have it both ways (Sherrie Tucker, *Dance Floor Democracy: The Social*

Geography of Memory at the Hollywood Canteen (Durham, NC: Duke University Press, 2014), xix).

13 Palermo's performance credits include: *How to Succeed in Business Without Really Trying* (1995), *Annie Get Your Gun* (1999), *Wicked* (2003) Off Broadway: *Little Fish* (2003). Choreography and musical staging in New York include: *Journey to The West* (2006), *Babes in Toyland* (2017), *Austen's Pride* (2017), *Of Thee I Sing* (2017).

14 Interview by author, July 6, 2018.

15 Megan Pugh, *America Dancing: From the Cakewalk to the Moonwalk* (New Haven, CT: Yale University Press, 2015), 235.

16 Early on in the show the Japanese term *Gaman* is introduced. In the author's note in the program, book writers Marc Acito, Jay Kuo, and Lorenzo Thione explain, "'Gaman' is a word we learned from George Takei, the inspiration and guiding light of this production. It's Japanese for 'endurance with dignity' and was a principle that sustained George, his family and the 120,000 Japanese-Americans unjustly incarcerated during World War II." "Allegiance," *Playbill*, accessed November 11, 2018, http://www.playbill.com/playbillpagegallery/inside-playbill?asset=00000150 -aea8-d936-a7fd-eefc72ea0009&type=InsidePlaybill&slide=6.

17 Juliet McMains and Danielle Robinson, "Swingin' Out: Southern California's Lindy Revival (2000), in *I See America Dancing: Selected Reading 1685–2000,* ed. Maureen Needham (Chicago: University of Illinois Press, 2002), 87. Italics theirs.

18 Following the "Heart Mountain Dance" number, Frankie and some of the young women internees perform the song "Paradise," a cutting parody of Mike Masaoka, the leader of the Japanese American Citizens League (JACL). Masaoka is a controversial player in the Japanese internment (and the only non-fictional character in the musical) as in general he felt it was counterproductive to fight back against incarceration.

19 Aragaki, *Swing-Power*, 21.

20 William Given, "Allegiance and the Construction of a New American Musical." *TheatreForum-International Theatre Journal* (2012): 44, 45.

21 Ibid., 45.

22 David Walsh and Len Platt. *Musical Theater and American Culture* (Westport, CT: Greenwood, 2003), 197.

23 Karen Shimakawa, *National Abjection: The Asian American Body on Stage* (Durham, NC: Duke University Press, 2002), 78.

24 Shimakawa, *National Abjection*, 10. It is also important to note that all military units segregated African Americans from White Americans during World War II.

25 Shimakawa investigates several Asian American playwrights that are doing this kind of work: Wakako Yamauchi's *12–1-A* (also about Japanese internment camps, and the conflict revolves around responses to the loyalty questionnaire); Elizabeth Wong's *Letters to a Student Revolutionary*; Frank Chin's *The Chickencoop Chinaman* and *The Year of the Dragon*, 163.

26 Shimakawa describes the stock figures often used in performance: the exotic and sensual Asian female, the Asian female who sacrifices herself for her child, the paralyzed or invisible Asian Male.

27 Shimakawa, *National Abjection*, 160.

28 Interview with author, July 6, 2018.

29 Notably, Rumi Oyama does take on the choreographic helm for the 2018 production of *Allegiance* produced by the East West Players at the Aratani Theatre in Los Angeles where the show was revived with some of the original Broadway cast members returning. Tara Overfield Wilkinson has directed and choreographed the U.K. premier of *Allegiance* at Charing Cross Theatre in 2023.

30 Correspondingly, in terms of casting, as seen in past Broadway shows such as the original *The King and I* and *Miss Saigon* (to name a few) "Asian" becomes a catch all term for all performers in audition posting and those with different cultural identities and backgrounds are often seen as "interchangeable," Donatella Galella,

"Artists of Color/Cross-Racial Casting," in *Casting a Movement: The Welcome Table Initiative*, edited by Claire Syler and Daniel Banks (New York: Routledge, 2019), 190. This practice is particularly common in histories told by and from a U.S. perspective. In 2015, the audition calls for *Allegiance* stated they were seeking Asian, South Asian/ Indian, Southeast Asian /Pacific Islander actors. "Allegiance," March 7, 2015. https://www.backstage.com/casting/allegiance-61119/. Please see the entire edited collection of essays, *Casting a Movement: The Welcome Table Initiative* for more on casting and representation in performance.

31 Liza Gennaro, *Making Broadway Dance* (Oxford University Press, 2021), 124.
32 Critics and scholars have pointed out that conditions in the internment camps were not as violent and forceful as they are portrayed on stage. See: Brian Niiya, "Allegiance: See the Film, But Watch for These Historical Inaccuracies," *Densho Blog,* February 10, 2017, https://densho.org/allegiance-see-film-watch-historical-inaccuracies/.
33 David Rooney, "'Allegiance': Theatre Review," *Hollywood Reporter,* November 8, 2015, https://www.hollywoodreporter.com/review/george-takei-lea-salonga-allegiance-838242.
34 It is not difficult to make this connection given Lea Salonga was the Tony Award winning lead in *Miss Saigon.* She has also played the roles of both female lead roles (Eponine and Fantine) in the Broadway production of *Les Miserables* in 1993.
35 Charles Isherwood, "Review: 'Allegiance' a Musical History Lesson About Interned Japanese-Americans, *New York Times,* November 8, 2015; Linda Winer, "'Allegiance' Review: George Takei on World War II Japanese-American Camps," *Newsday,* November 8, 2015; Jonathan Madell, "George Takei, Lea Salonga in a Musical About Japanese-American Internment," *DC Theatre Scene,* November 8, 2015; Jeremy Gerard, "George Takei, Lea Salonga Survive WWII Internment In Broadway's 'Allegiance,'" *Deadline,* November 8, 2015; Lily, "'Allegiance' Brings Japanese American Internment to Broadway," *8Asians: An Asian American Collective Blog,* November 24, 2015; David Finkle, "First Nighter: 'Allegiance' Attempts to Musicalize World War II's Japanese-American Internment Camps," *Huffington Post,* November 8, 2015.
36 To view images of the promotional materials for *Allegiance* see: https://web.archive.org/web/20190312151735/http://allegiancemusical.com/article/allegiance-broadway-review-ny-observer/.
37 Winer, "'Allegiance' Review"; Madell, "George Takei, Lea Salonga…".
38 Gerard, "George Takei, Lea Salonga Survive WWII Internment In Broadway's 'Allegiance,'" 2015.
39 Ibid.; Finkle, "First Nighter".
40 Jenn Fang, "'Allegiance' – George Takei stars in musical (and history lesson)," *Northwest Asian Weekly,* November 20, 2015.
41 Angela Yuki Proulx, *Decolonizing the Stage: An Analysis of Edward Sakamoto's Pilgrimage and Jay Kuo, Lorenzo Thione, and Marc Acito's Allegiance.* University of California, Riverside, 2018.
42 Ibid., 14
43 Fang, "Allegiance".
44 In the time line of *Allegiance*, the transmission of swing dance beyond the U.S. would be relatively small, and thus would be identifiable as an American dance. The swing dance did spread to Europe and the rest of the world with increasing intensity, but in the late 1930s early 1940s the dissipation was not yet rampant. Tucker, *Dance Floor Democracy*, xvii.
45 Niiya, *Densho Blog,* 2017.
46 Frank Abe, "Allegiance Fabrications Just Part of Larger Problem, Critics Say." Resister.com: Japanese American Resistance to Japanese American Internment. https://resisters.com/2015/12/23/allegiance-reviews/; Frank Abe, "Guardian of History Challenges Historical accuracy of 'Allegiance,'" Resisters.com, February 19,

2017, http://resisters.com/2017/02/19/guardian-of-history-challenges-historical-integrity-of-allegiance/#more-3158. Abe further explains, "Here are the facts. No resistance leader was hunted by guards like an inmate escaping Stalag 17. No one at Heart Mountain was beaten bloody by guards. And for god's sake, no guards shot and killed any white nurse in a jealous scuffle with a resister."

47 Emily Roxworthy, "Revitalizing Japanese Internment: Critical Empathy and Role-Play in the Musical *Allegiance* and the Video Game *Drama in the Delta*," *Theatre Journal* 66, no. 1 (2014): 109.

48 Ibid., 109.

49 Ibid., 109–110.

50 Palermo discusses the numerous rounds of cutting and different version of choreography that was kept or left behind particularly for "Get in the Game." Palermo explains, "'Paradise' is one of the songs, as well as 'Camp Dance,' that changed very little. From the first time I heard a demo, all the way through the Broadway production. Almost everything else got changed hugely or cut or whatever, but those two really stayed," Interview with author July 6, 2018.

51 The renaissance of swing dancing in the 1990s that embraced the music, fashions, and hairstyle of the time, serves to confirm how strong the nostalgic draw of the era is. For more information on this see: William Given: "Lindy Hop, Community, and the Isolation of Appropriation" In *The Oxford Handbook of Dance and Theatre,* ed. Nadine George-Graves (Oxford, UK: Oxford University Press, 2015), 729–749.

52 Ibid., 44.

53 Ted Gioia explains "The various Goodman splinter bands were not the first racially integrated jazz groups, but they were the most prominent of their day." *The History of Jazz* (New York: Oxford University Press, 2011), 134.

54 Svetlana Boym, *The Future of Nostalgia* (New York: Basic Books, 2001), xvi.

55 Marshall and Jean Stearns. *Jazz Dance: The Story of American Vernacular Dance* (New York: Da Capo Press, 1994), 1.

56 Ibid.

References

Abe, Frank. "Allegiance Fabrications Just Part of Larger Problem, Critics Say." Resisters.com, December 23, 2015. http://resisters.com/2015/12/23/allegiance-reviews/.

Abe, Frank. "Guardian of History Challenges Historical Accuracy of 'Allegiance.'" Resisters.com, February 19, 2017. http://resisters.com/2017/02/19/guardian-of-history-challenges-historical-integrity-of-allegiance/#more-3158.

Allegiance Musical. "Allegiance." http://allegiancemusical.com/#ahHdc3gocE76FSpM.97, accessed June 5, 2018.

"Allegiance," March 7, 2015. https://www.backstage.com/casting/allegiance-61119/.

Aragaki, Rachel. *Swing-Power: Music, Historical Learning, and Critical Empathy in Jay Kuo's Allegiance*. California State University, Long Beach, 2021.

Boym, Svetlana. *The Future of Nostalgia*. New York: Basic Books, 2001.

Cabalona, Jeremy. "How George Takei went from *Star Trek* to Social Media Superstar." *Mashable*, April 20, 2012. https://mashable.com/2012/04/20/george-takei-social-media/#3Pbxvz26Juq4.

"Entire City put on War footing," *New York Times*, December 8, 1941. https://nyti.ms/3uSyDOf, accessed April 18, 2022.

Fang, Jenn. "'Allegiance' – George Takei stars in musical (and history lesson)," *Northwest Asian Weekly*, November 20, 2015. https://nwasianweekly.com/2015/11/allegiance-george-takei-stars-in-musical-and-history-lesson/.

Finkle, David. "First Nighter: 'Allegiance' Attempts to Musicalize World War II's Japanese-American Internment Camps." *Huffington Post*, November 8, 2015. https://www.huffingtonpost.com/david-finkle/first-nighter-allegiance_b_8507490.html.

Gennaro, Liza. *Making Broadway Dance*. Oxford University Press, 2021.

Gerard, Jeremy. "George Takei, Lea Salonga Survive WWII Internment in Broadway's 'Allegiance.'" *Deadline*, November 8, 2018. https://deadline.com/2015/11/george-takei-lea-salonga-allegiance-broadway-review-1201614865/.

Gioia, Ted. *The History of Jazz*. New York: Oxford University Press, 2011.

Given, William. "Allegiance and the Construction of a New American Musical." *TheatreForum-International Theatre Journal* (2012): 40–45.

Given, William. "Lindy Hop, Community, and the Isolation of Appropriation." In *The Oxford Handbook of Dance and Theatre*, edited by Nadine George-Graves, 729–749. Oxford, UK: Oxford University Press, 2015.

Hertvik, Nicole. "An Interview with Jay Kuo, Composer and lyricist of 'Allegiance.'" *DC Metro Theatre Arts*, December 7, 2016. https://dcmetrotheaterarts.com/2016/12/07/interview-jay-kuo-composer-lyricist-allegiance-film-broadway-musical-will-show-theaters/.

Isherwood, Charles. "Review: 'Allegiance' a Musical History Lesson About Interned Japanese-Americans." *New York Times*, November 8, 2015.

Kahn, Robert. "Takei, at 78, Boldly Goes Into Painful Family History." *NBC New York*, November 8, 2015. https://www.nbcnewyork.com/entertainment/the-scene/Review-Allegiance-George-Takei-342666812.html.

Kuo, Jay and Marc Acito, LorenzoThione, *Allegiance*, 2015.

Lyon, Cherston M. "Loyalty Questionnaire." *Densho Encyclopedia*, https://encyclopedia.densho.org/Loyalty_questionnaire/, accessed June 15, 2018.

Madell, Jonathan. "George Takei, Lea Salonga in a Musical About Japanese-American Internment." *DC Theatre Scene*, November 8, 2015. https://dctheatrescene.com/2015/11/08/allegiance-review-george-takei-lea-salonga-in-musical-about-japanese-american-internment/.

McMains, Juliet, and Daniele Robinson. "Swingin' Out: Southern California's Lindy Revival (2000)." In *I See America Dancing: Selected Reading 1685–2000*, edited by Maureen Needham, 87–91. Chicago: University of Illinois Press, 2002.

Murphy, Mathew. "Get in the Game." Allegiancemusical.com, *New York Observer*http://allegiancemusical.com/article/allegiance-broadway-review-ny-observer/#odtAdLMMDoXRu5iq.97, accessed September 14, 2018.

Murphy, Mathew. "Heart Mountain Dance." Allegiancemusical.com, *New York Observer*http://allegiancemusical.com/article/allegiance-broadway-review-ny-observer/#odtAdLMMDoXRu5iq.97, accessed September 14, 2018.

Niiya, Brian. "Allegiance: See the Film, But Watch for These Historical Inaccuracies." *Densho Blog*, February 10, 2017. https://densho.org/allegiance-see-film-watch-historical-inaccuracies/.

Palermo, Andrew. Personal Interview, Los Angeles, July 6, 2018. Phone.

Playbill. "Allegiance." http://www.playbill.com/playbillpagegallery/inside-playbill?asset=00000150-aea8-d936-.a7fd-eefc72ea0009&type=InsidePlaybill&slide=6, accessed June 14, 2018.

Pugh, Megan. *America Dancing: From the Cakewalk to the Moonwalk*. New Haven, CT: Yale University Press, 2015.

Rooney, David. "'Allegiance': Theatre Review." *Hollywood Reporter*, November 8, 2015. https://www.hollywoodreporter.com/review/george-takei-lea-salonga-allegiance-838242.

Roxworthy, Emily. "Revitalizing Japanese Internment: Critical Empathy and Role-Play in the Musical *Allegiance* and the Video Game *Drama in the Delta*." *Theatre Journal* 66, no. 1 (2014): 93–115.

Shimakawa, Karen. *National Abjection: The Asian American Body on Stage*. Durham, NC: Duke University Press, 2002.

Stearns, Marshall, and Jean Stearns. *Jazz Dance: The Story of American Vernacular Dance*. New York: Da Capo Press, 1994.

Tran, Diep. "Broadway's Yellow Fever: From South Pacific to Allegiance, The American Musical Has Traveled From Well-Intentioned Orientalism to Something Like Authenticity." *American Theatre* 32, no. 9 (2015): 58.

Tucker, Sherrie. *Dance Floor Democracy: The Social Geography of Memory at the Hollywood Canteen*. Durham, NC: Duke University Press, 2014.

Walsh, David, and Len Platt. *Musical Theater and American Culture*. Westport, CT: Greenwood, 2003.

Winer, Linda. "'Allegiance' Review: George Takei on World War II Japanese-American Camps." *Newsday*, November 8, 2015. https://www.newsday.com/entertainment/theater/allegiance-review-george-takei-on-wwii-japanese-american-camps-1.11069303.

Conclusion "Just Like It Was Before"

The Promise Continues

At the opening of the 2017 Broadway musical *Bandstand*, Donny Novitski (Corey Cott) returns home from combat at the end of World War II with a heavy heart – he feels responsible for the death of his best friend from friendly fire. He stands stiffly downstage struggling to buy into the optimism the ensemble sings around him that somehow life will return to "just like it was before" he was deployed overseas.[1] The ensemble celebrates, "It's like they popped a cork, the clubs are full again. With all the good time girls and service men. So grab your sweetheart tight and take the floor. […] it it'll be just like it was before."[2] Other veterans tentatively enter the space with fists clenched around suitcase handles and shoulders rolled inwards. The transition back into civilian life is a visible burden; the ghosts of dead soldiers (played by men in faded army fatigues and cast in pale blue light) rest a hand on the backs of the survivors and follow them around the stage. Donny and his friends are broken from their experiences; one struggles with chronic pain, another with trauma from a POW camp, and all are haunted by the atrocities of war. For them, nothing is like it was before – the forced nostalgia is impossible and painful. Donny sings, "They want illusion and they achieve it. We all relive the past […] The world is ending. And we're pretending."[3] And yet, Donny in an effort to find a semblance of normalcy returns to his career as a jazz pianist. He convinces his fellow veterans to form a swing band and pursue a contest to write a hit song to salute the troops. The embodied ghosts fade into the darkness as the mental weight momentarily lessens for the men as they find meaning through music in their rag tag band.

The story of *Bandstand* challenges assumptions of the supposed joyous post-World War II years and explores how a group of mismatched friends, united by their trauma, use music and movement to create meaning in a world they cannot seem to find comfort in. I turn to *Bandstand* in summation because it is a recent musical that both builds upon and troubles the embodied nostalgia of social dance in the Jazz Age. Equally, *Bandstand* is emblematic of the case studies of this project where social dance has been shown to be the spark upon which choreographers build a unique movement signature that explores the visceral experience of a particular moment for a particular community. *Bandstand* director and choreographer Andy Blankenbuehler uses diegetic moments

DOI: 10.4324/9781003163688-14

of social dance (enhanced by his choreographic innovations) as a platform for the characters to work through their frustrations, anxieties, and personal conflicts in a post-World War II world. Furthermore, Blankenbuehler builds a mode of non-verbal communication that makes use of the embodied nostalgia in social dance-based choreography. This style is paired with gesture and moments of stillness from the ghost characters, adding profound resonance and meaning to the characters living with post-traumatic stress disorder.

As briefly described at the beginning of this project, promotional materials pitch *Bandstand* as a nostalgic escape to the world of swing music and heroes. The description of the show as "a truly American celebration of the men and women whose personal bravery defined a nation" illustrates musical theatre's ongoing and deep-seated relationship with history, memory, and ideologies of American exceptionalism.[4] While promotional materials make the most of conventions of the Swing Era (late-night swing dances in smoky bars, romance, and overflowing patriotism in the video trailers), the show's extended movement signature takes on the complexities of post-traumatic stress disorder and the tension between personal and national pride. By both pressing against and harnessing the backwards glancing currents of nostalgia in *Bandstand*, Blankenbuehler's use of two bodies to represent one character – the character and his soldier ghost – allows for a decentering of the some of the more commercial conventions of musical and thus adds a layering of multiple meaning and subtext achieved largely through movement.

In the band's journey, the after-effects of war – anger, alcoholism, mental illness, and survivor's syndrome – are placed alongside the surrounding community and everyday life in Cleveland, Ohio in 1945. The narrative weaves together the communal healing of the band members with a budding romance between Donny and his best friend's widow, Julia (Laura Osnes), the singer of the band. They perform at various dance venues and Blankenbuehler takes every opportunity to include social-dance based choreography. His movement signature establishes the feel of the era and also allows the characters to physically cope with their issues. At the song contest finals, when the band realizes they would be signing away the rights to the prepared song, they instead sing "Welcome Home," a deeply personal song derived from Julia's private poetry that exposes the harsh truth about issues soldiers and survivors face during and after the war.[5] The contest producers think the band will sing a sentimentalized song saluting to the troops and instead they sing the starkly honest eleven o'clock number: "Johnny made it home. Most of him at least. Had three operations. But the pain has not decreased […] Davy cracks a joke, claims to be alright. Drinks a fifth of vodka in his kitchen every night."[6] The clash between the bright swing songs of the 1940s and the band's cutting take on society's disregard for the repercussions of soldiers' experiences in war zones dismantles the nostalgia around the show and pointedly focuses in on the grievous effects of PTSD. Blankenbuehler begins in a reflective nostalgic register and moves towards a decidedly anti-nostalgic reckoning by the end of the musical.

Blankenbuehler uses physicalized efforts (such as the ghost soldiers) to generate awareness around post-traumatic stress disorder. As such he keeps the tension between collective memory and individual experience throughout his choreography (for which he won the show's only Tony Award). I take a brief look at Blankenbuehler's choreographic strategies in *Bandstand* to first emphasize and then bring together some of the tactics used to by the choreographers of the case studies of this project to physicalize the communities shown on stage.

In *Bandstand* Blankenbuehler dissects the features of swing dance to present a perspective on the post-World War II era that both draws on the zeitgeist of the time, and also questions the validity of a longing or nostalgia for that time as interpreted by the body in motion. He explains how he creates embodied meaning and excavates emotion in his work in the show, "I take artistic liberty to exaggerate elements of the social dance to make sure the audience is following the reason it's happening." This increased theatricalization of the social dance moves draws greater attention to the foundations of the dance and dovetails with the expectations of audiences for a thrilling movement experience, as seen in "Push Da Button" in *The Color Purple*. Blankenbuehler details, "For example I might ride the drums louder, or I might do a lot of stop time moves." He goes on to describe this effect, "so in just an instant, the audience can look around and like a close-up on film, see how that person's shoulders are riding up because they're enjoying it so much, or see they're letting out so much sweat and actually they're finding healing." By using social dance driven choreography, he is directing not only the audiences gaze but is targeting both their visceral experience and their understanding of the moment. He explains this maneuvering, "I change rhythm and tempo so that the audience doesn't miss it. Then when I go back to tempo again, they just know the meaning is embedded in there."[7] Furthermore, in his diegetic use of dance he establishes that social dance venues were where problems could be worked out and where much action of the musical takes place. He explains:

> Social dance is the lens for every social issue that is happening right there. Nobody says that out loud they are just hearing the music… they're drawn into it, they're magnetized into the fold. And they find a venue to scream out even if they don't have an answer.

Blankenbuehler brings the essence or "lifeblood of the community" *to* the story he wants to tell as opposed to vice versa.[8] He uses the example of the movement of the both the soldiers and "ghost soldiers" to explain: "Their physicality on the dance floor has to be the same as their physicality in battle. If you have to bend your knees to not be knocked over by the tidal wave of stress, what does that feel like? Then that's the position you do your social dance in." He connects a crouched low to the ground "flight or fight" physicality of the battlefield to the deep *plié* (or flexed knees) of the foundational roots of swing dance styles.[9] Additionally, in order to extend the diegetic sense of the production numbers, he rarely has dancers work in unison or perform facing the audience in a presentational style. While the moves are certainly theatricalized and polished, by avoiding a flat picture he is able to invite the audience into the community, as opposed to performing "at" them.

There are collective and individual moments of movement for the ghost soldiers. For example, when Donny is at the piano the ghost soldiers surround the piano and link to each other in a low crouch as if in a bunker. Conversely, one ghost soldier trudges behind a performer with a hooked arm over their shoulder, head down, dragging himself behind – the weightedness and agony is visible in the grounded stance and deeply curved spine. In a similar moment a character literally carries the solder on their back as they show the struggle of dragging another through the physical and mental fog of war. While the soldiers' ghosts come and go in the show as a reflection of the ebbs and flows of mental healing, they function as a point of contrast to bring the themes to light. In so doing, Blankenbuehler keeps the tension between collective memory and individual experience throughout his choreography.

A unique development in the process of exploring a story about veterans returning from war is the creative team, in their efforts put forth a meaningful and accurate narrative, connected with the organization Got Your 6. Got Your 6, is part of the Bob Woodruff Foundation, a non-profit foundation with the mission to "find, fund, shape and accelerate equitable solution that help our impacted veterans, service members, their families, and their

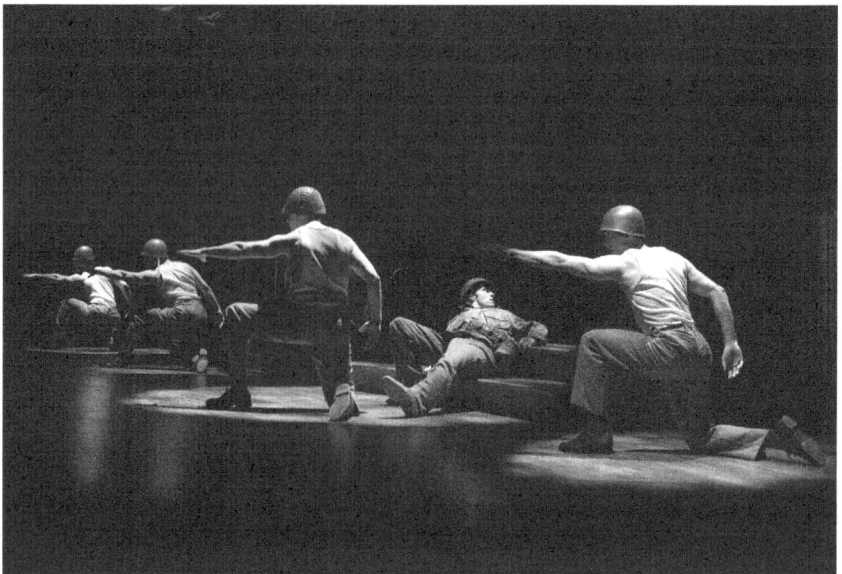

Figure 10.1 One of the only promotional images of the ghost soldiers in performance *Bandstand* (2017)
Source: Photo by Jeremy Daniel.

caregivers thrive."[10] This relationship resulted in conversations and dialogue between the cast and creative team and veterans. *Bandstand* now holds the honor of being the only Broadway musical to be "6 Certified" for its accurate portrayal of veteran experiences. Music and Lyricist Richard Orberaker explains his intent with seeking out the collaboration, "At the end of the day, our show is about taking adversity…and turning it into the very thing that gives your life purpose…the way they learn how to take this adversity and give their life purpose is by telling the truth."[11] As detailed, Blankenbuehler connects his choreography to an exploration of this truth telling. Pointedly, the creative team aimed to avoid any sentimentalizing or stereotypical tropes in regards to their narrative and thus formulated the central question of the musical as "What would veterans who came back from that experience… be dealing with, and, if they were musicians, what would they need to make themselves feel back at home in society again?"[12] In *Bandstand*, Blankenbuehler, as both director and choreographer, creates a world where movement and music function as a release, a reaction, an outlet, and ultimately a healing process.

Bandstand shares some commonalities with the previously discussed Broadway musical *Allegiance* in terms of repair and reconciliation. *Bandstand* has been filmed and screened on Memorial Day in the U.S. in honor of veterans with proceeds going to T.A.P.S (Tragedy Assistance Program for Survivors) that provides care for those who have lost loved ones in the line of duty. Both

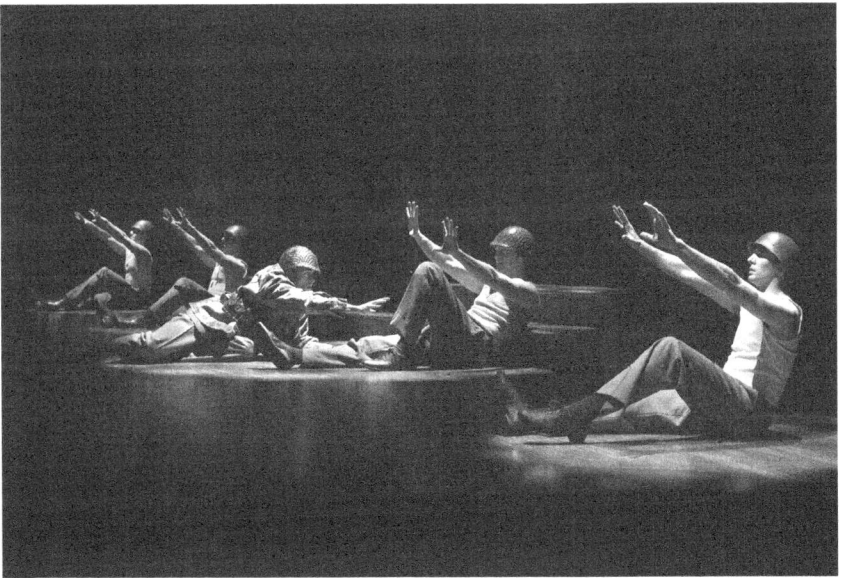

Figure 10.2 Bandstand (2017)
Source: Photo by Jeremy Daniel.

these shows put forth a uniquely embodied interpretation of experiences that can be difficult to articulate and discuss. The potential for choreography to open up spaces for reflection and healing is felt in these two instances. The compassion set forth in both these shows and their subsequent community engagements offers a potential in musical theatre worthy of further consideration, particularly as both shows, despite their short runs, experienced after-lives that played a productive part in the long road towards recovery and reconciliation both on individual and community levels. In *Bandstand* the movement is key in this journey.

In relation to the other choreographers discussed, Blankenbuehler's movement signature involves a loosening of the elements of the swing dance (timing, steps, musical accents etc.) and interlaces them with original moves and unconventional rhythms. This is how he builds a bridge between the physicality of the dance floor and the battlefield, thus layering the past and present for audience consideration. Graciela Daniele works in a similar and effective fashion in *Ragtime* by deconstructing the Cakewalk to problematize racial assumptions and conflict. Likewise, Savion Glover develops a comparable strategy of fragmenting historical dances from the 1920s and blending them with percussive and hard-hitting urban tap in *Shuffle Along*. Susan Stroman does not deconstruct the dance in *Steel Pier*, but rather, she juxtaposes the animated social dances of the 1930s with moments of intimate lyrical movement to express the internal states of mind of the marathon dancers. By fragmenting the social dance idioms, weaving together modern and historical styles, or by reflecting internal and external emotions through movement what all these choreographic strategies *do* is meld together subversive undercurrents in the dance with the historical template to produce impact decades later. The physicalization of community memories, longings, and historical meaning, what this project has termed "embodied nostalgia," demonstrates how social dance can embody implicit meanings in a story and thus elucidate racial, cultural, and political consciousness.

Historically, *Bandstand* takes place toward the end of the 1940s and close to the moment of transition of coupled dancing to more group based social dance. Though this transition did not happen overnight, the Swing Era faded with the approach of rock'n'roll and this shift changed the way people experienced music and dance. The Stearnses explain that with the decline of swing-styled dancing and the transition into Bebop music, there was less dancing.[13] There are a multitude of reasons for this, no singular one fully explaining the shift. As mentioned, there was a new federal tax on dance floors in the U.S. causing many dancehall owners to shut down, along with various recording bans in the 1940s that decreased circulation of music. Additionally, there was a distinct shift in jazz music to a more "Be-bop" style that was not as naturally conducive to dance styles as in the past.[14] While swing band leaders at the ballrooms tried to maintain bigger bands, with rising costs, smaller venues were becoming more prominent and bands decreased in size. Scott DeVeaux explains how this change in venue and rhythm created a less "popular" sound to jazz: "the rapid acceptance of bebop as the basic style by an entire generation of musicians helped pull jazz away from its previous reliance on contemporary popular song, dance music, and entertainment and toward a new sense of the music as an autonomous art."[15] Moreover, the growing popularity of rock'n'roll music, particularly with the younger generation increasingly opened up a space that allowed them to rebel from the older generation and their coupled social dance styles. Though many of the older generation thought that rock'n'roll was a "vulgar fad that would fade with time" it did the exact opposite.[16] Importantly, the "jukebox" played a key role in shifting how music was consumed and how dance and physicality were experienced. Owing to the invention of the "jukebox," the idea that music could be in diners, restaurants, schools, and gas stations was a novelty that became immediately popular. Social dances of the 1950s were experienced from a perspective that was mediated and self-curated (i.e. learning at home from the television) in a manner that allowed for a sense of self-expression that was both individual and connected to this newly forming sense of popular culture. The Stearnses succinctly describe the new generation, "Rock-and-roll supplies a temporary solution whereby the teenager has his cake and eats it. As a fan he protests as loudly as his phonograph will permit, or as grotesquely as the latest dance suggest (he knows his parents are unfamiliar with both the music and the dances)."[17] They explain there is an awareness that the older generation would not be familiar with the songs and dances, however, as the Stearnes state, "he belongs to a group with identical tastes in music and dance. He is both dependent and independent – he belongs and rebels simultaneously."[18]

What did this shift mean for social dance in musicals and what is the reflection of that shift in the contemporary era? When you begin to look at musicals set after the 1950s, in the era of rock'n'roll there is a different sort of nostalgia that emerges, where one may long for spirited group social interactions and explorations of social identity as in *Grease* (1971), or excitement and thrill around teen idols and fads as in *Bye Bye Birdie* (1960). On the whole, the popularity of radio and the obsession of the younger generation with the various radio programs, disc jockeys, and youth communities drew people together in a different way than going to a dance hall and hearing live music. When the Twist became the latest dance fad in the late 1950s, social dance was no longer about physical connection in the same way as swing dance. Social dance, while always about creating a community ethos, is defined in the second half of the twentieth century as something different, something both individual and communal, yet not coupled in the manner it once was. Choreographer Susan Stroman explains that, nonetheless, there may always be a longing for the era of partner dancing, "when people see dance historically, and see what it was like when two people actually touched in a dance, I think they even long for it, and wish it were the same today."[19]

The body in motion in ballrooms, dance halls, night clubs, bars, town centers, village squares will continue to offer a window into or lens by which to observe, participate in, comment on or critique, cultural, social, and economic politics. In particular, when these dancing bodies are theatricalized in musical theatre in diegetic, and thus narrative, moments of social dance, important insights and commentary on the "human predicament in the modern world" are made available.[20] In all, on the stage, choreographers have the opportunity to reflect back to the audience how we use our bodies to emotionally relate to each other, and to demonstrate how movement can embody our concept of home or homeland within the greater space of the world, and the significance of our physical presence as part of a community or nation. The term "embodied nostalgia" can be interpreted as an amalgamation of these factors as manifested in the body, whether through postures, movement, or dance. While the consequences of adapting social dances to suit the needs of the production are profound (loss of ownership and authenticity), it is equally clear that there is much to be gained (social and political awareness, personal reflection, and community empowerment) when the social dance is set forth as a structure to be cultivated by choreographers. In essence, how we embody our social activities and community identities on stage will continue to be an essential indicator self, society, and social politics.

It is my hope that *Embodied Nostalgia* will encourage others to rethink dominant theorizations and investigations of musical theatre that examine the material artefacts of the genre such as the libretto, score, and book and instead (or alongside) look to the body as an important site for the (re)performance of shared memories and emotions that musical theatre regularly taps into. By approaching musical theatre through this lens of social dance – always already deeply connected to notions of class and race – and the politics of the choreography therein, a unique and necessary method to describing, discussing, and critically evaluating the body in motion is put forth and encouraged in the analysis and understanding of musical theatre.

At the close of this project, a crop of nascent questions has begun to take shape, particularly in regards to choreographers who also take on the role of director in the twenty-first century.[21] This dual role was seen in several case studies of this book (*Bandstand* and *The Drowsy Chaperone*) by Andy Blankenbuehler and Casey Nicholaw respectively. Likewise, other choreographers in this study have since taken up the role (Susan Stroman, Graciela Danielle, Andrew Palermo to name a few). What does it mean when their directorial vision comes from an embodied place or bodily archive and how can an embodied way of knowing and working become part of the process of what Dorinne Kondo calls "reparative creativity"?[22] Described as, "the ways artists make, unmake, remake race in their creative processes, in acts of always partial integration and repair," – what does the choreographer, the choreographic process and social dance in musical theatre offer up in this regard? How are dramaturgical explorations from a place of "reparative creativity" enhanced when one is both the director and choreographer of a musical? Or, conversely, how do unique collaborative synergies, such as that between Savion Glover and George C. Wolfe, undertake similar artistic labor? How does a mode of embodied thinking transfer across genres as in the work of Camile A. Brown as director and choreographer of Ntozake Shange's *for colored girls who have considered suicide / when the rainbow is enuf*? Furthermore, when a Broadway director choreographer such as Brown puts "social dance at the heart of their work" and is dedicated to "the meaning and legacy of art form" what can we learn from and about the embodied experience of community?[23] In our highly mediated world, does the embodied experience brought forth by the director-choreographer and the possible "kinesthetic empathy" therein have the potential to work as a much-needed salve and a unique medium to raise critical consciousness?[24] I aspire to unpick these questions moving forward and hail others interested in any and all areas of movement and dance in musical theatre, theatre, and performance to join in – a 5, 6, 7, 8!

Notes

1   "Just Like It Was Before," *Bandstand*, music by Richard Oberacker, lyrics and book by Richard Oberacker and Robert Taylor, 2017. *Bandstand* was viewed live.
2   Ibid.
3   Ibid.
4   Promotional material for the 2017 musical *Bandstand* "Bandstand," www.bandsta ndbroadway. accessed March 25, 2017.
5   After World War II, the psychiatric disorder was overlooked, ignored, or dismissed as "combat fatigue" in favor of patriotic fervor and rekindled mythologies. "What is Post traumatic Stress-Disorder," *American Psychiatric Association,*https://www.psy chiatry.org/patients-families/ptsd/what-is-ptsd, accessed November 29, 2018.
6   "Welcome Home," *Bandstand*, music by Richard Oberacker, lyrics and book by Richard Oberacker and Robert Taylor, 2017.
7   Interview by author September 12, 2017. All further interview excerpts in quotations.
8   Julie Malnig, *Ballroom, Boogie, Shimmy Sham, Shake: A Social and Popular Dance Reader* (Chicago: University of Illinois Press, 2009), 4.
9   Of note, in all the promotional materials that highlight the movement and choreography throughout, there are no videos of the ghost soldier and only several production pictures.
10 "Our Foundations Mission" *Got Your 6,* Bob Woodruff Foundation, accessed June 1, 2022. https://gotyour6.bobwoodrufffoundation.org.
11 Debbie Gregory, "Broadway musical *Bandstand* about real struggles of war," April 17, 2017, https://militaryconnection.com/blog/broadway-musical-bandstand-rea l-struggles-war/
12 Gabriela Capestany, "Bandstand accurately display the postwar world of soldier through song," *Charleston City Paper,* January 29, 2020. https://charlestoncitypaper. com/bandstand-accurately-portrays-the-postwar-lives-of-soldiers-through-song/.
13 Marshall, and Jean Stearns. *Jazz Dance: The Story of American Vernacular Dance* (New York: Da Capo Press, 1994), 1.
14 Ibid.
15 Scott DeVeaux, "Bop (bebop, rebop)" October 16, 2013, *Grove Music Online,* http://www.oxfordmusiconline.com/grovemusic/view/10.1093/gmo/978156159 2630.001.0001/omo-9781561592630-e-1002248431?rskey=ga3C5b&result=4.
16 Elizabeth L. Wollman, *The Theater Will Rock: A History of the Rock Musical, from Hair to Hedwig* (Ann Arbor: University of Michigan Press, 2006), 13.
17 Stearns and Stearns, *Jazz Dance*, 2.

18 Ibid., 2.
19 Interview by author, June 22, 2018.
20 Svetlana Boym, *The Future of Nostalgia* (New York: Basic Books, 2001), 351.
21 The director-choreographer role is by no means a new phenomenon, as Liza Gennaro explains, "By the late twentieth century, the choreographer-director trend was firmly in motion," Gennaro, 141. For a detailed exploration of the director choreographer role in the twentieth century see Chapter 5 of Liza Gennaro's, "Taking the Reins: Emergence of the Director-Choreographer" in Liza Gennaro, *Making Broadway Dance* (Oxford: Oxford University Press, 2021).
22 I thank Donatella Galella for bringing this concept and Kondo's work to my attention in her keynote speech for the XVI Song, Stage, and Screen Conference at the University of Portsmouth (2022).
23 Salamishah Tilet, "The School that Camille A. Brown Built." *The New York Times,* September 2, 2020. https://www.nytimes.com/2020/09/02/arts/dance/camille-a -brown-pandemic-every-body-move.html.
24 Susan Foster, *Choreographing Empathy: Kinesthesia in Performance* (London: Routledge, 2010), 28.

References

American Psychiatric Association. "What is Post traumatic Stress-Disorder." https://www.psychiatry.org/patients-families/ptsd/what-is-ptsd, accessed November 29, 2018.

Bandstand Broadway. "Bandstand." https://bandstandbroadway.com/, accessed March 25, 2017.

Blankenbuehler, Andy. Personal Interview, New York City, September 12, 2017.

Boym, Svetlana. *The Future of Nostalgia*. New York: Basic Books, 2001.

DeVeaux, Scott. "Bop (bebop, rebop)," October 16, 2013, *Grove Music Online*, http://www.oxfordmusiconline.com/grovemusic/view/10.1093/gmo/9781561592630.001.0001/omo-9781561592630-e-1002248431?rskey=ga3C5b&result=4.

Foster, Susan Leigh. *Choreographing Empathy: Kinesthesia in Performance*. London, UK: Routledge, 2010.

Gennaro, Liza. *Making Broadway Dance*. Oxford University Press, 2021.

Kondo, Dorinne. *Worldmaking: Race, Performance, and the Work of Creativity*. Duke University Press, 2018.

Malnig, Julie, ed. *Ballroom, Boogie, Shimmy Sham, Shake: A Social and Popular Dance Reader*. Chicago: University of Illinois Press, 2009.

Oberacker, Richard and Robert Taylor, *Bandstand*, 2017.

Stearns, Marshall, and Jean Stearns. *Jazz Dance: The Story of American Vernacular Dance*. New York: Da Capo Press, 1994.

Tilet, Salamishah. "The School That Camille A. Brown Built." *The New York Times*, September 2, 2020. https://www.nytimes.com/2020/09/02/arts/dance/camille-a -brown-pandemic-every-body-move.html.

Wollman, Elizabeth L. *The Theater Will Rock: A History of the Rock Musical, from Hair to Hedwig*. Ann Arbor: University of Michigan Press, 2006.

Index

Page numbers in *italics* indicate Figures.

Abe, Frank 206
Acito, Marc 156n4, 198, 210n16
Acocella, Joan 71
Ahmanson Theatre 146n6
Ahrens, Lynn 49
Allegiance: background of 198–200; *Bandstand* commonalities with 219–220; "Camp Dance" 212n50; choreographic signature 206–207; choreographic strategies in 200–201; critical reception of 203–205; defining national identity 197; embellishments 205–206; film screening 207; "Get in the Game" 212n50; ghost characters 206; "Heart Mountain Dance" 196, *197*, 201, 205; historical inaccuracies 205–206; internment camps, portrayal of 196, 206; "Itetsuita" 205; "Paradise" 207, 210n18, 212n50; plot 199; revival 210n29; "Should I" 204–205; swing dance and 155; U.K. premier 210n29; U.S. identity crisis, focus on 201–202
Als, Hilton 38
American Dream 191–192
American identity 199–200, 208 *see also* nationalism
Anderson, Benedict 10–11
Andrews, Julie 105, 113n8
Aragaki, Rachel 198, 201
Aratani Theatre 210n29
Arias, Yancy 101n63
Arima, Stafford 13, 204
Arnaz, Desi 179n80, 179n81
Asato, Sono 162
Ashford, Rob 105–108, 111
"Asian", as catch-all term in casting calls 210–211n30

Asian Americans, theatricalization of 201–203
Astaire, Fred 84n60
Atkinson, Brooks 164, 165–166, 168, 173

Baber, Katherine 169, 170
Babylon Girls (Brown) 69
Baker, Josephine 98n19, 99n26
"Ballin' the Jack" 138
Bandstand: as "6 Certified" 219; about 1, 215, 216–217; *Allegiance* commonalities with 219–220; challenges assumptions of post-WWII 215; choreography 217–218; descriptive language in 2; ghost soldiers *218*, *219*; promotional images *218*; promotional materials for 216; PTSD focus 216–217; reflective nostalgia in 14n20; restorative nostalgia in 14n20
Barre, Gabriel 101n63
Baum, Vicki 101n62
Beat generation 165
"Beatnik Dance" 178n55
Beatty, John Lee 42n24
Beaumont, Ralph 175n4
Bebop music 220 221
Bechete, Sidney 122
belonging, sense of 14n17; *Allegiance* and 200; "Heart Mountain Dance" 197–198; Slow Drag and 30–31, 34; social dance creating 40, 115n37; *Steel Pier* and 184, 186, 189; swing dance creating 151; *Wonderful Town* and 161; *see also* nationalism
Bennett, Susan 137
Bernard B. Jacobs Theatre 31
Bernstein, Elmer 113n8

Bernstein, Leonard 156n2, 160, 161, 168
Bindas, Kenneth J. 151
Black, Eubie 65
Black Bottom (dance) 98n12; background
   of 120–123; copyright attempts
   130n32; description of 123;
   interpretations of 130n30; sensuality of
   122; stage directions 124–125; transfer
   to stage 124–125; transition from
   Charleston to 121–122; uniqueness of
   122–123; *see also Wild Party, The*
Black Broadway choreographers 42n19
Black communities: creating dances
   121–122; cultural continuation of
   8–10; as cultural innovators 69; Jewish
   immigrants' relationship with 129n21;
   migration north 30–31; ragtime dances
   21
Black dances: appropriation of 130n28;
   refinement by white artists 22,
   26–27n9; *see also* Castle, Irene and
   Vernon
Black dance teachers 92–94
Black minstrel shows 61–62n23
Black performers: absence from the stage
   169; *The Color Purple* and 34; as
   cultural agents 69; executing the
   Cakewalk 54–56; female dancers
   69–70; invisibility of 92–93; in
   minstrel shows 61n23; "new woman"
   and 115n31; reclaiming ownership
   106
Black women, white women imitating
   109
Blake, Eubie 75
Blankenbuehler, Andy 1, 215–217, 220
Bob Woodruff Foundation 218–219
body, the: as produced by its social
   environment 7; socialization through
   dance 24; transmission of
   choreography 7
box steps 139, 147n21
Boym, Svetlana 4, 5, 44n44, 145, 208
Brantley, Ben: *The Color Purple* review
   33, 36, 39; *Ragtime* review 49, 58;
   Shuffle Along review 72; *Steel Pier*
   review 190–191, 193; *Wild Party*
   review 126–127; *Wonderful Town*
   review 173–174
Bray, Stephen 31–32, 34–35, 43n36
breakaways 91, 110, 122, 130n36, 152,
   157n18, 196, 201
Broadway style of tap dance 78–79
Broadway Theatre, The 31

Brooks, Daphne 9
Brown, Buster 71
Brown, Camile A. 222–223
Brown, Jayna 9, 54, 56, 69, 93, 97n5,
   107, 109, 130n28
Brymn, Tim 122
Bunny Hug (dance) 26–27n9, 183, 188,
   194n18
Burke, Thomas 109
Burton, Humphrey 166, 171
Bush, John 98n13
Byrd, Donald 11, 31, 32

Cabalona, Jeremy 209n9
Cakewalk 11; background of 52–56;
   Black performers executing 54–56;
   Color Purple, The 25; connections to
   Africa 61n20; contests 54; dancers
   performing *53*; deconstruction of
   57–58; frictional sense of nostalgia
   57–58; infiltrating entertainment
   venues 54; as mockery 53; nostalgic
   contractions in 56; as a social situation
   55; on the stage 55; *see also Ragtime*
Calabria, Frank M. 185, 189
"Camp Dance" 212n50
Carlson, Marvin 147n24
Castle, Irene and Vernon 22, *23*,
   26–27n9, 97n5
Chaney, Lon 71
Chaplin, Sydney 175n4
Charleston, The: about 87–88;
   background of 91–92; dangerous for
   young women 94; economic/
   sociopolitical climate and 95–96;
   influences on 97n6; openness of
   movement in 91–92; as path to vice
   88; physicalizing whimsy and wildness
   of Jazz Age 95; in previous works
   97n1; sugars 196, 209n1; transfer to
   stage 88–89; transitioning to the Black
   Bottom 121–122; worldwide
   dissemination of 101n62
Charleston Knee 100
Chodorov, Jerome 156n2, 161, 175n9
choreographer-director role 222–223,
   224n21
chugging 123, 130n38
circular dance movement 27n18
Clorindy, or the Origin of the Cakewalk
   (musical comedy) 54, 62n30,
   83–84n44
Cohen-Stratyner, Barbara 7–8, 95, 122
Collette, Toni 101n63

Color Purple, The: about 31–32; Africa represented in 39; Byrd's choreography 32–34; Cakewalk 25; "Dirty Dozens" 43n38; Doyle's revival of 36–40; Doyle vs Byrd's interpretations 40; film 43n38; jook joints, use of 11, 32–34; London production 44n45; mixing musical styles in 35; movement style in 35; "Ms. Celie's Blues" 43n38; "Push Da Button" 33, 37–38, 43n38; revival 32, 36–40; set design for 42n24; sexual metaphors in 33; Yee's choreography 36–40; *see also* Slow Drag
combat fatigue 223n5
Comden, Betty 156n2, 161
commercialization of leisure 186
Conga dance 172–173, 179n80, 179n81
"Conga!" section 171–173
consumption, self-identification and 96
Conyers, Claude 157n18
Cook, Will Marion 54, 83–84n44
Crucible, The 161
cultural appropriations 8–9, 172
cultural front 162
Cultural Front, The (Denning) 162
Culture Makers (Koritz) 94–95

dance marathons: American Dream and 191–192; background of 185–186; banning of 192; cultural references to 193–194n4; on the stage 183–184; *see also* Steel Pier
Dance Marathons (Martin) 185
Dance of the Sleep Walkers (Calabria) 185
dance(s): movement style in 91–92; parody and 89–90; transmission of 92–94; *see also* social dance(s)
Daniele, Graciela 11, 50, 57, 60–61n9, 220
Darktown Follies 55
Davis, Luther 101n62
DeFrantz, Thomas F. 67, 69
Dendy, Mark 101n63
Denning, Michael 162
Depression era 150, 183, 188
DeVeaux, Scott 220–221
developpé style 52, 61n17
Dick, Bernard F. 175n8
Diggs, Taye 101n63
Dinah 122
director-choreographer role 222–223, 224n21
Dirty Dancing (film) 44n42
"Dirty Dancing" style 35, 44n42

"Dirty Dozens, The" 43n38
Doctorow, E.L., *Ragtime* 48–49, 58, 62–63n49
Dodds, Sherill 15n26
Dote, Janelle Toyomi 203
Doyle, John 31–32, 36, 44n48 *see also Color Purple, The*
Drabinsky, Garth 49
Drowsy Chaperone, The 89, 98n11, 98n15; audience, bringing in 136; Charleston, use of 138, 142–143; choreography 138–145; "Cold Feet" 140; as comical spoof 134–135; creating nostalgia onstage 12; dramaturgical strategy for 134–138, 145; escaping into fantasy world 137; final chorus 142–143; making fun of itself 135–136; opening sequence 134, 139; pedagogical strategy 135–136; "Toledo Surprise" 142

Ebb, Fred 183
Ellis, Scott 183
embodiment, concept of 6,7
embodied nostalgia, definition of 2, 5
Enchanted Nightingale, The 144
ethnic parody 107
"Everybody Dance" 188

Fancy Free 176–177n30, 176n29
Fang, Jenn 204, 205
Federal Bureau of Investigation (FBI) 197
female autonomy 12, 91, 114n28
female body: in 1920s 88; liberation of 90; in motion 90, 105, 106; objectification of 122–123; on stage 90, 146
female dancing body 88
female minstrelsy 93
Fields, Joseph 156n2, 161, 175n9
Finkle, David 204
Fitzgerald, F. Scott 26n8, 94, 112, 121, 128
Flaherty, Stephen 49
flapper 90
fluidity of dance 15n30
Forrest, George 101n62
Foster, Susan 6–7, 24
Foster, Sutton *104*, 108, 109, 110–111, 114n27, 141, 147n24
Fox, James 113n8
Frank, Jonathan 132n50
Franko, Mark 112

Funny Face 178n55
Furman, Roy 42n17

Galati, Frank 11, 50
Galella, Donatella 210–211n30
Gaman 200, 210n16
gangsters 95, 111, 135, 140, 142, 147n30
Gennaro, Liza 2, 72, 224n21
geopolitics 13
George-Graves, Nadine 34, 43n34, 43n39
Georgia Minstrels 61n23
Gerard, Jeremy 204
Gershwin, George 65
gestural style 57, 131n44
gestural vocabularies 70
"Get in the Game" 212n50
Giddons, Rhiannon 72–73
Gilbert, Douglas 107
Gioia, Ted 84n59, 212n53
Given, William 8, 201, 207
Glover, Savion 11–12, 65–68, 71–72, 83n28, 109, 220
Goodman, Benny 156n9, 208
Good Neighbor Policy 172
Gottschild, Brenda Dixon 8–9, 53, 71
Got Your 6 (organization) 218–219
Graham, Martha 163
Grand Hotel, The 101n62
Green, Adam 69
Green, Adolph 156n2, 161
Green, Chuck 71
Green, Jesse 37–38
Greenwich Village 159
Griffin, Gary 11, 31, 33
Grizzly Bear (dance) 65–66, 75, 183, 188, 194n18
Grody, Svetlana McLee 50
Grosz, Elizabeth 7
Gundlach, Daniel 163
Guys and Dolls 177n31

Halbwachs, Maurice 6
Harlem (play) 41–42n16
Harlem, New York: demographics 152, 157n19; notable ballrooms in 157n14; territorial behavior 152; *see also* Savoy Ballroom
Harlem Renaissance 84n51, 92–93
Harmony Kings 65, 82n3
Haskins, James 88, 97n6
Hazzard-Gordon, Katrina 30, 33, 34, 40, 41n6
Heap, Chad 99n30

"Heart Mountain Dance" 196, *197*, 201, 205
Heilpern, John 98n14, 119, 129n20
Hellzapoppin (film) 178n53
"hep" 167–170, 178n49
Hepburn, Audrey 178n55
Herrera, Brian 172
Hill, Constance Valis 77–78
Hill, George Roy 113n8
Hines, Gregory 71
Hoffman, Hans 159
hoofing 78–79
House Un-American Activities Committee (HUAC) 161, 162, 169
Hubbard, Karen 35
Hudson, Jennifer 36, 38
Hunter, Alberta 130n32
Hurston, Zora Neale 9, 121
Hutcheon, Linda 89, 98n15, 107, 146–147n12

identity formation *see* belonging, sense of
Illbruk, Helmutt 145
imagined communities 10–11
"I'm Just Wild About Harry" 75–76
Indecent (play) 82n16
Isherwood, Charles 108, 127
"Itetsuita" 205

Jacksonville Rounders 130n30
James, Brian D'Arcy 101n63
James, Henry 98n23
Japanese Americans 196, 201–203 *see also* *Allegiance*
"Jay Bird" 97n6
Jazz Age 26n8; Charleston, The (*See* Charleston, The); economic/sociopolitical climate during 95–96; embracing of "Blackness" in 92–93; Fitzgerald coining phrase 94; hedonism, fascination for 119; invisibility of the Black dancer 92; musicals exploring 97n10; societal changes in 84n51; thrills and highs of 121; *see also* Roaring Twenties
jazz hands 35, 44n43, 139
jazz music 75, 84n59, 147n21
jazz square 168
Jitterbug 153 *see also* swing dance
Jitterbug contests *154*
Johnson, James B. 87, 91
Jones, John Bush 176n20
Jones, Quincy 32, 43n38

jook houses 11, 30–34, 36–40, 41n6, 43n39, 121
Joplin, Scott: as king of ragtime composers *22*; "Maple Leaf Rag, The" 21, 26n1; in New York 21; "Ragtime Dance, The" 26n4; writing for the theatre 26n4
Juba (dance) 61n23, 81–82n2, 91, 99n27
jukebox 221

Kander, John 183
Keathley, Elizabeth L. 164, 170
Kerr, Walter 173
Kiss Me Kate 147n30, 176n16
Kitt, Eartha 101n63
Knapp, Raymond 1–2, 58, 62n48, 177n31
Kondo, Dorinne 222
Koritz, Amy 94–96
Kraut, Anthea 122, 130n32
Kuo, Jay 156n4, 198, 210n16

LaChiusa, Michael John 98n11, 101n63, 117, 119, 123, 129n16, 132n50
Lambert, Lisa 98n11, 134
Lane, William Henry 61n23, 81–82n2
La Touche, Lisa 66, 71, 73–74, 77, 81, 85n63
Lawrence, Paul 54
Lee, Michael K. 201
leisure time 100n52
Lindbergh, Charles 153
Lindy Hop 10–11, 16n40, 100n44, 152–155, 190, 196
Lion King, The 49
Lippa, Andrew 101n63, 129n16
Lipton, Brian Scott 33, 42n22
LiveEnt Inc 49
Loring, Eugene 178n55
loyalty questionnaire 209n11
Lyles, Aubrey 65

Mack, Cecil 87
Madell, Jonathan 204
Malnig, Julie 4, 14n10, 84n53, 157n17
Mandelbaum, Ken 60n5
"Maple Leaf Rag, The" 21, 26n1
March, John Moncure 98n11, 101n63, 117–118
Marks, Peter 37
Marshall, Kathleen 175n11
Martin, Bob 98n11, 134–135
Martin, Carol 91–92, 185, 191–192, 193
May Day Riots of 1919 94

Mayer, Michael 105, 111, 112
Mayor of Dixie, The (play) 65–66
McCarthy, Joseph 161
McCarthyism 173, 174
McDonald, Audra 72, 80
McKeever, Jacquelyn 175n4
McKellar, Don 134
McKeller, Don 98n11
McKneely, Joey 124–126, 101n63
McMillin, Scott 144
McNally, Terrence 49
McNulty, Charles 37, 66
Menier Chocolate Factory 42n17
Menzel, Idina 101n63
migration north 30–31
Miller, Arthur 161
Miller, Flournoy 65
mimicry 51, 53, 61n18
Minstrel Show Revisited, The 42n20
minstrel shows 32–33, 53–54, 61–62n23, 120
minstrelsy 93
Mirvish, David 146n6
Monaghan, Terry 35, 153, 155
Moore, Mary Tyler 113n8
Moriah, Kristin 67, 73
Morris, Richard 98n11, 105
Morrison, Greg 98n11, 134
Mosher, Stephen 191
"Ms. Celie's Blues" 43n38
Murney, Julia 101n63
Murphy, Donna 175n11
musical theatre: African American loves scenes in 42–43n28; "Asian" as catch-all term in 210–211n30; Black ownership of tap in 68–69; breaking fourth wall 144; choreographic strategies in 10–11; emotional connections of 2; emotional connections to 136; ephemeral nature of 73–74; Japanese bodies in 201–203; jazz music's impact on 75; narrative style, use of 163; pedagogical strategy 135–136; pornography and 137–138; standard conventions of 113n9; structure of 2; use of parody in 89–90; *see also* American Broadway musicals
music appropriation 65
My Sister Eileen (play) 161

Nakauchi, Paul 201
nationalism 13, 197 *see also* American identity
Nesbit, Evelyn 52, 57

New Deal 150–151
"new woman" 90, 98n23, 105, 108–112, 115n31
Nicholaw, Casey 12, 138–139, 143, 144
Niiya, Brian 206
Norton, Pauline 97n4
nostalgia: definition of 14n15, 15n24; pre-migratory 34–36; *see also* embodied nostalgia, reflective nostalgia, restorative nostalgia
"Nuttycracker Suite" 110–111

Oberacker, Richard 1, 219
Oja, Carol 163, 175n13
Oliver, Paul 33
"One Hundred Easy Ways" 165
On the Town 162, 163–164, 176–177n30
Orientalism 12, 107, 144
Orientalist stereotypes 107
Osnes, Laura 1
Oxman, Steven 114n24
Oyama, Rumi 203, 210n29

Palermo, Andrew 13, 197, 200, 203–205, 210n13, 212n50
Pao, Angela C. 107, 113–114n17
"Paradise" 207, 210n18, 212n50
parodic double coding 98n15
parody: ethnic 107; movement and dance as part of 89–90, 98n18; in *Thoroughly Modern Millie* 107; use of 146n12
partner dancing 91, 151, 221–222
pastiche 12–13, 89, 96, 109, 112, 123–124, 163, 175n9
Patinkin, Mandy 101n63
Patterson, Chris 189
patting 65, 81–82n2
Patting Juba (dance) 81–82n2, 99n27
Pennington, Ann 122
Perpener, John O. 41–42n16
Pinkins, Tonya 126
Platt, Len 150
Pollack, Sidney 193n4
popular dance, American cultural identity and 14n10
Popular Dance Studies 15n26
Popular Front 162
post-traumatic stress disorder (PTSD) 216–217, 223n5
pre-migratory nostalgia 34–36
Prohibition in the U.S. 12, 94–95, 100n53, 150
Proulx, Angela Yuki 204–205

Pugh, Megan 26–27n9, 54, 56, 200
"Push Da Button" 33, 35, 37–38, 43n38

race and ethnicity in popular entertainment 73
Rae, Patricia 161
Ragtime 11; about 49–50; Broadway Cast Recording Cover *59*; choreography 50–52, 58, 220; embodied tension in 51–52; film 60n3; finale 57–58, *59*–60; fragmenting the Cakewalk in 52; nostalgic contractions in 56; opening sequence 50–51, 56–57; prologue 51–52; reviews of 60n5; revivals 60n5; "Wheels of a Dream" 60; *see also* Cakewalk
Ragtime (Doctorow) 48–49, 58, 62–63n49
"Ragtime Dance, The" 21
Ragtime Dance, The 26n4
ragtime dance(s): about 21–22; shifting to the stage 24–25; *see also* Cakewalk, Slow Drag
ragtime music, as sound of a new age 21
reflective nostalgia: *Bandstand* and 14n20, 216; *The Color Purple* and 11, 40; definition of 5, 44n44; *Shuffle Along* and 67, 68, 80; *On the Town* and 163; *Wonderful Town* and 172
reparative creativity 222–223
restorative nostalgia: *Allegiance* and 202, 207; *Bandstand* and 14n20, 15n24; *The Color Purple* and 36; definition of 5–6; *Ragtime* and 50; *The Wild Party* and 128
Rhodes, Chip 96
Riis, Thomas 62n30
Roach, Joseph 16–17n53
Roaring Twenties 88, 90, 101n62, 119 *see also* Jazz Age
Robbins, Jerome 124, 166, 177n44
Roberts, John Storm 179n81
Robinson, Danielle 3, 8–9, 29, 30–31, 92–93
rock-and-roll music, growing popularity of 220–221
Rooney, David 39, 204
Roosevelt, Franklin D. 150, 172
Rose, Lloyd 58
rounders 130n30
Roxworthy, Emily 206
Rugg, Rebecca 36
Runnin' Wild 87, 91 *see also* Charleston, The

Russell, Brenda 31–32, 34–35, 43n36, 170, *171*
Russell, Rosalind 175n4

Saddler, Donald 159–160, 165–166, 170, 173, 177n42
Salonga, Lea 211n34
Sanders, Scott 42n17
Savoy Ballroom 26n7, 151, 152
Savran, David 2, 71, 75
Scandals of 1926 122
Scanlan, Dick 98n11, 105, 113n10
Seaton, Sandra 73
Seibert, Brian 68
Shimakawa, Karen 202, 210n25, 210n26
shimmy 41n6, 88, 91, 123
"Should I" 204–205
Shuffle Along, Or The Making of the Musical Sensation of 1921 and All That Follows 11–12, 25; 1921 original version 74–75; about 65–67; cast members *70*; cast of 80; changing dancing structure of shows 75; Charleston, The 97n1; choreography 220; as a counter-example 66; dramaturgical framework 67–68; ensemble dancers *74*; foundational construction of 66; Glover's choreography 66–67, 68–69, 80; as homage to tap 67; "I'm Just Wild About Harry" 75–76; shaping modernity 69–70; show's early closure 72–73; source material for 65–66; tap challenge in 76–78; vaudeville sequences 66; Wolfe's dramaturgical choice 75–76
Siegle, Barbara and Scott 111
Sissle, Noble 65, 70, 91
Slow Drag 11; background of 29–30; as coping mechanism 30; "Dirty Dancing" and 44n42; as diversion from public sphere 30; dividing Black communities 30–31; reimagined choreography for 35
slumming 99n30
Slyde, Jimmy 71
Smith, Helen 166, 168
Smith-Rosenberg, Carroll 90
Snake Hips 91, 99n26
social dance communities 10–11
social dance(s): Black Bottom (*See* Black Bottom (dance)); bringing out the "social" in 111; Charleston, The (*See* Charleston, The); circulation of 98n13;

as community experience 5, 6; creating nostalgic impulses 2; cultural appropriation of 8–9; from dance clubs 7–8; dance marathon (*See* dance marathons); as escapism 207–208; fluidity of 15n30; genesis of 6–7; identity formation and 115n37; illnesses associated with 94, 100n49; impact on everyday life 15n22; Juba 61n23, 81–82n2, 91, 99n27; Lindy Hop 10–11, 16n40, 100n44, 152–155, 190, 196; Malnig's definition of 4; moral panic around 97n5; Patting Juba 81–82n2, 99n27; as plot device 8; ragtime dance era 21–22; shifting to the stage 24–25; Slow Drag (*See* Slow Drag); Snake Hips 91, 99n26; Stroman on 186; transitions in 4; trends in 14n10; *see also* dance(s)
Sofer, Johannes 14n15
Somers, Elyse 126
South Pacific 176n20
Spamalot 138
Spectrum Dance Theatre 32
Spiegelman, Art 119
Spielberg, Steven 31
Spring, Howard 151–152, 156n9, 157n16
"Sprints" number 191, 193
Stearns, Marshall and Jean: on the Cakewalk 55; on The Charleston 91; on circular dance movement 27n18; on Harlem demographics 152; on Jacksonville Rounders 130n30; on patting 81–82n2; on rock-and-roll generation 221; on swing dance blackout 208; on vernacular dances 153; on Ziegfeld 85n62
Steel Pier 13; background of 182–184; challenges to choreography 190; choreography 184–185, 188–189, 220; communicating passage of time 184–185; critical reception to 190–191; dance marathon as a metaphor 183, 208; dramaturgical strategy for 184–185; "Everybody Dance" 188; narrative strategies 186–188; opening sequence 188; Playbill *187*; "Sprints" 191, 193; structure of 183; swing dance, use of 208; title image *187*; *see also* dance marathons
Stevens, Hugh 98n23
Still, William Grant 65

stock market crash 26n8, 94, 146, 149, 156n5, 185
Stowe, David W. 157–158n26
Stroman, Susan 13, 182–183, 186, 220, 221
Structures of the Jazz Age (Rhodes) 96
sugars 196, 209n1
surrogation 16–17n53
swing dance: athleticism of 157n18; background of 151–154; breakaways in 152–153; code of conduct 152–153, 157n22; emphasis on belonging 151; with Japanese American bodies 200–201; movement qualities of 167–168; moving beyond stereotypes in 202; in popular cinema 154; promoting national pride 155–156; racial appropriation of 154–155; racial integration and 208; renaissance of 212n51; renewed interest in 15n23; sugars 196, 209n1; at time of World War II 200, 207; transmission beyond the U.S. 211n44; whitening of 153; *see also* Jitterbug
swing music: American identity and 208; movies and 157–158n26; partner dancing and 151–152; transition to Bebop music 220–221; varieties of 157n16
"Swing!" section 169–170
Swing! That Modern Sound (Bindas) 151

tableaux 57
Takei, George 198, 209n3, 209n9
tap dance: as Afro-Irish fusion 78; background of 71–72; Broadway style 78–79, 140; challenge dances 77–78; as a conversation 76–78; in *Drowsy Chaperone* 138, 140; evolution of, in performance 79–80; Hines and 71; hoofing 78–79; intercultural fusions of 78; social nature of 77; style diversity of 85n63; in *Thoroughly Modern Millie* 107, 109–110; two styles of 78–80; *see also Shuffle Along, Or The Making of the Musical Sensation of 1921 and All That Follows*
T.A.P.S. (Tragedy Assistance Program for Survivors) 219–220
Taylor, Diana 7, 15n30
Taylor, Robert 1
Taylor, Scott 138, 147n18
Tesori, Jeanine 98n11, 105, 113n10
Texas Tommy (dance) 157n18

theatrical memory 147n24
They Shoot Horses Don't They (film) 193n4
Thione, Lorenzo 156n4, 198, 210n16
Thompson, David 183
Thoroughly Modern Millie 89, 96, 98n11; about 103–105; background of 105; cast of *104*; casts' racial makeup 114n23; choreography 105–108; finale 112; "new woman" and 108–112; "Not for the Life of Me" 106–107; "Nuttycracker Suite" 110–111; opening sequence 103–105; Orientalist stereotypes 107; pastiche quality of 112; racism in 1967 film 113–114n17, 114n24; wealthy character inserted into 108–109
Thurman, Wallace, *Harlem* 41–42n16
"Toledo Surprise" 142
Tomko, Linda 90
Tony Awards 176n16
Too Many Girls 179n80
Toronto Fringe Festival 146n6
Tran, Diep 198–199
Tucker, Earl 99n26
Tucker, Sherrie 209n12
Turner, Victor 61n18
Twine, Linda 32

Usner, Eric Martin 15n23

Van De Graaf, Janet 134
vaudeville idioms 138
vaudeville sequences 66, 107, 117, 123, 131n42
Viertel, Jack 73
Vogel, Paula, *Indecent* 82n16

Walsh, David 150
Walton, Lester A. 121–122
War Department 209n11
War Relocation Authority (WRA) 209n11
Waters, Daryl 66
Webb, Elida 91
Welch, Elisabeth 87
"Wheels of a Dream" 60
White, Herbert 152
white dancers: appropriation of Black dances 78, 79, 93; Black dances performed by 8, 22; Black dance teachers instructing 92–94; Charleston taken up by 90

white female performers 168–169
white women, imitating Black women 109
Wild Party, The 89, 92, 95, 98n11; about 117, 118–119; base material for 129n16; choreography 124–126, 131–132n49; creating vaudeville on stage 123–124; critical reception to 126–128; dramaturgical strategy for 119–120; finale 127–128; gestural style 131n44; music, tension in 118–119; *see also* Black Bottom (dance)
Wild Party, The (poem) 98n11, 101n63, 117–118
Wilkinson, Tara Overfield 210n29
Williams, Ethel 85n62
Williams, Vanessa 132n50
Willis, Allee 31–32, 34–35, 43n36
Wilson, August 73
Windman, Matt 37
Winer, Linda 204
Winfrey, Oprah 32, 42n17
Wolfe, George C. 65–66, 92; describing Glover 72; directing history 82n5; dramaturgical framework for *Shuffling Along* 75–76; Glover collaboration 68, 71; goal with *Shuffling Along* 72; previous works 67; *Wild Party, The* 98n11, 101n63, 117, 119, 123
Woll, Allen 42n28

Wollman, Elizabeth L. 98n18, 162, 177n31
women's suffrage 90
Wonderful Town 156n2; about 159–160; background of 161–163; choreography 159–160, 165–170, 173; chorus boys *171*; "Christopher Street" choreography 166, 177n44; comedic structure of 149; "Conga!" section 171–173, 179n81; critical reception to 173–174; freedom of movement in 166–167; homage to the 1930s 164–165; mixture of musical styles 168–169; "One Hundred Easy Ways" 165; opening sequence 165, 167; political undertones in 160–161, 175–176n14; revival 173–174, 175n11; show structure 164; stage directions 168–169; "Swing!" section 167–168, 169–170; telecast of 159–160; *On the Town* comparison with 163–164
World War II 155, 200, 207, 209n11
Wright, Robert 101n62

Yee, Ann 36, 42n17, 44n45
Yeston, Maury 101n62
"You have to be carefully taught" (song) 176n20
Young, Catherine M. 72–73

Ziegfeld, Florenz 85n62

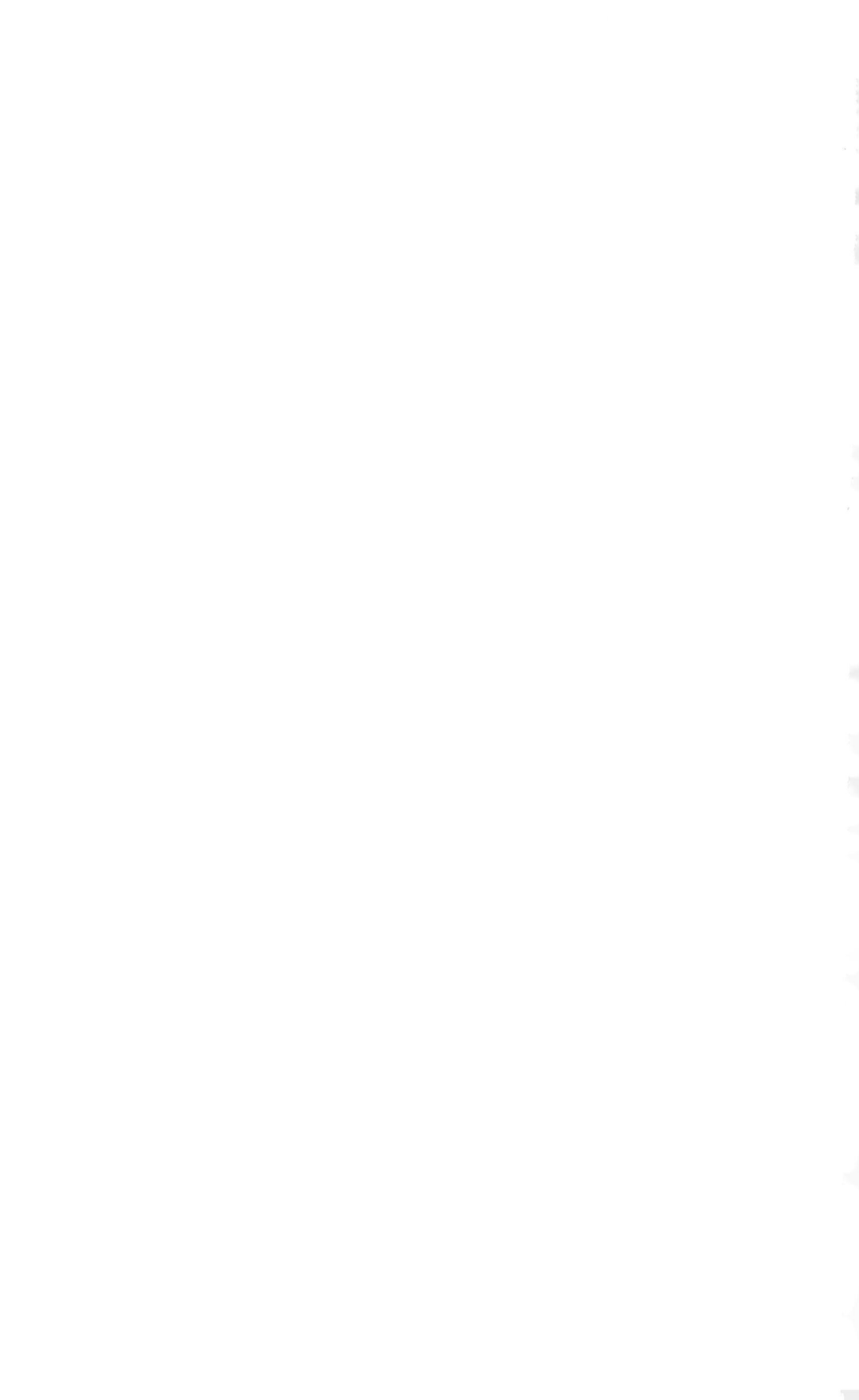